Soundscapes
of Liberation

Refiguring American Music

A series edited by RONALD RADANO, JOSH KUN, AND NINA SUN EIDSHEIM

CHARLES MCGOVERN, CONTRIBUTING EDITOR

Soundscapes of Liberation

AFRICAN AMERICAN MUSIC

IN POSTWAR FRANCE   CELESTE DAY MOORE

Duke University Press   *Durham and London*   2021

Project editor: Lisa Lawley
Designed by Courtney Leigh Richardson
Typeset in Garamond Premier Pro by Westchester Publishing Services

Library of Congress Cataloging-in-Publication Data
Names: Moore, Celeste Day, [date] author.
Title: Soundscapes of liberation : African American music in postwar
France / Celeste Day Moore.
Other titles: African American music in postwar France |
Refiguring American music.
Description: Durham : Duke University Press, 2021. | Series: Refiguring
American music | Includes bibliographical references and index.
Identifiers: LCCN 2021011636 (print)
LCCN 2021011637 (ebook)
ISBN 9781478013761 (hardcover)
ISBN 9781478014690 (paperback)
ISBN 9781478021995 (ebook)
Subjects: LCSH: Jazz—France—20th century—History and criticism. |
Blues (Music)—France—20th century—History and criticism. | African
American musicians—France. | African Americans—France—Music—
History and criticism. | African Americans—Music—Influence. |
Popular music—Europe—History and criticism. | Jazz—Europe—History
and criticism. | Blues (Music)—Europe—History and criticism. |
BISAC: MUSIC / Genres & Styles / Jazz | SOCIAL SCIENCE /
Black Studies (Global)
Classification: LCC ML3509.F7 M66 2021 (print) | LCC ML3509.F7
(ebook) | DDC 780.8996/073044—dc23
LC record available at https://lccn.loc.gov/2021011636
LC ebook record available at https://lccn.loc.gov/2021011637

Cover art: *Louis Armstrong and his orchestra at the Olympia in Paris,
France, January 1, 1955.* Courtesy Reporters Associes/Gamma-Rapho
Collection via Getty Images.

For my parents, Susan and Thad,
with gratitude

Contents

Abbreviations

ABSIE	American Broadcasting System in Europe
AEF	Afrique Équatoriale Française
AFCDJ	Association Française des Collectionneurs de Disques de Jazz
AFM	American Federation of Musicians
AFN	American Forces Network
AFNOR	Association Française de Normalisation
AMSAC	American Society of African Culture
AMGOT	Allied Military Government for Occupied Territories
AOF	Afrique Occidentale Française
ASE	Armed Services Editions
BBC	British Broadcasting Corporation
DOM-TOM	Départements d'Outre-mer–Territoires d'Outre-mer
ECA	Economic Cooperation Administration
ETO	European Theater of Operations
FLN	Front de Libération National
JMF	Jeunesses Musicales de France
MJC	Maisons des Jeunes et de la Culture

OCORA	Office de Coopération Radiophonique
ORTF	Office de Radiodiffusion-Télévision Française
OWI	Office of War Information
PAO	Public Affairs Officer
PWD	Psychological War Division
RDF	Radiodiffusion Française
RFE	Radio Free Europe
RN	Radiodiffusion Nationale
RTF	Radiodiffusion-Télévision Française
SAC	Société Africaine de Culture
SHAEF	Supreme Headquarters Allied Expeditionary Force
SORAFOM	Société de Radiodiffusion de la France d'Outre-mer
UNESCO	United Nations Educational, Scientific, and Cultural Organization
USIA	United States Information Agency
USIS	United States Information Service
USO	United Service Organizations
VOA	Voice of America
WPA	Works Progress Administration

Acknowledgments

I have loved researching and writing this book, in large part because of the extraordinary people I have met along the way. I want to begin by thanking Tom Holt and Leora Auslander, whose support, friendship, and writing continue to mean the world to me. You are the models to which I aspire in every way. The book was likewise transformed by the mentorship of Adam Green, Travis Jackson, and Phil Bohlman, whose discerning questions have continued to inform this project, as well as Paul Jefferson, who first taught me how to think about Black history in global terms.

I am grateful for the generous support of the National Endowment for the Humanities; National Humanities Center; Center for the Study of Race, Politics, and Culture; France Chicago Center, Department of History, and Social Sciences Division at the University of Chicago; and the dean of faculty at Hamilton College. I was also fortunate to receive research and writing support as an Exchange Fellow at the Institut d'Études Politiques in Paris, where I had the good fortune of being mentored by Emmanuelle Loyer and Pap Ndiaye, and as a Predoctoral Research Fellow at the Carter G. Woodson Institute for African American and African Studies at the University of Virginia, where Deborah McDowell deserves particular thanks for her own brilliance, generosity, and expertise in bringing together colleagues and friends. I also want to thank Jacqueline Goldsby for the opportunity to work with an amazing group of archivists, librarians, and graduate students in the Mapping the Stacks project; through this, I met the late Michael Flug, whose passion for social justice and commitment to archiving African American history inspire me still.

I am further indebted to the many archivists and librarians who made this research possible, especially Teddy Abebe and Joellen Elbashir at the Moorland-Spingarn Research Center at Howard University; Nicole Bertolt at the Cohérie Boris Vian; Pierre Pichon and Anne Legrand in the Audiovisual Collection at the Bibliothèque nationale de France; Sarah Frioux-Salgas at the Musée du Quai Branly; Daniel Alogues and the late Patrick Brugel at the Médiathèque municipale in Villefranche-de-Rouergue; Djibril Gueye and Oumar Sarr at the Archives of Radiodiffusion Télévision Sénégalaise; and Kirstin Kay at the Special Collections and University Archives at the University of Massachusetts at Amherst. I'd like to express a particular note of gratitude to Robert Peyrillou, Geneviève Bouyjou, and Hélène Pare at the Bibliothèque municipale in Souillac, where this project first took root.

At Duke University Press, I am so thankful for the support and vision of Ken Wissoker and his (encouraging!) admonitions to be bolder, and to the anonymous reviewers, whose comments and critiques have transformed the book. I want to acknowledge the phenomenal series editors Ron Radano, Josh Kun, and Nina Eidsheim, as well as the expert guidance of Ryan Kendall and Lisa Lawley in getting the book into production. I am grateful for the editorial assistance of Matt Somoroff, whose keen eye, questions, and enthusiasm got me to the finish line.

At Hamilton College, I have been fortunate to have found deep wells of intellectual support and camaraderie. I want to offer particular thanks to my department; my departmental colleagues Maurice Isserman, Kevin Grant, and Alfred Kelly, who generously read and commented on the manuscript; as well as Jennifer Ambrose, Quincy Newell, and Benj Widiss, whose valuable feedback enriched the book. I have taught so many extraordinary students, but I would like to thank in particular Cam Blair, Sean Henry Smith, Chidera Onyeoziri, and Syon Powell for their probing questions, and Eleni Broadwell, Shaneil Dacosta, Pascal Dafanis, Sarah Malard, and Allie Zuckerman for being expert research assistants (and wonderful students).

I am grateful to everyone who read drafts of this work in various forms. I want to thank especially Penny Von Eschen for her early support and encouragement, Paul Kramer for his guidance and generosity, and Tyler Stovall for pointing me in the right direction. I am grateful to Pap Ndiaye, Kennetta Perry, Barbara Savage, David Suisman, and Emily Thompson for their critical feedback, as well as the many colleagues who offered advice and support: Jennifer Boittin, Rashida Braggs, Fadeke Castor, Jay Cook, Naomi Davidson, Baz Dreisinger, Andy Fry, Pim Higginson, Michelle Hilmes, Jim House, Rachel Jean-Baptiste, Erik McDuffie, David Murphy, Jann Pasler, Alexandre Pierrepont, Julie Saville, Rebecca Scales, Jim Sparrow, Lester Spence, Jennifer Stoever, Ludovic Tournès, and Derek Vaillant. At UVA, I received expert guidance and feedback from Kandioura Dramé, Claudrena Harold, Sandhya Shukla,

Bonnie Gordon, and Eric Lott as well as from my fellow fellows. My thanks to Joshua Clark Davis and the contributors to the German Historical Institute's workshop on the globalization of African American business and consumer culture, particularly Davarian Baldwin, Brenna Greer, and Donna Murch, and to Saliou Mbaye and Ibrahima Wane for the opportunity to participate in the Colloque Cinquantenaire du 1er Festival Mondial des Arts Nègres in Dakar. I want to acknowledge the African American Intellectual History Society, especially its cofounders Keisha Blain, Chris Cameron, and Ashley Farmer, and the wonderful scholars I have met through it, including Reena Goldthree, Stephen Hall, Guy Emerson Mount, Sandy Placido, David Romine, and Quito Swan. Finally, a note of thanks is due to the CNY jazz and culture writing group— Ben Givan, James Gordon Williams, Darren Mueller, Fritz Schenker, and Ben Baker—for their insightful comments and suggestions.

I am grateful to the colleagues and friends in France who opened up their memories and homes: Jean and Richard Copans; Dominique, Étienne, and Jean-Louis Achille; as well as Philippe Baudoin, Michel Brillié, Philippe Carles, Laurent Clarke, François Desbrosses, Joël Dufour, Eric Dussault, Christian Gauffre, Yann Gillot, Michael Haggerty, Jean Hébrard, Jacques Muyal, Jacques Joyard, Hilary Kaiser, Jacques Périn, Gilles Pétard, Michel Poulain, Bernard Vincent, Jean-Claude Zancarini, and Michelle Zancarini-Fournel. I also offer thanks and remembrances to the late André Clergeat, Jacques Demêtre, André Francis, Jean-Marie Masse, and Alain Tercinet. I am so grateful to have met the late Michelle Vian, whose friendship—and lessons in French and feminism— enriched this book and my time in France. I offer particular thanks to Daniel Richard and Thérèse Chasseguet, who have been such faithful friends and advanced this project in innumerable ways. In Senegal, my profound thanks to Ousmane Sow Huchard, Marthe Ndiaye, Mamadou Thior, Ousmane Sene, Bouna Ndiaye, and Cheikh Amala Doucouré, who all offered generous assistance and support for my research in Dakar, and to Ricardo Niasse, Gibril Gaye, Alioune Diop, and Moustafa Sene for sharing their experiences and expertise. A special note of thanks too goes to John Betsch, Georges Collinet, the late Bobby Few, Famoudou Don Moye, Steve Potts, Archie Shepp, and Val Wilmer, whose memories and music have enriched this project.

None of this would be possible without the collegiality and comradeship of dear friends I have met along the way, whose insights have informed this book in ways that are hard to even discern now and whose friendship has sustained me. My particular gratitude to Sarah Miller-Davenport, Venus Bivar, Jake Smith, Gwyn Troyer, Monica Mercado, Sam Lebovic, Tyler Fleming, Emily Marker, Susannah Engstrom, Chris Dingwall, Eleanor Rivera, Alexsia

Chan, Pavitra Sundar, Faiza Moatasim, Sam Rosenfeld, Erica De Bruin, Dave Morton, Jane Lynch, Tyler Fleming, Kate Adelstein, Kate Brown, Claire Moufflard, Alex Plakias, Heather Sullivan, and Joel Winkelman. Rebecca Vandiver has offered support, advice, and (necessary) tough love at too many moments to count: thank you for it all. Thank you to Dey, Sarah, Anna, and the NEDAP crew for grounding my own work in social justice. Thanks to Cara, Hannah, Ellen, and Lucy for being critical sounding boards and steadfast friends. I am so grateful to my family: my parents—Susan and Thad—for modeling compassion and curiosity, and for your unconditional support and love; my brother, Spencer, for keeping me honest; and Barbara, for her incredible generosity.

I owe Peter everything. Thank you for your humor, intellect, and strength; for reading endless drafts, for traveling with me when you could and taking care of our children when you couldn't; and for being part of this joyful journey. And finally, a note to Agnes and Meridel, whose births have brought great happiness and now disquiet as I look at the world that surrounds us. It is for them that I write and work—but also fight—for a just future for all.

INTRODUCTION

Making Soundwaves

———

Over the course of five days in October 1961, Ray Charles gave six electrifying, sold-out performances at the Palais des Sports in Paris.[1] Although Charles had been relatively unknown in France just a few years earlier, his fame had skyrocketed in the previous months. Thanks to the commercial success of his recordings and the transnational media networks that broadcast his music, Charles's concerts attracted a record-breaking thirty-five thousand attendees, who squeezed into the sports stadium to hear and see him, now accompanied by a sixteen-member band and the backing vocals of the Raelettes. Charles's triumphant debut in Paris, however, came close to being canceled altogether. Until the eve of the first scheduled concert, the Palais des Sports served as a temporary detainment facility for seven thousand people arrested on October 17, 1961, in the midst of the Algerian War. That night, the Paris police descended on tens of thousands of North African men, women, and children as they attempted to demonstrate peacefully in the city center, killing dozens and detaining (and torturing) fourteen thousand people at sites across the city.[2] Two days later, fearing the public outcry and financial repercussions if the concerts were canceled, officials moved the detainees from the Palais to the nearby Parc des Expositions, where thousands of North Africans remained detained.

On Friday, October 20, the Palais opened its doors, guarded by a phalanx of police forces and still reeking of disinfectant. For Ray Charles, as well as the twenty performers who accompanied him, the hours leading up to the concert were disorienting. Charles himself claimed later that the Algerian National Liberation Front (Front de Libération Nationale, or FLN) assured him and the band they would have safe passage to the Palais, while tenor saxophonist Leroy Cooper recalled their terror in anticipating the invasion of armed police at any moment.[3] Even though one report noted the "impressive deployment of police," who seemed better suited to "quell demonstrations of a political nature than the enthusiasm of the spectators," there was no mention in contemporary accounts of the detention center at the Parc des Expositions.[4] Likewise, few concertgoers recalled the sounds of the nearby detainees, though latecomers could have heard their hymns of resistance. Instead, they thrilled to the sounds of Ray Charles and his big band, who performed nightly for a largely—but not entirely—white crowd in the cavernous space of the Palais des Sports.

The big band began each night's performance with musical arrangements by Quincy Jones, Charles's longtime friend and collaborator, before Charles himself appeared on stage, prompting an explosive response from the restless audience. In the concert recordings, the audience can be heard singing joyfully along to lyrics likely memorized after constant radio play and repeated listening to records distributed in France. Each concert ended with an encore performance of "What'd I Say," a call-and-response song whose play on the secular and spiritual was deepened by the accompaniment of the Raelettes, whose vocal responses to Charles helped re-create the dialogic sound of the gospel tradition.[5] An unofficial civil rights anthem in the United States, the song now thrilled a European crowd less than a hundred yards from an illegal internment site holding several thousand of their fellow citizens. The intimacy and immediacy of the soundscape created in the Palais des Sports were then broadcast over state-run networks to transistor radios throughout France and North Africa, where combatants on both sides of the war listened to the evening transmission.

While the immediate coverage of the concerts made little mention of the ongoing violence in Paris, Charles's performances themselves soon became a medium to express injustice. A few weeks after the concerts, a group of Algerian students published an open letter critiquing the French belief that a love of African American music exempted its audiences and critics from accusations of racism.[6] Instead, they argued, the conditions for this particular performance had simultaneously buttressed and obscured the state's enactment of racial violence. The concerts—and their attendant sounds and silences—echoed throughout France and its crumbling empire.

I begin here, in the transnational and imperial soundscape of the Palais des Sports, to introduce the conceptual and methodological stakes of *Soundscapes of Liberation*, which tracks the transatlantic networks of musical production, distribution, and performance that converged in postwar France to make African American music a signifier of power and protest. Surveying a wide range of musical genres, forms, and media, this book shows how African American music became a critical means for French and Francophone audiences to comprehend the transformations of the postwar period—in particular the convergence of decolonization, the expanding global economy, the Cold War, and worldwide liberation movements.

While the French interest in African American culture is most often associated with the interwar period, when Josephine Baker's performances in *La Revue nègre* thrilled Parisian audiences, this book presents a new narrative of African American culture's appeal. Baker's performance may have epitomized the dynamics of interwar negrophilia—and the vogue for Black performance and culture in Paris—but the historical currents that defined the postwar period are discernible in a very different set of historical actors and venues: the US military's own wartime record and radio distribution, the translation and promotion of "racial passing" memoirs, the French record industry's catalogues of blues, jazz, and R&B recordings, the emergence of a provincial choir that specialized in Negro spirituals, and the millions of listeners stretching across the French empire who heard jazz programs hosted by US State Department officials. These moments exemplify the historical and material conditions that defined an era when new sound technologies, expanding media networks, and changing political climates radically transformed French encounters with African American music. These new conditions, and the changing terms and technologies, helped African American music sound like liberation, but in contradictory ways that simultaneously undergirded state power and insurgent protest.

In making sense of the sounds and silences that defined the postwar world, I turn to the conceptual framing of a soundscape, which has offered scholars a way not only to consider the specific conditions of an acoustical environment but also to show how that same environment in turn transforms the means and modes of perception.[7] This scholarly tradition echoes Jacques Attali's own formulation that music might be understood not simply as an "object of study," but instead as a "way of perceiving the world."[8] Likewise, *Soundscapes of Liberation* is committed to uncovering the material conditions of musical production, casting a wide net to reconstruct the different technologies, networks, and producers who created specific soundscapes and acoustical spaces in which listeners encountered African American music.[9] Within these soundscapes, African American music was not simply a sonic diversion or background music to the tumultuous events of the postwar period. It demanded new modes of discernment and perception, conjured distinct racial visions and fantasies, bolstered competing notions of liberation and freedom, and trained the "listening ear" to distinguish African American music from the "noise" of a dying colonialism.[10] Through the analytical framework of the soundscape, we thus not only discern the structural dimensions of sound production and distribution but also comprehend how these same spaces formed competing notions of liberation in postwar France.

These soundscapes, I argue, were constructed by a cohort of cultural intermediaries—record and radio producers, book publishers, translators, writers, and educators—whose fluency in French and familiarity with African American culture gave them privileged positions from which to interpret, disseminate, and racially encode this musical tradition for Francophone audiences.[11] Some, like record producer Nicole Barclay and critic Boris Vian, were motivated by personal gain. Others, like educator Louis Achille and radio producer Sim Copans, imagined a different political future sustained through intercultural and international dialogue. While the work of these intermediaries was firmly embedded in the new media technologies and political circumstances of the postwar world, I contend that these intermediaries were inheritors of mediating traditions that were formed within the Atlantic world and its transatlantic brokers, interlocutors, and *passeurs,* as well as by the Black Atlantic, whose paths, routes, and grooves were critical to the circulation of Black music in the twentieth century.[12]

Whether by creating a print market for Black literature, launching new record companies to distribute jazz and blues LPs, introducing US State Department–sponsored programs on jazz to the French radio, or redefining the political power of Negro spirituals within the burgeoning networks of postwar and postcolonial Black internationalism, these mediating figures were instrumental in defining the sonic and political power of African American music after World War II. Compounding—and at times misreading—complex musical meanings as they conveyed it across national and imperial boundaries, these intermediaries imbued African American music with new racial value and political power.[13] Conscious of their own inability to fully embody the African American musical tradition, they often accomplished their interventions through nonmusical means: photographs, liner notes, prefaces, artwork, and physical gestures. With the addition of visual, experiential, aural, and discursive clues, they demonstrated both their fidelity to African

American culture and their commitment to racially "marking" this cultural tradition and making it legible to audiences in France and beyond.[14]

It was the work of these intermediaries that made possible the emergence of distinct yet overlapping soundscapes of liberation, in which African American music gained new meaning and value. Some of these were formed in physical spaces: the villages of liberation-era Normandy in which jazz was broadcast from mobile broadcasting trucks, the provincial concert halls that welcomed touring blues and gospel performers in the 1950s, the Lyonnais classroom where students gathered to learn and perform Negro spirituals, or the Parisian *foyer*, where African laborers gathered to hear performances by the Art Ensemble of Chicago in the early 1970s. Other soundscapes were constructed through Cold War, commercial, and colonial media networks, which brought these sounds into the everyday lives of listeners across the nation and empire: in the *disquaires* and jukeboxes that sold recordings of blues, jazz, and R&B; the millions of listeners who tuned in nightly to hear US State Department–sponsored jazz programs on the French radio; and the Caribbean and African students who listened to these same programs and concerts while noting the contradictions that defined postwar and postcolonial France. Within these new media, African American music no longer simply implied the slippage between the modern and the primitive for French audiences, as it had in the interwar period.[15] It instead simultaneously connoted the threat of American hegemony, the growing ubiquity of mass consumerism, the waning influence of French colonialism, and the cultural power of a minority population.

Performance and Power

Though attentive to these intermediaries' privilege—and their particular empowerment within the conditions of the postwar world—*Soundscapes of Liberation* also shows how their power was experienced and contested.[16] White French audiences may have comprised the majority of consumers and listeners, but these networks of musical mediation also reached Black and other nonwhite Francophone audiences, whose sharp observations, interpretations, and interventions would further transform the political power and value of African American music.[17] Moreover, while cultural intermediaries and audiences may have invested liberatory potential in African American music, Black musicians, interlocutors, and performers recognized that this was distinct from any investment in Black liberation. Put simply, listening to African American music did not necessarily entail a heightened consciousness of (or commitment to) Black people's struggles for liberation.[18] Nevertheless, African American, African,

Caribbean, and Afro-European observers found ways to navigate these spatial spheres of influence. In some cases, Afro-European musicians found that adopting the African American musical tradition could be a means of claiming expertise or an "authentic" musical identity, even if they were viewed by white contemporaries as facsimiles of "real" jazz performers. At other moments, African and Caribbean listeners, writers, and performers used the vibrant public discourse surrounding both jazz and African American identity to initiate different (and at times riskier) debates about the nature of French colonialism and racism. They did so in a nation and a language that was resistant to conversations about race, rendering the discourse that surrounded African American music a key mode of expression and dialogue.

The stakes for African American musicians were different. Some musicians, like blues pianist Memphis Slim and drummer Kenny Clarke, came to France to secure a steady income and a life that was free of the constraints imposed by anti-Black US racism. Others, like the actress and pianist Hazel Scott, traveled to Paris after being blacklisted in the film and recording industries during the McCarthy era. Unlike her contemporaries Paul Robeson and W. E. B. Du Bois, whose passports were revoked, Scott was able to live in Paris for three years, a period of "much needed rest, not from work, but from racial tension." Scott went on to clarify, "I do not mean that I never run into racism. . . . I'm not going to say that France is paradise, but I will say this: You can live anywhere if you've got the money to live."[19] For Scott, Paris offered a space in which to create and to construct a different kind of life.[20]

While Scott found that her experiences with French racism were mitigated in part by her success as an African American performer, others were less convinced. In the course of an evening's conversation at the Café Le Tournon, where Richard Wright, Art Simmons, Larry Potter, Ollie Harrington, James Baldwin, Gordon Heath, and Chester Himes would often gather to drink, reconnect, and swap stories, William Gardner Smith transcribed a lively debate about life in France. After Wright offered the group his well-worn aphorism that "there's more democracy in one square block of Paris than in the whole of the United States," they all began to share their own perspectives on expatriate life.[21] In response to one man's claim that all white people were "potential crackers or Afrikaners if you put them in the right circumstances," conductor Dean Dixon replied: "Probably. But the thing is, we don't have those 'right circumstances' here at the present time. So you and I can live in relative peace for a change. That's already something."[22] In this, Dixon underscored the "relative" conditions of success for African American expatriates, who recognized that they were living on borrowed time.

And indeed, the lived experience of racism in France was shifting throughout the postwar period alongside departmentalization and decolonization. While interwar Paris was populated by a relatively small number of African and Caribbean students, the postwar period was marked by increased migration from the newly formed departments of Martinique, Guadeloupe, and French Guiana as well as from the African continent. Following decolonization in Africa and the formation of the Bureau pour la Migration des Départements d'Outre-mer (Bumidom) in 1962, the number of migrants from the Caribbean and Africa soared, establishing in France for the first time a Black working class.[23]

The centrality of these transformations, as well as the ongoing battle for colonial power in Algeria, was not lost on African American musicians, who closely observed the similarities and differences between racism in the United States and France. Tenor saxophonist Frank Wright, for example, perceived the effect of heightened racism during the Algerian War, noting the "police patrolling the streets, stopping mostly Algerians and Africans."[24] However, the increased migration also meant that African American musicians had more opportunities to work with African and Caribbean musicians. For Nina Simone, for example, these collaborations were musical and diasporic, offering her a way to "create my own Africa in the heart of Europe."[25] Similarly, African American drummer Famoudou Don Moye, who performed regularly in Paris with the Art Ensemble of Chicago, was especially drawn to partnerships with African drummers and opportunities to raise money for African municipal workers.[26]

Sidney Bechet, whose own journey has been defined as a kind of archetypal narrative for jazz in France, found in postwar France a critical space not only to perform but to craft his own account of jazz history. Through his long-standing relationship with the French record label Vogue, Bechet purportedly averaged fifty thousand dollars a year from recording royalties as well as from his extensive tours throughout Europe, France, and its overseas departments.[27] When Vogue hosted a free concert in Paris at the Olympia Theater in 1955 to celebrate the sale of over 1 million copies of the 1950 hit record "Les oignons," more than five thousand people crowded into a concert hall meant to hold only half that number.[28] But even as he relished his success, Bechet was loath to romanticize postwar France as either racially colorblind or as an idyllic space for artistic production. While he too found in France a link to his imagined African past—describing his life in France as "closer to Africa"—he was critical of its colonial policies.[29] He explained to an *Esquire* interviewer in 1958: "I live in France because that's where I can make a living. If I could make out with money back home, I'd be back in New York tomorrow." Moreover, he maintained, "The

French have no call to crow over Americans. I've told them so. I've told them I've been in Dakar and I've seen what they do to Negroes there, and Frenchmen are no better than anyone else."[30] Clear-eyed in his accounting of French racism, Bechet still recognized in France a market that could not only sustain the last stages of his career but also give him access to the necessary financial, symbolic, and cultural resources to write his own autobiography.[31]

While their reasons for living in France varied, African American musicians were frequently read as emblems of resistance, for their identities were already defined within a global economy that traded in representations of their suffering, political consciousness, and liberation.[32] They remained, of course, performers who determined their set lists, performance styles, and creative output. But their own musical and aesthetic decisions were made within a shifting discourse in France, some of which they understood and some of which was translated (or mistranslated) for them. While Ray Charles and Sidney Bechet occupied vastly different positions in the French musical landscape, each found himself invoked in the service of a range of narratives, some affirming colorblindness and some directly defying it. The popularization of African American music depended on the presence of musicians, but these musicians were excluded from the mechanisms of mediation. The products of their labor—and the mobility of their musical creations in a global marketplace—frequently depended on the musicians' own immobility within French society.[33]

To succeed, African American musicians needed to navigate the complex conditions of musical production and distribution in France. Sometimes they directly challenged how their artistic creations were redeployed. In other cases, their responses required more restraint but nevertheless became what Stuart Hall has described as sites of "strategic contestation," comprising a range of "subterranean strategies of recoding and transcoding, of critical signification, of signifying."[34] Performing at the Salle Pleyel in 1969, jazz saxophonist Julian "Cannonball" Adderley introduced his quintet to the crowd. The dulcet tones of Adderley's distinctive voice would likely not have prepared his audience for his comments. Adderley said: "Thank you very much, ladies and gentlemen. I could say something like 'it's so wonderful being back in Paris again' or 'it's a pleasure being here playing for you' when obviously everyone understands that it's our pleasure being here because we are *employed*. We are being compensated for our presence, so naturally it's wonderful."[35] Improvising on the script of expected pleasantries, Adderley clarified instead that his own enjoyment derived from compensation and employment. In so doing, he located himself within a system of commerce and claimed (for himself and his bandmates) the right to create, define, and control the musical creations of African Americans.

While this book is transatlantic in its narrative arc and archive, it is grounded mainly in France, which has long claimed a special—and in some ways foundational—place in the history of African American music and culture.[36] This history has its roots in *la belle époque*, but it was the outbreak of World War I that ushered in a new era for African American expatriates and culture in France. Beginning with the arrival of James Reese Europe's Harlem Hellfighters band, African American performers were phenomenally successful in interwar Paris, where Josephine Baker and Ada "Bricktop" Smith attracted fervent audiences. Against this backdrop, African American artists, musicians, and writers found in Paris not only opportunities for financial success and artistic creation but also a space of diasporic connection and collaboration. These overlapping histories are perhaps most vivid in the lives they shaped: writers like Richard Wright, Angela Davis, James Baldwin, and Chester Himes; performers like Hazel Scott, Memphis Slim, and the Art Ensemble of Chicago; artists like Loïs Mailou Jones, Herbert Gentry, and Barbara Chase-Riboud; as well as the less-publicized sojourns of journalists, soldiers, chefs, and students. Each of these figures helps to reveal how the contours of African American history have been influenced by the real and mythical voyage to Paris, where racial codes and violence did not determine every life decision. Reflecting on the African American investment in this narrative, Tyler Stovall has argued that the history of exile in France has served as an important "success story" for African Americans and a rejoinder to the traditional narrative of Black impoverishment and struggle.[37] In these cases, Black Paris was a significant *lieu de mémoire*, a site of memory and critical archive of a moment, life, or career in which American racism did not triumph.[38]

While it is clear that France has played a critical role in the lives of African American performers and writers, this narrative has unfortunately upheld a set of mythologies and misunderstandings that are endemic to French history and historiography.[39] Indeed, as Stovall himself and others have noted, the romanticization of French colorblindness (even when used strategically by African Americans) has obscured the extent of French racism and the impact of colonial racial ideology on all dimensions of French society.[40] This was clearly evident to African American observers, who took note of the parallels and correspondences between their experiences, whether in the treatment of colonial troops, the racial division of labor, or the state-sanctioned violence against African and North African communities. The recognition of French racism, and its parallels to other imperial and settler colonial systems, was likewise critical to the emergence of decolonial, anticolonial, pan-African, and Black internationalist movements.[41] While these converging movements developed a global critique of colonialism and empire, their own insights were frequently ignored in France, where a range of power brokers sought to minimize the significance of race and racism in discourse, politics, and policy.[42]

For a long time, the dominant myth of colorblindness was woven into the histories of jazz in France, where, in James Baldwin's memorable phrasing, audiences imagined that all African Americans arrived "trumpet-laden and twinkle-toed, bearing scars so unutterably painful that all of the glories of the French Republic may not suffice to heal them."[43] This exceptionalism in turn hindered the construction of the kinds of critical readings that defined the scholarship on "global jazz"—including work on Great Britain, Germany, Japan, China, and South Africa—whose national histories are not as weighted by narratives of rescue and liberation.[44] In recent years, however, a range of scholars, including Jeremy Lane, Andy Fry, and Eric Drott, have debunked this narrative and drawn attention to the intersections of jazz fandom and performance with structures of colonial racism and racist policies in France.[45] Their insistence on the centrality of French colonialism to jazz history has strengthened an already rich scholarly field, which has illuminated not only the lives of individual musicians but also the range of debates that occurred within the world of jazz criticism.[46] This work has effectively demonstrated how these internal quarrels—which focused on questions of jazz authenticity and ownership—reflected concurrent social and political debates in France. However, as Fry has argued, the focus on processes of integration, acculturation, and civilization tends to replicate and reproduce the narratives of assimilation that have long defined French politics and culture.[47] Given that, it may be less important to locate the precise moment in which jazz was assimilated into French culture than to pay closer attention to how (and why) African American music occupied a changing—if continually contradictory—position in French society throughout the twentieth century. These contradictions have been at the center of recent scholarship, including work by Elizabeth MacGregor, who considers how jazz intersected with a range of postwar social questions, and Tom Perchard and Rashida Braggs, who have brought attention to the performers and performances that challenged the nationalist and racist narratives of jazz.[48]

While indebted to this work, my book takes a different approach to historicizing the twinned discourses surrounding African American music and racial consciousness in France. First, while jazz has been the focal point in most discussions, this book looks at a wider range of musical genres. I discuss jazz but also track the history of other genres—blues, spirituals, gospel, rhythm and blues, and soul—which proliferated alongside other forms of French popular music. In broadening the frame, I am informed not only by musicians' own critiques of these market-driven taxonomies, but also by a range of scholarship that has foregrounded the shifting discursive terrain for defining and selling African American music in the United States.[49] Second, this book seeks to move beyond the world of jazz critics to uncover the material history of musical production and distribution, whether in the construction of radio networks, the production of records, or the development of political and social institutions. In forming this methodological approach, I draw on the rich social and cultural histories of African American music in the United States that have offered important strategies for historicizing the materiality of music and sound.[50] While the dynamics in France are distinct, these US-based studies have offered critical insights into how the changing social, political, technological, and economic conditions for musical production can give rise to new forms of racial consciousness and political activism.[51]

This book is also committed to expanding its analysis beyond metropolitan France. It builds in part on critical interventions in French and French colonial historiography, which have clarified not only the troubled history of departmentalization and the unequal allocation of political power in the postwar period, but also recent work that has brought attention to the ways in which decolonial thinking preceded *and* followed the formal end of empire.[52] The broader push for liberation occurred throughout the French empire, where the linked demands for sovereignty, human rights, and the end of empire were frequently met with violence and intimidation. In these spaces, Afro-European activists built political movements that simultaneously claimed citizenship rights and diasporic belonging, remapping what Annette Joseph-Gabriel has described as the "geographies of resistance."[53] Within this context, liberation was given new meaning as an emancipatory, anticolonial, and antiracist project.

In addition to rethinking the boundaries of France and its real—and imagined—power in the postcolonial Francophone world, this book also reassesses the linked histories of modernization, decolonization, and Americanization.[54] As Penny Von Eschen has shown, it is not possible to consider the global impact of African American music without paying attention to the networks of US diplomatic power in the Cold War, wherein the linked fates of anticolonialism and civil rights were brought to the fore.[55] While attentive to diplomatic infrastructure and archives, this book shows how the work of US State Department officials was embedded within French cultural institutions, including those in metropolitan France but also those whose influence extended into Francophone Africa. In so doing, *Soundscapes of Liberation* joins a range of historical work that has contested conventional histories of US power—particularly those that privilege US sources and archives—to focus instead on the dialogic reproduction of American culture and identities overseas.[56] Within this expanded history of diplomacy, this book clarifies how and why African American culture was a critical venue in which the "American century" was constructed and contested.[57] Broadcast within these overlapping networks, African American music was linked to American and French power, which simultaneously sustained a French belief in France's own antiracism and a US belief in the liberating power and democratic vigor of American music.

While the power of African American music was frequently co-opted through these different political networks and agendas, the transatlantic routes of production and distribution nevertheless made its deployment especially resonant to listeners within the African diaspora. As Ron Radano and Tejumola Olaniyan have argued, sound was not only produced by imperial and Cold War structures—which helped to "modify and produce qualities of hearing"—but also played a key role in hastening the dissolution of those same powers.[58] Likewise, the presence and active participation of African American, African, and Caribbean musicians and critics in Francophone and Cold War cultural networks reminds us that while this story was given its initial shape by a cohort of (largely) white intermediaries, it is still one that belongs in the global history of Black culture. As scholarship by Alexander Weheliye, Shana Redmond, and Paul Gilroy has shown, the sonic has a privileged place in African diasporic histories.[59] Whether by revealing the persistent exclusion of Black people from narratives of progress and technological innovation or by underscoring the myriad forms of "sonic Afro-modernity" that have defined Black politics, culture, and sociability in the modern era, this work has demonstrated that sound is critical to understanding the liberatory projects formed within Black histories. This book shares that commitment to writing a diasporic history of Black music but shifts the focus to colonial, commercial, and Cold War networks of musical production and distribution. This infrastructure, I argue, was not simply background or context; instead it can serve as a means of expanding the accepted boundaries of Black cultural production. Indeed, the networks of mediation that defined this world—and continue to refine and regulate the meaning of African American culture—were likewise redefined by Black artists, writers, and performers, who found in them new sites of contestation and creation.

The narrative begins in 1944, when US military officials transformed the sonic and racial experience of liberation through new recording technologies and radio networks. Rather than accept the preordained relationship between jazz and liberation, this first chapter instead interrogates the space in which this symbolic connection was forged. In particular, the chapter tracks the broadcasts of US military and diplomatic officials, who reintroduced jazz as an American cultural form through performances by segregated military bands, the distribution of military-issued Victory Discs, and the widespread diffusion of the American Forces Network. In this context, alongside immense sexual, racial, and retributive violence, as well as the mobilization of an unprecedented number of African American and French colonial soldiers, the military imbued jazz with new racial and political value and helped enshrine it as a symbol of postwar freedom. In this, African Americans played a limited yet critical role, frequently desired as a means of authentication yet continually surveilled—and in some cases punished—for crossing racial lines.

Building on this new value for African American music—and simultaneous anxiety about the role of Black people in constructing this valuative system—the second chapter examines the integration of jazz narratives, and their links to African Americans, into postwar intellectual culture. I focus on two books, both of which drew on the authors' own purported links to African American spaces and subcultures to sell their "insider" accounts of African American identity. The first, French jazz critic Boris Vian's novel *I Will Spit on Your Graves* (1946), popularized the social practice of racial passing. The second, Mezz Mezzrow and Bernard Wolfe's memoir *Really the Blues* (1946), was translated into French in 1950. Featured prominently in the postwar media landscape, the books made African American subjectivity both visible *and* salable in postwar French culture. While the authors themselves were critical to this process, this chapter reveals how those around it—the coauthors, publishers, translators, and publicists—made African American music sound like a path toward existential and political liberation for a range of readers.

This new marketability of African American identity and culture would in turn transform the record industry, whose unprecedented profits are the focus in the third chapter. Two record labels—Vogue and Barclay—transformed a small, niche industry into a mass market for jazz, blues, gospel, and spirituals. In so doing, however, they were not simply selling records; rather, they marketed these commodities as conduits to African American culture and the Black freedom struggle. The new valuation was again facilitated by the work of a range of intermediaries, whose knowledge of international regulations, fluency in English, and familiarity and intimacy with African American musicians gave them a privileged position through which to sell African American music in France and its overseas territories and departments. In considering the critical yet sometimes obscured role played by African American musicians in this industry, this chapter challenges accepted narratives of African American musicians' success in France. Some African American musicians did benefit from these developments, which offered new opportunities to tour and record, and even revitalized or launched some careers. But many others were excluded from profits while French producers and moguls capitalized on their musical creations and racial identity.

The profit motive behind the commercial industry is put into sharp relief by the fourth chapter, which considers how the diasporic network of Black internationalism cultivated new venues for postcolonial musical performance and debate. This history begins in the interwar period of Black internationalism, but follows its influence into the postwar period, when Black internationalist politics were reshaped by new media and political pressures. This chapter illuminates the work of Martiniquan educator Louis T. Achille, whose ties to the *négritude* literary movement and experience teaching at Howard University in Washington, DC, helped form a lifelong commitment to translating and performing the African American spiritual in postwar France, where it connoted both French and diasporic identities. Although Achille shared some of the characteristics of other intermediaries in this book, his experience was unique; his own racial identity simultaneously enabled and constrained his capacity to embody the African American musical tradition. Building within and through this ambiguity, he sought to transform the Negro spiritual into a means of achieving spiritual freedom and liberation in the Francophone world.

Turning from the Black internationalist sphere, the fifth chapter considers the history of African American music in the context of the Cold War, when visual and aural representations of African American culture became important tools with which US officials propagated a vision of America as colorblind, universal, and equitable. In this chapter, I deepen this history of statecraft by attending to the radio, lecture, and print networks that linked Cold War diplomacy to the colonial interests of the French government, which itself broadcast US State Department jazz radio programs nightly to millions of listeners across the French empire. The central figure in this chapter is Sim Copans, the Voice of America's official delegate to the French radio, whose radio programs and lecture tours introduced millions of listeners in metropolitan and overseas France to jazz and spirituals. Copans's voice in particular shaped the French encounter with African American music, whose Blackness was understood in relation to his own white, authoritative, and American accent. In this capacity, Copans made clear African American music's potential political value for US State Department officials as well as for state and nongovernmental officials in France. While invested in propagating the liberatory potential of African American music—and indeed affirming its global roots and routes to Africa— Copans still partook in a political project that sought to constrain and limit the possibility of African self-determination in the postcolonial period.

Building on these case studies, and the increasingly global frame in which African American music was produced, the last chapter represents, to some extent, the culmination of the processes detailed in the previous chapters. It demonstrates that the economic, political, spiritual, and cultural value once ascribed to African American music in postwar France was incorporated into postindependence sites of political and cultural expression. This included well-known events like the 1966 First Festival of Black Arts in Dakar and the 1969 Pan-African Cultural Festival in Algiers but was also visible within other media and spaces: the postcolonial and Cold War radio networks, which broadcast the voice of DJ Georges Collinet; the construction of commercial sites and informal trading networks; and the individual performances of musicians like Duke Ellington, Archie Shepp, and James Brown, whose success depended on a range of political and commercial interests. Yet even as commercial interests and diplomatic authorities envisioned—and traded on—a particular understanding of the racial meaning and political power of African American music, there were competing sounds, unexpected encounters and alliances, and new listening practices of African audiences who were attuned to this musical tradition in different and unexpected ways. In this regard, the final chapter also represents a point of departure, a tentative step in understanding how these same transatlantic routes of musical creation in turn shifted the conditions for diasporic encounters.

By centering on France, and the intermediaries who worked within its national, imperial, and diasporic structures, this book reveals a wider web of forces that defined African American music after World War II. It revises the older narrative of African Americans in Paris—and the associated tropes and mythologies that have sustained a narrative of exceptionalism—to instead argue that France is a unique locus and a rich source from which to consider how the racial meaning, political power, and economic value of African American music were transformed in the twentieth century. While honoring the labor of African American musicians to define the politics and value of their music, it calls particular attention to the intermediaries—the networks and agents whose mediating work encoded African American music in new ways.

By uncovering their work, as well as the responses, revisions, and radical reappraisals they engendered among African diasporic listeners and readers, *Soundscapes of Liberation* offers a new way of understanding the sounds and silences that have attended the production of African American music in the twentieth century. Recalling again the Palais des Sports, and the competing sounds that surrounded Ray Charles and the accompanying musicians, it becomes clear that African American music was not only shaped by the conditions of the postwar world but was also critical to perceiving—and ignoring—these same transformations.

1

JAZZ EN LIBERTÉ

The US Military and the Soundscape of Liberation

————

Jacques Chesnel's memoir, *Le jazz en quarantaine* (*Jazz in the Forties*), is an evocative portrait of young jazz fandom in Normandy in the small commune of Venoix, just west of Caen. The memoir's title refers to the decade itself, the 1940s, but it also intentionally gestures to the isolation, or quarantine, from American culture that defined this period. Chesnel felt the double meaning of *quarantaine* particularly in terms of jazz. Well before he had ever heard the music, Chesnel was fascinated by the word "jazz." The silences and unfamiliar phonemes—the unexpected "zz," the "a" that was not really an "a," and the "d" present on the tongue before the word—all alerted him to something new.[1] But jazz remained largely intangible for him until the summer of 1944. While playing a record in his room, Chesnel suddenly heard through the window: "Hey, jazz! Jazz!"[2] He looked out and saw a "tall black man in an American army uniform" who beckoned to him and asked if he liked jazz. They began to talk and laugh, and soon Chesnel realized that this African American GI was none other than Joe Louis, the world-famous and world-champion heavyweight boxer. On learning Louis's identity, Chesnel invited him into his home, where his incredulous parents brought out cake and their best Calvados liquor to welcome the boxer. After asking if he liked Count Basie, Louis offered Chesnel 78 rpm Brunswick records of Basie's "Boogie-Woogie" and "Jumpin' at the Woodside" as well as one of the "famous V-Discs," government-issued Victory Discs intended for American servicepeople. Chesnel "preserved this priceless gift like a relic," but he still could not resist listening to the V-Disc record until it could no longer be played.

In many ways, this story personifies the popular account of the "return" of jazz, which seemed to sound the liberation from Vichy rule and German occupation. Although Chesnel's memory is full of wonder and promise, the liberation was in fact a period of tremendous violence and uncertainty. Even before the arrival of the Anglo–North American forces on June 6, 1944, Norman residents had been bombed heavily by Allied warplanes for nearly two months. The liberation itself continued for months after, resulting in the destruction of property, livestock, and infrastructure, as well as the loss of nearly twenty thousand civilian lives in Normandy alone.[3] Adding to the uncertainty of this period was the precariousness of French sovereignty. With plans to install the Allied Military Government for Occupied Territories (AMGOT) in France, the Anglo-American coalition did not recognize the authority of the Free French leader Charles de Gaulle until October 1944. Moreover, the presence of these new occupants deepened the fractures already wrought by the war, occupation, and collaboration. The resulting fear and anxiety of French civilians was manifest most clearly in their response to the presence and perceived threat of African American soldiers, who were arrested and executed for rape at alarming rates.[4] While Chesnel's response to an African American soldier seemed to have been welcoming, his neighbors' responses were decidedly less so.

Returning to Chesnel's memory, we see the material conditions that would have made it possible—if still unlikely—for Joe Louis to introduce jazz to a young French boy. By this point, Louis was arguably the most recognized African American figure in the world, a position that was cemented following his two fights with the German boxer Max Schmeling. After Schmeling beat Louis in 1936, his victory was hailed by Nazi propagandists as evidence of Aryan superiority. When Louis then beat Schmeling in one round in 1938, his victory made him a hero in the United States among Black and white Americans alike. The image of his animated body—masculine, strong, proud, and poised to fight—was drafted into the service of the US military in 1942, when Louis became a spokesman for the war effort, participating in exhibition matches and visiting American troops on the front.[5] In addition to his embodied connection to US military power, Louis offered Chesnel a V-Disc, one of the military-issued commodities that flooded postwar Europe. These records, along with the sponsorship of military band performances and the widespread diffusion of the American Forces Network (AFN) radio, broadcast a very particular version of jazz to audiences throughout France and the Francophone world. New technologies integrated African American music into the soundscape of liberation, mingling with strange accents and voices, the concussion of artillery and bomb blasts, and constant humming of warplanes.

These technologies, and the military infrastructure that produced them, are the subject of this chapter, which argues that the imagined link between jazz and liberation was forged within a landscape in which African Americans (and Black French soldiers) were met with fear and violence. While both Black Francophone and African American soldiers were constrained in their labor and participation in the war, and subject to judicial and extrajudicial violence, African American music was far more mobile. Its mobility depended on a range of technicians, producers, and cultural intermediaries, who worked within the US military's infrastructure to transform the ways in which French audiences heard African American music. By virtue of their work and the structural conditions of World War II, the real *and* imagined presence of Black people defined the experience of liberation-era France and in turn the world that African American musicians would inhabit.

Mythologies of Jazz in France

By most accounts, French audiences first encountered jazz during World War I, through the performances of James Reese Europe's Fifteenth Infantry Regiment (later the 369th Infantry Regiment, or Harlem Hellfighters) band. Beginning in January 1918, the band performed at train stations and in town squares throughout France (see figure 1.1).[6] Their success in syncopating military music—and, notably, "jazzing up" "La Marseillaise"—helped ignite an explosion of new interest in Black music and culture in interwar Paris.[7] While this period of negrophilia, or *le tumulte noir*, was manifest in art, consumer goods, literature, and philosophy, it had a particular impact on the livelihood of African American performers, including Louis Mitchell's Jazz Kings, Will Marion Cook's Southern Syncopated Orchestra, Ada "Bricktop" Smith, Sidney Bechet, and Josephine Baker.[8] Parisian audiences were especially thrilled by Baker, whose performances in *La Revue nègre* seemed to simultaneously enact and destabilize French notions of primitivism, playing on the thin lines separating racial and national identity in colonial Paris.[9]

African American performers' impact on white French audiences is particularly well documented, but their performances and presence in Paris also transformed the relationships among African and African-descended people in the metropole. Since World War I, France had promulgated assimilationist policies that encouraged African and Caribbean students, workers, and intellectuals to

FIGURE 1.1. James Reese Europe and his Harlem Hellfighters Infantry band performing at American Red Cross Hospital number 5 in Paris, ca. 1918. Photo courtesy of the Collection of the Smithsonian National Museum of African American History and Culture.

pursue educational opportunities in Paris. Once there, these newcomers saw firsthand the ways in which African American culture in particular was valorized, a fascination that stood in stark contrast to the experiences of Black Francophone people, who struggled to gain any form of political or cultural recognition. In this way, the history of interwar negrophilia is fundamentally linked to the history of the contemporaneous movement of *négritude*, which was rooted in a growing international consciousness of racism and empire.[10] In Paris, Black writers worked across the racial identities ascribed by nation and empire to challenge the racist associations with Blackness. Whether by publishing new magazines or attending the weekly salons at the home of the Nardal sisters, Black writers—including Aimé Césaire, Léopold Sédar Senghor, Paulette and Jane Nardal, and Léon Damas—redefined the political meaning and value of Black culture.

French jazz criticism was born out of this particular moment, when its earliest critics sought to identify the racial meaning and power of jazz in the modern age. In this world, the preeminent place of African Americans as jazz creators was not a given; instead, jazz offered a new realm in which to debate the meaning of modernity, consumerism, and national identity. In response to this, some critics—including André Schaeffner and Hugues Panassié— emphasized the racial authenticity of African American jazz performance, not as a mechanism for antiracism but instead as part of the "same anti-American, antimodern agenda" that promoted jazz as authentically French.[11] These debates over authenticity were also linked to jazz's increasing commercialization and its growing links to mass media. Broadcast on the low-wattage Poste Parisien and Radio-Cité stations, jazz could be heard alongside other musical genres, including dance, variety, and tango.[12] In 1932, critics Panassié and Charles Delaunay helped to create the Hot Club de France as a space in which to debate the quality and authenticity of jazz records and performance.[13] In 1935, they launched the jazz journal *Jazz hot*, whose early bilingualism evinced its commitment to defining the history and future of jazz across linguistic and national borders. In the magazine, as well as in essays, discographies, biographies, and books, Panassié and Delaunay introduced their small yet committed fan base to "real jazz": an authentically "hot," Black sound that jazz critics contrasted with the "sweet," commercial orchestral music heard on the radio.

Just as the racial meaning and power of African American music had been shaped by the First World War, its meaning was fundamentally transformed by the onset of the Second World War and the German occupation, when new systems of racial classification and anti-Semitism were enforced by both German officials and the collaborationist government based in the spa town of Vichy. Manipulating gender, reproduction, and family, this regime promoted a racial understanding of French identity that was built on previous anti-Semitic policies and older colonial models.[14] The new racial regulations had a unique impact on jazz, which was associated with both Jewish and African American performers. By 1941, French radio officials in the German-occupied and Vichy zones had mandated that musicians could not be "Jewish in race or religion."[15] They demanded the removal of any albums, performers, and employees with Jewish names, including George Gershwin and Benny Goodman.[16] Moreover, by 1943 the Hot Club had directed its members in Paris and the provinces to be discreet and avoid associations with American music and culture, lest the authorities pick them up for idleness. They also feared association with the *zazous*, young people who embraced "swing" as a mode of sartorial and linguistic resistance during the war. Sporting large pleated pants and "long jackets with high collars," the *zazous* appeared to have borrowed their name and aesthetic from American "zoot suiters," whose style was first introduced by Mexican American and African American youth and later popularized by the jazz singer Cab Calloway.[17] The racial associations with the *zazous* were also noticed by contemporaries, who bemoaned the "youth with long hair and high-collared shirts who wiggle to the *rythme nègre* of swing music."[18]

Jazz was never banned in Paris or in any other part of France in this period. Contrary to what some contemporaries and historians have suggested, jazz flourished during the war, gaining broader circulation through performances on Vichy and German-sponsored radio stations.[19] With the absence of American musicians, French musicians like Gus Viseur, Raymond Legrand, Alix Combelle, Aimé Barelli, and Django Reinhardt became national celebrities.[20] In fact, the Hot Club grew enormously during the war: it even added new chapters in German-annexed Strasbourg and the Stalag VI-B prison camp. The Hot Club sponsored seventy-six concerts over the course of four years in addition to lectures, recordings, and festivals, including the 1940 Festival du Jazz Français and the 1941 Concert du Jazz in Paris.[21] After years of limited success, the Hot Club also helped Django Reinhardt find national celebrity with his 1940 recording of "Nuages."[22] Indeed, the popularity of this *manouche*, or Romany, musician helps clarify why jazz was successful during the war. Even though the Romany people were subject to persecution and deportation, Reinhardt's performances were made palatable and profitable because he was presented as French.[23]

The Hot Club effectively reformulated the meaning and history of jazz as a French cultural creation in keeping with Vichy's ideological formulations. Yet both Panassié and Delaunay remained concerned with the growing popular interest in jazz. Whereas the Hot Club had once been a small, elected minority, now thousands were listening to jazz on the radio and attending concerts. To counter the potential degradation wrought by mass fandom—and in keeping with Vichy-era practices—Delaunay and others (who had previously acknowledged the central role of African Americans as creators) defined jazz as a *French* folk music in both lectures and publications.[24] Despite his previously stated convictions about the African American roots of jazz, Delaunay did not reference the United States or African Americans in his jazz lectures in 1941; instead he emphasized the genre's French origins.[25] Hugues Panassié, by contrast, drew on his well-known commitment to African American authenticity in jazz, a critical position that had been cemented during his time in the United States in the 1930s and through his friendship with Milton "Mezz" Mezzrow.[26] Building on this, Panassié advanced his belief—on Radio Paris and in print— that jazz had been corrupted by commercial forces and that it was necessary to promote an authentic jazz as an antidote to the modern age.[27] Furthermore,

André Coeuroy claimed in his 1942 *Histoire générale du jazz* that jazz was a French folk music, which fit the Vichy regime's commitment to regenerating French culture and identity.[28] This critical position not only insulated the Hot Club from the associations of jazz with American and Jewish cultures but also transformed French jazz musicians into national celebrities and expanded the club's own membership base.

This new vision, which intimated that jazz could contribute to national regeneration and racial purity, offered a precarious place for Antillean and African jazz musicians in Paris.[29] As in World War I, large numbers of soldiers from the French empire were recruited by the military for its campaign against Germany, with the expectation that broader citizenship rights would be extended to colonial subjects.[30] Following the 1940 surrender, some Antillean and African soldiers were captured and interned in German labor camps, while others found themselves in occupied France with no work or clear path home.[31] Among these colonial soldiers were jazz musicians, whose limited options in the wartime labor market were further constrained by curfews and closed public venues. By February 1942, Guadeloupian saxophonist Felix Valvert decided to leave Paris to tour the free zone and brought with him Guadeloupian musicians Albert Lirvat and Claude Martial and Martiniquan performers Robert Mavounzy and Eugène Delouche. Though the tour was cut short after a violent incident with German authorities in Dijon, the group began anew on the Mediterranean coast, touring from May to September 1942. This tour went more smoothly, thanks to the addition of the German-speaking Cameroonian boxer "Malapa," who helped the band cross the demarcation lines and liaise with German authorities. In June 1942, Mavounzy left the tour early to join a new Parisian band led by Cameroonian drummer Fredy Jumbo, who, having been raised in Cameroon and previously worked in a German circus, also had the cultural and linguistic fluency to secure permits. Jumbo's band performed regularly at the Cigale club in Montmartre and featured Mavounzy, Lirvat, and Martial, as well as Henri Godissard of Guyana, Sylvio Siobud of Guadeloupe, and Maurice Thibault of Haiti. After a recording session, both the Swing and Polydor record labels promoted "Fredy Jumbo's marvelous black band and swing ensemble" to "swing fans" throughout France.[32]

In 1943, seeing the difficulties encountered by "musicians of color," trumpeter Abel Beauregard founded the Club Artistique et Musical des Coloniaux, which sought to "tighten the bonds of camaraderie and solidarity among members, to bring them needed moral aide, to help in the perfection of their music, and to defend their professional interests." In 1943, on behalf of the club,

Beauregard wrote to officials at the Vichy-controlled Radiodiffusion Nationale (RN) asking for a place on the program for his "authentically French colonial" group, which included Valvert, Mavounzy, and Martial. He presented his band as a manifestation of true "Antillean folklore" that "could be of great service to French colonial propaganda."[33] By carefully accenting their roots in French folklore and avoiding any American connotations, Beauregard demonstrated the possibilities of cultural assimilation in the process of national renewal.[34]

On December 19, 1943, the Hot Club sponsored an afternoon concert at the Salle Pleyel of the Hot Club Colonial featuring Felix Valvert's band and a smaller ensemble led by Robert Mavounzy. The concert was advertised as the Festival de Musique Nègre and, as later reported, "presented for the first time a large black band and soloists in a program which had to alternate between jazz and Antillean folklore" (see figure 1.2).[35] The relative success of this performance was significant for the musicians themselves, whose wartime popularity helped them gain employment, fame, and at least a limited opportunity to fight unequal treatment. In January 1944, for example, they hosted another concert in Rennes to raise money for colonial prisoners of war.[36]

For white French critics and audiences, however, the performance of the Hot Club Colonial facilitated an affirmation of French identity, folklore, and musical contributions while still retaining its racial signifier, now a French racial minority. Seeking perhaps to counteract the tendency of white French audiences to immediately welcome "the first *nègre* who can drum on a box," the Hot Club officials highlighted the youth and inexperience of the musicians in publicity materials.[37] As one reviewer noted, there would need to be a great deal of work to "reach the average level of continental white musicians." However, this "young school of black French musicians" had "shown the qualities of [their] race: enthusiasm, warmth, and a *bon-enfant* naturalness that puts the listener at ease."[38] Highlighting the "warmth" and "naturalness" of these Black musicians, the French reviewer reinforced the tropes of French colonial racism in a new context. Black Francophone musicians were granted provisional access to the jazz tradition not as cocreators of an African diasporic music but instead as those whose natural warmth might offer an ersatz Black *American* performance for French audiences. By signifying Black culture and invoking French folkloric traditions, Afro-European musicians were, at least for a moment, welcomed to the stage and given a temporary (if highly constrained) pass to African American cultural identity. While this temporary arrangement might have worked for the moment, it would be transformed in June 1944, when the arrival of the Americans generated competing claims on the racial identity of jazz.

SALLE PLEYEL
DIMANCHE **19** DECEMBRE, à 14 h. 15
LE HOT CLUB DE FRANCE
présente :
LE HOT CLUB COLONIAL :

FESTIVAL
DE
MUSIQUE NÈGRE
avec
GRAND ORCHESTRE
sous la direction de Félix VALVERT
*
QUINTETTE ET ORCHESTRE TYPIQUE
*
ROBERT MAVOUNZY
et son nouvel orchestre
LOCATION :

PRIX DES PLACES :
de 40 à 125 frs

FIGURE 1.2. Circular for a concert by the Hot Club Colonial, 1943. Photo courtesy of the Fonds Charles Delaunay, Bibliothèque nationale de France.

Warring Soundscapes

War correspondent Ollie Stewart of the *Baltimore Afro-American* began his reports on the liberation of France with high hopes. In June and July 1944, he recommended the Norman hard apple cider, complained good-naturedly about the fickle weather, and reassured his readers that "colored Americans have been seen taking part in every advance in almost every branch of service."[39] By August 5, 1944, however, he was less enthusiastic: "Apology to readers, if any: If I keep mentioning colors and races in this and other articles, I'm sorry. But everywhere I go it pops up. I'm sick of the subject, and wish I never heard it again, but the army functions on racial lines."[40] Stewart's observations illuminate what remains a powerful elision in both French and American history. The liberation is frequently recalled through images of American GIs offering chewing gum and cigarettes from the backs of trucks, but this focus on smooth political transition and consumer exuberance has obscured an extended period of physical, retributive, sexual, and racial violence, much of which was directed at African Americans, who were disproportionately accused of violent crimes by both French and US officials.

As Stewart reported for his *Afro-American* readers that summer, African Americans comprised 10 percent of the US military, or approximately 126,000 Black soldiers in the European Theater of Operations (ETO) in June 1944, on the eve of the invasion.[41] Though the majority of the 73,000 American troops who landed on the Omaha and Utah Beaches on D-Day were white soldiers, African American soldiers participated as members of the port battalions (490th and 494th) unloading supply ships on D-Day, in the antiaircraft balloon battalion, and in the subsequent waves of troops. Most, however, were assigned to noncombatant labor positions within segregated units in the service and supply corps, where they were largely responsible for the reconstruction and cleanup after the liberation, under conditions that deteriorated quickly as the summer progressed. As African American veteran Bruce McMarion Wright recounted, everywhere were "apples and bodies of cows rotted in the sun." French farmers continued to make their Calvados liquor, which "helped all of us to move forwards under optimum sedation of fear, if not immunity, through the soft apple slush, the dung, and the bodies we used to know."[42] Wright's account underscored the nightmarish conditions, which were exacerbated by segregationist policies. As one of the few Black officers stationed in France, Lieutenant Thomas Russell Jones recalled that "in this era, the American army was still almost totally segregated," with African Americans confined to inferior duties.[43] The continued segregation in the armed forces and defense industries concerned both GIs and civilian African Americans, prompting the *Pittsburgh Courier*'s Double V campaign for victory against enemies at home and abroad. While some African American leaders had pushed for participation in the war, hoping it would ensure full citizenship in the postwar world, others recognized the ways the war had built on and then exacerbated global systems of racism.[44]

Race-based classifications were, in principle, a matter of US military policy, but they nevertheless figured in the lives of many French civilians as well. In November 1945, at the Chanor base in Lille, discrimination complaints were lodged by African American GIs after the words "white" and "colored" were used over the public address to "designate segregated periods for use of shower facilities." The report further pointed out that "a French civilian waiter" was told "to direct one of the . . . officers (colored) to eat outside of the Officers' Mess with the enlisted personnel."[45] French civilian encounters with enlisted

African American men and women were not limited to US military encampments. Stationed in a provincial town in southern France after the Dragoon Allied landing, Lieutenant Jones, mentioned above, described acceptance and humanity during his stay with a French family.[46] Junior officer Joseph O. Curtis described his travels in the south of France with three other "spook officers," who "drew all eyes: male, female, military, and civilian." He recalled, "Don't know when I've been on the other end of so many flirtations."[47] Other Black Americans remembered being met with distant curiosity. In May 1945, the 6,888th Central Postal Directory Battalion, the only African American Women's Army Corps unit to serve overseas, was assigned to Rouen. As one of the 824 enlisted women remembered, "They stared at us. . . . It seemed like they had never seen black women before in their lives."[48]

There is also evidence that the presence of African American troops deeply unsettled the local population. While general complaints about US troops were lodged in several regions, reports from Normandy were most explicit about local concerns with African American troops.[49] The highest number of complaints was centered in Normandy's Cotentin Peninsula, where African American servicemen had been brought for repair and service work following the period of most intense fighting in July and August 1944.[50] According to military reports, "thousands of Negro port battalion troops were billeted in and around" the city of Cherbourg, where residents loudly complained about their presence, stating that "when they've had something to drink, they behave worse than beasts."[51] In September 1944, after reports circulated of an attack on a young girl by a group of Black soldiers, local French officials discussed the imminent hanging of the "three negroes of La Pernelle," just east of Cherbourg. They remarked that "public feeling is very high against the troops and they wish to show the population the measures they are taking against it, but in order to have the hanging public, they will have to have Eisenhower's permission."[52] In this case and many others, they had it.

In a military with a Black membership of roughly 10 percent, Black soldiers were accused and convicted of 77 percent of reported rapes of French women. Of the 181 charges of rape between 1944 and 1946, 139 were levied against African Americans, 18 of whom were executed.[53] Though interpretations of these statistics vary, it is clear that the number of African American soldiers charged and convicted of rape was vastly disproportionate to their numbers in the military. Moreover, witnesses, victims, and prosecutors described these crimes in terms of sexual depravity, bestiality, and deviance, suggesting that the environment in which Black soldiers were charged was racially coded, located within what Heide Fehrenbach has identified in postwar Germany as new "zones of contact."[54] It was not "racial ignorance" that was operationalized in these zones but instead new kinds of "racial knowledge," a "combination of pre-war anti-black racism and exposure to US segregation" that was born out of contact, coercion, and limited communication.[55]

It was in this context—darkness, misinformation, violence, and fear—that American jazz was reintroduced in Normandy, broadcast from the mobile truck of Simon J. Copans. While Copans eventually become one of the best-known radio hosts in France, he was in fact born in Stamford, Connecticut, the son of Jewish immigrants from Lithuania. He had become fluent in French language and culture through extensive academic training in French literature and his marriage to a French woman.[56] Copans had first traveled to France in the 1930s to conduct research for his dissertation on nineteenth-century Franco-American relations.[57] Active in a socialist organization based in Chartres that supported anti-Franco forces in Spain, he then met Lucienne Godiard, whom he married in 1939.[58] One year later, they returned to New York, where Copans taught French at Columbia University and completed his dissertation. In 1944, he was recruited by Pierre Lazareff to join the Office of War Information (OWI) as a civilian radio officer.[59] The OWI had been established in 1942 to reach civilian and military populations through radio, film, press, and other media. Its radio broadcasts were popularly known as the Voice of America (VOA), a program name that had originated with the Foreign Information Service and seemed to capture what Derek Vaillant has described as the "U.S. broadcast techno-aesthetic."[60] Throughout the war, the OWI generated short-wave broadcasts that were relayed from its New York office to stations in Tunis, Algiers, and Italy, to ultimately reach audiences in the rest of Europe with news and American music.[61]

In France, the OWI successfully reached the southern coast with short-wave broadcasts in 1943. However, enemy jamming and poor signal strength stymied the OWI's ability to provide "a consistent flow of fresh American music," which officials had identified as "one of our greatest needs abroad."[62] Given this continued difficulty, in April 1944 the OWI opened a new relay program and broadcasting facility in London known as the American Broadcasting System in Europe (ABSIE), which became a powerful weapon of information for the Allies. Through medium-wave and short-wave transmitters, ABSIE broadcast news and music directly to listeners throughout Europe.[63] Copans had arrived for training at the London facility at precisely the moment of ABSIE's inaugural broadcasts.[64] In June 1944, he received orders to join the Psychological Warfare Division (PWD), whose civilian and military personnel were attached to the First Army. The PWD was created to distribute the "propaganda of liberation" through leaflets, loudspeakers, and radio programs in France and Germany to civilians and deserters alike.[65] Copans was then assigned to the Second Mobile Radio Broadcasting Company, which arrived in France on June 26, twenty days after the Allied landing.[66] Whereas his ABSIE colleagues Irving Berenson and Bravig Imbs were assigned to the task of rebuilding local radio stations, Copans's unit was charged with distributing news and information to French civilians.

When Copans and his fellow PWD officers arrived in Normandy in late June, they followed a trail of destruction that extended from the landing beaches to the coastal towns to the interior of the region (see figure 1.3). Before the liberation, German troops were ordered to seize radio sets in the coastal zone, leaving residents with very little information on what had transpired. Furthermore, without electricity in most towns, the remaining radio sets struggled to capture signals from France and neighboring countries. As they were driven from town to town in trucks equipped with radio transmitters, the PWD officials prepared news bulletins in French based on broadcasts from the British Broadcasting Corporation (BBC) and ABSIE. They delivered the bulletins in approximately twenty towns per day, where they were "usually the first bearers of such information."[67] As one report noted, well before the arranged time, "crowds appeared in the squares, watching the empty road that wound between the hedgerows, eagerly awaiting the Allied town crier." Many such officers would "themselves become figures of note in the countryside." On Sundays, they would sometimes visit towns for the purpose of retransmitting concerts aired on the BBC or ABSIE, which American officials found to be particularly useful in cultivating goodwill.[68] Copans similarly described his own aims to "advise and orient the civilian population" by broadcasting news and information.[69] Throughout the summer of 1944, Copans traveled on a regular basis to at least twenty-five towns throughout the Cotentin Peninsula in the Normandy department of La Manche, among them Carentan, Saint-Côme-du-Mont, Ste-Marie-du-Mont, Ste-Mère-Église, Picauville, Cherbourg, and Barneville-Carteret, most of which were within ten kilometers of one another.

As an unknown person appearing in towns traumatized by recent violence, Copans needed a strategy to draw in, reassure, and win over his audiences. On entering the town of Valognes, then "in the middle of ruins," Copans "parked in a deserted location, and put on a record." Against a soundscape of fearful silence, punctuated by the explosion of artillery or the distant sound of an airplane, Copans played a V-Disc recording of Tommy Dorsey's rendition of Irving Berlin's "Blue Skies," which was, according to Copans, a very effective means of "announcing his arrival."[70] While he turned to jazz in order to bridge the gap between liberator and liberated, Copans was not a jazz aficionado. As

FIGURE 1.3. Sim Copans next to his mobile broadcasting truck in Normandy, ca. June–July 1944. Photo courtesy of the Copans Family Archives.

he put it later, in a turn of phrase typical of his long career in public broadcasting, he "arrived in France with a doctorate in letters but not a doctorate in jazz." In fact, he claimed to have been "obliged" to think about the needs of his French listeners, who had been "cut off during the war" and were "thirsty for American music."[71] In reality, his choice was largely determined by the conditions of wartime musical production as well as the popular shift to swing that began in the late 1930s, when the word "swing"—which had previously referred to a particular form of rhythmic emphasis—became synonymous with white popular bandleaders like Dorsey and Goodman.[72] As David Stowe has written, it was seen by some in the Depression-era US as the "preeminent expression of the New Deal . . . accessible, inclusive, distinctively democratic," and thus distinctly American. Its popularity was further heightened by the onset of World War II, in which the unprecedented mobilization of technology led what Stowe has termed the "militarization of swing."[73]

While obscuring the creative work that African American musicians had done in *making* music "swing," this new genre received widespread dissemination through phonograph players, radio sets, and USO tours, as well as the production and distribution of Victory-Discs, or V-Discs, the same records that Joe Louis had purportedly distributed in 1944. The V-Disc was created in the wake of the 1942 recording ban by the American Federation of Musicians, which sought royalty payments to musicians for concert, radio, and jukebox performances.[74] While it resulted in a two-year hiatus of commercial recording, this recording ban did not prevent the state's involvement in the production or distribution of records. Beginning in 1943, the Army Special Services Division hired recording engineers and producers from Columbia and RCA Victor to produce recordings of musicians and bandleaders—including Glenn Miller, Benny Goodman, Lionel Hampton, Louis Armstrong, and Count Basie—which were then shipped in "waterproof and pressure-resistant cartons of 20 twelve-inch disks" to eight thousand foreign bases, at a rate of 250,000 individual recordings a month.[75] They were nonstandard records, "made of an 'unbreakable' plastic,'" and, because of their larger size, could play six minutes per side rather than the usual three or four minutes.[76] With radio posts and phonographs present in both the barracks and service centers, "soldiers who had not previously heard it were becoming fans of swing and jazz." One bandleader believed more men had become "jazz conscious" during the war, while serviceman called swing a "great morale music."[77]

As a radio broadcaster, Copans had full access to large collections of these V-Discs, including Dorsey's "Blue Skies," which featured a young Frank Sinatra, whose smooth and easy voice alternated with a slightly up-tempo rhythm section and a men's chorus (the Pied Pipers) crooning about bluebirds and happy days ahead (see figure 1.4).[78] This song had been first popularized in the film *The Jazz Singer* (1927) by Al Jolson, whose character signals his liberation from Jewish traditions by performing Tin Pan Alley music in blackface.[79] Nearly twenty years later, it signaled a very different form of liberation. Before the vocals even begin, a muted trombone strikes a light, optimistic note, and then with the first refrain of singing—and the chorus's "Look up, look up"—it transforms the sky's threats into spaces of possibility. We can perhaps imagine its sonic reverberation in the village as it bounced off the rubble of what once was. Copans later remembered that as the song continued, more and more people came to hear and see the source of this music, and "after several minutes," he was "astounded to see 150 people" gathered around his truck.[80] Copans later recalled a "small boy around 11 years old who came 'to hear the American who gave the news, because of the music.'" He claimed that for this boy, "it was love at first sight for American music."[81] The sounds were thus inflected by their visual counterpart: a slight, balding white man in an American uniform poised next to a military truck, whose presence now signaled the end of war.

FIGURE I.4. Victory
Disc of Tommy Dorsey
and His Orchestra,
"Blue Skies."

These events occurred in a French village square, whose bells were immortalized in Alain Corbin's landmark study of sound in social life. Whereas the bells once held a "monopoly" over aerial and aural space and "made manifest the power of the constituted authorities," their importance had faded by the early twentieth century.[82] At war's end, the soundscape was filled with air-raid sirens and German trucks and voices, as well as the profound and fearful silences that infused rural life and occupied the lives of listeners.[83] And in June 1944, it was the loudspeaker microbroadcast of Tommy Dorsey's band that redefined time and space and made manifest the power of the Allied authorities. These new technologies—the V-Disc and the military-operated broadcast truck—altered the soundscape of liberation in Normandy.

In this space, the racial "signals" embedded in these broadcasts were distorted, remade, and redefined by the "noise" of war and reconstruction, obscuring—for the moment—the racial history that preceded and followed these records.[84] Indeed, just five months after Copans's own arrival in Valognes, three African American soldiers were removed at gunpoint from the same village square.[85] Their transgression of the racial hierarchy was then reported to both French and American officials, a reminder that while the co-opted sounds of the African American musical tradition might signal a joyful liberation, its progenitors remained under close surveillance.

While intended for armed forces radio stations and GIs, the 8 million V-Disc records sent around the world reached many unexpected ears. Jacques Chesnel's own V-Disc, which he guarded as a sacred object, was one of thousands of records that entered the French market, were traded in Parisian flea markets, and grew in value following the postwar destruction of the master recordings. The first postwar issues of *Jazz hot* included advertisements in the classified section for V-Discs in "reasonable condition."[86] By April 1946, a section of the fan journal was created to review V-Discs "at the request of numerous readers."[87] In addition to the popularity of V-Discs, many American soldiers carried and traded jazz books published on a mass scale by the Armed Services Editions (ASE) and printed by the Council on Books in Wartime for distribution to the American military.[88] According to reports, the soldiers who boarded invasion barges and landing craft frequently discarded inessential items but kept these sturdy, compact books, including the 1944 edition of *Esquire's Jazz Book*, which instructed listeners on the "extremely complex yet basically savage rhythms" of jazz.[89] Much like V-Discs, the ASE books did not remain in the hands of GIs and were soon scattered throughout Europe. Charles Delaunay, for example, learned about wartime jazz developments by reading the ASE edition of *Esquire*.[90]

The unrestricted movement of new media and technology stand in stark contrast to the limited mobility of African American soldiers, who nevertheless played a key role in reintroducing jazz to French audiences. In fact, there were a number of African American musicians stationed in the Normandy region as service and supply troops. One of the busiest transit sites until 1946 was in the Basse-Seine region. This included Rouen and Le Havre, where hundreds of thousands of American troops were stationed in the so-called cigarette camps, transit camps named after American brands like Old Gold and Lucky Strike.[91] As had been the case in Cherbourg, there were reports of high civilian anxiety regarding the presence of African American soldiers.[92]

Yet it was from within this same region that African American soldiers were frequently solicited as jazz performers and audiences. One of the best-known was drummer Kenny Clarke, who by October 1944 had been transferred via Le Havre to the Thirteenth Special Service in Rouen, where he formed a twelve-member band that toured active service units before audiences of US GIs and French civilians in Rouen and in Paris (where he met Charles Delaunay). It was in Rouen that Clarke met John Lewis, with whom he later formed the Modern Jazz Quartet.[93] Because there was no official military band in Le Havre, US officials frequently called on local French jazz musicians to perform, drawing from well-established chapters of the Hot Club de France in both Le

Havre and Rouen. In December 1944 and January 1945, for example, the jazz band from Rouen played nearly a dozen times at the Philip Morris camp and at a local pool occupied by the American army.[94] Moreover, correspondents later reported that these French bands benefited from the occasional participation of African American musicians stationed in the region.[95] In many cases, the presence of African American GIs authenticated the jazz performance and made clear the transition from previous racial regimes.

Another central transit site was near Marseille, whose local Hot Club noted with excitement the "great number of musicians and American bands stationed there."[96] In 1945, after allegedly finding himself among "thousands of black Americans" and before "revues entirely played by blacks," Hugues Panassié declared Marseille the "new capital of jazz." Overwhelmed, he wrote: "I had the impression of finding myself in Harlem. There was the kind of ambiance of when a good black band plays for black dancers."[97] As Panassié's response reveals, African American soldiers and musicians helped create the "kind of ambiance" that was sought in this particular moment. While this "ambiance" was in fact secured by US segregationist policies—which separated Red Cross clubs for white and African American GIs to avoid "racial clashes"—French audiences reveled in this approximation of a "black and tan" milieu.[98]

The embodied presence of African American musicians on US military bases was also crucial to the orchestration of recording sessions. In September 1945, Panassié supervised a recording session with a "colored all-star band" from the Delta Base Section at the local American Forces Network station.[99] And between 1944 and 1945, the French folklorist Paul Arma hosted and recorded several concerts featuring African American "Negro spirituals" quartets, recordings that he would later include on his Parisian radio program *Rhapsodies noires*.[100] He claimed that these singers "spontaneously formed" ensembles in the military, including Harmony Wonders, Secret Star, Jubilee Four, and Harmony Four. In organizing a series of five concerts from April to July 1945 in Paris, Arma claimed he had difficulty securing official permits because "some white officers" were offended by the quartets' success. In contrast to the US officials, Arma claimed to have directly engaged his new "black friends" in discussion of "racial problems in the United States." He drew on these relationships in promoting the concerts, which, he argued, represented the "hope born in the period of slavery, sustained across generations." The concerts, as he recalled, drew "long and frenetic" applause from the French audiences.[101] After identifying these performers as nonprofessionals who "sing when it pleases them," one reviewer defined their music as the "songs of the oppressed" and "almost songs of resistance."[102] Later reviews of the recordings remarked that the musicians had no musical training but were instead "natural musicians" and that the recordings themselves were "a faithful translation" of the "natural harmonizations" of Black singers.[103] These characterizations reveal little about the musicians themselves, who may in fact have been professional performers, but do exemplify the prevailing jazz discourse, which privileged "natural" performances over those deemed too commercial or professionalized.

The liberation of Paris opened up new opportunities for jazz performance. The reopening of the Hot Club in Paris on September 1, 1944, was reported to be a particularly special event, witnessed by French fans, musicians, and numerous African American GIs, including trumpeter Arthur Briggs, who had returned to France (where he had lived throughout the 1930s) after being imprisoned in a German labor camp for four years.[104] On October 15, 1944, at the École Normale de Musique, the Hot Club presented its first concert of the season, featuring Briggs and banjo player Dick Griffith, another former GI.[105] Rudolph Dunbar of the *Chicago Defender* and Ollie Stewart of the *Baltimore Afro-American* described the young crowds who gathered to see "Briggs, the ace colored trumpeter" and "to welcome his return into the ferment of swing music after four and a half years of internment." Dunbar credited the Hot Club with educating its membership on the Black roots of jazz and the foundational work of Black musicians.[106] He wrote: "The music in all of them [the Montmartre night clubs] is hot and good for swing music is now the vogue in Paris. It is amazing to see how the French musicians have adopted themselves to the rhythmic exuberance of swing."

Stewart and Dunbar were joined by other African American war correspondents in witnessing the "rebirth of swing music in this music-loving city."[107] In 1945, Roi Ottley of the *Pittsburgh Courier* described walking at night in Montmartre, whose "shuttered windows" and empty streets seemed menacing until he heard "an old familiar tune." At first, he could just pick up the "strains of a saxophone," but Ottley soon recognized a recording of Coleman Hawkins's "Body and Soul." The song "seemed to suggest that the French were reasserting their traditional independence—and this included their love for Negro music." While Ottley believed that the presence of Black soldiers had reinforced the already "profound influence" of African American culture, Allan Morrison, correspondent for *Stars and Stripes*, was equally struck by the novelty of postliberation jazz, which he referred to as "free jazz."[108] Reporters also delighted in the international character of Parisian jam sessions, which featured Django Reinhardt, André Ekyan, Hubert Rostaing, Robert Mavounzy ("a colored lad"), and "many other colored swing musicians," most of whom were left unnamed.[109] Having weathered the war, these Caribbean and African musicians represented the rebirth of swing. For white French observers, these racialized performance spaces were thrilling to enter and observe. In 1945, the *Bulletin du Hot Club* reported that American soldiers had been attracted to "several bands *de couleur*" in Pigalle, particularly the Cigale, which featured Fredy Jumbo's band. One French observer wrote, "Sometimes it seems that we find ourselves plunged into . . . the ruckus of Harlem," for the "black musicians made of this place their general neighborhood"; and "despite the cries from the owner who presides powerless over this unleashing," the Black soldiers "danced in all corners of the room."[110] Whether as performers or dancers, African Americans were critical—if obscured—features of the liberation soundscape.

Outside of direct encounters in which jazz was embodied by African American GIs and tinged with new forms of fear and excitement, the US military continued to broadcast a racialized vision of jazz through its expanding radio networks. Indeed, this is where the conflict over the racial provenance and affiliation of jazz would play out in its most prolonged form. While the US military had been broadcasting radio programs to its domestic troops since the war began, it established the American Forces Network (AFN) in 1942 to broaden its diffusion. On July 4, 1943, the AFN had begun broadcasting out of London to troops in Western Europe.[111] The AFN stations played V-Discs as well as recorded transcriptions of variety programs (with fifteen minutes of programming on each side) produced in Los Angeles in front of live audiences. In addition to variety shows like *Hit Parade, GI Jive, Command Performance*, and *Mail Call*, the AFN regularly rebroadcast programs of jazz recordings, including *Condon's Jazz Session* and weekly broadcasts featuring Duke Ellington.[112] One of the more popular programs was *Jubilee*, an all-Black variety show that featured host Ernie Whitman and performers including Count Basie, Duke Ellington, and Lionel Hampton. Some guests, as Lauren Sklaroff observes, made "both subtle and overt references to American racial tensions," but the show was not described as African American programming and thus drew in audiences throughout the AFN listening network.[113] It was the network's fourth most popular show and was consistently featured on peak evening hours.[114]

According to contemporary reports, during the eighteen-month period following the liberation, "American popular music and American radio programs were heard continuously for twenty hours a day" in France.[115] On January 9, 1945, for example, listeners could hear *Hit Parade, Amos 'n' Andy*, and *Condon's Jazz Session* on a local AFN station. By mid-June 1945, with the new recording studio on rue François 1° in Paris, even French jazz critics got involved. Charles Delaunay, for example, hosted the "Hot Club Corner" during the jazz program *Beaucoup de music*, which was broadcast on AFN on Friday afternoons until

February 1946.[116] Moreover, the AFN studios captured and broadcast live performances of military bands, including Django Reinhardt's performance with the Air Training Corps (ATC) Band in 1945.[117] To the chagrin of *Jazz hot*, Reinhardt's collaboration with the ATC band—which was reported to evoke a "style *nègre*"—did not receive nearly as much attention as Glenn Miller's band, which played at the Opéra and the Pleyel.[118]

Just as the V-Discs were distributed far beyond their intended audiences, the AFN reached beyond the ranks of US military camps. In August 1945, *Radio revue* noted that the AFN had become a "godsend" for jazz fans, even though some questioned its interpretation of "real jazz."[119] While the daily broadcasting program was accessible to American military personnel in copies of the newspaper *Stars and Stripes*, the "thousands of French fans" for whom these programs and "daily jive" had become "indispensable" had no program guide. Therefore, the French audience was likely composed of committed fans who obsessively followed the weekly schedule, and casual listeners who happened to find the programs while scanning the dial.[120]

On vacation in Brittany with his family in 1945, Yann Gillot and his brother would huddle over a refurbished radio set to listen to the AFN radio station. He remembered: "It was in the course of these programs that we first heard jazz bands recorded in public, with ambient sounds, applause, presentations by the announcer, almost always the dynamic and jovial Ernie 'Bubbles' Whitman and his famous 'tank you tank you.'"[121] Much like Chesnel, Gillot remembered vividly the sounds around the music. For him, Whitman's "tank you" was a distinctly African American articulation. The voices and applause authenticated his experience as a listener, even though he was far away from the originating concert. Gillot could not always understand the words, but he picked up on the dialect and speaking style. He recalled listening to *Jubilee* around 8:30 at night. Each broadcast dedicated thirty to forty-five minutes to jazz, and began and ended with Count Basie's "One o'Clock Jump" (1937), which combined the catchy riffs, blues forms, and big-band arrangements that were typical of Basie's Kansas City style. While the opening number would change in different programs, it remained a V-Disc, meaning that listeners might also, in addition to "One o'Clock Jump," catch Charlie Barnet's "Skyliner" (1944) or Count Basie's "On the Upbeat" (1945).[122]

The AFN's success in reaching French listeners was sustained not only by the programming itself—which was monitored and reviewed in French magazines and newspapers—but also by the continued challenges facing the French radio. The "liberated" French radio had begun broadcasting to Parisian listeners on August 20, 1944, but with only one station in the entire country transmitting at 5 kilowatts, listeners with limited electrical power, and regular power out-ages, it was not sufficient to reach listeners outside Paris. Moreover, French officials were in the midst of "cleansing" the radio from the stain of collabora-tion through massive purges of personnel. Hoping to create a radio system that would "unify, enlighten, and entertain the entire nation," they sought to es-tablish a state radio monopoly, henceforth known as Radiodiffusion Française (RDF).[123] In this effort to restructure the mass media, American military and government officials were well positioned and eager to help.

By October 1944, the reconstruction of French radio had begun with the aid of politically and culturally invested American officials from the OWI who had already discovered the power of broadcasting in Normandy, including Sim Copans and his colleague Bravig Imbs. Already well-known in the Parisian in-tellectual scene in the 1920s, Imbs had been recruited by the OWI in 1944 to oversee the first postliberation radio broadcasts in Normandy.[124] Once in Paris, both Copans and Imbs worked to secure cooperation between the French radio and the American government. According to internal reports, the Americans intended to "consolidate, intensify, and perpetuate Franco-American friend-ship and cooperation" and, ideally, not trample (too much) on French "ter-ritorial integrity."[125] In exchange for programmatic consultation, equipment, and technical assistance for a French-produced news program relayed over American networks, French radio officials agreed to relay the Voice of Ameri-ca's own French-language programming.[126] As one news agency noted, the OWI soon made "vigorous use of the possibilities of the 'international language'" of music.[127] In a 1945 article on the OWI's new "cultural formula," the *New York Times* detailed its musical broadcasting efforts, noting that "a good part of the commercial platters is of jazz music, which the OWI points out 'America inven-ted and popularized all over the world.'"[128]

Given that short-wave broadcasts were poor transmitters of music, Copans and Imbs prepared variety and jazz broadcasts at the Paris office to serve as an interlude during the evening French news hour. Indeed, while the Voice of America–produced radio program *Ici New York* arrived by shortwave from New York, the technical work of this musical diplomacy was conducted on the ground. In their preparations, Copans and Imbs drew on the rapidly expand-ing Voice of America record library and a new studio at 11bis rue Christophe Colomb (see figure 1.5). Imbs created the record library out of the thousands of American records that arrived from the American military—some V-Discs, some for the AFN—but all in the new "33 *tour*" format. These were not the same long-playing (LP), microgroove records that entered the commercial sphere in the early 1950s; they were made out of plastic, not vinyl, by transcription

FIGURE 1.5. Sim Copans alongside technical director Richard Condon in the Voice of America studio at the Hotel Scribe in Paris, 1945. Photo courtesy of the Copans Family Archives.

services at NBC, Thesaurus, and Music from America. Like the AFN transcriptions, each turned at 33 1/3 revolutions per minute, rather than 78, but measured 50 centimeters in diameter (not the later 30 centimeters, or 12 inches).[129] In exchange for free access to this library of over four thousand records, the French radio offered space in recently acquisitioned buildings.[130] As Copans remembered later, the AFN provided many new jazz records, including records created uniquely for the use of the US Army.[131]

Imbs began broadcasting American jazz on AFN in October 1945 with *Toujours du jazz*, which was broadcast three to five times per week on the French radio's Chaîne Parisienne. In December 1945 he began hosting *Musique populaire américaine* on Saturday evenings, as well as *Music-Hall Franco-Allié*.[132] Based on some contemporary accounts, Imbs was a well-known and generally well-liked jazz broadcaster who received four hundred fan letters each week in response to his programs.[133] However, Imbs was not a favorite among the Hot Club membership or the editorial board of *Jazz hot*, who, in their first issue after a wartime hiatus, asserted that while "jazz was born in the United States," it was "in Europe that it received its titles of nobility." They claimed that "well before the Yankees realized its significance, the intellectuals of the Old Continent were interested in this new music."[134] By establishing European preeminence, the editors were responding to real changes in the jazz landscape following the Allied landings. They were concerned about the general public's capacity to recognize good jazz: most audiences seemed to think any musician was good if he was "smudged with black." While ecstatic that their own assessment of jazz had "triumphed" in the postwar period, the Hot Club grew increasingly anxious about the growing commercialization and popularization of what had been a niche fanbase.[135]

In the same issue, the editors commented directly on the American influence on the postwar radio soundscape. After the indignity of listening to American military bands, "which no American station in even the most remote town of the forty-fourth state would want," they could not believe the audacity of the French radio in choosing *Americans* to host its jazz programs. They went on: "It would be too simple to call on Hugues Panassié or Charles Delaunay, whose competence is internationally recognized." Instead, the RDF featured "the indefatigable M. Bravig Imbs." After surmising that it was the "nationality of this M. Imbs" that granted him a place on the radio, the editors asked: "Does he forget . . . that France is not still an American colony?"[136] By redefining France as a colonized nation, though not actually aligning themselves with colonial subjects, the editors reframed the liberation as a kind of *colonial* occupation. With many American troops transferred from France to Germany, the airwaves had become the site of this continued, misguided colonial presence. They pushed back against this new colonial power, arguing, "It is not sufficient to belong to the American Information Service, nor to read *Esquire* in order to know jazz."[137] In a related article in the same issue, Jean Michaux wrote that while it might be amusing to listen to these so-called specialists, whose "deft ears confuse the trombone and trumpet," the initial amusement "disappears as soon as one remembers that their crack-pot ideas reach perhaps millions of listeners who, intelligently guided, could have become real fans of jazz, and that these gentlemen are going to forever turn them off of this music."[138] It was clear that the moment was ripe for instituting informed jazz enthusiasm among the growing number of fans. However, the Americans did not appear to be equipped for the job.

In this and future issues, the critics at *Jazz hot* expressed particular frustration with Imbs over the question of race. Though Imbs did not claim jazz as white, he appeared to have "resolved *la question nègre*" by "erasing it." Michaux mocked him, asking, "White jazz, jazz *nègre*? What madness! There is only 'popular American music.'"[139] In presenting jazz as an American music, Imbs appeared to have flattened the cultural traditions of racial groups and nations by insisting that jazz was a universal language, provided that the question of race was put aside. This criticism echoed earlier concerns of Delaunay, who worried whether jazz, "emerging from the misery of an oppressed race," had lost its "original character" over the course of the war. His own jazz heroes—Duke Ellington, Louis Armstrong, and Sidney Bechet—were missing; in their place, the "champions of the hour" were the "white bands of Harry James, Glenn Miller, Tommy Dorsey, Benny Goodman."[140] However, Delaunay's dismay at the whitewashing of jazz during the war becomes more curious when one considers that he had, until 1944, been a vocal supporter of a *French* nationalistic jazz history that elided African American contributions. Amid the domestic turmoil of liberation, French critics pointed to outside oppression in trying to absolve the country of its own wrongdoing.

While Imbs's own jazz programs would end with his untimely death in a jeep accident in 1946, the American presence on the French radio was sustained when US officials (including Copans) brokered a deal with French officials to give an abandoned AFN transmitter, record library, and studio to the French radio in exchange for the continued transmission of US-sponsored programs even after the departure of most American military personnel.[141] Though initially only powerful enough to reach listeners in the Paris region, the former AFN transmitter would eventually become Paris Inter, a nationally broadcast station. By early 1947, the station would feature Copans as the Voice of America on weekly US State Department jazz programs, which endured through the mid-1950s.[142] Through these programs, the US government continued to locate jazz at the center of a political project, making way for the literal and metaphorical Voice of America. While this conceptualization of jazz as the sound of American democracy, power, and authority would later be put to use by the US State Department in waging the Cold War, in the mid- to late 1940s this political maneuver was more startling—for French jazz fans as well as African American musicians and journalists—who remained uncertain as to the political potential of African American music.

Within its first few months of publication, the postwar intellectual journal *Les Temps modernes* had featured essays by Jean-Paul Sartre, Maurice Merleau-Ponty, Richard Wright, and Simone de Beauvoir, but also a rather curious short story by Nathalie Moffat in December 1945.[143] In this fictional account, Moffat describes the experiences of a French woman named Jouka, who works as a prostitute in the GI camps in Paris, where American soldiers beckon her with "Hello Blondie!" and ask, "You zig-zag?"[144] While navigating this new postwar world and the sexual advances of American men, Jouka is invited into the truck of a young Texan farm boy named Albert. She is keenly aware of his body, taking note of his "warm voice," "dark complexion," "big shiny eyes," and "large nose." As they listen together to music from his truck's radio, she observes how, in the dim lighting of the truck, Albert appears Black: "'He's almost a *nègre*,' thought Jouka with emotion." Shrouded in the truck's shadows, Albert becomes an ersatz African American GI, whose potential threat is mitigated by the music of the military radio until Jouka's fear becomes too much, prompting her to flee.

While fictional, the story underscores the ambiguous role of African American identity in the period of liberation. In this strange soundscape, even as African Americans were excluded, feared, and executed, their musical traditions buoyed the sounds of American power, drowning out the noise and soothing the cacophony of war. African American observers were likewise conscious of the precarious place of Black identity in postwar France. With the "weight of the American Army" now gone, Ollie Stewart had begun to "look with a jaundiced eye upon the so-called equality and fraternity of the French people." He wrote, "Without my uniform and my chocolate bars and cigarettes, I am just another black man."[145] In June 1945, Edward Toles of the *Chicago Defender* went further, stating that racism continued to thrive in Cherbourg. Comparing anti-Semitic racism to anti-Black racism, he argued that Jews had "merged into the community again" but that "the Negro who wore no prison garb, no star yet unmistakably marked with a badge of color which he cannot shed, retains to some extent all of the burdens that went with his badge of color."[146]

While Toles's account vastly overstated the ease of Jewish reintegration after Vichy, both journalists recognized the ways in which the value ascribed to African American or Black identity was contingent on the context in which it appeared. It was clear that African American identity was most valued as a source of entertainment. In September 1946, the *Afro-American* noted that while "the stage is set . . . the nucleus of attraction, American colored musicians and entertainers," was still absent. As the war had "robbed" France of her best musicians, new musicians were needed as soon as possible to "restore normal conditions." In this new paradigm—in which "American colored musicians and entertainers" were at a "premium"—African American identity had become increasingly enticing.[147]

2

WRITING BLACK, TALKING BACK

Jazz and the Value of African American Identity

———

In his 1946 memoir, Mezz Mezzrow described an evening spent at Moskowitz & Lupowitz, a Jewish Romanian restaurant and club on the Lower East Side of Manhattan. While there, Mezzrow noticed two women in the chorus line who appeared white but whose "spirits weren't tied up in straitjackets" like the other performers. He was confused until it hit him: "Goddamn, those girls were too good—they must be colored kids passing for white!"[1] Mezzrow's Black companion, Columbus Covington, agreed: "'Man,' he said, 'how in the hell did you dig that? I been suspicioning the same thing myself.'" After "wising up all the boys on 131st Street," they took the women out to a ribs restaurant in Harlem, where other Black friends joined to test the women's authenticity with "added sly little innuendos" that "no white girl" could have understood. After this racial test, "the kids had to break down and confess, and when we came to take them home damn if they didn't live right in Harlem, on 109th Street." To Mezzrow's delight, the women then accused him of passing for white because "they couldn't believe that any white man could be as hip to the jive as I was" or play jazz the way he did. His friend Columbus concurred: "'Man, why don't you come clean, don't nobody fault you for makin' out you's ofaginzy.'"[2] Mezzrow ended the story wistfully: "How I wished they were right."

This episode comes in the middle of *Really the Blues*, a best-selling memoir that recounts Mezzrow's evolution from a Jewish jazz musician in Chicago to an "ex-white man" and "voluntary Negro" living in Harlem.[3] It was cowritten by Mezzrow and Bernard Wolfe, who offered their readers a purported insider account of African American culture and jazz musicians. While the memoir was celebrated for its jive language and interracial escapades, its success was also clearly tied to its literary reinvention of the social practice of racial passing. Due to the rules of racial hypodescent in the United States, where a person with only "one drop" of African blood was still legally considered Black, passing had historically referred to the movement of light-skinned African Americans across the color line into white society.[4] By contrast, this memoir presented an account of *reverse* passing, or the movement of a white person across the color line into African American society.

While Mezzrow and Wolfe's memoir was successful in the United States— where it prefigured future articulations of the "hipster"—its influence was equally profound in postwar France. Translated in 1951 as *La rage de vivre* (*Lust for Life*), the memoir was promoted on French radio and in jazz magazines, newspapers, and intellectual journals as a glimpse into how Mezzrow had "crossed the color line in reverse."[5] For French audiences, *La rage de vivre* opened up the possibility that African American identity could be claimed as their own, making its associations with authenticity and intrinsic political engagement a part of French culture. But Mezzrow's was not the only account of racial passing to reverberate in postwar France. This practice had first been introduced to French audiences in 1946 by the jazz musician and novelist Boris Vian, who claimed to have discovered a hard-boiled racial thriller set in the American South. The book—*J'irai cracher sur vos tombes* (*I Will Spit on Your Graves*)—depicted a light-skinned African American man named Lee Anderson, who passes for white to infiltrate the white world and then rapes and kills two wealthy white women with the intent of avenging the lynching of his younger brother.[6] Whereas Mezzrow and Wolfe defined passing as an act of playful transgression, Vian transformed it into a means of revenge. While the subject matter alone was enough to titillate French audiences, the fact that its alleged author, Vernon Sullivan, was himself an African American GI seemed to underscore its authentic social critique. By the time the novel had become a best-seller in 1947, however, the hoax was up. Boris Vian was widely suspected to be the real author of *J'irai cracher sur vos tombes*, having successfully duped the French public and sold a half million copies in the process.

These two books—and their multiple authors—are the subject of this chapter. While they presented different accounts of race and African American culture, both resonated in postwar France, where "racial passing" had neither the same sociocultural nor the same literary history as it had in the United

States.[7] Without the same social context for comprehending African American strategies of survival, the act of passing instead was presented as a means for white people to inhabit, or apprehend, the Black experience. To do so, the various authors, publishers, translators, and promoters sold the books as direct links to fantasies of jazz communities: be it Vian's well-known exploits in the *caves* of Saint-Germain-des-Prés, where existentialism seemed to go hand-in-hand with jazz, or Mezzrow and Wolfe's evocations of an underworld of hipsters, jazz musicians, and drugs. In these spaces, African Americans were imagined to embody a particularly defiant and emancipated posture, which might enable their readers to likewise liberate themselves from the past and remove the shackles of society's expectations. In these spaces, jazz appeared to facilitate a more intimate relationship to African Americans, such that the enjoyment of African American music might offer a sonic approximation of liberatory politics.

The versions of racial passing peddled by Mezzrow, Wolfe, and Vian were simulacra of a social strategy used to maneuver within—and subvert—the powerful fictions of racial identity in the United States. But they were sold as faithful interpretations of Black life and vernacular, verified—as it were—by the authors' purported links to African American spaces.[8] Given this, the response of Black Francophone readers was decidedly more ambivalent than that of their white counterparts. While many rejected these literary claims to Blackness on the grounds that they caricatured African American life and history, Black readers nonetheless found in them a range of allies and strategic essentialisms, which they in turn used to define the contours of colonial cultural politics.

Black like Boris

The origin story of *J'irai cracher sur vos tombes* may be as infamous as the book itself. In July 1946, Jean d'Halluin, the editor for the publishing house Éditions du Scorpion, was in deep financial trouble and looking for a best-seller. He had in mind not only the revived popularity of American novelists like William Faulkner and Erskine Caldwell, but also the enormous success of French publisher Gallimard's new publishing imprint, the Série noire, which had been launched by Marcel Duhamel in 1945 to publish "hardboiled" crime fiction (and later published the work of African American novelist and expatriate Chester Himes).[9] While searching for a crime thriller that had somehow escaped his eye, d'Halluin met a young musician and novelist named Boris Vian, who played trumpet in a jazz band with d'Halluin's brother in Saint-Germain-des-Prés. Vian could not provide d'Halluin with an original American crime thriller, but he offered to write one himself. Intrigued by Vian's claim that he could write a best-selling American novel in less than two weeks—having never actually traveled to the United States—d'Halluin took the bet. Vian completed *J'irai cracher sur vos tombes* in August 1946; it soon became a best-seller, giving its author and publisher unforeseen profits and infamy in the French literary world.

Vian's decision to write *J'irai cracher sur vos tombes* was shaped by his long-standing interests in jazz and American culture (see figure 2.1). Born to a bourgeois family in the Parisian suburb of Ville-d'Avray in 1920, Vian spent his youth managing severe medical problems, his family's financial struggles, and the onset of World War II.[10] During the war, he became involved with the *zazou* subculture, in which young people resisted the mainstream political culture by embracing American and British fashion, mannerisms, and music. He also met and married Michelle Léglise, who had spent her childhood summers in England and taught Boris to speak and read English.[11] In 1941, exempted from military service because of a heart condition, Vian earned a degree in engineering from the École Centrale in Paris. With a family to support, he immediately began working for the Association Française de Normalisation (AFNOR). After the liberation, Vian continued to play regularly in Claude

FIGURE 2.1. Boris Vian and his double, n.d. Photo courtesy of the Cohérie Boris Vian.

FIGURE 2.2. Michelle Vian, Miles Davis, and Boris Vian, 1949. Photo courtesy of the Cohérie Boris Vian.

Abadie's jazz band, frequently before audiences of US military personnel. In addition to facilitating their relationships with American GIs, the Vians' fluency in English frequently made them hosts for African American musicians on their arrival in Paris (see figure 2.2).[12]

Soon, the Vians were central figures in Saint-Germain-des-Prés, where young people gathered to dance and drink in a nascent network of jazz clubs, including the Tabou, Club Saint-Germain, Vieux-Colombier, and Lorientais, as well as the Rose Rouge and La Rhumerie, where African and Antillean youth gathered as well.[13] As a habitué and performer in many of these same clubs, Vian played a key role in propagating the mythology of Saint-Germain-des-Prés and presenting himself as the necessary escort to this new avant-garde space in which jazz and existentialism were linked up.[14] Vian's self-proclaimed role as intermediary is evident in his own guide to the neighborhood, the 1951 *Manuel de Saint-Germain-des-Prés*, as well as in the publication of *Jazz 47* (a special issue of the journal *America*), which defined jazz as the "music of our era."[15] Sponsored by the Hot Club de France and edited by Charles Delaunay, it included essays by Jean-Paul Sartre, Jean Cocteau, and Vian, further cementing the close relationship of this American musical form and the French intelligentsia, as well as the firm link between jazz and liberation.[16]

In 1946, spurred by some literary success and the growing interest in American culture, Vian left AFNOR to focus on writing. To craft his own hard-boiled thriller, Vian drew from the American press, clipping articles on lynching, race riots, and racial passing in the United States. Vian was particularly intrigued by passing, which appeared in the mainstream American press in sensational terms. In 1946, *Time* reported that "more than 2,000,000 U.S. Negroes have crossed the color line," contributing to an "ever widening stream of black blood to the white native stock." This article, clipped by Vian, introduced him to the term "white negroes," who were defined as those who appeared white but had at least "one drop of blood" that made them Black.[17] While Vian's direct access to American media sources facilitated his preoccupation with race, it mirrored the growing interest of French intellectuals in US race relations and racial violence. In fact, it was in this same period that Jean-Paul Sartre wrote and produced a play, *La putain respectueuse* (*The Respectful Prostitute*), which recounted the mob justice and attempted lynching that accompanied the infamous 1931 Scottsboro case. In addition, Sartre had recently founded the journal *Les Temps modernes* (*Modern Times*), which frequently included African American writers and subjects.[18] Not only had the first issue's call for "engaged literature" been immediately followed by a short story by African American writer Richard Wright, but the journal's special issue in August–September 1946 on the United States had also focused on race relations, including an excerpt on racial passing from Horace Cayton and St. Clair Drake's *Black Metropolis* (1945).[19]

Building on their close friendship with himself and Simone de Beauvoir, Sartre had invited both Boris and Michelle Vian to contribute essays and translations to *Les Temps modernes*. In June 1946, Sartre asked Vian to contribute his own "impressions of America" for the special issue on the United States, even though Vian had never traveled there. Vian's essay, which would have appeared as part of his regular "Chronique du menteur" ("Liar's Column"), describes his arrival—accompanied by his friend Alexandre Astruc, a filmmaker—in New York City by submarine. There the two find a surreal vision of New York. The Empire State Building is destroyed but still features an elevator that one can take to the roof. Soon after, the two discover the famed French surrealist poet André Breton in Harlem, at a "small grimy club called Tom's." Even more shockingly, they find that Breton has become Black. Vian observes, "There's no doubt, it was him. But what a camouflage! He had passed to black; one could absolutely say a real *Nègre*, he even had a *Nègre*'s big lips and frizzy hair, and he spoke like a *Nègre*. He called himself Andy, the others didn't seem to have a lot of respect for him." Asked if he plans to return to France, Breton responds, "Man. Ah'll stay wid' ma black gal and ma black kids. I'am't no use, man, goin'all' round de world an' catchin' sea sick, crabs an' claps an'looking' always for fuck. Lawd don't likes that man, sure Lawd don't likes that." Shocked that Breton "knew words like that," and bemoaning the "loss for surrealism," Vian and his companion leave the club. They soon find the rest of their Parisian contingent, who had been waiting "all morning in front of the hotel in the hopes of seeing a *nègre* lynched."[20]

Framed by a voyeuristic search for racial violence, Vian's "impressions" of America are riddled with racist fantasies. In his reimagining, Breton had become the physical embodiment of a caricatured, diseased, and hypersexualized Black man, a transformation that Vian defined as an act of racial passing. But the account is also constructed to satirize these same illusions. Vian mocks the French fascination with lynchings, perhaps even poking fun at the pending premier of Sartre's own play, which staged a lynching for eager French audiences. Moreover, by rendering Breton Black, Vian satirizes the primitivist undercurrents in French intellectualism that had long kept Black culture at arm's length. This satire was made specific to Breton for several reasons, not the least of which was the fact that Breton had spent most of World War II in exile in New York, where he allegedly "sulked, hating America," and engaged in an "almost compulsive rejection of everything American." One biographer noted that he was "careful not to learn even three words" of English "for fear of dulling the edge of his own exquisite writing instrument."[21] It was also during this time that Breton had famously "discovered" the Martiniquan poet Aimé Césaire during a trip to Fort-de-France. While this encounter had launched an arc of patronage and preface writing that was premised on the hope that Césaire's poetry would save Europe, Breton nonetheless remained blind to its fundamental critique of Western imperialism.[22] It mirrored in many ways Sartre's own relationship to *négritude* poetry, which he would claim as "the sole great revolutionary poetry" while still defining it as a mere "stage" in the path to liberation, little more than "a flavor, a taste, a rhythm, an authenticity, a cluster of primitive instincts."[23] Vian's provocative "impressions" were immediately rejected by the editorial board at *Les Temps modernes* and left unpublished until 1974.

Building on his growing fascination with US race relations and increasingly strained relationship to French intellectuals, Vian decided to focus his allegedly American crime novel, *J'irai cracher sur vos tombes*, on the act of racial passing. Seeking revenge for the death of his youngest brother, who was lynched for sleeping with a white girl, the main character, Lee Anderson, decides to pass into the white world. Unlike his other brother, who was "too meek and resigned" to enact violence and too "Black" to pass, Lee's apparent whiteness affords him a path to retribution.[24] Lee claims in the novel, "I know some men more or less like me who try to forget their blood and who go over to the side of the whites for all purposes, not even having the decency to refrain from knocking the colored race when the occasion demands it."[25] As this suggests, Vian has taken the act of racial passing—a social practice whose primary aim was assimilation and survival—and turned it into a way to enact violence.[26]

Lee moves to the town of Buckton, where he soon meets a group of young, wealthy white teenagers. The novel then narrates Lee's exploits with them and his systemic manipulation and seduction of white teenage girls. While Lee's physical characteristics do not immediately betray his racial identity, his white companions frequently compare aspects of his body to those of Black people. His singing voice, for example, is likened to Cab Calloway's, while later a companion remarks that Lee has the "same kind of drooping shoulders as a colored prizefighter."[27] One of his most desired conquests, Lou Asquith, compares his voice to those of the Black men she heard while living in Haiti. Indeed, music is an important site of racial imagining in the novel. When Lee suggests that Black music is the "source of all American music," Lou refutes it, noting that all of the new dance orchestras are white. In response, Lee says: "Of course—the whites are in a better position to exploit the Negro's inventions."[28] He then tells her about all of the great African American composers, including Duke Ellington, and asserts that George Gershwin and other white composers had merely "plagiarized" their work. Lou responds: "'You're funny,' she said. 'I just hate the colored race.'"[29] Asquith's own racism is underscored by the source of her family's fortune in Haitian sugarcane plantations. Lee describes them as "a fine pair of crooks who had inherited a lot of money," which they used to "exploit people whose only crime is that they have a different color skin than theirs."

The recognition of this familial exploitation is ultimately what motivates Lee's plan to seduce and kill the Asquith daughters.[30] Once this plan is in place, the narration shifts to third person, at which point Lee rapes, impregnates, and kills the two girls. He imagines that his brother "would squirm in his grave with joy."[31] Even though Lee succeeds in avenging his brother, his racial identity is revealed and he himself is killed by the police, then hanged by a mob. The novel ends with a brutal scene: "The townspeople hanged him anyway because he was a *nègre*. Under his trousers, his crotch still protruded ridiculously."[32] Throughout the text, Vian simultaneously employs and subverts a wide range of racist and racially essentialist tropes, which in turn reinforce the mythologies of Black hypersexuality and sexual violence. The essentialism of these strategies is deepened by the profound violence and misogyny in the text. But there

FIGURE 2.3. Cover of original edition, with Vernon Sullivan listed as author, of *J'irai cracher sur vos tombes*, 1946. Photo courtesy of the Bibliothèque nationale de France.

are also hints of antiracism, whether in Lee's corrections on the source of Black music or his critiques of the Asquiths' exploitation of Haitian workers. Early on, Lee encounters one of the book's few sympathetic white characters, who claims that his sole desire is to write "best-sellers . . . where colored men sleep with white women and don't get lynched."[33] Indeed, while *J'irai cracher sur vos tombes* itself ends with the lynching of the main character, here the text evinces a deeper interest in using literature to combat such depictions.

While the book was set for publication in October, it was not officially released by Éditions du Scorpion until the end of November 1946 (see figure 2.3). In publicity materials and in later accounts, Vian claimed to have met the purported African American author, Vernon Sullivan, while he was playing in a US military jazz band, writing that the two hit it off immediately once Sullivan discovered that Vian played trumpet.[34] After introducing Sullivan to a French publisher in July 1946, Vian then claimed he decided to translate and publish the text himself. As he indicated in the preface, it was "not surprising that [Sullivan's] book should have been refused in America: we wager it would be banned the day following its publication."[35] In France, he reminded his readers, "we strive for more originality."[36] In introducing the text, Vian also drew on the same US news reports on passing, referencing the "several thousand negroes (so designated)" who "disappear from the census lists and pass to the opposite camp." According to Vian, Sullivan was one of these "white negroes." But he noted that Sullivan "considered himself to be more a *nègre* than a white man, despite having passed the 'line.'"[37] Reiterating the novel's revenge thesis, Vian defined Sullivan's book as the "manifestation of a desire for revenge in a race still, whatever one may say, over-worked, badly treated, and terrorized."[38] He furthermore described it as a kind of "exorcism" against the domination of "good whites" and a way of voicing Sullivan's contempt for "good negroes," those whom "white people tapped affectionately on the back in literature." By contrast, Vian claimed, Sullivan wanted to write a Black figure as "tough" as white men and then put this vision in print.[39]

Perhaps owing to this introduction, initial reviews focused on the racial themes in the novel. In some cases, its appearance was linked explicitly to the broader interest in US race relations, although reviews found Vian's text to be more "pornographic" than political.[40] Reviews also focused on the racial identity of the purported author, who was "what one calls in the United States a *nègre blanc*," which is to say "a man having in his veins an eighth of black blood, but in whose physical appearance one detects absolutely none of the characteristics of his race."[41] The novel spurred more intrigue by early 1947, when there was growing suspicion in the press that Vian himself was the author. By February 1947, the novel had become the subject of an investigation by the Cartel de l'Action Social et Morale, which had already banned works by Henry Miller, John Steinbeck, and William Faulkner.[42] In response to the Cartel's inquiries, the publisher Jean d'Halluin claimed that they had merely wanted to shed light on the racial persecution of Blacks in the United States.[43] Reinforcing the sense that Vian's work was antiracist, another review suggested that the novel spoke to the subject of slavery, "which [France] has never yet taken seriously," and made it central to the "French conscience."[44]

Amid increasing speculation about the true authorship of *J'irai cracher sur vos tombes*, Black Francophone writers became invested in debates over its authenticity. In February 1947, the editors at *Afrique Magazine* determined that it most certainly was "the work of a *nègre*," who told the tale of those who did not pass but instead "stayed faithful to their race."[45] The article specifically referenced Jean Boullet's illustrations in the 1947 Scorpion edition—which included captions such as "to avenge his brothers" and "[a] *noir* rapes the whites"—in heralding the book's unconventional account of Black people.[46] The editors seemed to appreciate that Sullivan had shown how *nègres* could "also know how to be cruel" and could "avenge themselves" if need be.[47] In 1947, the novel was reviewed in *Présence Africaine*, a new journal founded by Alioune Diop to introduce African diasporic culture and build Pan-African connections in the metropole. The journal's *comité de patronage* included a number of influential white intellectuals, like Sartre and anthropologist Michel Leiris, but also Hugues Panassié, who likely orchestrated the invitation of *Présence Africaine* to Gallimard's welcoming party for Louis Armstrong and Duke Ellington when they visited Paris in 1947.[48] In his review, the Senegalese philosopher Jacques Howlett alluded to ongoing suspicions regarding the novel's authorship. Despite the probability of mass deception, he argued that the novel nevertheless contained some kind of "hidden truth" about the nature of colonialism.[49] In presenting the story of a *nègre* who avenges the racist acts of whites, the novel suggested to Howlett a kind of foreboding, of premonition of a "victorious vitality" among Black people. Howlett's review also intimated that *J'irai cracher sur vos tombes* had been banned in the African colonies.[50] While he recognized that Vian's text was likely a hoax, Howlett suggested that it still could be mined for revolutionary potential to threaten colonial power structures. Juxtaposed against a review of Richard Wright's *Native Son* by critic and translator Madeleine Gautier, who underscored that one "could not doubt the authenticity" of Wright's novel, the racial veracity of Vian's text was less clear.[51]

One of the most penetrating criticisms of *J'irai cracher sur vos tombes* came from Martiniquan writer Joseph Zobel, who had recently published essays critiquing the French colonial project in Martinique.[52] In his review in *Les Lettres françaises* in July 1947, Zobel asserted that the novel was "neither *nègre* nor American."[53] He was even loath to call it a novel, given that Vian seemed to have written it out of sheer boredom. Among his many objections, Zobel was most offended that Vian had been "taken to be a great specialist of Afro-American culture" and that the novel was believed to be an "authentic specimen of *nègre-américaine* literature." As Zobel noted, *J'irai cracher sur vos tombes* seemed to "indict racial injustice," while at the same time playing on "the worst stereotypes" held by white people about "violent and sexually predatory black behavior." By contrast, he pointed his readers to the literary contributions of African American writers, whose "struggles, joys, and needs" have been manifest in "testimonies of struggle," "calls for justice," and "persuasive appeals."

He furthermore contended that these same characteristics "already mark the new work by Black Antillean writers." He urged his readers to stay alert to the "cultural awakening of *nègres*, Americans and French alike" and to reject all manifestations of both visible and "disguised" racism. As Zobel underscored, Vian had been permitted to act as an authority on African American identity and culture, which privileged him to claim, define, and assess Black identity in others. Not long after, Vian's literary excursions as an African American met sharp critique by African American journalist James W. Ivy, who, as a "student of Afro-French literature," was not convinced that it was written by an African American author. He concluded, "It is my considered guess that 'Vernon Sullivan,' if he is not *Boris Vian*, is some French Existentialiste who sees a literary gold mine . . . in the so-called American race problem."[54]

While Zobel's critique was not alone in this period, it was his that Vian singled out in the afterword of his second Vernon Sullivan novel, *Les morts ont tous la même peau* (*The Dead All Have the Same Skin*). He bristled at the critique from an "individual who claimed to be a black man from Martinique," suggesting bizarrely that "his name alone is a half-Arab, half-archaistic insult to public decency." Vian asserted that this Black man was as "qualified to comment upon his American brothers as a Chinese resident of San Francisco is capable of resolving the current upheavals in Shanghai."[55] Vian appeared to be less offended by the substance of the critique than by his belief that Zobel had used his *own* Black identity to criticize Vian's claims to Blackness. Vian rejected Zobel's capacity to assess racial authenticity and bristled at the idea that a Black Frenchman could speak on behalf of Black people outside France. To that end, Vian ridiculed Zobel's authority as a Black or French author by referring to him as a "half-Arab," which seemed simultaneously to disallow his Blackness and to ascribe a kind of mixture that was undesirable. Given the satiric quality of Vian's writing, it is possible that this too was meant as parody. But while sympathetic to the African American struggle and interested in jazz, Vian appeared appalled by the possibility that a Black Frenchman might question his authority on the subject.

Within a year of this review, a group of Antillean writers responded to Vian. They were interviewed at a club called the Rhumerie, described as a kind of Antillean "Tabou" in Saint Germain-des-Prés.[56] The article in *Samedi soir* suggested that one of the club's habitués, a writer named Raphaël Tardon, had just published "the antidote to *J'irai cracher sur vos tombes*." Whereas "Sullivan (or Boris Vian) creates scenes in which whites are raped by blacks," Tardon's novel, *Starkenfirst*, depicts the "rape of blacks by American slave traders in the nineteenth century." In addition, the article reported that Tardon, "who has in his veins as much black blood as white," had reproached Vian (or "Sullivan")

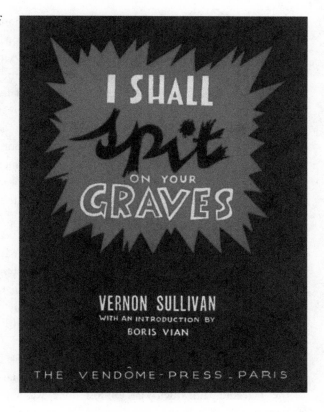

FIGURE 2.4. Cover of the English-language "original" of Boris Vian's novel, *I Shall Spit on Your Graves*, 1948. Photo courtesy of the Bibliothèque nationale de France.

for doing nothing for the "cause of blacks," which was apparently an opinion shared by his companions. While noting that Tardon was Martiniquan, the article also stressed that Tardon had chosen to be "faithful" to his "black blood," highlighting a particular form of Black identity in France. Moreover, the article contrasted Vian's apparent political inaction with Tardon's activism, which was rooted in his Blackness. Just two years earlier Tardon had interviewed the writer Richard Wright, who expressed concern with the "good Negro" image of African Americans that was propagated in France. Available "for export," these popular cultural representations seemed to suggest African Americans were "as happy as a child."[57] Like Wright, this group of writers was concerned with the question of representation in France, where the truth of African American identity was the subject of much debate.

In April 1948, Vian decided to respond to the growing intrigue surrounding the novel by presenting it in its "original" English version, which would prove Sullivan's existence (see figure 2.4). With the help of his wife Michelle, Vian found a former GI named Milton Rosenthal, with whom he cowrote an English version of *I Shall Spit on Your Graves* for publication by Vendôme Press in 1948.[58] But by the time it was published, the Cartel de l'Action Social et Morale sued the author and publisher, forcing Vian in November 1948 to admit that he was in fact the author of the text. A December 1948 article in *Opéra* noted, "We now know 'officially' that Vernon Sullivan, the so-called Black American author of *J'irai cracher sur vos tombes* and *Les morts on tous la même peau* ... is in fact M. Boris Vian." It ended by asking, "Will Boris Vian stay his own *nègre*?"[59] Playing on the double meaning of the term, which was a racial epithet as well as a common term for "ghostwriter," the reviewer's comments underscore the ways in which the racialization at work in this moment was both endemic and foreign to the French language.[60]

The publisher Marcel Duhamel later wrote that it was difficult to defend Vian's books, particularly given the ways in which the author so clearly added "grist to the racist mill."[61] But nearly three decades later, one of Vian's most prominent defenders was James Baldwin, who argued that the characterization of the novel as "pornographic" was precisely because it featured "the vindictive sexual aggression of one black man against many white women."[62] This, he suggested, was compounded by the fact that the "black G.I. in Europe was a genuinely disturbing conundrum" during the late 1940s. Baldwin further suggested that the novel was informed not just by its "sexual fantasy" but instead by the "rage and pain which Vian (almost alone) was able to hear in the Black American musicians, in the bars, dives, and cellars, of the Paris of those years." He argued that while Vian would have likely learned this from the literary work of William Faulkner, Richard Wright, and Chester Himes, he also "*heard* it in the music, and indeed, he saw it in the streets."[63] In "spite of the book's naïveté," Baldwin contended, "Vian cared enough about his subject to force one into a confrontation with a certain kind of anguish. The book's power comes from the fact that he forces you to see this anguish from the undisguised viewpoint of his foreign, alienated one." For Baldwin, Vian's transracial excursions had revealed a defining truth of African American identity in France, where the legacy of African American GIs had transformed the perception of Black sexuality. [64]

While the scandal had ended Vian's literary ambition as a Black American author, it nonetheless boosted his career as a jazz critic. Soon his satirical voice was featured in *Jazz hot* and *Jazz news*, as well as in the communist newspaper *Combat*. In his jazz criticism, he continued to mock any and all efforts by white critics to define jazz. His 1947 review of the film *Jammin' the Blues* expressed horror at seeing Fred Astaire in blackface. In response, Vian wrote, "Cab [Calloway]? He's perfect. At least he's wearing his own skin, not blackface, and we hear his own voice. . . . Whereas that imbecile Astaire, with his Negro costume and his silent trumpet. A monkey, I tell you, *that's* the monkey."[65] Elsewhere, Vian reiterated his firm belief that jazz was first and foremost the cultural product of African Americans. In addition to claiming that "blacks are necessarily right when it is a question of jazz," he titled one 1948 column "Must We Kill the Whites?"[66] It was a provocative title for a serious essay, in which he admitted that he selfishly enjoyed the opportunity to play with Black musicians but nevertheless wondered, "Who benefits? Surely not them."[67] In 1948, during a concert by Dizzy Gillespie, Vian reported in *Combat* that spectators had yelled at the musicians to go back to Timbuktu, shouting at Duke Ellington, "Why don't you learn French, dirty *nègre*?"[68] While his colleagues ignored issues of race and French racism, Vian seemed to constantly return to them.

Writing the Blues

Although Vian mocked the condemnations and pronouncements of many French jazz critics, he was particularly offended by Hugues Panassié, whose defense of "real jazz" was as laden with racial essentialisms as Vian's own writing but lacked the self-conscious satire. By 1947, Panassié arguably had become one of France's best-known and most-resented jazz critics, having expelled from the Hot Club de France all those who embraced the so-called commercial forms of jazz. He was particularly opposed to bebop, a musical style born out of the 1940s and marked by more complex rhythmic changes, faster tempo, and harmonic-based improvisation. Panassié argued that these new developments in jazz had betrayed the spontaneity, freedom, and authenticity of traditional New Orleans jazz. Instead, he endorsed "real jazz," preferably played in the New Orleans style by African American musicians who had not "abandoned their natural instincts."[69] In fact, the birth of bebop was far more complex than Panassié's reading suggested: it was rooted in new kinds of politics and aesthetics among professional jazz musicians.[70]

Notwithstanding his profound misreadings, Panassié was an enormously influential figure in the jazz world in this period. Because of his critical influence and financial power, these aesthetic battles in France reverberated among visiting and resident African American musicians, whose imprimatur was sought by both sides to authenticate the different positions.[71] Moreover, Panassié was influential among Black Francophone writers, in large part because he had joined the editorial committee of *Présence Africaine* in 1947. Léopold Sédar

Senghor was among those influenced by Panassié's readings of jazz, evidenced in what Tsitsi Jaji has described as Senghor's "negritude musicology."[72] An October 1948 *Jeune Afrique* review of an essay by Panassié in *Présence Africaine* had noted his "conservative position," but nevertheless conceded that "none is more qualified than he to speak of Louis Armstrong."[73] By contrast, Joseph Zobel noted Panassié's pronounced tendency to keep "company with *Nègres*," mocking the "perpetual state of grace" that Panassié had found through his "incessant study" of jazz.[74] They offered distinct impressions of the critic, but both accounts underscore the profound influence that Panassié wielded in postwar discussions of jazz.

While Panassié continually sought to align himself with African American musicians, his critical perspective was most fundamentally shaped by his relationship with Mezz Mezzrow, whom he met well before the publication of *Really the Blues*. Born Milton Mesirow in 1899 to middle-class Russian Jewish immigrants in Chicago, Mezzrow developed a lifelong devotion to New Orleans–style jazz.[75] After playing clarinet for several years in Chicago, in 1929 Mezzrow traveled to France, where he first met and befriended Panassié.[76] Mezzrow returned to New York in the early 1930s, married an African American woman named Johnnie Mae Berg, and settled in Upper Manhattan. There he became best known for selling opium and high-quality marijuana, which led to his incarceration at Rikers Island in 1941.[77] Based on their acquaintance, Panassié featured Mezzrow in his 1936 *Hot Jazz*, and in 1938, visited Mezzrow in New York, where they recorded a number of New Orleans–trained musicians, including Sidney Bechet, Tommy Ladnier, and Pops Foster.[78] This recording session in turn helped launch a revolt among jazz critics, who rejected the growing popularity of swing and called for a return to a supposedly "authentic" form of jazz based in New Orleans.[79] This revolt against modernism and commercialism—which would eventually frame critical debates about bebop—had economic and personal consequences for musicians. While some were blacklisted by critics and recording labels, many New Orleans musicians found new opportunities to record after years of obscurity. Recording sessions like Panassié and Mezzrow's in New York in 1938 had an even more profound impact in France, where a new generation of musicians was inspired to become imitators and stewards of New Orleans jazz. In 1945, Mezzrow started his own record label, King Jazz, to provide "uncorrupted" New Orleans jazz for collectors.[80]

In most accounts written by fellow musicians and critics, Mezzrow's identification with African American music was ridiculed as cartoonish.[81] While other white musicians openly criticized his paternalism and affected southern accent, most African American musicians did not publicly voice concerns. They likely felt unable to, for fear of endangering their professional relationships with Panassié and Mezzrow. In 1945, Mezzrow's particular racial affectation piqued the curiosity of journalist Bernard Wolfe, who was then living in New York, where he worked as a science journalist, ghostwriter, and pornographer and was marginally a member of a cohort later known as the "New York intellectuals."[82] In this period, Wolfe began "independent research on race relations in the field of jazz," a project that he would later title "The Role of the Negro in American Popular Culture."[83] In writing, Wolfe drew on recent publications on race relations in the United States, including Gunnar Myrdal's *An American Dilemma* (1944), as well as existentialist philosophy, particularly work published by Jean-Paul Sartre on anti-Semitism. Building on this research, Wolfe claimed that African American culture was fundamentally a form of mimicry that reflected the *white* aspirations of African American performers.[84] In this vein, he argued that bebop—the newest form of jazz born out of late-night jam sessions in New York—was merely Black pandering to the racist fantasy of white jazz fans. While the modern jazz enthusiast might mistakenly believe that bebop was more authentic than blackface minstrelsy, and believe that in this form the "Negro appears as *himself*," Wolfe argued that the musical developments in jazz were due to white influences and that all commodified representations of Blackness (including jazz) were in fact constitutive components of the Black image *as* made by whites.[85]

While ostensibly legitimated by social science and philosophy, Wolfe's reductive contention that Black culture was fundamentally a form of mimicry was grounded in the life of Mezzrow. As Wolfe recounted in an unpublished letter, Mezzrow "occupied a unique position in Harlem and . . . seemed to me to typify in a dramatic way the Negrophilia often encountered in and around the jazz world. It seemed to me worthwhile to record Mr. Mezzrow's story, and I undertook to write it."[86] While Wolfe recognized that Mezzrow "was not alone in hanging around with blacks, moving physically into the closed black world, marrying a black girl and having a child with her," he nonetheless found that his "personal 'negrification'" was unique. In the afterword to the memoir, Wolfe wrote,

> You'll never turn up another case of a man who after extended immersion in the ghetto came to believe he had actually, physically, turned black. Mezzrow, after his long years in and under Harlem, did truly think his lips had developed fuller contours, his hair had thickened and burred, his skin had darkened. It was not, as he saw it, a case of transculturation. He felt he had scrubbed himself clean, inside and out, of every last trace

of his origins in the Jewish slums of Chicago, pulped himself back to raw human material, deposited that nameless jelly in the pure Negro mold, and pressed himself into the opposite of his birthright, a pure Black.[87]

As this description suggests, the poetics and politics of Mezzrow's racial transformation were very much tied to Wolfe's particularly vivid writing style and scholarly interest in the psycho-sociological aspects of race relations. For Wolfe, Mezzrow's life was the truest form of mimicry, a mechanical transformation formed in "the pure Negro mold."

On April 23, 1945, Wolfe and Mezzrow signed a contract to cowrite what was initially titled *A Multitude of Sins* but would be published as *Really the Blues* in November 1946.[88] The exact parameters of this writing relationship were contested by the two writers, as well as by observers and colleagues. However, based on their own writings, private correspondence, and their known intellectual agendas, it is likely that Wolfe played a central role in writing *Really the Blues*. Moreover, it was Wolfe's larger intellectual project on the meaning and authenticity of African American culture that defined its power for French intellectual audiences, which would prove critical to both of their careers.[89]

The memoir begins with Mezzrow's early incarceration at the Pontiac Reformatory outside Detroit, where he first identified as Black; the text thus immediately cements the popular associations of jazz with illegality and social rebellion. It then traces Mezzrow's life from his Jewish middle-class youth to his adventures with Al Capone in Prohibition-era Chicago to his life in Harlem, where he married a Black woman, developed an opium addiction, and was jailed for selling marijuana. It continues in this manner. In addition to claiming that drugs are crucial to jazz performance, Mezzrow and Wolfe defined jazz as "one gigantic harmonic orgasm."[90] They also claimed that "nice people" still turned up their noses at this "whorehouse music."[91] The narrative then details Mezzrow's incarceration at Rikers Island for selling marijuana. Mezzrow asks to be housed in the Black block, telling the warden, "I'm colored, even if I don't look it."[92] He was eventually moved to Hart's Island and, on meeting a fellow inmate, was asked: "What's your story? I heard of many a cat passin' for white, but this is the first time I ever heard of a white man passin' for colored, and in jail too."[93] The memoir concludes with Mezzrow's full racial transformation after his imprisonment, after which he could play jazz better than ever because "now they were inside my skin, making my fingers work right so I could speak my piece."[94]

In addition to presenting an account of reverse racial passing, the book was also promoted as a sociological and linguistic introduction to jive language, which Mezzrow and Wolfe defined as "the tongue of a *beaten* people."[95] This new jive language was, in their estimation, the hipster's response to the "ounce-brained tongue-tied stuttering Sambos of the blackface vaudeville routines" and the "Old Mose's of the Southern plantations." By speaking jive, the hipster "reverses the whole Uncle Tom attitude of the beaten-down Southern Negro," a "satire on the conventional ofay's gift of gab and gibberish."[96] Wolfe and Mezzrow described jive as the aural resistance to "outsiders—detectives, square ofay musicians, informers, rivals from white show business, thrill-hungry tourists who come slumming up to 'savage' and 'primitive' Harlem to eyeball and gape."[97] They positioned themselves against this particular way of accessing Black life, highlighting their own insider status in this African American space and their capacity to translate it for their readers. Further reinforcing the authors' importance as translators were the original appendices to the book, including a glossary of hipster terminology and a translation of a transcribed "jive" conversation, which would presumably help the white, nonhipster reader understand these private "inner-racial jokes."[98] In contrast to the conceptions of the outsiders and "thrill-hungry tourists" who went slumming in Harlem, this book was an insider account of a man who had passed into African American society.

White American reviewers were scandalized and hooked. The memoir was, according to its publicity materials and reviews, an "authentic," "anthropological," and "sociological" text, a strong indictment of racism and "intolerance," and a "surreptitious glimpse of things never meant to be seen."[99] According to Bucklin Moon in *New Republic*, the book made "all novels with jazz backgrounds seem as phony as an Eddie Condon concert."[100] Reviewers in the Black press were equally intrigued, with *Negro Digest* describing it as "one of the raciest, rawest books ever written on race."[101] While a December 1946 profile in *Ebony* was careful to point out that "physically speaking, Mezzrow couldn't pass for Negro by any stretch of the imagination," it nevertheless gave credence to his claims to have "passed" into Black culture and society (see figure 2.5).[102]

It was this same *Ebony* profile that first alerted Simone de Beauvoir to Mezzrow. In January 1947, Beauvoir arrived in New York to begin a four-month journey across the United States that included a lecture tour through elite college campuses, a Greyhound bus trip across Texas, and stops in New Orleans, Chicago, Los Angeles, and Santa Fe. While the account of her travels was later published in 1948 as *L'Amérique au jour le jour* (*America Day by Day*), dispatches from her trip were serialized in 1947 in *Les Temps modernes*. In keeping with the journal's avowed interests in US race relations and African American culture, a recurring subject in the memoir was her encounter with "authentic

FIGURE 2.5. Milton "Mezz" Mezzrow posed among copies of *Really the Blues*. On the desk is a copy of a 1946 issue of *Ebony* that featured Mezzrow and his family in Harlem. Photo courtesy of Getty.

jazz." Beauvoir was no stranger to either recorded or live jazz performance, but her time in the United States convinced her that these previous experiences had been mere simulacra of the real thing, whether it was the "real jazz played by blacks" in New Orleans, the Black dancers at the Savoy, or the sounds of a Harlem preacher, whose sermon seemed to Beauvoir to be a kind of "'hot' improvisation," and thus "the most authentic jazz."[103]

Frustrated by the seeming inability of white Americans to recognize its genius, Beauvoir found that *Ebony*'s photographic account of Mezzrow's day-to-day life included "the most singularly moving images" she had seen in the United States. She was particularly taken with scenes of Mezzrow "laughing in the streets of Harlem," noting how this "white musician" had not only married a Black woman but "had lived for twenty years among blacks." Moreover, Beauvoir delighted in meeting Wolfe and Mezzrow in New York and, in particular, discovering that they "love jazz with fervor" yet opposed "American capitalism, racism, puritanical moralism—everything I detest in this America."[104] In them, she had found a way to claim the existential engagement and political power of African American identity while still rejecting America.

Beauvoir was not the first French visitor to report on this exciting new memoir. During a trip to New York in the summer of 1946, *Jazz hot* editor Charles Delaunay wrote to readers to describe his excitement after attending a book reading of *Really the Blues* at an "intimate meeting reserved for musicians" on New York's Fifty-Second Street. He described the memoir's style as the "pure jargon" of a jazz musician and claimed that "no one other than Mezzrow, who has lived among black and white musicians in Chicago and New York, is more qualified to write such an account."[105] Delaunay's endorsement of Mezzrow was surprising not only because Mezzrow was the protégé of his rival but also because of the increasing concerns about the effect of returning foreign musicians on the French jazz scene.[106] The Hot Club simultaneously needed to express its support of French musicians while still reasserting its defense, "above all," of "the great black musicians without whom jazz would not exist."[107] Against this backdrop, Mezzrow offered an intriguing alternative. He was a self-proclaimed Black man who loved New Orleans jazz but was also clearly white, a self-styled curator and protector of African American music. By January 1947, critic Frank Ténot had cited Mezzrow in *Jazz hot* as the only white musician who had "entirely assimilated to the 'black' idiom." He added: "All of those who love only the music of blacks love Milton."[108]

Most invested in Mezzrow's reputation in France were Panassié and his partner Madeleine Gautier, whose skill in English made her an invaluable collaborator for Panassié in forging direct relationships with jazz musicians.[109] Panassié and Gautier had, for both financial and aesthetic reasons, moved away from Delaunay and *Jazz hot* and thus were interested in finding new ways to establish authority in the French jazz world and reassert the primacy of New Orleans–style jazz. Mezzrow was the obvious choice, and throughout this period Panassié plugged his music and memoir in newspaper articles, magazine features, and books, as well as on the French radio. In March 1947, one young radio listener, who had previously bemoaned that commercial jazz had neither "heart, soul, blood, nor sperm," was thrilled by a radio program produced by Panassié that featured "the life of Mezz Mezzrow." He noted with particular astonishment that Mezzrow claimed to be Black.[110] In February 1948, Panassié invited Mezzrow to come to France for the first jazz festival in Nice, where he was introduced as the "white musician who knows most perfectly how to assimilate the black style" and as an "honorary black."[111] Panassié attributed this honorific to Mezzrow's musical fidelity to the New Orleans style as well as to his marriage to a Black woman. News reports quoted from the forthcoming book, pointing out that his last imprisonment had opened up his spirit to "real jazz music" and suggesting that "Milton Mezzrow had completely 'passed the line' in reverse."[112] As this report suggests, Mezzrow's passing was openly affirmed by and for French audiences.

By virtue of Panassié's inclusion in the patronage committee at *Présence Africaine*, Mezzrow was also featured in the first issue of the journal. In the short essay "Le mal blanc," Panassié introduced Mezzrow as "one of the very rare white musicians to have learned to play exactly like the Blacks in the United States, that is to say to make authentic jazz."[113] Panassié also described Mezzrow as one of the few musicians to join in the fight against racism, which he once again attributed to Mezzrow's mixing with them and marriage to a Black woman. In addition, Panassié suggested that Mezzrow loved Black people not only for their music but "because he found them more human than Whites." Panassié then used this assertion to make a far broader claim about the relationship of white "civilization" to Black culture. While whites believed that they had somehow given to Black people the fruits of civilization, white people had in fact been brutalized by this so-called progress and had thus lost their sense of community and "joie de vivre." Meanwhile, despite being brutalized, Black people had retained the same joy. This, Panassié argued, was because "the *Noir* lives in the present," much like a "child."[114] Whereas most contributors to *Présence Africaine* sought to valorize African civilization—and demonstrate its primacy to modernity—Panassié relied on primitivist tropes of timelessness and immaturity.

While Panassié continued to promote Mezzrow in various venues, Gautier and Wolfe organized the translation and publication of *Really the Blues* in France. As early as 1946, Wolfe had traveled as a literary scout for Random House to France. In addition to meeting other writers and intellectuals, Wolfe met with French publishers interested in translating *Really the Blues*, as well as those who might be interested in publishing his own manuscript on Black popular culture.[115] In fact, in 1946 the editors at *Franc-Tireur* wrote on behalf of Wolfe's visa application to the US State Department to reiterate their interest in publishing *Really the Blues*, which they claimed would "help French men to understand Americans and develop further amicable relations." Moreover, given the "problems of language peculiar to this book (Jive and Negro talk)," they wanted to bring Wolfe to France as soon as possible.[116]

In the end, Wolfe decided to partner with Marcel Duhamel, the well-known French publisher of crime novels that had first inspired Vian's *J'irai cracher sur vos tombes*.[117] In addition to his series, Duhamel had also become Richard Wright's primary French translator, whose work included a serialized translation of *Black Boy* in *Les Temps modernes* from January to June 1947.[118] Duhamel's particular affinity for translating this material was formed by his love of jazz during the war as well as travels in the United States immediately after the war.[119] In addition to being fluent in English, his cotranslator, Gautier, was well-known for her translations of blues lyrics, which appeared regularly in *Jazz hot* in 1946, and poetry, including a translation of Gwendolyn Brooks's "Ballad of Pearl May Lee" in the first issue of *Présence Africaine*.[120]

While Gautier was charged with the primary work of translating the book, she, Wolfe, and Duhamel were all involved in publicizing the memoir. Following the publication of an excerpt in *Les Temps modernes* in June 1950, Mezzrow's memoir was officially published in 1950 by Le Club Français de Livre and then widely distributed by the Editions Corrêa as *La rage de vivre* that same year (see figure 2.6).[121] As part of this publicity scheme, and perhaps hoping to trade on the growing interest in Mezzrow's life, Wolfe began to publish some of his own work on "negrophilia" in French intellectual journals. In May 1949, *Les Temps modernes* featured his essay "Uncle Remus and the Malevolent Rabbit," which was translated as "L'Oncle Rémus et son lapin."[122] In the essay, Wolfe considered the proliferation of Black figures in American popular and consumer culture: Aunt Jemima, Mammy, Beulah, Br'er Rabbit, and Uncle Remus, all stock characters in the stories popularized by white southern folklorist Joel Chandler Harris. While white readers might see Br'er Rabbit as a mischievous "prototype of the Negro grinner-giver," Wolfe argued that the figure instead represented Black resentment and revenge. It was, he argued, "the white man who manufactures the Negro grin."

This skeptical reading of the "grin" was left untranslated in the French text, which instructed readers to instead imagine the Pullman porter's "wide teeth-baring smile."[123] Wolfe's essay would in turn be taken up by a number of Francophone intellectuals. It was reviewed in the seventh issue of *Présence Africaine*, which noted with interest his argument that "black consciousness" was enslaved to the "white master."[124] Just a few years later, Frantz Fanon cited from Wolfe's work on Br'er Rabbit to critique the psychology of racism in his *Black Skin, White Masks*. Building on Wolfe's arguments regarding the fundamental mimicry of Black culture, and the "grin," Fanon argued that the mechanisms of colonial domination had created a sense of dependency and inadequacy for the colonized subject, who was then compelled to appropriate, imitate, and put on the white mask.[125]

Within a year, Wolfe again appeared in *Les Temps modernes*, this time with a translation of his "Ecstatic in Blackface" in the September 1950 issue.[126] In this essay, he drew on his earlier unpublished work to critique jazz fans' belief that

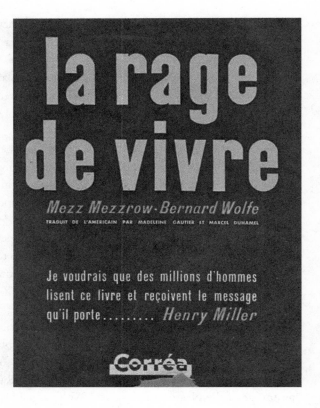

FIGURE 2.6. Cover of the French translation of Mezz Mezzrow's *Really the Blues*, which was published with Bernard Wolfe as coauthor as *La rage de vivre* in 1950.

they had witnessed "the Negro as he really is" ("the essential, distillate Negro, propelled by trance, emotionally supercharged, spontaneous"). Instead, he contended that "every Negro is to some extent a performer." Influenced by Sartre's own work on anti-Semitism, Wolfe argued that Black expression was satiric and reactive. Wolfe was particularly critical of jazz enthusiasts who, "feeling crushed by circumstance themselves," preferred to "see the Negro as a pre-social creature in whom the romping subjective is king" and who persisted in believing that "the Negro is lucky to be a pariah." Though distinct from Panassié's interpretations of bebop, and indeed critical of its same essentialism, Wolfe's essay nevertheless revealed his inability to see African American performance as capable of exceeding the limits of mimicry or minstrelsy. Indeed, he continued to foreground the role of the white critic: "*We* may be creating, via the Negro, what we could not create in our own persons."[127] It also perpetuated another illusion: that white observers could and should maintain critical control of Black art and that African American performers were merely reactive.

This particular framing was amplified in the publication of the memoir, which foregrounded the importance of the white authors and translators. In a letter—which was reprinted (in translation) as the introduction to the memoir—Henry Miller highlighted the "glorious things" that Mezzrow and Wolfe had done for this "sad, worn-out white man's language."[128] Throughout the text, the translators attempted to mimic the explosive power of the original, both in their translations of Black vernacular and in their notes to the reader, which help explain key terms like "Jim Crow," "blues," and "passing the line."[129] In translating the "jive" passage that had so entranced readers in the United States, Duhamel and Gautier offered a note to the reader. They indicated that this was a "very free adaptation" of the original, given that "the majority of words and expressions are a double entendre." The note continues, "Thanks to jive, the *blacks* can effectively say anything they feel when they are around a *white*, under the guise of perfectly anodyne comments."[130]

In promoting the book on the French radio, Madeleine Gautier spoke candidly about the difficulty and pleasure of translating Mezzrow, and the *décalage* (lag or gap) that existed between American and French argot.[131] While Gautier focused on the literary labor, cotranslator Duhamel was given center stage to locate himself in the writing process, reinforcing the gendered division of labor and recognition. In its final form, the memoir was followed by Duhamel's own postface, which highlighted his own first encounters with jazz in France (complete with a sexualized account of Josephine Baker and his first "racial brawl").[132] As a European "unaffected by the problem of racial segregation," he had always vaguely sensed that "real jazz, with its seizing rhythm and aching accents, was likely the ultimate means of poetic exteriorization of a people to whom free vocal expression had been denied."[133] After meeting Mezzrow in New York City in 1948, Duhamel claimed that he was immediately entranced by the book—which was at once an autobiography, a documentary of the South Side of Chicago and Harlem, a study of manners, and a jazz history—and asked to do the translation himself.[134] He spent the rest of his time with Mezzrow, who facilitated firsthand encounters with African Americans in the "black capital."[135] This racial fantasy of immersion in Black life was reinforced in advertisements for the novel, which superimposed an image of Mezzrow over the head of jazz drummer Warren "Baby" Dodds.

French reviewers were particularly excited by the memoir's capacity to make visible—and audible—the culture, language, and politics of Black people. In *Le Monde*, the reviewer wrote that it was "a history of jazz, of course, but it also was something else: a moving testimony, an indictment of racial discriminations. It screams, the words are formed, slow, tearing, bursting."[136] The review in *Action* also focused on the language, noting its translation of "the argot of blacks and jazz musicians, the jargon of Harlem and the sense of verbal intervention," where "humor and tragedy are confounded."[137] In *Franc-Tireur*, the reviewer noted, "There are not fifty books to read today. There is only one: that's *La Rage de Vivre*."[138] French reviews consistently underscored the ways in which this new book had successfully translated the language, emotion, and political power of African American culture into French. Echoing Beauvoir's own account, the jazz world became, for its French readers, a space where they too might claim African American existential liberation without necessarily capitulating to American power.

In 1951, the translation of *Really the Blues* was reviewed in *Présence Africaine* by Jacques Howlett, who had previously discussed Boris Vian's *J'irai cracher sur vos tombes* in 1947 in the inaugural issue of the journal.[139] While Howlett had found in Vian's novel a premonition of simmering anticolonial resentment, Mezzrow's embodiment of Blackness and rejection of assimilation also struck the reviewer. Howlett believed that Mezzrow—in his words, his identity papers, his marriage, and life—exemplified a fidelity to *négritude*, the "ultimate otherness." While Howlett's praise might appear to us now as misguided, or at the very least misdirected, it nevertheless reveals something of this moment, when uneasy alliances were critical to the articulation of Black Francophone cultural power. While *Présence Africaine* would become a powerful publisher and proponent of decolonization by the mid-1950s, in this moment it was very much constrained in terms of its political ambition and message, and its writers engaged in various forms of what V. Y. Mudimbe has termed "surreptitious speech."[140] Bennetta Jules-Rosette has cautioned against conflating *Présence Africaine* in its early years with a form of revolutionary pan-Africanism. By contrast, she argues, it offered a space for collaboration between Black writers and French anthropologists that "was uneasy at best."[141]

In this context, while *Really the Blues* and *J'irai cracher sur vos tombes* were each sold as a means for white people to access Black identity, they were nonetheless read and reinterpreted by nonwhite Francophone people. Those readers in turn laid claim to the texts, finding new inroads and strategies to critique, revise, and push against colonial models and, moreover, to lay claim to the means of their own racialization. While distinct from Brent Hayes Edwards's account of Black internationalism, this moment nevertheless echoes his point, that it is "as though certain moves, certain arguments and epiphanies, can only be staged beyond the confines of the United States, and even sometimes in languages other than English."[142] Likewise, the purportedly foreign provenance of these texts created a new discursive space for Francophone audiences, who found new opportunities to surreptitiously critique empire and bolster the value of *négritude*. Several years later, when describing the colonialist's own impulse to define authentic indigeneity, Frantz Fanon compared it to the "reactions of white jazz specialists" to bebop. In their eyes, "jazz should only be the despairing, broken-down nostalgia of an old Negro who is trapped between five glasses of whisky, the curse of his race, and the racial hatred of white men." In contrast to the whites "who are faithful to this arrested image," Fanon argued that "as soon as the Negro comes to an understanding of himself . . . it is clear that his trumpet sounds more clearly and his voice less hoarsely." For Fanon, the jazz metaphor continued to hold a "certain measure of importance" precisely because "the real nature of colonialism was not involved."[143] In Fanon's hands, these racial explorations, while intended to lay claim to Black identity, were transformed into a new discursive tool, one of many that Fanon would use to subvert colonial rule and to articulate new languages of nationalism and identity.

The texts' immediate impact, however, was their immense success in selling not only the African American experience, but also the color line itself. Playing on the thin yet critical borders of race, the authors, translators, and publishers made clear that while the Black experience was at the core of the marketability of African American culture and music, African Americans (or Black Francophone people, for that matter) were not necessary to its sale. Indeed, this remained the province of white writers and publishers. Owing to this literary phenomenon's direct ties to jazz, future purveyors of African American music would continue to draw from the embodied African American experience. In short, Mezzrow, Vian, and Wolfe had inaugurated a new postwar economy of racial nostalgia, which reevaluated and capitalized on modern African American subjectivity while maintaining the residuals of its supposed primitive and slave past. This would grow considerably in the years to come, but in all cases, African Americans found themselves marginalized, and at times invisible, even as their experiences gained economic and social value.

3

SPINNING RACE

The French Record Industry and the

Production of African American Music

———

Archived within the collections of the Bibliothèque nationale de France in Paris is an undated, handwritten manuscript, signed by Marge Creath Singleton, titled "The Truth about Mezz Mezzrow."[1] Marge Singleton was the wife of African American jazz drummer Zutty Singleton, a New Orleans–trained musician who began performing with Mezzrow in New York in the 1930s. Their close personal and professional relationship was featured in Mezzrow's infamous 1946 memoir, *Really the Blues*, which recounted his life as a "voluntary Negro." Soon after the book's enormously successful translation into French in 1950, Mezzrow invited Singleton and trumpeter Lee Collins for a six-month tour of Europe and North Africa. Initially pleased by her husband's opportunity to join what would likely be a lucrative tour, Marge Singleton soon suspected a more "sinister motive" for Mezzrow's living in Harlem, among African Americans. She was especially suspicious of the contract her husband had to sign, for Mezzrow—citing their long friendship and trust—had specified that Singleton could not accept "any kind of work or personal appearance" in Europe without his consent. Tempering these fears with optimism for a high-paying gig, in November 1951 the Singletons joined Mary and Lee Collins on a ship to Le Havre, where they were greeted by Mezzrow, as well as critic Hugues Panassié and his collaborator Madeleine Gautier. After touring metropolitan France and French North Africa, as well as Belgium, Switzerland, and Spain, they returned to Paris, where the musicians participated in a two-day recording session with the record label Vogue, which subsequently released five 78 rpm records derived from the session.[2]

Nearly a year later, neither Singleton nor Collins had received their expected royalties. During a return visit to Paris, Mary Collins requested the royalties from Vogue. The label claimed that Mezzrow had the money, which prompted Collins to demand remuneration at the American embassy.[3] Meanwhile, Marge Singleton claimed that Mezzrow had dropped Zutty from the tour while still owing him five weeks' salary and return airfare. After sending for financial help in the United States, the Singletons returned home, where Singleton had some professional recourse. He filed a complaint that led to Mezzrow's expulsion from the American Federation of Musicians (AFM) in September 1952, citing his failure to pay Singleton an estimated $1,615 in back wages.[4] Reflecting on these experiences, Marge Singleton concluded that Mezzrow was "not a friend to the Negro, as he would have the public believe," but rather that he was "using the Negro, for his own selfish purpose, to write books about them and make money and give concerts in Europe and make more money." If Mezzrow truly cared for African American musicians, she wondered, "Why does he bring them to Europe for $150.00 a week" when he himself earned $3,000? This breach of faith—and contract—was made all the more painful for her as she watched Mezzrow announce in concert, with "crocodile tears" in his eyes, his devotion to African American musicians.[5]

While Mezzrow's unique capacity to attract and alienate African American musicians should not be discounted, this particular account offers more than another chapter in his strange and storied career.[6] It sheds light on the specific conditions facing African American musicians as they attempted to navigate the postwar French recording industry.[7] While exploitation was endemic to the recording industry, the vulnerability of musicians was heightened in foreign countries, where a lost contract meant that a musician was still a one-week passage or a multistop transatlantic flight away from home. New technologies may have ensured a wider circulation for jazz in the postwar era, but musicians were often prevented from fully benefiting from this market expansion because of the particular conditions of copyright law in the United States.[8] Indeed, jazz improvisation and performance had fewer claims to "ownership" than the original composition did, even though the specific performances were frequently the reason for a particular record's success. Any musician's welfare overseas depended on the presence of cultural intermediaries and interpreters, but African American musicians—by virtue of their ties to especially profitable musical genres—were more often targets of industry deception. When Singleton did not receive the promised royalties, the recording company shrugged off its responsibility, leaving Singleton, a foreign visitor whose own visa and employment depended on the same people who had absconded with his money, with few options. While Zutty Singleton appealed to the AFM, Marge Singleton appealed to the reader (whoever that might be), hoping that Mezzrow's infamous reputation as a "voluntary Negro" might elicit some kind of public pressure to pay her husband.[9] The Singletons did not live in France, but they still needed to navigate the transnational economy of musical production and distribution, which required different forms of currency.

The ordeal of the Singletons and Collinses helps to illustrate the stakes of this chapter, which examines the growth of the transatlantic record industry after World War II, when new technologies, trade agreements, and licensing laws made possible an explosive growth in sales and cultural influence of African American music. The chapter focuses on the women and men whose mastery of English and firsthand knowledge of African American culture facilitated the transatlantic movement of labor and commodities. Out of a relatively small jazz fan base in interwar Paris, these record producers created national markets for African American music, including jazz, blues, rhythm and blues, and gospel, which would in turn transform these same labels into successful multinational businesses. This transformation was made possible by their representations of African American culture. By virtue of the political, cultural, and military networks established during the liberation period, African American subjectivity had become politically and existentially valuable in France. Thus, the symbols of that experience were frequently incorporated into the records themselves; through written, visual, and aural means, representations of African American life were included in the marketing of these cultural commodities, further enhancing the prospects for sales and profits. But industry marketing also relied on the physical presence and labor of African American performers, many of whom were living in France as short-term visitors or as long-term residents.[10]

In some cases, African American musicians benefited from these new opportunities to record in Paris, which was a central transportation hub for touring other European capitals and offered regular performance opportunities in local clubs. The opportunity to record in France launched and even revitalized careers, as was the case with blues guitarist Big Bill Broonzy. For jazz clarinetist Sidney Bechet, the French record industry offered the opportunity not only to profit from the revived interest in his New Orleans style but also to help define his own place in jazz history. For some musicians, including drummer Kenny Clarke, a steady income in France provided him with the means to live and perform free from the everyday encounters with American racism. For Quincy

Jones, it offered a way to reclaim the means of musical production. However, while the industry valued the embodiment of African American identity for its own ends, it did not necessarily recognize African American claims to subjectivity and self-possession. In this way, the French industry seemed to exemplify Ornette Coleman's claim that "in jazz the Negro is the product."[11] Taken together, African American musicians' varied experiences reveal the workings of this industry, whose profits depended simultaneously on the visibility *and* invisibility of African American people. It built on the soundscapes formed after liberation—and the increasing marketability of African American subjectivity—but in this case, the commodity form itself promised consumers a share in this emancipatory history.

From Niche to Mass Market

From their emergence during the interwar period, both the jazz critical world and recording industry in France were premised on commodity scarcity. Early fans sought out in vain "hot jazz" records featuring Louis Armstrong and Fletcher Henderson in the French marketplace, the rarity of which was even more frustrating given the surfeit of "sweet," symphonic jazz records by the likes of Paul Whiteman. Many joined the Hot Club de France, which had been formed in 1932 to facilitate access to "hot" jazz. Members of local Hot Club chapters listened collectively to 78 rpm phonograph records imported directly from the United States that they might otherwise not be able to find or purchase.[12] This mode of listening, which emerged in conjunction with growing radio distribution, was adopted in response to both the scarcity of and the particular challenges presented by the 78 rpm record, which was made from a shellac compound that made it fragile, heavy, difficult to ship, and relatively expensive.[13] Not only did each record offer just three to five minutes of playback per side, the fidelity of the recording also rapidly deteriorated with each revolution. Finally, the record itself only listed the title and bandleader's name, leaving the listener with no information on the identity of other musicians or the details about the recording session. French listeners were left with the recording sounds themselves, which they heard as mere echoes of African American music, made in faraway, exotic places like Harlem, New Orleans, and Oklahoma. For these fans, the record thus brought the elusive and "inherently ephemeral art of improvisation" out of "the black ghettos" and into the world, where it could be "studied, dissected and analyzed."[14] In addition to Hugues Panassié's innovation of *conférences-auditions* (or "listening-lectures"), Charles Delaunay pioneered the practice of discography, the painstaking cataloguing of all details regarding the recorded performances of a musician or the recordings of a label.[15] As these supra-aural excursions suggest, the pleasure of jazz could not be disentangled from the ethnographic acquisition of detailed knowledge initiated by jazz listeners.[16]

In 1937, still frustrated with extant networks of jazz record distribution, Hot Club cofounders Panassié and Delaunay created Swing, the first French record label specializing in jazz. The label was a subsidiary of Pathé-Marconi (and therefore EMI), which financed and distributed its records. In Swing's first few years, the small label recorded local orchestras like the Quintette du Hot Club de France as well as visiting American musicians like Coleman Hawkins, Bill Coleman, and Rex Stewart. During the German occupation, with few American musicians left in France, the label had focused exclusively on French musicians and expanded the French audience for jazz. After the war, still unable to get new recordings, fans sought out old records in flea markets. Though Swing was interested in distributing new records from American catalogues, EMI-Pathé-Marconi was reluctant to distribute new material that might compete with its own recordings.[17] To remedy this problem, in July 1948 Delaunay traveled to New York to seek out distribution deals with independent labels like Apollo, Keynote, and Savoy.[18] In addition to acquiring masters from those labels for Swing—which would enable their manufacture and distribution in Europe—Delaunay hoped to create an affiliate of Swing for distribution in the United States, an ambition that in the end did not materialize.[19]

Delaunay's keen interest in establishing Swing's market share on the continent was also spurred by the arrival of new competition, Blue Star, a jazz label created in 1945 by Nicole and Eddie Barclay.[20] Born Edouard Ruault, Barclay had renamed himself following his immersion in the occupation *zazou* culture. During the war, Barclay played piano at Pierre-Louis Guérin's Parisian club, which became known as Eddie's Club following the liberation and soon attracted American GIs, musicians, and avid jazz fans. The postwar club most frequently featured Eddie himself, joined by African American trumpeter Harry Cooper (who had spent part of the war in an internment camp), French musicians Bobby Guidott and Jean-Pierre Sasson, and a singer named Eve Williams, the first pseudonym of Nicole Vandenbussche, who took Eddie's surname when the two married several years later.[21] One of the frequent visitors to Eddie's Club was Allan Morrison, a Canadian-born Black journalist who served as a war correspondent for the American military newspaper *Stars and Stripes*.[22] The Barclays and Morrison talked for hours about jazz while listening to American-made, noncommercial Victory-Discs, all of which helped cement their own interest in producing jazz records. In February 1945, the Barclays created Blue Star, with Eddie as *président directeur general* and Nicole as *directeur financier*, at their home on rue Pergolèse and began recording French musicians, like Jerry Mengo, and African American GIs, like Arthur Briggs, at the Technisonor Studio, a studio still managed by the American Forces Network.[23]

The fates of these fledgling labels converged in late 1946, when tenor saxophonist Don Byas arrived with Don Redman's big band, the first African American civilian orchestra in France since the war's end.[24] Delaunay organized a December 1946 recording session for Byas with Swing, but while Delaunay was in New York, Panassié returned to Paris (from his new residence in southwestern France) to organize a separate recording session for Byas with Blue Star in January 1947.[25] This duplicity marked the bitter end of Panassié and Delaunay's personal and professional relationships, culminating in Delaunay's decision in September 1947 to terminate all financial agreements between them. In turn, Panassié (now excluded from *Jazz hot* and Swing) denounced Swing's sessions with Byas as "inferior to those on Blue Star" and in October 1947 ousted Delaunay from the Hot Club de France.[26] At this point, Panassié terminated his own contract with Swing to sign on as artistic director with Blue Star, where his plan was to "reclaim [his] independence."[27] In addition, Panassié played a role in extending Pathé-Marconi's technical and financial support to Blue Star. This meant that EMI-Pathé-Marconi then manufactured records for both labels at its factories in the suburban town of Chatou, which was one of the few record businesses in operation at a time when materials were still scarce.[28]

Although the split was articulated in aesthetic and racial terms, at root it was a struggle over market power. This new battle was bound up in different maneuvers to claim the fruits of Byas's labor, making him simultaneously critical to yet fundamentally invisible in the production process. And because this press coverage was resurrected at every major concert and record release, it helped reinvigorate the market for both New Orleans and bebop records, which in turn had important consequences for African American musicians.[29] While some visiting jazz musicians maintained equanimity among the battling critics, it was more difficult for musicians like Bechet, who was represented in business dealings by Delaunay, and who pointed out in 1948 that the musicians themselves most suffered from this "childishness."[30] Pressured by critics to embody their critical claims, African American musicians needed to tread carefully in the French musical world.

Perhaps owing to the increasingly competitive jazz market, the business fortunes of both labels improved quickly. In the early days, the Barclays stored records in their bathtub and distributed orders by bicycle in Paris, with Nicole Barclay responsible for most financial and business dealings. For the next two years, they "didn't make a cent" but continued to have records produced at

Chatou, selling "at a rate of 15,000 a month." As the story was told in 1948, "by drastic economies" they saved enough for Nicole to sail third-class across the Atlantic to New York, where she stayed for two weeks "in a dingy hotel near Harlem," in search of masters.[31] She returned with bebop masters and licensing deals with three new independent labels: Circle, Gotham, and Dial. Through these deals, the Barclays released twenty 78 rpm records, the most significant of which were reissues of Charlie Parker's 1940s Dial Sessions.[32] In December 1948, with a total of two hundred titles in the Blue Star catalogue, the Barclays created their own jazz magazine, *Jazz news*. Edited by Boris Vian, the journal poked fun at the internal battles of jazz critics and soon distinguished itself from Delaunay's rival magazine, *Jazz hot*.

Whereas other contemporary jazz magazines featured photo spreads and interviews with Black musicians, *Jazz news* frequently focused on the glamorous lives of the Barclays and their direct ties to the African American community. These photo essays not only featured Blue Star's own jazz records but also visually displayed the Barclays moving among African Americans and within Black spaces, all of which underscored to readers their familiarity with and fidelity to African American culture. This was possible in part because they had stayed in touch with war correspondent Allan Morrison, who had left France to become the New York editor of *Ebony*. In October 1949, *Jazz news* reported the couple's arrival in New York, where they were welcomed by musicians Lester Young, Coleman Hawkins, Mary Lou Williams, and J. C. Heard, "all alerted by [their] friend Allan Morrison, editor of 'Ebony' (the great black newspaper)."[33] The magazine included photographs of the Barclays as they were picked up by Charlie Parker in a "magnificent Cadillac" and escorted to Harlem's Savoy Club. By sharing the "extraordinary feeling" of being in Black spaces—and highlighting their own intermediary role—the Barclays invited their French readers (and consumers) to share in their intimacy with African Americans.[34]

In addition to demonstrating their access to African American life in the United States, these transatlantic trips to New York continued to link the Barclays to new distribution deals. In the November 1949 issue of *Jazz news*, Blue Star placed an advertisement for its new series, "Super-Rythme 1950," which featured exclusive recordings from eleven American labels: Aladdin, Atlantic, Century, Circle, Comet, Dial, Gotham, Manor, Mercury, Sunrise, and Wax.[35] Blue Star also released its first print catalogue, which included new categories for jazz—"Dance Orchestra, Hot Jazz, New Orleans, and bebop"—and listed Eddie Barclay as the *directeur du production* and Hugues Panassié as *superviseur*.[36] Though the catalogue made clear the categories of jazz and the new business associations, it nonetheless obscured the crucial role played by Nicole Barclay in expanding the label's repertoire. One of her biggest accomplishments was a March 1949 deal with impresario Norman Granz, who was an artists and repertoire (A&R) representative at Mercury. Through this new deal, Barclay would have exclusive distribution rights of Mercury's catalogue as well as the rights to distribute recordings of Granz's own *Jazz at the Philharmonic* concert series in France, Switzerland, Italy, and Belgium.[37] Furthermore, in exchange for sending etchings of visiting American stars and classical recordings to Atlantic, Blue Star had acquired "several instrumental jazz masters, principally bop, to be issued in France" and would also distribute a new "Atlantic series" for export to Argentina, given that trade restrictions made it impossible to ship directly there.[38]

Meanwhile, Charles Delaunay was also engaged in the acquisition of new recording and distribution opportunities for Swing. In July 1948, building on increasing sales by Swing in France, its colonies, and Europe, he joined in a new partnership with Léon Cabat and Albert Ferrari to record and distribute records in Europe.[39] They created the Association Française des Collectionneurs de Disques de Jazz (AFCDJ), through which they planned to rerelease older blues and jazz recordings by acquiring masters from other jazz fan associations.[40] Soon they secured the licensing rights from the King label's "race records" catalogue as well as recordings from the Hot Record Society. After acquiring the rights to reissue an Odéon recording of Louis Armstrong and His Hot Five, in December 1948 they pooled their profits (and sold Ferrari's car) to create a company called Jazz Disques, also known as Jazz Sélection. Delaunay was in charge of publicity, Ferrari was artistic director, and Cabat was the *president directeur général*, effectively running the business.[41] The new company then broke from EMI-Pathé-Marconi and had its records manufactured by independent French company Sofradis.[42]

In 1949, Delaunay and Nicole Barclay were both in New York, where they attempted to recruit musicians to join in rival jazz festivals in Paris. The previous year, in February 1948, the city of Nice had hosted the first international jazz festival, organized by Hugues Panassié and Madeleine Gautier. Befitting Panassié's own preferences, the lineup included Louis Armstrong, Mezz Mezzrow, Baby Dodds, Pops Foster, Velma Middleton, and Sammy Price—all of whom were considered "traditional" jazz musicians—and had been broadcast across Europe via radio.[43] That same month, Dizzy Gillespie's hugely successful concert in Paris had likewise demonstrated that modern jazz could also bring in profits, driving the interest of both Blue Star and Swing/Jazz Disques to follow suit. After discovering they had inadvertently signed the same musicians, Barclay and Delaunay decided to create a unified festival for May 8–15, 1949, at the Salle Pleyel in Paris, headlined by bebop giants Charlie Parker and Miles Davis in addition to New Orleans native Sidney Bechet, Mary Lou Williams, and drummer Kenny Clarke, whom Nicole Barclay had recruited in New York.[44]

Although Parker and Davis were successful, Bechet's triumph in France was unmistakably unique. By virtue of his French Creole–speaking family, Bechet seemed to embody the imagined French connection to jazz. Furthermore, his clarinet's sinewy sound was the *ur*-sound of the New Orleans revival, which was launched in part by Mezz Mezzrow and Hugues Panassié in the late 1930s in the United States and gained fervent French fans in the late 1940s. Indeed, throughout the May festival, Bechet was "plagued by discographers eager to check on the personnel of various recordings."[45] Afterward, both Blue Star and Swing/Jazz Disques brought him in for recording sessions, but after returning to the US, Bechet discovered that even after his success in France, he was, in the words of a contemporary, "just another jazzman scuffling."[46] A few months later, Bechet returned to France, where he made a recording with Delaunay's label that would launch him into superstardom. The 78 rpm record, "Les oignons," was released by Vogue (the new name of Swing/Jazz Disques) in December 1949, and it received almost continuous airplay on the French radio. It would go on to become the best-selling record in French history, eventually selling over 1 million copies at a time when most jazz records sold five hundred copies.[47] Andy Fry has described "Les oignons" as the "perfect introduction to traditional jazz, whose noisy polyphony can leave newcomers perplexed."[48] Due to its simplicity and regularity, many self-identified "serious" jazz fans, including the reviewers at Delaunay's own *Jazz hot*, despised the recording.[49] Nevertheless, its success assured Bechet's continued collaboration with Delaunay, who had already secured him a high payment (a total of 525,000 francs for five performances) for the May festival, as his European manager and agent.[50]

The Barclays and Delaunay joined forces once again in early December 1950, when they organized the first International Salon du Jazz at the Maison de la Chimie in Paris. The industrial and commercial trade show in Paris drew in thirty thousand visitors from throughout the world. Though the state-run Radiodiffusion Française and French Ministry of National Education were cosponsors of the trade show, the overriding rationale was unquestionably commercial.[51] The published program, written by Delaunay, heralded the jazz industry's extension into the "domain of records, radio, and spectacle" and its employment of "thousands of French craftsmen" who, by creating the instruments of jazz, made clear to the world "the renown of the French industry."[52] Furthermore, within the program were advertisements for record labels, record

FIGURE 3.1. Photograph from the 1951 Salon du Jazz in Paris, where fans listen to records beneath an advertisement for a Decca record featuring Louis Armstrong. The advertisement specifically promotes the new *microsillon* 33 rpm record. Photo courtesy of Getty Images.

FIGURE 3.2. An advertisement for a new record by Sidney Bechet, the "talisman" of Disques Vogue, looms over the 1951 Salon du Jazz in Paris. Photo courtesy of Getty Images.

stores, and even "existentialist" clubs like the Vieux Colombier. After paying the fifty-franc entrance fee, visitors could wander through a commercial exhibition hall of booths, each selling the wares of record labels like Blue Star, Vogue, Odéon, and Pathé-Marconi, manufacturers of record players and instruments such as Hohner and Pierret, and book publishers like Corrêa, which prominently featured its new translation of Mezz Mezzrow's memoir.[53]

This unmistakably commercial sphere was also defined by various depictions of the African American body and reconstructions of African American life. The program's cover featured an enslaved Black man with chains around his ankles, a figure who stooped as though struggling under the weight of history.[54] In the commercial hall, the booths were peopled by African American musicians as well as life-size models of Black musicians advertising instruments and records (see figures 3.1 and 3.2).[55] The exhibit hall featured "art work inspired by jazz music," which included abstract sculptures by African American expatriate artist Harold Cousins, as well as drawings and engravings of jazz orchestras, blues singers, and the Mississippi River by French artist Pierre Merlin.[56] According to some reports, visitors could also peruse a reconstruction of a New Orleans street in the Salle Pleyel or ride on a Mississippi riverboat on the Seine.[57] The presence of these racialized bodies and places, many of which recounted a history of enslavement and struggle, clarifies what was at stake in the commercialization of jazz in France.[58] The depictions of African Americans had facilitated the transformation from what had been the province of a small group of committed fans into a mass medium of popular music. Though couched in terms of emancipation, the Salon du Jazz inaugurated the mass commoditization of African American music and African American musicians' labor in France.

Marketing the *Longue Durée*

While these transformations were specific to France, they were closely tied to developments in the US recording industry, where business was booming. Unfettered by postwar reconstruction, the US record industry had recovered from a wartime strike of the American Federation of Musicians to produce more records than ever before.[59] It was spurred by the mass movement of laborers to industrialized cities, where their earnings allowed them to become consumers accustomed to buying the records they heard on the radio and jukeboxes. Critical to this urban migration were African American consumers, whose tastes were now catered to by "rhythm and blues" (R&B), a record marketing nomenclature that replaced the old genre of "race records."[60] These jazz and R&B records were produced by a new crop of independent labels, including Atlantic,

Savoy, King, Chess, Sun, Vee Jay, Prestige, Blue Note, and Riverside, as well as Mercury and Capitol, which navigated networks controlled by the "majors," among them Columbia (CBS), RCA-Victor, and Decca.

The expansion of the market for African American music was also facilitated by the introduction in 1948 of two new record formats: the twelve-inch, 33 rpm long-playing (LP) record, launched by CBS; and the seven-inch, 45 rpm single, launched by RCA. These new record formats transformed record listening, which no longer involved a heavy, fragile shellac record but instead a light, sturdy, easily transportable vinyl LP record, which could hold up to fifty minutes of music.[61] Just as the 78 rpm record had engaged senses beyond the aural, the microgroove record was likewise a multisensory object. In addition to the smell of vinyl, there was the sound of the *microgroove*, with its noises, scratches, and reverberations, sonic annoyances that nevertheless defined the experience. These sensual experiences continued to mix as one progressed through the rituals of listening: pulling out the album, reading the liner notes, and listening to a long-awaited recording. Whereas the typical 78 rpm shellac record had no cover art or liner notes, the vinyl album's cover made bold visual claims of modernity, authenticity, and history through its designs, photographs, and words penned by familiar critics and writers. And with the jazz or blues LP, each stage of consumerism constituted a direct engagement with race, whether in the texture, style, or tone of the photograph or how the liner notes' author defined the music's production.

In the United States, the introduction of the LP and the 45 rpm single led to expanded production of records as well as record players; moreover, it expanded listening audiences, who bought new and reissued albums. However, in Europe, where EMI was slow to introduce the new vinyl technology, the market was still dominated by the heavy and expensive 78 rpm record. As *Billboard* reported in 1949, "Monetary restrictions, and the fact that shellac must be imported, have prevented sizeable increases in production, and have delayed reduction of disk prices."[62] This meant that Blue Star and Swing were well positioned to not only compete with the majors in selling 78 rpm records but also to introduce these new formats to French audiences. In 1951, the Barclays had incorporated as Productions Phonographiques Françaises and had begun to acquire the new technology necessary to distribute the LP format. According to Eddie Barclay's own lore, they learned about the *longue durée* (LD) record through their old friend Allan Morrison, who sent a telegram saying, "Eddie. Most important discovery since Einstein. A revolutionary record, unbreakable and each side can last thirty minutes!" The Barclays left immediately for New York to seek out the long-playing record, which appeared, "black as ebony, solid, miraculous, a 33 LP," a description that underscored once again the racialization of the record commodity.[63] The Barclays returned to France with Mercury's masters in hand. Although Pathé's factory in the Parisian suburb of Chatou was not initially equipped for this new technology, the Barclays prevailed and finally introduced the *microsillon* to French audiences in the summer of 1951.[64]

In September 1951, *Jazz hot* reported that the new format had appeared "just before the summer vacation." The article continued, "It goes without saying that the appearance of these records in the market poses serious problems to French listeners, who in general do not yet have players equipped to handle 33 revolutions."[65] While heralding the arrival of cheaper, sturdier, and more attractive records, the article underscored the enormous shift for consumers, many of whom had invested in older technology. As one memoirist recalled, "The appearance of the microgroove record" was "a genuine revolution." He continued, noting that "one could listen to a symphony without changing the record every five minutes and with a purity of sound that appeared to us clearly miraculous."[66] This technological innovation in turn catapulted Blue Star into a hugely successful business, earning Eddie Barclay the moniker "king of the microgroove."[67]

However, Blue Star was not the only label that was peddling the *microsillon* record. By 1951, Jazz Disques, Jazz Selection, and Swing had been unified under the label Vogue, the commercial name for the Productions Internationales Phonographiques (PIP).[68] The continued success of Bechet's 1949 recording of "Les oignons" had almost single-handedly launched Vogue as a major industrial force. Higher demand for records had prompted the label to abandon its "traditional" methods to achieve distribution on a much larger scale within France and the empire.[69] Through these new profits and an expanded audience, Cabat and Delaunay began to rerelease and record a wider variety of genres. In many ways, this marked a return to the collectors' desire in the 1930s and 1940s to amass the full range of African American musical expression, but now this work was driven by a desire for profit as well as preservation.

One of the most significant moments in this period of acquisition was September 1951, when Vogue organized a two-day recording session with blues singer and guitarist "Big Bill" Broonzy, his first in three years. In 1950, Broonzy was living in the college town of Ames, Iowa, and working as a janitor at the state university.[70] By this point, his career had already undergone a number of transformations. Broonzy faced an increasingly volatile recording industry in the postwar United States, where the music industry struggled to adapt to changes in recording and to the decline in live performance due to the increasing popularity of jukeboxes and radio. In response, Broonzy had transformed himself from a southern fiddler to a solo blues guitarist in the style of Blind Lemon Jefferson to an early progenitor of jump blues to (more recently) a regular feature of the folk music circuit, which had brought him to Iowa. It was the relative security of this position, as a minor celebrity among local folk music fans, that likely made Broonzy hesitate when he received a phone call from Hugues Panassié in 1950 inviting him to tour in France. Panassié had first heard the blues singer perform in 1938 at the "Spirituals to Swing" concert in New York, where Broonzy was dressed in overalls and introduced as coming straight from Mississippi. Quite taken with the performance, Panassié began to promote Broonzy to the many adherents of the Hot Club de France. In 1949, he encouraged jazz fans in particular to listen to Broonzy, a "natural" singer who, he claimed, had learned to sing "in the South, on street corners or river-banks."[71] Eschewing Broonzy's urban and northern trajectory, Panassié painted a portrait instead of the "natural" southern blues musician.

After receiving repeated inquiries—and a promise to triple his fee—in 1951, Broonzy finally agreed to a tour of France, Belgium, Switzerland, Germany, and Holland under the sponsorship of the Hot Club de France. He toured France for approximately one month, accompanied by two African American musicians (trumpeter Merrill Stepter and pianist Wally Bishop) and three white French musicians, performing in twenty-six towns.[72] Many of the stops were in summer resorts, where Gautier claimed that "people are now real crazy about blues singers," especially "the old school ones, the real ones."[73] She clarified that unlike the "modern ones, who leave the audiences over here just cold," that Broonzy's tour was a "tremendous success."[74] Immediately following the 1951 tour, Panassié coordinated a recording session for Broonzy with Vogue, which resulted in a total of twenty-five sides, including the first commercial recording of Broonzy's song "Black, Brown, and White."[75] While Broonzy first wrote the song in 1939 and had performed it throughout the 1940s, he had faced difficulty in attracting a record company's interest. In the song, he details the distinct economic experiences of African Americans, whether in the work-place (where they were paid different rates for the same work), in spaces of lei-sure (where one could not count on being served), or in the eyes of state (whose employment office followed a racial hierarchy). The song ends by describing the labor of rural African Americans in fighting the war, and calls the listener to arms in ending Jim Crow. The chorus, repeated after every verse, outlines the racial hierarchy that connects each of these disparate experiences: "They say, if you is white, you'll be all right / If you is brown, stick around / But as you is black, oh, brother, get back, get back, get back." In the months following the recording session, Vogue released the song first as a 78 rpm single (Vogue 134) and then as part of a two-volume vinyl LP album, whose iconic cover quickly made it a valuable commodity.

In some respects, the recording session and trip were successful for Broonzy, who found not only a new market for his music but also an opportunity to stage his own critique of American racism on foreign soil at a moment when some of his contemporaries—including Paul Robeson and Hazel Scott—found themselves surveilled and circumscribed by the Cold War.[76] In 1952, Broonzy was interviewed by Alan Lomax in Paris and spoke frankly about racial prejudice in the record industry and compared the racism facing African Americans and "French negroes."[77] He also formed a long-standing professional relationship with Belgian blues researcher Yannick Bruynoghe, who worked with Broonzy in writing his own memoirs, which in turn established his critical position on the blues.[78] But like Zutty Singleton, Broonzy had difficulty securing remuneration from the Hot Club, which owed him 125,000 francs following a subsequent tour. In 1952, he too was forced to go to the American embassy for help.[79] Broonzy also made a written declaration of his ill treatment, which was then published by Panassié's rival Charles Delaunay in his magazine *Jazz hot* in July 1952. His artistic empowerment was thus circumscribed by his vulnerable economic position in France, where the Hot Club's recognition of artistry was sometimes proffered in lieu of just compensation. And while the recording of "Black, Brown, and White" was a point of professional pride—and would influence his performance style in the years to come—Broonzy did not share in the financial profits that Vogue would later claim from record sales or by expanding its blues catalogue. In 1958, Broonzy died impoverished, while Vogue had become the preeminent producer and distributor of African American music in Europe.[80]

Following the 1951 Broonzy recordings, Delaunay's partner Cabat sought out new licensing deals with small, independent record labels in the United States, including Chess, Key, Modern, Peacock, Apollo, Blue Note, Savoy, and Atlantic, all of which specialized in Black popular music.[81] By 1952, the Vogue catalogue had identified its holdings for consumers within the following categories: "the Kings of boogie-woogie," the "favorite stars of the black American public," "jazz records that make you dance," "historical documents," "jazz recorded in France," "Negro Spirituals," "Antillean folklore," "Accordion," and "Hammond Organ." In addition to instruments and musical genres, this classification referenced the sites of production, creation, history, and performance. By advertising the "favorite stars of the black American public" in particular, Vogue aligned French fandom with the preferences of African Americans, thus offering authenticity alongside mass commodities. The new catalogue included recordings by Sir Charles Thompson, Charlie Parker, Coleman Hawkins, and Mahalia Jackson, who in 1952 found her "first all-white audience" in France.[82] These recordings were all part of a new series of long-playing microgroove records that would eventually include over two hundred titles (LD 001 to LD 222). Some of these records were shorter than the traditional LP and comprised ten-inch 45 rpm vinyl records that featured two tracks per side. Most were jazz, blues, or gospel.[83] These included, for example, Vogue's own recordings of pianist Sammy Price, whose "varied repertoire of blues and jump" was advertised to customers.[84] In addition, Vogue was in contact with Charles Mingus, to whom Delaunay wrote in 1952 to reiterate his interest in "creating new sounds."[85]

Further distinguishing this particular record series were its covers, all of which were designed and drawn by trumpeter, collector, and artist Pierre Merlin. In the late 1930s, while enrolled at the École Municipale des Beaux-arts in Bordeaux to study architecture, painting, engraving, and decorative art, Merlin discovered jazz on a portable gramophone. After receiving a scholarship in 1942 to attend a fine arts program in Paris, he began performing New Orleans–style jazz at parties and in clubs in Saint-Germain-des-Prés. In his scrapbooks, he describes this world with wonder and precision, whether by recounting a chance meeting with Richard Wright at a jazz nightclub or listing every American film he had seen.[86] Merlin was also drawn to Black figures, first in his sketches of the well-known *tirailleur sénégalais*, or Senegalese sharpshooter, the famed colonial soldier who gained familiarity and infamy as the face of the breakfast drink Banania. Though Merlin may have seen actual colonial soldiers, his drawing more closely resembles the figure as it appeared in the consumer commodities then commonplace in French homes.[87] The scrapbook also includes images of the walls of the Hot Club de Bordeaux, which were covered with his own drawings of Louis Armstrong. A few years later, Merlin's sketches of jazz musicians were featured at the 1950 Salon du Jazz in Paris, where one jazz journalist noted that his rendering of a blues singer, *Chanteur de blues*, seemed to "embody, simply and unpretentiously, the depth of a blues song."[88]

After the salon, Merlin was asked by Vogue to design its new record liners, which featured line drawings (in black and red) of jazz musicians, and soon after, to design cover art for its new *longue durée* series. Merlin recalled that he was given very little direction in making these covers: often only the title of the record, the title of some of the songs, and occasionally photographs from which to capture the meaning and impact of the music.[89] These early LP records did not feature liner notes, meaning that Merlin's own attempts to capture genre, feeling, and "style" were especially critical to the aural experience for many fans, most of whom did not have the opportunity to see African American musicians in person. A review of a 1948 Erroll Garner concert, for example, noted that while "the record has given us a very accurate idea of the music" of Garner, what it "cannot reveal to us is the power that emanates from his entire person when he is in action. One *sees* his music."[90] Unable to hear or see Garner perform, most listeners relied on Merlin's evocations of the racial meaning and aesthetic power of African American performance.

In representing African American jazz musicians, Merlin drew in part on the work of David Stone Martin, an American designer whose iconic covers for Mercury and Clef Records had also been featured at the 1950 salon in Paris. Martin's work was imbued with humor but also emphasized the bodies of the musicians: their size, their tired eyes, their particular clothing choices, or, in the case of Charlie Parker, by transfiguring his body entirely into "Bird," the nickname that characterized his seemingly effortless melodies on the saxophone. While Merlin borrowed many of Martin's techniques and also invested his images with levity, he established his own visual vernacular. His work would prompt a reviewer at *Jazz hot* to claim that French albums, "for once, rival the work of the best American designers."[91] Like Martin, Merlin's covers emphasized the physicality of the musician, yet they consistently blurred the line between the materiality of the person and the instrument, producing a kind of embodied instrumentality. On the cover of Earl Hines's *Encores* (LD 053) the pianist seems to disappear into the piano and a cloud of smoke, his face only visible by virtue of his cigar (see figure 3.3).[92] On the cover of an eponymous recording (LD 005), Coleman Hawkins appears to be almost entirely saxophone, his fingers growing out of the instrument. The cover of a record featuring pianist Bud Powell's trio (LD 010) displays the musician in a performance posture, though the instrument itself is transparent. The figure of Mahalia Jackson (LD 097) is drawn within a hand, reminding the viewer that her own body was her instrument, perhaps also a reference to religious feeling or ecclesiastical response.

By obscuring, transforming, or melding the subjects and objects in his images, Merlin's representations simultaneously underscore the mastery of the musician and the particularity of the African American figure. On the one hand, the heightened bodily connection between the artist and his instrument could suggest a kind of artistic transcendence. The musician's modern subjectivity takes in all around him, disrupting the lines between the person and the art. On the other hand, the body-instrument connection could also reinforce an erroneous belief in the "natural" Black self. The Earl Hines cover, for example, is dominated by a container of cigars, whose phallic centrality persists even

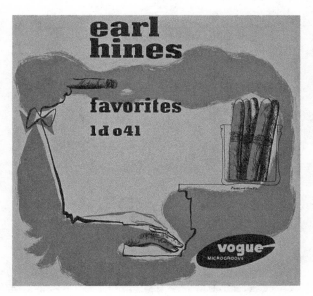

FIGURE 3.3. Album cover of Earl Hines's *Encores* (Vogue, LD 053) designed by Pierre Merlin.

while the rest of the image seems to float away in a cloud of smoke. This is also true of the Hawkins cover, which places the saxophone, mouth, and fingers front and center. In all three covers, the musicians' eyes are absent, removing any possible confrontation in the returned gaze.[93] Acting as an intermediary between the listener and the music, Merlin's artwork reinforces Black particularity as a way to distinguish this commodity from any other and reassure the audience that they have encountered a faithful representation of Black life.

The cover featuring Big Bill Broonzy (LD 030 and LD 072), which accompanied the two-volume record release of the 1951 Vogue sessions, is the most lifelike of all: Broonzy's closed eyes and parted lips give it a quiet strength, and his full figure is on display, masterful and manly (see figure 3.4). Its particular power is likely due to Merlin's own experience performing with Broonzy in 1952, which gave him many opportunities to sketch the singer's face, some of which were preserved in his scrapbook. On the cover, Broonzy is surrounded by the material of modern life: the electric guitar, the liquor bottles, an ashtray, and lit cigarette, all of which encode Broonzy as the displaced urban "blues singer." The frame is interrupted by the microphone and the nameplate, which not only identify the musician and label but also call attention to the technologies of recording. The white outlines of Broonzy's body foreground his presence on the black background yet also render him as an invisible figure who might disappear behind the table or guitar—an aesthetic choice, to be sure, but

FIGURE 3.4. Album cover of Big Bill Broonzy's *Blues Singer*, vol. 1 (Vogue, LD 030) designed by Pierre Merlin.

one that also provides a potent metaphor. For even though the likenesses of African American musicians graced covers and guaranteed profits, the musicians themselves had little power or visibility in economic dealings.

In the coming years, Vogue's catalogue continued to grow, thanks not only to Merlin's covers but also to the continued popularity of Bechet. He had followed up "Les oignons" with new releases on *microsillon*, including "Promenade aux Champs-Elysées" and a 45 rpm single, "La nuit est une sorcière."[94] In January 1952, Vogue released what would become Bechet's second most popular recording, "Petite fleur."[95] The recording was accompanied by a major publicity campaign, featuring Bechet posed with Dizzy Gillespie on board a riverboat in the Seine, as well as a concert series in Paris in February 1952 with Zutty Singleton, Mezzrow, and Blind John Davis.[96] Bechet's visibility in performances, photographs, and album covers was key to Vogue's continued growth. Whenever a new Bechet album was released, it increased the sales of other albums released in the same series, all of which in turn served as capital for "significant investments for the company."[97] In Cabat's words, Bechet functioned for Vogue as a "talisman"; elsewhere, he was described as a "kind of lucky-charm, a mascot."[98] Once objectified, Bechet's presence added magic and value to the commodity, the commodity series, and the label itself.

Bechet's popularity was in many respects unprecedented. One American visitor noted that "Sidney could have become mayor of Paris if he wanted to.

Crowds of people followed him through the streets. I was never so surprised in my whole life as when I discovered that a compatriot, whom I had barely heard of, had become the darling of the French."[99] In addition to his regular gig at the Vieux Colombier, between 1954 and 1958 he gave nearly two hundred performances throughout France, Europe, and France's overseas departments in North Africa.[100] He drew large crowds and enthusiastic responses, particularly to his show-stopping performance of "When the Saints Go Marching In," in which he led his band in a mock second-line march as if through the streets of New Orleans. Bechet also toured with visiting musicians, including Albert Nicholas, whom he introduced to Delaunay and "various other French entrepreneurs," making it "easy for Albert to find enough work to settle in Europe."[101] In many ways, this success was a tremendous boon to Bechet, given that regular tours and recording made it possible for him to live a financially comfortable life. He was also able to publish his autobiography, *Treat It Gentle*, which affirmed his own place in jazz history as well as the importance of France, where he claimed he felt nearer to his ancestral family.[102]

Locating Authenticity in a Mass Market

In November 1955, when Vogue had sold 1 million copies of "Les oignons," Bechet, Delaunay, and French impresario Bruno Coquatrix organized a free concert at the Olympia in Paris. Though the hall was intended to accommodate 2,800 concertgoers, reports were that more than 5,000 young people crowded in, breaking down doors and windows along the way. By the time Bechet sang "When the Saints Go Marching In" at the end of the show, the concert had "degenerated into a riot," and the noise was so loud that after "the fifth row, no one could any longer hear the music." Journalists reported that fans threw oranges and roasted chestnuts at the band, while others "hoisted a refrigerator" from the balcony. Reflecting on the events, *Paris Match* surmised that fans "were sacrificing to their god Bechet while wrecking the music hall."[103] After several arrests and at least two serious injuries, the concertgoers left in their wake seventy-nine broken seats, a floor full of pieces of wood, shoes, and broken umbrellas, and, according to one report, one very dazed hot dog vendor.[104] One police officer noted, "I had seen venues after political protests before but never like that."[105] Two years later, Bechet toured Algeria, Tunisia, and Morocco with André Reweliotty's band, stopping in Oran, Algiers, Tunis, and Casablanca, where they played to strictly white European crowds.[106] Reportedly, these "unleashed fans" gave Bechet the "strongest ovation of the year," providing the kind of atmosphere "that we have lost the habit of knowing in Algiers." Fearing for either the fate of the seats or the possibility of more sustained unrest, officials established order by enlisting *gendarmes* to "hold in the tide of young people."[107]

For young people in both metropolitan and overseas France, the concert venue was a site of emotional and physical release, which was particularly resonant at a moment of heightened political tensions during the Algerian War. But the size of these concerts, and the extent of the response, also demonstrate that the mid-1950s marked the beginning of mass popular music fandom in France. For some jazz critics, the Bechet concert spoke to an unsettling trend in popular music. While pleased that Bechet had gained such acclaim, they distrusted the violent rage lurking in the audience, and particularly feared that the public would begin to see jazz as the "music of savages" once again.[108] Ultimately, jazz fans would coalesce around a shared distrust of what became known as rock'n'roll, in which they heard repetitive riffs and a lack of rhythmic complexity that marked it as a commercialized version of African American music, but might nevertheless inadvertently introduce young people to Black American music.[109]

In this same period, jazz fandom expanded beyond the prototypical jazz fan—white, male, urbane—to include larger and more diverse audiences in France. Whereas there were roughly ten thousand attendees per year at concerts in the mid-1940s, this number had grown to eighty thousand by the late 1940s and then to more than three hundred thousand in 1954.[110] This growing fan base was brought to jazz, blues, and gospel through the record, played on state-run or commercial radio, in jukeboxes in clubs and cafés, or at home.[111] Reflecting the rapid expansion of postsecondary education in postwar France, jazz fans represented a much wider range of students: young women, suburban working-class youth, as well as African and Caribbean people who were either working or studying in France.[112] Cameroonian students Manu Dibango, Francis Bebey, and Mongo Beti fell "deeply" into jazz culture in the 1950s, an experience later enhanced by their encounter with Miles Davis's iconic 1957 record *Birth of the Cool*.[113] Some Francophone students threw "jazz parties" to help raise financial support for their studies, given that the "complementary funding" from their home governments and the Ministry of Education rarely arrived on time.[114]

By the mid-1950s, there were more African American musicians living and working in France than ever before, performing gospel, jazz, blues, and spirituals for thousands in Paris and in provincial towns.[115] Though resident jazz musicians like Sidney Bechet, Bill Coleman, Art Simmons, and Kenny Clarke have received the most scholarly attention, there were numerous other musicians who made a living in France. Pianist Mary Lou Williams and jazz singer Hazel Scott both spent considerable time in France, where they found new opportunities to record and perform. This musical community also included rhythm and blues performers like Mickey Baker; gospel groups like the Golden Gate Quartet and the Delta Rhythm Boys; jazz musicians Dexter Gordon, Earl Freeman, and Johnny Griffin; and vocalists like folk singer Gordon Heath, gospel singer John Littleton, and pop singer Nancy Holloway, who opened up her own club in 1959.[116] Holloway's success built on a longer tradition of Black women's clubs in Paris, including Chez Inez, founded by Inez Cavanaugh after her arrival in Paris.[117] This world also included musicians whose work would become better known in avant-garde circles, like Marshall Allen, who first arrived in France during the war and would, like many others, study at the Conservatoire de Paris. In addition to performing with musicians like James Moody and Kenny Clarke, Allen relished the opportunity to perform with musicians from Africa and the Caribbean.[118]

The same period marked a growing interest in the blues, sustained in part by the number of rereleases on LP records as well as by Vogue's own efforts to secure distribution rights from independent labels like King, Chess, Apollo, and Peacock. It was also aided by French writers like Jacques Demêtre, whose surveys of urban blues (and interviews with musicians in New York, Chicago, and Detroit) were published in *Jazz hot* in 1959 and 1960. In these accounts, there was a palpable desire to make sense of African American music in context, with reports on civil rights, photo essays of the urban ghetto, and in particular, descriptions of Black church life, and its attendant customs, clothing, and codes of behavior. At the heart of Demêtre's inquiry, and other contemporary blues journalism in France, was a deep longing to be part of the world that African American musicians inhabited. In 1962, blues pianist Memphis Slim would settle permanently in France, in large part because of this growing blues fandom and the financial success he found as a result. In 1966, he reported to the readers of *Ebony* that he was "enjoying life, living better than ever, making enough to support my habits."[119] Several years later, members of the Art Ensemble of Chicago met Slim in Paris. Bassist Malachi Favors noted that he had long wondered why the blues musician had left Chicago—which had the "greatest entertainment section in the world, right there on the South Side"—for Paris. But once he arrived, and "checked out Memphis Slim in his Rolls Royce," he "never would have thought it" again.[120]

For many of these musicians, Paris offered the freedoms to perform and record regularly, work with other musicians, rest in between European tours, make money, and socialize freely. This was particularly important for gay musicians, including Heath and jazz pianist Aaron Bridgers, and for Hazel Scott, whose opposition to segregation had brought her before the House Un-

American Activities Committee in 1950, effectively ending her career in the United States as a singer and actress.[121] In all cases, these musicians were keenly aware of their distance from the ongoing struggles of African Americans to gain civil rights. Some traveled back to help raise money, some held sympathy rallies in Paris, and others engaged in the global freedom struggle by way of African anticolonialism.[122] However, there were others for whom political engagement seemed impossible, as they feared being deported from France, being subjected to retribution by American officials, or possibly alienating their audiences.[123] With a large music community in place, as well as visiting luminaries like Louis Armstrong, Duke Ellington, Count Basie, Mahalia Jackson, and Miles Davis, African American performers were consistently covered by French magazines and newspapers. According to one observer, "Even the staid, government-sponsored *Le Figaro* ... devotes liberal space to descriptions and pictures of Negro jazz artists."[124] Though most African American musicians were based in Paris, many tours included stops in provincial cities, particularly those with large student populations. By 1956, students in Lyon, for example, had seen Ellington, Bechet, Gillespie, Big Bill Broonzy, Armstrong, Coleman, Mahalia Jackson, and Kid Ory.[125] In addition to touring hexagonal France, many musicians—including Armstrong, Buck Clayton, and Lionel Hampton—toured Algeria, where European fans flocked to concerts.[126]

In 1956, *Baltimore Afro-American* journalist Ollie Stewart, who had developed a keen eye for French racial politics during the liberation, reflected on this growing enthusiasm for African American performers: "Colored entertainers mean money in the till in Europe—especially in France. Just the name on the program, or the face on the marquee in front of a theater or night club, is a guarantee of good business and a flood of cash!"[127] Yet he could not merely revel in the financial spoils of African American performers. He wondered, "What makes the difference? What is it about the character of the French people that makes the theater managers sure that almost any colored entertainer will be good for the box-office?" Although French stars like Edith Piaf and Maurice Chevalier were easily understood by their audiences, "somehow they don't have the kids storming the doors and breaking up the theater seats." In reflecting on the difference, he determined that it was due to "a certain conviction. A conviction coming from years back ... the belief that a colored entertainer performs with his soul. Everything he does comes from inside of him." Though "nobody seems to know" why, when Ellington plays, they know "that's the true rhythm. When Marian Anderson sings, that's what a spiritual should sound like."[128]

This "conviction" was borne out in the liner notes, album covers, and reviews that accompanied the production and distribution of African American music, which was increasingly defined by the representation of the Black figure. The certainty that Ellington or Anderson's performance was what it "should sound like" did not necessarily emerge from musical knowledge or literacy. Instead, it emerged from the visual clues and racial knowledge that was fundamental to this industry's marketing. Moreover, though launched within a small jazz fan base, this conviction was at the root of both Vogue and Barclay's expansion into national and eventually international industrial powers. By 1956, Vogue had created its own factory in suburban Paris, in the town of Villetaneuse, that was entirely devoted to vinyl production. Furthermore, the company now controlled all levels of record production, including manufacturing, storage, delivery, recording, and marketing, which further ensured its transformation into a major market force.[129] Likewise, the Barclays had also moved all production to the Parisian suburb of Neuilly-sur-Seine, where they manufactured records for several new subsidiary labels and drew in profits nearing $5 million per year.[130] In addition, the Barclays had partnered with Norman Granz to host his Jazz at the Philharmonic concert series in France and had started a new magazine, *Jazz Magazine*. In 1955, they sold it for a "quasi-symbolic sum" of money to Frank Ténot and Daniel Filipacchi in exchange for running free advertisements for the record label.[131] The magazine would become a huge success, setting up Ténot and Filipacchi's publishing empire and radio dominance on Europe 1, which broadcast *Pour ceux qui aiment le jazz* and *Salut les copains*. The label continued to distribute recordings from Mercury, whose collection had grown to include early doo-wop and R&B groups like the Platters. In 1955, Barclay— which was now the commercial name of the business—distributed the Platters' hit single "Only You," which went on to sell 1 million copies in France in one month.

In contemporary and historical accounts of the couple and their business, Eddie is most frequently the star, known as a "playboy, host of mad extravagant parties, obsessive champion of gimmicks and gadgets, protagonist of balmy days and wild nights in Saint Tropez, and advocate of abandoned and almost interminable gaiety."[132] When speaking of his wife and partner Nicole, Eddie highlighted her capacity "to receive, improvise and charm the musicians (be they French or American) to speak English, and to dance."[133] However, among industry insiders, Nicole Barclay's business acumen was more quickly acknowledged, earning her such titles as "recording baroness" and "fem wax tycoon."[134] As her contemporaries noted, Nicole was frequently at the center of distribution deals or negotiations for concert series. In 1956, *Billboard* recognized her alone, not Eddie, in the introduction of "rhythm and blues" to European audiences, after her negotiations with Mercury in New York.[135] In addition, she possessed a skill for recognizing and recruiting talent. In 1956, she brought in German sound engineer Gerhard Lehner, who built an "ultramodern studio" (complete with a magnetophone Ampex 300 stereo smuggled in Nicole's luggage) on avenue Hoche and whose engineering skills and passion for jazz attracted new talent.[136] In 1956, after meeting photographer Herman Leonard in the United States, she hired him as official photographer at Barclay, where he would spend the next four years.[137]

Nicole frequently socialized with African Americans in the United States and France, where her presence was noted by members of the Black media. In the late 1950s and early 1960s, *Jet* magazine and New York's *Amsterdam News* reported on the social life of "the ultra-rich French beauty and recording company moneybags," seen out in Chicago in 1957 with Billy Eckstine.[138] In 1962, *Jet* noted that Barclay had "planed in from Paris, and, without unpacking, went straight to Harlem on Sunday morning in search of authentic gospel music."[139] As African American expatriate journalist Ollie Harrington recalled, Nicole was a fixture at Haynes's soul food restaurant in Pigalle "among the gentlefolk working on their fried chicken or ribs." He described her as the "completely unpredictable Frenchwoman who heads Barclay Disques," noting that "more famous Negro musicians work under a Barclay contract than any other."[140] In 1960, longtime Paris correspondent Edgar Wiggins reported that "negroes in Paris" had created "Our Inner Circle," whose founding members were Josephine Baker, the Peters sisters, Bill Coleman, Art Simmons, the Golden Gate Quartet, Delta Rhythm Boys, and Leroy Haynes, and whose honorary committee included Nicole Barclay and Hugues Panassié.[141]

Just as her trips to Harlem and socializing with African American musicians in the 1940s helped solidify Blue Star's position, Nicole Barclay's relationships with African Americans were a means of establishing new distribution and recording deals and to bring in African Americans into Barclay's employ. Nicole's longtime secretary, for example, was an African American woman named Mamie Wheatley (née Brown).[142] In the 1950s, Barclay recruited crime fiction writer Chester Himes to write a "complete history of jazz to be presented in a series of albums."[143] Though the Himes project never materialized, in 1959 Barclay, through "her great charm," successfully recruited novelist Richard Wright to write liner notes for the label.[144] Though Wright was skeptical of joining in this commercial enterprise, he needed extra income to cover the expenses of his daughter Julia's education.[145] He wrote some essays that were never published, including "It's Louis Jordan All the Way" and "Another Heroic Beginning," which described the influence of classical composers on Quincy Jones's musical development.[146] He also wrote an ode, "So Long, Big Bill Broonzy" for a posthumous recording titled "The Blues of Big Bill Broonzy," which was eventually distributed by Mercury.[147] At first, Wright seemed apologetic for this commercial activity, noting to a friend that he was simply writing a "few hundred words for the buyer to read while trying to make up his mind if he wishes to buy or not."[148] The following month, however, he wrote: "I'm not doing any serious writing at the moment, but the writing I'm doing for the records does say something. Not much, but a little something."[149]

Nicole Barclay was also the central intermediary in negotiations with African American musicians living in France, including jazz stars and the gospel group the Delta Rhythm Boys and doo-wop group the Platters, who followed up with their 1955 hit by recording with Barclay in 1957.[150] According to musician René Urtreger, "People knew they had a friend when they came to Paris."[151] In response to this support, in 1954 Mary Lou Williams dedicated a song—"Nicole"—to her "best friend, Nicole Barclay, who has done so much for jazz in France."[152] Williams explained, "She was such a fabulous friend to musicians, she always helped musicians when they were stranded or in distress. She'd see they got money or a ticket back to America." But years later, Williams complained that she "got no money by making the disc nor received any royalties."[153] Again, lest one imagine that the desire for proximity to musicians guaranteed fair dealings, this example reminds us of the economic vulnerability of African American musicians and underscores the economic motivations of their "patrons."

One of Nicole Barclay's most significant decisions came in 1957, when she hired Quincy Jones as musical director, arranger, and conductor for Barclay. At that point, Jones had been working in New York, where he had already established himself as "one of the top arrangers in the world" by the age of twenty-five. Bobby Tucker, the arranger and musical director for Billy Eckstine, recalled that Eckstine had first recommended Jones to Nicole Barclay. She then called Quincy Jones and invited him to France, and "the first thing Quincy asked her was 'Can I write for strings over there?'"[154] This was not an insignificant query. In fact, according to Bobby Tucker, "the easiest way to starve in America [in the 1950s] was to be a black arranger writing for strings. You could've been Mozart, Stravinsky, Wagner, and Beethoven all rolled into one, but if you came from Harlem, U.S.A., and had nappy hair and black skin, your ass went to the blues and jazz department of every record company and I don't give a hoot if you were God. Strings were considered sophisticated and for whites only."[155] This was, Tucker continued, a period in which "classical was still considered *that* kind of music and jazz was considered *this* kind of music."[156] Frustrated by this racial codification of musical arrangement, Jones was quick to ask Nicole

Barclay about the opportunities at the label. In response, she reportedly said, "My dahling you can write for whatever you want in France."[157]

Though he intended to stay in Paris only three months, Jones ultimately stayed for five years and wrote arrangements for an estimated 250 recording dates. He worked closely with composer Nadia Boulanger, whose lessons paid off in real time. Jones observed, "This all fit together with my work at Barclay records. They had an excellent 55-piece house orchestra that I could use to practice everything I was learning!" (see figures 3.5 and 3.6).[158] In that time, Jones grew to greatly admire Nicole Barclay, who had "built an empire from nothing."[159] Jones's description of Nicole, like most other accounts, highlighted her charisma, sexual exploits, alcoholism, and drug use, but he also reveled in her capacity to follow up a bottle of Preludin with a successful meeting with record company executives. Reflecting on his later professional and artistic success, Jones wrote,

> I'll always be grateful to Nicole, to Eddie [Barclay, her husband], and to France. In France, the yoke of black and white was off my shoulders. . . . I was able to envision my past, present, and future as an artist and as a black man; I took a wider view of the human condition that extended to both art and life, and later helped me to take stock of global markets in business dealings. I became comfortable as a citizen of the world. France treated me like an artist. . . . France made me feel free, and glad to be who I was.[160]

According to Jones, this professional experience helped him to secure artistic authority and economic power on a global scale, while also living "free" and like an "artist."

Once ensconced in the label, Jones helped the Barclays recruit Kenny Clarke for its resident orchestra. Clarke, a pioneer in bebop drumming, had first recorded with Vogue in 1948. It was then that he met and befriended Nicole, who had invited him to join the 1949 festival.[161] After working in New York with the Modern Jazz Quartet in the early 1950s, Clarke returned to Paris in 1956 to become the house drummer at the Club St. Germain and then later at the Blue Note.[162] Clarke's presence at these clubs was central to enabling him to gain his financial equilibrium in this period. The Blue Note in particular was an important place for Clarke, as universities and conservatories could always reach him there. It was, he said, "like an office for me."[163] In addition to regularly joining tours in Europe, North Africa, and Senegal, Clarke found numerous and regular recording sessions with Barclay Records.[164] As Clarke's biographer noted, "While he was earning considerably less money than he could have

FIGURE 3.5. Quincy Jones at Barclay Studios in the late 1950s. In Chasseguet, *Barclay*, 142–43. Photo reproduced with permission from Thérèse Chasseguet,

made in New York, the lack of pressures and the more leisurely pace of life in France were substantial compensations."[165] Of the four years that Quincy Jones was at Barclay, Clarke would later recall, "I was recording almost every day. Every day! I couldn't believe it."[166] Allegedly he urged Charlie Parker to come to France, saying, "You may never make a hundred thousand a year, but you'll be around a long time and people will appreciate your music. Over here you will be treated as an artist."[167] Later, when Dizzy Gillespie reflected on Clarke's time in France, he was adamant that there were significant financial benefits: "I don't *think* Kenny is doing better in Europe than he would be over here. I *know* so. He could not get that kind of money here. I know so. He records in Europe—that's where he lives. And everybody respects him over there. . . . He is the king. He is not a local musician; he is not a local yokel."[168]

For all the freedom working in France offered artists like Jones and Clarke, however, other musicians recognized the embedded limitations. Jazz trumpeter Donald Byrd first traveled to France in 1958. That same year, he was featured in a concert at the Olympia organized by Frank Ténot and Daniel Filipacchi (the entrepreneurs who bought *Jazz Magazine*), which was relayed on their jazz

FIGURE 3.6. Quincy Jones joins Eddie Barclay and Gerhard Lehner in the engineering booth at Barclay Studios in the late 1950s. In Chasseguet, *Barclay*, 25. Photo reproduced with permission from Thérèse Chasseguet.

program on French commercial radio and then distributed by Brunswick and then later Polydor.[169] Byrd spent time in Paris over the course of his career, but he never became a long-term resident like Jones or Clarke, given his concerns about exploitation on the continent. While blatant racism defined the US recording industry, Byrd found that a "more discreet exploitation" took place in Europe. He believed that African American musicians—himself included— were deceived by this myth of European respect for the artist. Underlying both industries was "the same bullshit." Byrd continued, "Given the presence of the jazz purists in Europe and the entrenched myths of respect, African American musicians were fooled into believing they were respected."[170]

As Paul Gilroy notes, both Byrd and Jones "played powerful roles in the remaking of jazz as a popular form in the early 1970s," working as musicians, producers, teachers, and advisers.[171] After receiving his doctorate in music education, Byrd taught at North Carolina Central, Howard, Oberlin, and Cornell, forming and supporting groups of student musicians at each institution. Jones would go on to become the most successful African American producer of the 1970s and 1980s and would be one of the first African American musicians to enter into the American film and music industry as a producer. Furthermore, he was a man whose "personal narrative of racial uplift has . . . become something of a cipher for black creativity in general and black musical genius in particular."[172] Living, working, and producing in France helped Jones envision and ultimately enact a much broader trajectory as an African American performer and artist. This new context, in which history could be reshaped and reconfigured, helped him imagine a different future. In this transition, it was France—but more specifically the French recording industry—that recognized his artistry. These new technologies and networks had brought into being both new mobilities and immobilities, and through them a store of potential cultural, economic, and political value.

Taken together, the varied experiences of Jones, Clarke, and Byrd clarify the possibilities and contradictions in the French music industry, whose profits depended on both the visibility and invisibility of African Americans. On the one hand, the emergence of new French record labels provided a venue for a wider range of African American musicians, who found new opportunities to record and new venues through which to form an aesthetic rebuke to American racism. On the other hand, many African American musicians were excluded from the ensuing profits, even as their racial visibility authenticated the proliferation of mass commodities and ensured revenue for the growing French record industry. The French industry's valuation of African American music frequently came at the expense of the musicians, who either never received their share of the profits or whose value as authenticators was never rewarded.

4

SPEAKING IN TONGUES

The Negro Spiritual and the Circuits of Black Internationalism

————

When Howard University professor Mercer Cook arrived in France in 1951 on a Fulbright fellowship, he was already well acquainted with the French love of jazz. As the son of composer Will Marion Cook and singer Abbie Mitchell, he had heard more than one African American performer recount stints in Parisian nightclubs or time spent in France during European tours. While living in Paris as an exchange student in the 1920s, Cook recalled that he "could almost bet" that any African American musician he saw in Montmartre "had been in Dad's orchestra."[1] But in 1951 it was neither jazz nor vaudeville that captured his ear. Instead, it was the Negro spiritual that had found "a place in the hearts of the French people."[2] Writing in 1952 for *Music Educators Journal*, Cook declared, "No longer are the Negro's religious folk songs familiar only to a select group of French concert-goers." Now this music had "seeped through to a large segment of the French public," spread by American military networks, national tours, new radio and recording technologies, and even religious groups. Cook had himself been invited to the University of Bordeaux to give an illustrated lecture on spirituals to an audience of one hundred French students.[3] In what was certainly a most uncanny experience, Cook described walking down the rue Bonaparte near the École des Beaux-Arts in Paris, only to hear behind him "a young Frenchman whistling 'Swing Low, Sweet Chariot.'" When Cook asked him how he had learned it, the young man replied: "Oh . . . we sing it at our Catholic Youth meetings."[4]

Reflecting on this experience, Cook recalled his former colleague Louis T. Achille, who in 1948 had formed a Negro spirituals choir in Lyon, France. While Achille was born and raised in Martinique, the two men had first met in Black intellectual circles in interwar Paris and then again in 1932, when Achille began teaching French at Howard University in Washington, DC. After teaching at Howard for nine years, Achille joined the Allied military effort in World War II and subsequently returned to France to teach English in Lyon. It was there that he formed the Park Glee Club, a student choir whose specialty for nearly thirty years was the performance of Negro spirituals. As a longtime observer of African American music in France, Cook understood immediately that Achille offered a unique vantage point from which to assess the growing popularity of Negro spirituals. Unlike the majority of French people and jazz fans, Achille had lived among African Americans in the United States, where he not only became fluent in English but also became intimately familiar with African American society. In addition, Achille was a devout Catholic, which was increasingly remarkable at a moment when church attendance and authority had declined precipitously.[5] Finally, as a light-skinned Martiniquan man, Achille had personally reflected on racism and racial thinking in France, its overseas empire, and the United States, and he could think critically about the differences. Indeed, if Cook sought to explain how the religious music of enslaved people had come to flourish in France amid secularization, Americanization, and decolonization, he could not have found a more insightful interlocutor.

Moving from Cook's contemporary account, this chapter considers Louis T. Achille's efforts to introduce and redefine the Negro spiritual in post–World War II France. While Achille's life and work span the twentieth-century Atlantic world, and have marked the transnational and national histories within it, he has thus far remained at the margins of the history of Black internationalism, one of the many "overlooked Francophone intellectuals from Africa and the Antilles."[6] Born in Fort-de-France, Martinique, to a bourgeois Antillean family, Achille wrestled throughout his life with a system of racial hierarchy that proffered the possibility of racial assimilation while denigrating African and Antillean people and their cultural contributions. Having gained entry at an early age to Black internationalist circles in Paris and Washington, DC, Achille soon encountered distinct forms of racism and different racial ideologies with which to evaluate the meaning and value of Black culture.

Within this transatlantic context, Achille was particularly drawn to a concertized form of African American religious music, the Negro spiritual, which demonstrated for Achille the possibility that African and European traditions could be melded into a recognizably "civilized" cultural form. As a choir leader, essayist, and teacher, Achille sought to articulate the music's universalist themes of liberation and spiritual redemption while nonetheless insisting on its racial and religious specificity, a claim that he grounded in his own racial identity and experiences in the United States. Although Achille's earlier commitment to racial assimilation might not seem to prefigure his transformation into a champion and protector of African American authenticity, his approach to the spiritual helps explain this transition. The concertized spiritual was at its root a form of translation, a transcription and approximation of a religious music that was forged without written arrangements. Achille worked within this tradition, seeking to make it visible and audible for a wider audience and in turn revealing the liberatory value of African American music. By making himself—and his embodiment of Black identity—central to the presentation of the Negro spiritual, Achille ensured that his audience could not ignore the linked histories of race and colonialism in France.

Transatlantic Formations

Louis Thomas Eugène Achille was born on August 31, 1909, in Balata, a commune of Fort-de-France in the French colony of Martinique. He was the son of Marguerite Ferdinand and Louis Achille, whose own father had migrated from Guadeloupe to raise Louis and his sister Louise among the highly educated Martiniquan bourgeoisie.[7] The first Antillean to pass the *agrégation*—the degree required for the highest-ranking teaching positions in the French educational system—Louis Achille (senior) taught English at the Lycée Victor Schoelcher in Fort-de-France, where his students included future *négritude* writers Léon Damas and Aimé Césaire. The younger Achille, his siblings, and his cousins from the Nardal family were known throughout the island "for their intelligence and good breeding," heirs to the modern-day "aristocracy of the Antilles."[8] After completing primary school in Fort-de-France, Achille began studies in Paris in October 1926 as an *élève de khâgne* at the prestigious Lycée Louis-le-Grand, which prepared students from throughout France and its overseas empire for the entrance exam required to attend the École Normale Supérieure. As a boarder at Louis-le-Grand, Achille joined an elite cohort that included Georges Pompidou, Maurice Merleau-Ponty, Pham Duy Khiêm, Aimé Césaire, and Senegalese student Léopold Sédar Senghor, who entered in 1928 and was Achille's classmate and close confidant.[9]

Senghor and Achille were drawn to each other for various reasons: their Catholic upbringing, their strong drive for academic success, and, most of all, their shared yet distinct experiences as subjects of the French empire.[10] Like other wealthy, light-skinned Antillean students, when Achille arrived at Louis-le-Grand he considered himself French. After meeting his classmates, however, he "saw clearly" that he "was not French in the same manner that they were."[11] While Achille did not identify race specifically, this feeling of difference was part of the broader set of race-based distinctions built into the colonial administrative practices of assimilation and association that distinguished African and Antillean students from one another and from the so-called unevolved colonial subjects.[12] For his part, Senghor found that in Paris, he was more conscious of what he was not.[13] Excluded from white French identity, both men began to define themselves in terms of a broader world inhabited by students, laborers, writers, performers, and artists from throughout the African diaspora, who were drawn to Paris as a center of education, employment, and culture.[14]

Unlike other colonial students who were in Paris on scholarship, Achille benefited from his family's wealth and social connections in the metropole. His parents owned an apartment in the 5th arrondissement overlooking the Jardin des Plantes, where they welcomed a steady stream of visitors to a "cultured home" that radiated "the cultural influences of the arts and social graces." One visitor's comment—that the nearby "Mahommedan Mosque" lent "a bizarre and alien effect to an otherwise sedate and homelike environment"—suggests that the family must have carefully presented its assimilated Frenchness.[15] The family of Achille's aunt also rented an apartment in the Parisian suburb of Clamart, where his cousins Jane, Alice, and Paulette Nardal lived while they pursued their respective degrees in classics, music, and English. By the late 1920s, the Nardal sisters had begun hosting biweekly salons for their friends and family, who ventured out to the suburbs to join in discussions of literature, music, and politics.[16] This practice continued a tradition initiated in Fort-de-France, where the cousins hosted a biweekly youth literary association to discuss literature and listen to music.[17] As Achille recalled later, the Clamart salon offered a distinctly "feminine" space in which to engage modern French life, particularly its "colonial and interracial problems."[18] Achille also underscored its British qualities: the "English armchairs," the fact that "only English tea" was served, but most of all, the conversation itself, which took place "rather naturally in English."[19] Along with his cousin Paulette, who studied English literature at the Sorbonne, Achille helped facilitate conversations among those from the Francophone world and those from the United States, England, and the British Caribbean. In fact, it was either here or at his apartment that Achille first introduced his classmate Senghor to Antillean students René Maran and Léon Damas as well as visiting African American writers, including Alain

Locke, Claude McKay, and Countee Cullen, and academics, including Mercer Cook, Carter G. Woodson, and Dorothy and James Porter.[20] These salons offered a place in which participants could locate a Black identity within the French imperial nation-state and within the broader network of Black politics and culture in the Atlantic world.[21]

What had been initiated in the intimate space of the salons gained a much broader audience in November 1931, when the Nardal sisters and the Haitian physician Leo Sajous launched the bilingual journal *La Revue du monde noir*. While there were only six issues, this self-consciously elite publication—the creators called themselves the "intelligentsia of the black race"—was formative in the development of *négritude* in the late 1930s and 1940s.[22] They also declared in these pages a new "Afro-Latin" identity that distinguished them from America and Africa. Achille contributed to the first issue an article titled "L'art et les noirs / The Negroes and Art," in which he argued that "Negroes are essentially artists," in contrast to Western rationality.[23] Appearing within months of the 1931 Colonial Exposition in Paris, Achille's essay is a reminder that he was embedded in colonial racial ideology.[24] In addition to his essentialist readings of Black performance, Achille's essay underscored his perceived distance from African people, whose "long mysterious stagnation" had left "little energy for intense political, economical, or intellectual effort."[25] In the third issue, he edited a collection of responses to the question "How should the negroes living in Europe dress?" For his part, Achille argued that "Negroes should follow European fashions when they live in Europe, if they don't want to feel uneasy or to introduce a false note in the harmony of the civilization in which they come to dwell." Following his own assimilatory advice, Achille was known for dressing like a "real dandy" in Paris, seen sporting "knickerbockers" on the boulevard Saint-Michel.[26]

In the midst of these struggles to reconcile his attraction to Western and African cultures, Achille discovered African American religious music. While he was well acquainted with other forms of African American music, Achille was especially drawn to the Negro spiritual. This was due in part to his growing religious devotion. Raised as a Catholic, Achille had recommitted himself to Catholicism at Louis-le-Grand and subsequently joined the Compagnons de Saint-François, a Catholic organization that organized walking pilgrimages for French and German young people.[27] Achille was still a student at Louis-le-Grand when he first heard the spirituals performed by nine Black singers, "eight of whom were born slaves," during a concert at the Théâtre du Châtelet in Paris. He remembered vividly the music snobs sitting nearby who were initially skeptical that African American music could appear in such a refined venue ("Come on, jazz here? Scandalous!") but by the third song were applauding wildly.[28]

Observing the audience's conversion from suspicion to enthusiasm, Achille became convinced that this kind of performance was a powerful way to demonstrate the refinement and civilization of Black people. The spirituals were markers of difference *and* assimilation, connoting the slave experience as well as assimilated Christianity. Achille next encountered the spiritual through his cousins Jane and Paulette, who had themselves first heard African American tenor Roland Hayes perform at the Salle Gaveau in Paris in 1924.[29] They subsequently decided to include opportunities to listen to records during their biweekly salons, where the Negro spiritual epitomized the assimilated, Christian, and African-European identity that Achille desired. Like the jazz listening parties that had defined the early Hot Club de France, these gatherings were a powerful means of mediating African American music. However, within these Black internationalist soundscapes, Black Francophone audiences would have heard in it a distinct racial value and political power.

By 1931, Achille had finished his studies at Louis-le-Grand and begun work at the University of Paris (Sorbonne) on a master's thesis on the African American poet Paul Lawrence Dunbar and the uses of African American dialect in music and literature.[30] After completing his diploma of *études supérieures*, he decided to pursue a career as an English teacher at the secondary level. But before the completion of the final degree, which necessitated passing the difficult *agrégation* exam, Achille was required to spend at least a year living in an Anglophone country. While he had initially chosen a post in Great Britain, an anticipated offer was withdrawn for "racial reasons"; apparently, the director feared that British families would not accept a "teacher of color."[31] Achille was at first wary that the United States would offer a worse racial environment. However, after some encouragement by his friend Mercer Cook and an interview with Alain Locke, in 1931 Achille accepted an offer to teach French language and literature courses in the Department of Romance Languages at Howard University.

He had initially intended to stay for one year, but Achille remained on faculty at Howard for nine years, leaving only to complete mandatory military service in France and to prepare for the *agrégation* exam in Paris (see figure 4.1). Within days of his arrival in Washington, DC, Achille decided to attend an early mass at the closest Catholic church.[32] When he returned to the African American boardinghouse, the proprietor expressed incredulity: "But that's a white church!" Believing that she had referred to its white stones, Achille initially agreed, but after he was asked to sit in the back pew during a subsequent

FIGURE 4.1. A portrait of Louis T. Achille taken in 1938 at a studio in New York City. Photo courtesy of the Achille Family Archives.

visit he understood her real meaning. The humiliation of this request was deepened when he saw that the French ambassador was able to sit in the front "even though we were both Christian and French."[33] This moment marked a shift in Achille's racial consciousness. Though he had previously remarked on his secondary status in Paris, he was nonetheless mortified by the realization that a religious space, particularly one inhabited by French people, could also be racially segregated. Henceforth, Achille's letters home were peppered with references to the racial character of venues, underscoring his own self-consciousness when attending a "church of color" or a "negro cinema."[34] His descriptions also reveal Achille's growing sense of racial and social distinction, whether as a foreigner or as a recognizable person of color. In May 1932, Achille remarked to his mother in a letter, "The colored race is splendid; I understand the attraction that they hold for white Americans."[35] Rather than identifying with African Americans, Achille placed himself within white American culture's complex "attraction" to Black culture. Though drawn to African American musical performances—a touring Tuskegee Institute choir, late-night broadcasts from Harlem nightclubs, the "aristocratic tenor" Roland Hayes, the blues and jazz vocalist Ethel Waters at the Apollo, or a performance of *Porgy and Bess* on Broadway in 1936—Achille remained in the audience.[36]

Achille's relationship to Howard was marked by geographical and social distance, in part because he initially chose to inhabit international spaces rather than attend African American gatherings. Achille lived about a mile away from Howard in Washington's Gold Coast neighborhood, which was populated by foreign embassies and diplomats. Likewise, at Howard he was involved in the Catholic students' association, the French-language theatrical society, and the foreign student choir, all of which drew from the school's international student population.[37] Outside Howard, he taught conversational French and hosted musical-cultural soirées at the Washington International Student House, which he later claimed was "the only place in the nation's capital where people of different races come together to chat."[38] By the late 1930s, Achille had developed relationships with fellow Howard faculty members, including Cook and artist Loïs Mailou Jones.[39] Through his relationship with Cook, Achille spent several summers teaching French at Atlanta University's summer school, where he was drawn into a world of pedagogical practice that located in French-language instruction the possibility for new forms of Black internationalism (see figure 4.2).[40] He was delighted by the experience; in 1939, after being dubbed "glamour boy no. 1" on campus, he concluded that "I had more fun in six weeks in Atlanta than five years in Washington."[41] It was also in Georgia that Achille had some of his most direct experiences with Jim Crow racism. In 1936, when he drove to Atlanta with Cook, they only dared stop when they could stay with friends, knowing that it was "impossible for us to stop" at white hotels or inns.[42] During his visits to Atlanta, he also saw that many poor Black families lived in "miserable neighborhoods . . . under the law of Dixieland."[43] Achille concluded that it was not possible to "live as a man of color in the United States and maintain one's dignity if you did not constantly stay alert."[44]

In this context of growing racial consciousness, Achille was once again drawn to the spiritual. While he encountered this musical tradition in a range of venues, Achille was most influenced by the inclusion of spirituals in the repertoire of Howard University's men's Glee Club, which had been founded in 1912 by Roy W. Tibbs and included in its repertoire a mix of "folk songs," classical music, and spirituals.[45] The Glee Club's own performance style was distinct from the musical tradition that had first originated among enslaved people in North America as they adapted Christian hymns in worship.[46] In-

FIGURE 4.2. Louis Achille's graduating class of master's students, including (from left to right) George Jackson, Edna Burke, Louise Taylor, Achille, Pearle Walker, Virginia Harris, and Raúl Perez, at Howard University in 1933. Photo courtesy of the Achille Family Archives.

deed, in the decades prior to Achille's arrival at Howard, the genre expanded to include a wide variety of performance styles, ranging from Marian Anderson and Roland Hayes's classicized solo performances to the call-and-response format still found in churches. In many cases, the spiritual was performed at the end of a repertoire of classical music performance. Moreover, urban "sanctified" churches included African American folk music in religious settings, where it was transformed into a popular and profitable musical genre known as gospel.[47] Against this changing liturgical and musical backdrop, African American writers, scholars, musicians, and religious practitioners continued to debate the meaning and future of the spiritual as a form of "Negro art." And many of these same debates occurred at Howard, where students were expected to know and perform the spirituals. In 1915, the Howard University student body famously refused to sing "plantation melodies" during chapel services, believing them to be old-fashioned and demeaning.[48] By contrast, Howard alumna Zora Neale Hurston publicly renounced the stylized arrangement and "trick style of delivery" of the concertized spiritual, regarding it as an inauthentic rendering of the slave songs.[49] In 1926, Alain Locke argued that the spiritual was "the most characteristic product of the race genius as yet in America."[50] In response to Locke's characterization, Langston Hughes critiqued those African American churchgoers who would never "dream of employing the spiritual," preferring instead the "drab melodies" found in white hymnals.[51] Invoked toward radically different political and aesthetic ends, the spiritual remained a powerful means of envisioning the past, present, and future of Black life.

Achille arrived at Howard soon after these debates had been initiated, which meant that he likely heard many of these same arguments in classroom discussions, faculty gatherings, and public debates. But he especially liked Howard's

Glee Club, which appeared regularly at university events, including the annual concert at Rankin Memorial Chapel, and was featured at the White House, in prominent African American churches, and on local radio programs.[52] Achille was immediately drawn to the choir, whose formality and mastery of Western modes of performance resonated with his commitment to French models of assimilation. In addition to his attraction to the solemn musical performance, Achille was also likely impressed by the sight of forty men dressed in tuxedos, who exemplified the sartorial "harmony of civilization" that he had earlier espoused (see figure 4.3). In fact, an African American choir's potential to model assimilation had already been noted by both American and French officials. In 1930, the US ambassador to France sponsored a European tour of the Hampton Institute Choir to raise money for the implementation of the Hampton-Tuskegee educational model in the French administrative zones in West and Equatorial Africa.[53]

Years later, when an interviewer surmised that the spirituals had been Achille's music "since childhood" due to his Martiniquan heritage, Achille quickly corrected him. While many people imagined that the spiritual was his "maternal music," he emphasized instead that it was an interest he had

FIGURE 4.3. A 1936 photograph of the Howard University Glee Club, whose formal dress would play a formative role in Achille's own approach to the presentation of the Negro spiritual. In Maud Cuney-Hare, *Negro Musicians and Their Music* (1936).

"acquired" and, indeed, "discovered in Paris while studying at Louis-le-Grand." It was in the United States, within a "black world," that this sacred music was made his own, "because it sang of the heavenly bliss that we are promised while at the same time it sang in the African rhythms whose memory my muscles had preserved, even though my memory is hardly furnished by memories of Africa. For alas! I have only spent one week on the black continent."[54] This reflection both clarifies and obscures the attraction of the spiritual for Achille. When listening, something stirred in him as well, something "so moving, so captivating" that he believed himself transported simultaneously to Africa and the United States.[55] Like Frederick Douglass, who described how the "wild notes" filled him with an "ineffable sadness," or Du Bois, who claimed, "Ever since I was a child these songs have stirred me strangely," Achille shared in a sense of the uncanny, drawn to music that was unknown to him.[56] By serving both as a conduit to his African identity and heritage and as a means of spiritual fulfillment, the spiritual helped unite Achille's divided sense of self.

Having discovered the spiritual "within this black world," Achille was inspired to make it his own. While on a religious pilgrimage in the early 1930s, he was asked to sing a song from his home country. Achille chose instead to sing an African American spiritual, claiming that Antillean songs were in fact not at all religious. A few years later, Achille made two separate recordings of spirituals on 78 rpm records with the Lumen and Odéon labels. The 1934 Lumen recording included an English-language rendition of "Swing Low, Sweet Chariot." He was accompanied by Roger Guttinguer's jazz orchestra, whose use of a lap steel guitar signaled a departure from the stylistic standards of university choirs.[57] In 1938, Achille made another recording with Odéon that featured performances of "Deep River," "I Want to Be Ready," "I Am Traveling to the Grave," and "Old Time Religion."[58] All of these recordings made clear that Achille was eager to test and perform his own interpretation of this musical tradition. Following a short visit to France, Achille returned to the United States after France was defeated and occupied by German forces. Achille temporarily abandoned his plans to take the *agrégation* exam and in 1941 entered a doctoral program in the Department of Religion at Catholic University in Washington to continue his study of interracial Catholicism.[59] In this period, he also began to write about the relationship between Catholicism and French colonialism, concluding that colonial policies had in fact emphasized the merits of native cultures and attempted to cultivate a "Franco-African culture."[60]

Initially, Achille did not enlist in the Allied effort in World War II. Writing for the *Washington Post* in May 1940 just weeks before the French surrender, Achille lamented that this "ruinous war" might result in the "loss of national identity" for West Indian populations. He was concerned about the possibility of ceding the French colonies to the United States as a guarantee of war debts.[61] In addition, Achille's time in the Compagnons de Saint-François also made him reluctant to fight his fellow pilgrims from Germany. It was, as he said later, "not my war."[62] Just a few months later, Achille gave a talk for Atlanta University's summer school students in which he contrasted the experience of "French Negroes" with the experience of the "American Negro" in war, focusing on the persecution that African Americans faced in war service.[63]

While initially reluctant to fight, in 1943, Achille joined the French army. He spent three months at a training camp in Fort Benning, Georgia, where one of his strongest memories was being refused access to the mess hall by white US soldiers, while his "French compatriots, because they were white, had access."[64] While at Fort Benning, he met a "fellow student-officer," whose work on "Eskimos" prompted Achille to write to the president of the Tuskegee Institute. Achille contended that this work would be especially valuable to "American Negro youth ... who live *in* the white man's world without being *of* it" and were thus, "like the Eskimos," able to "look at this Western civilization critically." He also emphasized that both groups still held "some of the primary (not to say primitive) virtues." Furthermore, Achille noted both his and the author's admiration for the "Spiritual," not only for its "musical quality" but "also as a heritage of intense human suffering and hope." Achille ended by noting that he was "proud of sharing with you and your students in the spirit and blood which made the 'Spirituals' possible."[65] In war as in peacetime, Achille's experience in the United States continued to be deeply contradictory. He rejoiced in the discovery of Black culture and his own Black heredity but was deeply unsettled once again by the experience of racial segregation and racism.

Following his training in the United States, Achille left the United States to be an interpreter for the US and French forces in North Africa, where he was impressed by the significantly better treatment, "despite the colonial situation."[66] He was nonetheless conscious of losing access to Black spaces. In a resonant moment, Achille described arriving in Algeria—"that is, my return to French soil"—and needing a haircut. His first thought was: "My God, there's no black barber!" He described this as a "reflex" learned in the United States, because "whenever one travels you have to know where to find a black barber, you had to know all of that." But Achille then admonished himself: "No, you are here in the land of liberty, you are going to present yourself to the next barber you see, even if he destroys your beautiful hair."[67] While thrilled to be seen as French, Achille mourned that his hair's specificity would no longer be valued or acknowledged.

Achille stayed in North Africa through the end of the war and by 1946 had at last succeeded in passing the *agrégation* and was ready to take an English teaching post in a French *lycée* (see figure 4.4). His first choice was North Africa, where he believed he would be most useful given his experience in dealing with "interracial conflicts in the United States."[68] However, Achille was eventually assigned to the Lycée du Parc, a prestigious public secondary school in the large provincial city of Lyon, known for a strong wartime resistance network as well as its ties to numerous progressive Catholic organizations, including the Compagnons de Saint-François.[69] On receiving his work assignment, Achille had no time to return to the United States to collect his personal things. Still without his civilian clothes yet no longer mobilized in the French military, he arrived at the Lycée du Parc in Lyon in February 1946 wearing a US military uniform. He was self-conscious about the uniform itself, which seemed a "little bit too beautiful" given the continued clothing rationing, but also cognizant of its emblematic power.[70] Appearing before his students "after four years of occupation" and an American-led liberation, the uniform introduced to the classroom an "atmosphere of the New World, with its *joie de vivre*, its efficiency, and its simplicity and honesty between students and teachers."[71] In contrast to the formality that characterized teacher-student relations in postwar France, his American uniform connoted a different—but not altogether clear—set of social and racial relations.

This moment would mark Achille's memory for another reason. Clothed in American power, Achille encountered the Negro spiritual once again in the assigned English grammar textbook *L'Anglais vivant* (*Living English*) published by Carpentier Fialip. As he recalled, this introduction to English language and literature included the lyrics of the spiritual "Nobody Knows the Trouble I've Seen," popularized through its arrangement by Harry Burleigh and performances by Paul Robeson. Seeing the lyrics, Achille remembered wondering how his new students, "at the end of a long period of occupation, marked by the rhythm of German boots and military songs with their sudden breaks," would "receive these melodies from overseas . . . songs that were also born out of a sort of captivity?" Equating the German occupation and American slavery, Achille wondered whether they might see themselves in this narration of "captivity" or, instead, reject it. Achille also worried for his new and precarious place in the school's hierarchy, fearing that an "imprudent opening" gesture of "misplaced frivolity" would destroy the professorial authority he held. Moreover, by revealing his "profound familiarity with this black music," would he "emphasize a racial and foreign heritage in this scholastic setting"? Finally, he wondered

FIGURE 4.4. Louis Achille with his family, ca. 1943 or 1944. From left to right, Achille's mother, Marguerite Ferdinand Achille, his brother Pierre Achille, Achille himself, his sisters Marguerite Achille, Jeanne Achille, and Isabelle Achille, and his father, Louis Achille. In the front row are the grandchildren. Photo courtesy of the Achille Family Papers.

whether it was possible to present the spirituals in a secular, state-run institution without overemphasizing their "spiritual meaning."[72] Emboldened by his students' "tireless curiosity for this immense and powerful country that had dressed me in her beautiful flag to help win our war," Achille decided to sing the spiritual, "Nobody Knows," without accompaniment. Each line—"If you get there before I do" and "Sometimes I'm up, sometimes I'm down"—was followed by the same response: "Oh yes, Lord," which he gave himself.[73] To Achille's apparent surprise, the "songs of black American slaves" resonated profoundly with his young students.[74]

Given Achille's desire to establish a narrative of the spiritual's immediate resonance, this story might provoke some skepticism. It nevertheless suggests that Achille's ambiguous racial embodiment of African American religious

FIGURE 4.5. Louis Achille directs a concert of the Park Glee Club in Lyon, 1952. The choir was mixed in age, but in this era it was limited to male students. Photo courtesy of the Achille Family Papers.

music was important to his own memory of this encounter. Perhaps most significantly, it inspired him to continue. In 1948, two years after he began teaching at the Lycée du Parc, Achille decided to form a glee club explicitly modeled on the choir he first encountered at Howard in the 1930s. For thirty years, the Park Glee Club (the *Parc* of the school was purposely Anglicized) sang almost exclusively Negro spirituals in the original language, with the occasional inclusion of French Creole songs. According to Mercer Cook, who saw the group perform during his 1951–52 Fulbright year, the choir was initially composed of "twenty-five white French students," all of whom were enrolled at or had recently graduated from the Lycée du Parc, and would remain so until the 1960s (see figure 4.5). By then, changes in French education and immigration patterns meant that the choir later included women and people of color, including Achille's own children.[75] During his 1951 trip, Cook noted that Achille directed another choir "composed of French colonial students" who performed at various functions, including at a Paris ceremony honoring African American diplomat Ralph Bunche.[76]

While no other record of this colonial choir exists, there is ample evidence that Achille knew North African students living in Lyon, including Frantz Fanon, who was there studying medicine and psychiatry. Though Achille and Fanon came from different generations, they were both Martiniquan men educated in France and living in a town "notoriously unfriendly to strangers," and thus shared in the experience of racial designation.[77] In his 1952 *Black Skin, White Masks,* for example, Fanon recalled a moment when Achille was asked by a priest during a religious pilgrimage in June 1950: "Why you left big savanna and why you come with us?"[78] By responding to the question in perfect and polite French, Achille demonstrated to the priest and fellow pilgrims the falsity of racial stereotypes and, moreover, provided Fanon with a resonant example of the power of language in the reproduction of race and racism.[79]

In May 1951, both Achille and Fanon were featured in a special issue on Black life in Africa and the United States in *Ésprit*, a leftist intellectual and Catholic journal.[80] The volume, titled *La plainte du noir*, included Fanon's first publication on the "lived experience of the black man," which he based largely on his own experiences in Lyon.[81] It was there that Fanon first heard, "Look, a negro!," which served as the opening line of the essay.[82] While Fanon investigated how racial designations and racism entered into everyday life, Achille's essay in *Esprit* included a historical overview of the spiritual tradition as well as his own translations of nine Negro spirituals. Before doing so, Achille made a jarring declaration to his readers: "The following translations of spirituals are absolutely not intended to be sung."[83] While presumably Achille was confident in his own capacity as a translator, he believed that, due to the "rhythmic harmony" that exists "between words and music," any intoned translation would lose the original meaning.[84] A translation might retain the "spiritual tone" of the original, but the song would nonetheless lose its "authentic message" in translation.[85] Furthermore, Achille argued that the "syncopated rhythm" of the arrangement would clash with the rhythm of the French language and "modern French religious sentiment." Thus, he reminded any reader who might be tempted to sing his translation of "Go Down Moses" ("Libère mon peuple") or "Were You There?" ("Étais-tu là lorsqu'ils mirent en croix Jésus?") or "Sometimes I Feel like a Motherless Child" ("Parfois je me sens tel un pauvre orphelin") that they would be missing entirely the "authentic message of these songs."[86] While other translators rendered the Negro spiritual into Creole, Achille did not, careful to distinguish African American vernacular from Caribbean languages. Bound by a commitment to root African American music in its own context, Achille contended that its meaning inhered in the original language.[87]

The Park Glee Club in Lyon exemplified Achille's commitment to this mode of performance. Each year, the choir—which had between fifteen and thirty members—performed spirituals in numerous public concerts, including Rotary Club functions as well as the school's annual *fête du lycée* and the December *fête des lumières* in Lyon. During a typical two-hour concert, the group performed fifteen hymns drawn from a repertoire of seventy-two songs, each of which was prefaced by commentary and a French translation to help the audience make sense of the lyrics. They would usually start their concerts with the spiritual "Every Time I Feel the Spirit," which set a serious yet hopeful tone for their concerts.[88] During performances, Achille conducted the choir and sang most of the solo parts, while the student participants sang the background parts. Achille's son, Dominique Achille, was a member of the choir in the early 1960s. He recalled the special significance of performing "Were You There," a spiritual that was first published in James Weldon Johnson's 1926 collection.[89] The song's questions—"Were you there when they crucified my Lord? Were you there when they nailed him to the tree? Were you there when they pierced him in the side? Were you there when the sun refused to shine? Were you there when they laid him in the tomb?"—were interpreted by his father, who mimed with his body the crucifixion of Jesus while the choir "created a kind of background sound without uttering any words." Achille's son recalled that even when it was performed in a secular environment, "no one laughed."[90] In this way, the Glee Club created a sacred soundscape for both its participants and audiences.

By law, Achille had to maintain the secularity of the choir because it was connected to a state-run school. In 1957, for example, when he and the choir were invited to sing in Louvain, Belgium, by Ad Lucem, a Catholic relief organization that focused its work on African colonies, he was careful to underscore that the choir, students, and school were strictly secular.[91] But he never disguised the lyrics, which were translated so "there was no ambiguity" even at school and secular celebrations. Achille said later: "I always expected criticism, but my reply was all ready, I could respond to people who were 'secular,' very often on the left, and say to them: you are not really going to prevent us from singing the liberatory songs of the black slave."[92] This suggests that the performance of the spiritual was exempted from French rules regarding religious display or practice in secular settings. It also suggests Achille's skill in presenting the Negro spiritual as a nonthreatening mode of cultural contact and his capacity to translate a religious practice by a minority population from another place and time into a kind of universally liberatory performance.

As a rule, the choir did not accept payment for its performances, except when a host organization covered the travel costs. For Achille, the choir's professed "poverty" was a "tremendous asset," for it allowed the choir to exist in the "spirit of the times, to sing in the same state of poverty and with the same natural methods as the black slaves, creators of these songs."[93] This troubling comparison was nonetheless tempered by his insistence that the choir could not replicate the songs of enslaved people. As he wrote, "The Park Glee Club never had the naiveté to believe that it could imitate the warm and resonant timbre . . . of the black voices of the United States, nor their subtle rhythms and typical harmonies." He referenced the emergence of other French Negro spiritual choirs, like the Compagnons du Jourdain, a group of four white French men who modeled their singing style on recordings from overseas. Achille deemed their performances only "somewhat convincing pastiches." By contrast, by seeking out "its own harmonies in a French interpretation," he believed that the Park Glee Club had found a path "as natural to the French as the black American style that characterizes African Americans."

To achieve this "natural" sound, Achille eschewed the use of written arrangements and sheet music. While this approach reveals his own tendency to essentialize the natural capacity of African Americans to sing expressively and spontaneously, it was also a practical way to include those participants who could not read music. Though he acknowledged that the spirituals typically required "knowledge of music theory," Achille wanted to include anyone who was interested, whether they were musically literate or not.[94] In fact, the Glee Club was officially part of the school's Club d'Anglais, whereas the school's choral groups were directed by music teachers, underscoring the fact that the choir was not intended to be a space of formal musical training. Furthermore, he believed this practice to be integral to "liberty" and "improvisation." As he told an interviewer, "We sing according to traditional methods of jazz without sheet music and with the right of improvisation and spontaneous harmonization."[95]

Alumni from the Glee Club emphasized these formal qualities as well. In a 1978 program celebrating the thirtieth anniversary of the choir, one member recalled the choir's role in his "discovery of rhythm," a "different" music, and the "feeling of responsibility" that came through membership. Another participant was grateful to have been able to "discover Afro-American civilization without needing to cross the ocean."[96] Yet another recalled the "warmth of moments spent together . . . the knowledge of the Negro spirituals, and the problems concerning those of the Blacks, the beauty of the songs, the original method of apprenticeship," and the "liberty of improvisation." One former student was struck by the manner in which Achille led the choir. While he was not religious himself, he was awestruck by Achille, who "was joyful yet also very rigorous," and who "communicated his enthusiasm with all." Echoing the other memories of the choir's practices, in which participants learned to sing by first understanding and speaking the words, the student further suggested that these explanations helped to clarify that one was "really participating in something."[97] By virtue of his identity as Antillean and his experiences at Howard, Achille seemed to give the choir a kind of legitimacy. In the students' eyes, Achille "was the child of slavery," born of a people whose emancipation was not so far in the distant past, yet had shown exceptional intellectual and political power. "We knew," the student recalled, "that we didn't sing negro spirituals for simple amusement." By singing spirituals, they came to have some understanding of "all that had passed in those years."[98]

By virtue of Achille's commitment—and perceived legitimacy—the space was one in which his white and nonwhite French students could enact a form of what Kyra Gaunt has called "musical blackness."[99] This dynamic was, of course, linked to the ways in which white audiences and performers profited—economically, psychically, socially, and aesthetically—from African American musicians and music.[100] However, rather than merely providing "spectator knowledge" of Black musical creation, Achille helped create "black musical identifications through an embodied practice," making the classroom and concert hall a site of experimental, situated learning.[101] In this regard, the choir might be considered in terms of Shana Redmond's work on Black anthems and the ways that, as a "participatory enterprise," music created "collective engagement in performance."[102] However, as E. Patrick Johnson also writes, the performance itself denotes a kind of ephemerality that denaturalizes race yet also offers a brief, "authenticating" experience for the participants, who access Black culture in the moment of performing.[103] Certainly, the thrill of racial appropriation remained, but the choir's rehearsals and performances may have enabled students to reimagine and enact spheres of multiracial assembly or interracial solidarity.

By the mid- to late 1950s, the Park Glee Club's popularity was amplified by the growing interest in the Negro spiritual in France. Promoted by the growing record industry, there were numerous African American performers who specialized in the genre and were featured regularly on French radio and television programs.[104] One such performer was John Littleton, who had first traveled to France during World War II and stayed to become the "ambassador of the negro spiritual in France."[105] In February 1956, Littleton was featured on Jean-Christophe Averty's public television program *À la recherche du jazz* (*In Search of Jazz*), which began with footage of Littleton chopping wood and singing "Water Boy," a spiritual popularized by singer Paul Robeson.[106] Also appearing frequently on French television programs was Gordon Heath, a Black American performer who in 1949 had founded L'Abbaye, an intimate folk music club in Saint-Germain-des-Prés.[107] Born to a Barbadian immigrant father and African American mother in New York in 1918, Heath had pursued acting and landed his first Broadway role in 1943. In 1945, he was cast in the lead of Elia Kazan's *Deep Are the Roots*, which dramatized the experiences of an African American GI returning from Europe to the Jim Crow South. While Heath's performance was widely acclaimed, he soon found that the theater offered limited options for African American performers and moved first to London and then, in 1948, to Paris.

Like Achille, Heath initially had a strained relationship to Blackness, careful to distinguish himself from African Americans and, on one occasion, delighting in the gift of a Golliwog from a British woman.[108] His time in Paris changed this perspective and instilled in him a greater consciousness of African American culture and Black pride. He remarked later on how "positively chic" it was to be a Black American in Paris (but still noted that he would "not care to be a black African in France").[109] In 1949, Heath met Big Bill Broonzy, who taught him how to play guitar, as well as Huddie "Lead Belly" Ledbetter, who had traveled to France under the sponsorship of the Hot Club.[110] Unconvinced by what he perceived to be a false promotion of Ledbetter as "polished," Heath devoted himself to presenting instead an authentic version of folk music and Negro spirituals.[111] With his partner Lee Payant, he founded the L'Abbaye, which was known for cultivating a church-like reverence for musical performance (see figure 4.6). Others described a kind of "prison discipline" in the space, in which "inattention and frivolousness" were "frowned upon, requests rejected, Stephen Foster barred, *Old Man River* inacceptable."[112] While the club featured a range of musical genres, including folk songs, ballads, and religious music, Heath gained particular fame for his nightly performance of the "Negro spiritual" (see figure 4.7).[113] Building on the success of the club, Heath released three records featuring folk music and toured throughout France and its overseas departments and territories, bringing his own renditions to eager audiences.

While these performers were integrated within the French culture, language, and landscape, US State Department officials sought to counter such visions with their own sponsored performances of the Negro spiritual. In addition to being featured in the weekly radio broadcasts of the Voice of America's Sim Copans, the spiritual was also promoted by the US military infrastructure. In 1952, the public affairs officer (PAO) at the Bordeaux US Information Service

FIGURE 4.6. A portrait of Gordon Heath and Lee Payant. Photo courtesy of the Gordon Heath Papers, Department of Special Collections and University Archives, W. E. B. Du Bois Library, University of Massachusetts Amherst.

FIGURE 4.7. Gordon Heath performing at the L'Abbaye Club in Paris, n.d. Photo courtesy of the Gordon Heath Papers, Department of Special Collections and University Archives, W. E. B. Du Bois Library, University of Massachusetts Amherst.

(USIS) office "conceived of the idea of presenting a group of Negro GIs" from the Captieux Ordnance Depot near Bordeaux. Twenty-two African American servicemen were enlisted to form a spirituals choir that toured southern France, including Angoulême, Bordeaux, St. Jean de Luz, and Biarritz, performing to "capacity houses."[114] In 1956, there were reports of a small quartet, the Golden Jubaleers, which had been formed on a US Army base and specialized in the performance of "Negro spirituals."[115] According to publicity materials, Leroy Anderson, Curtis Williams, Martin Gettis, and John Clayton came from "four different regions in the United States" and became friends "thanks to their love of singing."[116] A report in the local paper noted that immediately following the concert, the four singers were "literally besieged by a throng of young admirers in the quest of autographs."[117] Whether propagated within US military circuits or sold in the French record industry, the Negro spiritual was a highly contested aesthetic form, whose spiritual value was frequently asked to legitimate commercial and political projects in the 1950s.

Return to *Négritude*

While Achille was dedicated to the spiritual as a means of achieving certain political goals in postwar France, he maintained a commitment to its *négritude*. Writing in *Présence Africaine* several years later, he critiqued a new collection of translated Negro spirituals edited by Marguerite Yourcenar, noting that because they were intended to be sung in French, they had "lost their *négritude*."[118] By contrast, Achille believed the Park Glee Club was exemplary in maintaining this commitment (despite the choir's racial composition). This certainty in turn provided Achille with the experiential basis for his own interventions in Black internationalist politics. The most important venue for these was *Présence Africaine*, which had, since its creation in 1947, served as a critical space for defining the history and future of Black culture. In 1950, Achille had himself contributed to a special issue on the "black world," focusing on the history of race relations in North America.[119] Since then, he had remained in contact with the editorial board—which included former classmates Léopold Sédar Senghor and Aimé Césaire—and observed the transformation of the journal into one that more openly critiqued French colonialism.

In September 1956, Achille joined several hundred delegates and observers in the first International Congress of Black Writers and Artists (Congrès International des Écrivains et Artistes Noirs), which was sponsored by the journal.[120] For three days, an unprecedented gathering of Black intellectuals, artists, and writers, including sixty delegates from twenty-four countries, gathered in the Sorbonne's Amphitheatre Descartes in Paris.[121] In addition to the official delegations from the Caribbean, Africa, South America, and North America, hundreds more crowded into the amphitheater, "already unbearably hot" by ten o'clock in the morning.[122] As James Baldwin reported on the first day, the room "was hectic with the activity attendant upon the setting up of tape recorders, with the testing of ear-phones, with the lightening of flash-bulbs. Electricity, in fact, filled the hall." There were messages from those unable to attend, including an unnamed "group of black women," a group of Algerian militants, Josephine Baker, E. Franklin Frazier, and George Padmore, as well as W. E. B. Du Bois, who angered the American delegation by implying that any Black American delegate would only be speaking as a pawn of the US State Department.[123] In addition to the delegates and observers, print and radio journalists from around the world bore witness to this "cultural Bandung," alluding to the previous year's Asian-African Conference in Bandung, Indonesia.[124] In contrast to Bandung's explicit anticolonialism, the delegates to the 1956 Congress did not address political questions, whether the struggle for civil rights in the United States, the ongoing Suez crisis in Egypt, the developing conflict in Algeria, or the imminent declaration of formal independence in Ghana, the first sub-Saharan nation to throw off its colonial yoke. But if the Congress was inward looking, it was in no way insulated from the political and social events of the moment. As Baldwin noted, "Hanging in the air, as real as the heat from which we suffered, were the great specters of America and Russia."[125]

Against this backdrop, the founder of *Présence Africaine*, Alioune Diop, welcomed to the Congress these "men of culture," bound together by a common ancestry as well as by the shared experience of colonialism and racism.[126] Diop heralded the possibility that the Congress would "declare and assess together the richness, the crisis and the promises of our culture."[127] The papers were varied, covering Yoruba poetry, Fula culture, Haitian art, Christianity and Africa, West African nationalist movements, and the NAACP, as well as more wide-ranging presentations on culture, colonialism, and racism by Léopold Sédar Senghor, Aimé Césaire, Frantz Fanon, Jean Price-Mars, and Jacques Rabemananjara. Out of these presentations, and the discussions that followed, emerged two central debates. The first concerned the relationship of African American people to the proceedings. The US delegation, which included James W. Ivy, Horace Mann Bond, Mercer Cook, John A. Davis, William Fontaine, and Richard Wright, questioned not only the African American relationship to Africa but also the very idea that African Americans might be considered a colonized people.[128] Following Léopold Senghor's presentation on the need to root Black civilization in Africa, Richard Wright wondered:

Where do *I,* an American Negro, conditioned by the harsh industrial, abstract force of the Western world . . . where do *I* stand in relation to that culture? If I were of another colour or another race, I could say, "All that is very exotic, but it is not directly related to me," and I could let it go at that. *I can not.* The modern world has cast us both in the same mould. *I* am black and *he* is black; I am an *American* and he is *French,* and so, there you are.[129]

Wright's articulation of Black identity in this moment likely resonated with Achille, who saw clearly the different racial "moulds" that existed in France and the United States. In response to Wright, Senghor reiterated the possibility of an underlying cultural affinity and argued that an "African Negro civilization," consciously or not, still animated African American art and literature. He even claimed Wright's own poetry and novels as part of the African canon.[130] The next day's panels concluded with Césaire's own presentation on culture and colonization, followed once again by a closed-session debate and discussion. At this point, Cook raised objections to the political nature of Césaire's presentation, in particular his statement that "American Negroes have a semi-colonial status," while Davis reiterated the historical "anti-colonist position" of the United States.[131] Though unresolved, these debates nevertheless remain in the record. They serve as a reminder of the powerful mythologies that sustained Cold War liberalism, the immense pressure faced by African American political leaders, and, finally, the uncertainty and misunderstanding that followed discussions of culture and colonialism, even though earphones allowed all participants to listen to simultaneous translations in French or English.[132] As Baldwin asked, could there even be a culture shared by "so many millions of people"? Was a shared history of oppression "enough to have made of the earth's black populations anything that can legitimately be described as a culture? For what, beyond the fact that all black men at one time or another left Africa, or have remained there, do they really have in common?"[133]

The concerns of the American delegation have long been central to the historical treatment of the Congress, perhaps owing something to Baldwin's inimitable writing.[134] However, the Congress's attendees were also agitated by an entirely different question: the role of Christianity in African culture.[135] Indeed, one of the most controversial speakers was Thomas Ekollo, a Cameroonian priest whose presentation on Christianity's importance to the development of African culture was met with "hooliganism from the spectators."[136] For many delegates and observers, the Catholic Church represented the most insidious side of Western imperialism. Other delegates questioned whether Catholicism or Christianity could ever play a positive role in the formation of Black culture, given that Catholic missionaries had already done their best to destroy the temporal, cultural, physical, and spiritual components of indigenous African religions. In response to these claims, African priests at the Congress contended that the Catholic Church had adapted, becoming more African in Africa and more Haitian in Haiti.[137] These debates, and the shouts audible in the recordings, document the lingering anger toward Catholic missionaries and colonial religious doctrine in Africa.

Presenting the morning after these battle lines had been drawn, Achille gave his own presentation on the Negro spiritual, a cultural amalgamation, he suggested, that augured the "expansion of black culture" throughout the world.[138] He began by conceding that his subject was "a bit peripheral to our principal preoccupations," as it concerned the "offspring of African culture." His main focus was "Afro-American culture and its influence in Europe," and more specifically the "cultural masterpieces" born during a period of "odious colonization . . . a slavery devoid of any humanity."[139] In this statement, Achille affirmed the role of colonization in the United States while still appeasing the American delegation by placing it in the past rather than in the contentious present. Seen in relation to the global popularity of jazz, the spiritual was perhaps "less spectacular," he said, but its influence was nonetheless "more profound."[140] Achille contended that the "same inspiration" that first shaped the spiritual was "still sufficiently living" that new modern spirituals could be "born in our own time, nearly ninety years after emancipation."[141] Furthermore, he believed that they had "been taken up and adopted by free men who have never known slavery" precisely because they expressed the "universal expression of human suffering and Christian hope."[142] Achille found this resurgence to be particularly true in France, where he saw a "fertile and living implantation" and an "authentic assimilation" of a music whose new proponents were quite distinct from its original creators.[143] After describing its interwar introduction, Achille outlined the secular introduction of the spiritual in postwar France, drawing attention to African American GIs and the regular radio programs of Sim Copans. In addition, he underscored that an "evolution that was taking place in the heart of Christian spirituality in France," wherein the spiritual was now more than just "an exotic flavouring" for church choirs and offered, instead, a "new and richer nourishment" of Christianity.[144]

Achille once again asserted his belief that the incorporation of the spiritual into church choirs was a "delicate and difficult" process because of the issues of maintaining fidelity to the "subtlety of the rhythms and harmonizations."[145] Choirs either kept the melody but sang in French or created "imitation, pure and simple"; even in the original language, such imitations were, he argued, not very "black" or American." Achille presented the Park Glee Club as a counter-example, arguing that it had succeeded because it was based on Achille's own experience in the United States. Once again, Achille determined that his racial identity and experience had empowered him "to transmit the tradition of the Negro Spiritual orally and in direct fashion," serving as an intermediary of the spiritual for his white students.[146] What resulted, he argued, was "a grafting of Negro culture on to the White singers of the Park Glee Club." While Achille drew on his own religious beliefs, his training, and his racial experience to successfully "mix" Black and white cultures, he also used this self-positioning to assess the fidelity of other choirs. In positioning himself in this way, Achille mirrored some of the strategies that had been infamously employed by Mezz Mezzrow several years before. In fact, Achille even compared this "*métissage*" or "grafting" to Mezzrow's own experiences as a "voluntary Negro," which was likely familiar to the assembled delegates. In his most explicit acknowledgment of the Park Glee Club's engagement in cross-racial identification, Achille noted that the choir's willing assumption of the mantle of race was "admirable" precisely because it was "voluntary, mindful, and subjective."[147]

Beyond this exploration of the Negro spiritual in France, Achille offered another form of "proof" of the spiritual's continued relevance and development outside its original context. He next presented to his audience a spiritual of his own creation, the "first Negro Spiritual to see the light in the heart of a white community and in France," which was inspired by the 1955 bus boycott in Montgomery, Alabama. It was called "I Will Walk on My Own Legs 'til Kingdom Come!" After reading the lyrics in French, he then switched to English to speak directly to the US delegation:

> I wish to propose to the English-speaking delegates this very humble attempt at this type of music, which is entirely foreign to the country and to the people among which it sprung. It is the first time that it is being presented and I hope that the American delegates, when they happen to return to the United States, especially those who are in charge of the magnificent National Association for the Advancement of Colored People, will bring it back, bring it back to the people of Montgomery and tell them we are with them.[148]

By presenting his own spiritual to the American delegation in this moment of international solidarity, Achille hoped that his "humble attempt" might demonstrate his own solidarity with civil rights activists. He was unable to play a recording and so decided to sing it in English for the assembled delegates and observers:

I will walk on my own legs 'til Kingdom come. (*repeat*)
I will walk on my own legs 'til my brother shakes my hand
I will walk on my own legs 'til Kingdom come.

"Go'n sit back," he said to me 'til Kingdom come (*repeat*)
"Go'n sit back where you belong" and my brother didn't shake my hand.
"Go'n sit back," he said to me 'til Kingdom come.

My Lord said: "Come'n sit front 'til Kingdom come" (*repeat*)
My Lord said: "Come'n sit front, And I'm going to sit by your side"
My Lord said: "Come'n sit front 'til Kingdom come."

I will walk on my own legs 'til Kingdom come (*repeat*)
I will walk on my own legs 'til my brother shakes my hand.
I will walk on my own legs 'til Kingdom come.[149]

Throughout Achille's performance, his foot kept the beat, setting the rhythm for his AABA melodic structure. The lyrics themselves extended the boundaries of civil rights to the spiritual realm, positing that social action would eventually be rewarded with spiritual salvation. The bus boycott became the metaphor through which he defined the heavenly "seat" next to God. In this construction, Achille built on familiar themes in the spiritual tradition, rendering the lived experience of oppression as a means of liberation. By situating his spiritual in response to present-day racism, Achille also reaffirmed his argument that the spiritual's power was not tied to a distant time or place. Although he sang it without accompaniment and without amplification, the performance was later rebroadcast by Radiodiffusion Française throughout France and its empire, making Achille's translation and transformation of the Negro spiritual part of a colonial and anticolonial soundscape.

When Achille concluded the song, there was an eruption of thunderous applause and stomping feet. Unlike the earlier shouts of frustration and admonishment, now the crowd released its enthusiasm for this musical enactment of solidarity across language, religion, race, and nation. While the song might have served as a fitting conclusion to his presentation, Achille ended with some questions of his own, which he reiterated in later sessions. He wondered whether the African delegates recognized their own "musical genius" in these songs, "despite a clear Anglo-Saxon *métissage*," and, furthermore, whether Catholic or Protestant evangelization in Africa had led to similar creations.[150] To the American delegates, he queried the possible effects of desegregation— which he of course welcomed—on African American culture. Would it be able to "preserve its authenticity," or would it be "completely merged or diluted in the entirety of American culture?"[151] This series of questions demonstrated Achille's belief that the spiritual represented the best possible consequence of the encounter between Western and African civilizations, but also his own lingering questions about the meaning and political value of Black culture.

In late March 1966, Martin Luther King Jr. toured Europe to raise funds for the Southern Christian Leadership Conference, traveling to Sweden as well as France, with stops in Paris and Lyon. In Paris, he was joined by gospel singer Queen Esther Marrow and singer Harry Belafonte for *La nuit des droits civiques* on March 28 at the Palais des Sports, where over five thousand people gathered.[152] Reporting from Paris, longtime correspondent Ollie Stewart noted the large assembled crowd before observing that the "Embassy crowd" had stayed away "to keep from being tarred with the equality brush."[153] While the event was a clear fund-raising success, it had run into political trouble when the US ambassador, Charles E. Bohlen, chose not to attend, suggesting that it might be "construed as a gesture of favoritism for King's organization rather than of support for the whole civil rights movement," and allegedly instructing Belafonte to "keep the civil rights movement within national borders."[154] The political scene in Lyon the next day was far less volatile. Perhaps eager to link Lyon's own past as the capital of the French wartime resistance to the American civil rights movement, city officials welcomed King at the Bourse du Travail.

While King was greeted by a number of different religious and political organizations, the event also featured a performance by the Park Glee Club, who offered their own renditions of Negro spirituals for the assembled crowd (see figure 4.8). King then gave his own speech, in which he described the comfort he felt in being in France. He ended by leading the audience in singing "We Shall Overcome."[155] In all likelihood, Achille would have relished the opportunity to meet and perform before King, whose presence reaffirmed the political and religious importance of the Park Glee Club. However, he had already promised his former classmate and then president of Senegal, Léopold Sédar Senghor, that he would attend the First World Festival of Negro Arts in Dakar, which opened on April 1. Achille had been invited specifically to present on the Negro spiritual at the Colloque International sur les Arts Nègres, an event that opened the festival on March 30, 1966.

Achille's decision to travel to Dakar is most likely a testament to his friendship with Senghor and his commitment to the project of Senghorian *négritude* that he helped nurture in interwar Paris. However, it may also elucidate Achille's broader commitments. Although the concert in Lyon was organized to raise funds for the US civil rights movement, it was still an occasion on

FIGURE 4.8. The Park Glee Club performs for Martin Luther King Jr. during his visit to Lyon, 1966. Photo courtesy of the Achille Family Papers.

which a largely white French audience could affirm its own dedication to the African American political struggle while continuing to ignore a political and racial struggle at home. It was yet another moment in which the Negro spiritual would have been subsumed within a deeper and more insidious project to distance France from its own colonial and racial past. Indeed, while others sought to profit and gain political power by promoting the Negro spiritual, Achille saw in it a means of affirming Blackness and thus found himself not in Lyon but in Dakar, where he would root the spiritual in African culture. Although Achille, too, sought to redefine the value and political power of the spiritual, he was spiritually and racially bound to a diasporic community, which reaffirmed that Black people were the creators of African American sacred music and should thus benefit from its popular appeal.

5

THE VOICE OF AMERICA

Radio, Race, and the Sounds of the Cold War

———

In early February 1958, a large crowd gathered in the southeastern French town of Hyères for a lecture on the history of jazz. Some of the attendees were established "fanatics," while others were merely curious, but all came to see in person a man whose radio voice was already very familiar. The local newspaper even asked rhetorically, "Is it really necessary to introduce Sim Copans?"[1] And indeed, by 1958, Copans was one of the best-known and most trusted voices on the French radio, a man whose "name could no longer be separated from jazz history."[2] Since 1947, his weekly radio programs on folk music, jazz, and Negro spirituals had reached millions of listeners throughout France, in "French homes from Montmartre to Marseille."[3] This audience included young people, housewives, soldiers, priests, and politicians—even the French president, Vincent Auriol, who told Copans that his voice was "well known" at the Élysée Palace.[4]

This beloved jazz expert, however, was neither a musicologist nor a critic by training. In fact, Copans was not French but instead was born in 1912 in Stamford, Connecticut, the son of Jewish immigrants from Lithuania.[5] Intrigued by France from an early age, Copans enrolled in a doctoral program in French at Brown University. He lived for several years in France while he conducted research for his dissertation on nineteenth-century Franco-American relations, returning to the United States in 1940 with his wife, Lucienne Godiard, a

French woman whom he had met through socialist, anti-Franco organizations in the 1930s.[6] Following the onset of World War II, Copans was recruited by the Office of War Information to serve as a mobile radio broadcaster during the liberation of Normandy. Fluent in French, though still new to radio mechanics, he sought a new means of entertaining and reassuring the residents of rural villages and turned to jazz.[7]

Having seen firsthand the power of African American music as a means of cultural reconciliation, in 1947 Copans joined the newly reorganized US State Department to produce three weekly radio programs featuring Negro spirituals, jazz, and folk music. While these programs were broadcast over French state-run radio networks, they were produced and distributed by a US agency known throughout the world as the "Voice of America."[8] Copans left the State Department in 1954, but he continued to broadcast these programs (albeit with new titles) on the French radio, reaching millions of listeners throughout hexagonal France as well as the French empire, transforming its soundscape on the eve of decolonization. Building on his popularity, in the mid- to late 1950s Copans gave over two hundred lectures on the history of jazz throughout metropolitan France, and later the postcolonial Francophone world. Audiences and listeners alike marveled at the unexpected sonic connections: the comparison of recordings made by children in Alabama and Liberia, the combined sound of arranged spirituals and contemporary gospel, or the almost heretical juxtaposition of traditional and modern jazz.

While the recorded sounds of African American music were critical to his lectures and radio programs, it was not simply the musical content of Copans's programs that engaged his French listeners. It was also his voice. As hundreds of letters and memoirs attest, the particular timbre and tenor of Copans's voice resonated among listeners, who heard in his lightly accented French the informal allure of American power yet also an affirmation of French culture. Indeed, at the same time that his colleagues in the US State Department created the global radiophonic infrastructure for the "Voice of America," Copans created *la voix de l'Amérique*, nestled within French language and its national-imperial radio network. That relationship—between the sound of African American music and Copans's authorial voice on his Cold War radio programs—is the focus of this chapter. Through a close analysis of the work of Sim Copans, and his ties to both formal and informal networks of political power, the chapter shows how the history of the Cold War altered the conditions for musical production in the Francophone world. While Copans—a white, Jewish man— was the "voice" of America, he nevertheless drew on the sounds of African

American music. Translating this musical tradition for his French audiences, his voice conferred American power and authority through the sound production of its minority population, whose own voices and musical creations were subsumed under the sonic power of American broadcasting. While Copans was able to freely move throughout this period, African American musicians' own mobility was highly constrained, and their own critical positions were surveilled by both US and French officials.[9] Indeed, in a period when African American artists, musicians, and activists like Paul Robeson, Hazel Scott, and W. E. B. Du Bois were limited in terms of their capacity to represent and challenge the United States, it is important to recall that Copans had a privileged voice: he benefited not only from his whiteness but also from the material and symbolic power that came from his associations with US authority.

By examining his career within this frame, this chapter demonstrates how African American music became central to the sound of American power in the postwar period, despite (or perhaps due to) the absence of African American interlocutors. For over thirty years, Sim Copans worked within Cold War and colonial networks to disseminate and popularize the history of jazz in France and in Francophone Africa, which in turn facilitated new kinds of cultural and political value for African American music for American, French, and African diasporic observers. To his State Department colleagues, he revealed the potential political power of African American music, which in turn became a key tool in the United States' cultural Cold War. For French observers, he modeled the ways in which Black music might be cultivated, challenging the fears of many that this presumed primitive form had no place within the French patrimony. But he also revealed new kinds of value that would be taken up—in complicated ways—by another generation of listeners in Francophone Africa, where his valorization of the African roots of jazz would have a different resonance.

Broadcasting the Voice of America

Just as Copans's first broadcasts to French audiences in Normandy were from a military truck in the midst of the American-led liberation, the next stage of his career was likewise made possible by the entrenched presence of American forces in France's postwar reconstruction. While this effort was initiated by the US military, its departure in 1946 (until its return in 1950 under the North Atlantic Treaty Organization) meant that the bulk of this reconstruction was led by private and state-run relief agencies. Most worked under the Marshall Plan, or the Economic Cooperation Administration (ECA), which established its Mission France in the late 1940s to advise and assist in reconstruction efforts.[10] Following the dissolution of the Office of War Information (OWI) in 1946, Copans joined the US State Department to assist in the reconstruction of the state-run radio station Radiodiffusion Française (RDF), later known as Radiodiffusion-Télévision Française (RTF).[11] One of his first accomplishments was brokering the transfer of an abandoned US military transmitter, record library, and studio to French control in exchange for the continued relay of US programming on the French radio.[12] Following the agreement, the US State Department could rely on this new station—Paris Inter—for rebroadcast of American programming.[13]

By brokering American war matériel for access to French airwaves, Copans not only established a way to extend American sonic power but also created a platform for his own career as a radio host. Copans's debut was in September 1946, when he drew from the nearly four thousand records donated by the US military to produce several short jazz segments to accompany US-produced programs sent via short-wave relay from New York to Paris. Then, in April 1947, Copans was invited to produce and host his own programs for the French radio: *L'Amérique et sa musique*, *Negro Spirituals*, and *Panorama du jazz américain*. All three programs were produced in the former American studio using American records but were broadcast on Paris Inter, the radio station that had been until very recently maintained by the US military.[14] *L'Amérique et sa musique* (*America and Its Music*) was broadcast for thirty minutes on Sunday afternoons to introduce American history and culture through music. After the opening theme—the minstrel song "Turkey in the Straw"—each episode focused either on a musical genre (work songs, blues, musical comedy, folk songs, college fight songs), a specific region (New England, Route 66, the Mississippi River basin), or a theme (rivers, railroads, or the end of the day's work).[15] By contrast, the *Negro Spirituals* program was just fifteen minutes long and broadcast on weekday evenings, either Monday or Tuesday, at eight o'clock or eight-thirty.[16] It featured a broad range of African American religious music, including gospel quartets, classical soloists, choral ensembles, and recordings made of African American church congregations. Each episode began with a thirty-second clip of William Levi Dawson's arrangement of "Deep River," performed by the Tuskegee Institute Choir, which set the somber and spiritual tone for each broadcast.[17]

While all of his programs attracted large audiences, the most popular program was *Panorama du jazz américain* (*Panorama of American Jazz*), which was broadcast on Saturdays at midday (12:18 or 12:20). As its name suggests, the program featured a wide range of American jazz, including New Orleans, swing, and modern, all pulled from Copans's vast library of commercial and noncommercial records. Its opening *indicatif* was "Metronome All Out," a 1946 big band recording arranged by Duke Ellington and Billy Strayhorn. This program was the first to attract both the attention and the ire of French listeners, many of whom were sharply divided between the adherence to traditional and modern jazz. Just a few months earlier, this same rift had led to the permanent fracture of the Hot Club de France and the creation of rival fan clubs, critical magazines, and even radio programs that propagated different genres and musicians. By late 1946, RDF regularly broadcast jazz programs by Hugues Panassié, the leader of the traditionalists, who was joined on the radio in 1947 by Charles Delaunay, the recognized figurehead of the modernists and editor of the fan magazine *Jazz hot*.[18] Mindful of these polarizing debates over what constituted "good, real, and authentic jazz," Copans was initially focused on not alienating his diverse audience of critics, collectors, musicians, and fans.[19] To achieve this balance, he gestured toward American expertise, citing in his first broadcast those records chosen by American critics and musicians in a recent *Esquire* poll.

As wary of his relationship to the US State Department as they were about his musical choices, the readers and editors of *Jazz hot* were not impressed. Reporting on *Panorama* in early 1947, one reviewer compared him unfavorably to Bravig Imbs, Copans's former OWI colleague whose passion for jazz was matched by his enthusiasm for American exceptionalism.[20] By limiting his definition of jazz expertise to US critics, Copans had insulted French critics, fans, and musicians and personified the arrogance of Americans, who, "since they think they won the war and discovered the atomic bomb—but didn't suffer the bombings and occupation—now believe that anything is permissible!" The reviewer ended by suggesting that "Mr. Simon X" read the work of French critics, "who first revealed to the world, and to the United States" an art form that white Americans "disdained because it was created by blacks." While this review referenced a long-standing position of French jazz critics—who juxtaposed American racism with French colorblindness to establish their own aesthetic credentials—it responded to a new set of political and cultural conditions established by the Cold War. Indeed, Copans had joined the State Department just as the United States inaugurated a foreign policy platform in which the quest to eradicate the purported threat of communism justified unprecedented expenditures in the US military and propaganda services. While the reverberations of the Cold War were widespread (and were particularly devastating in the nonaligned "Third World") this policy shift was felt keenly in France, which was seen as the "keystone of continental Western

Europe" in the effort to combat communism.[21] Because of its size and power, and the recent success of the French Communist Party in national elections, France was the largest recipient of American aid, totaling approximately $2.9 billion, allocated by the Marshall Plan (or ECA) for reconstruction in Europe. Both the ECA's Mission France and the State Department's office at the Paris embassy funded publications, lectures, exhibits, and radio programs, all of which aimed to show American culture and society in the best light possible.

Further amplifying its policy aims were the direct broadcasts of Voice of America (VOA) programming, which, US officials claimed, reached 20 percent of the French adult population by 1949, roughly 4.5 million people.[22] Indeed, French observers were concerned about this direct form of "Trumanian propaganda," but they were most alarmed by the presence of American VOA officials on the French radio itself, referring to "an American occupation that one hears."[23] In this regard, Copans was not simply an exemplar of Yankee arrogance but also of American power. Introduced before each of his weekly programs as the official "delegate of the Voice of America" to RTF, he was frequently the direct target of news outlets associated with the French Communist Party, including the weekly magazine *Radio revue,* as well as daily newspapers *Ce soir* and *Humanité.* In 1950, *Ce soir* reported that French culture had been "systematically and progressively excluded" from radio programs since January 1947, "to the benefit of diversionary programs of the genre of those created by M. Sim Kopans [*sic*], official delegate of the 'Voice of America' in Paris."[24] As the article declared, the "radio is no longer French but . . . American. It is necessary to liberate it." Articulated within the discourses of liberation and occupation, this critique found in Copans the embodiment of American power. While the communist press continued to critique VOA's imperial ambition, it appeared increasingly resigned to its subtle power. Indeed, Copans's programming of Negro spirituals, jazz, and folklore had simply become too good.

Writing with evident frustration in 1948 regarding recent jazz and Negro spirituals programming, one author described how, "very subtly, America has produced excellent programs, whose propaganda is so nuanced that you swallow it, surprised at yourself upon further reflection."[25] In 1949, a *Radio revue* journalist's own springtime reverie of the diverse sounds of the state-run radio was tarnished by the knowledge that RDF had for so long "been cheating on him with America . . . in the arms of Simon Copans."[26] While the communist press critiqued the insidious yet seductive power of the US propaganda machine, critics in the center-right press unabashedly celebrated the large number of "jazz fans who find themselves glued to the radio set on Saturdays" to hear the "judicious and impartial choices of M. Simon Copans."[27] That same year, after comparing Copans to other jazz programs, a reviewer in the Protestant weekly *Réforme-Paris* endorsed *Panorama* for fans of classical music who wanted to "encounter black music."[28] In 1951, the weekly arts journal *Opéra* remarked that "no one can deny any longer that jazz is a valid and authentic musical language," noting in particular the programs of Copans.[29] In all of these accounts, Copans appears to have effectively domesticated jazz within the French soundscape, where his "impartial" choices had demonstrated the validity and value of jazz.

Against this critical backdrop of passionate defectors and enthusiasts, Copans cultivated a wide-ranging audience of listeners for *Panorama du jazz américain*. In all cases, his listeners benefited from the programs' prime broadcasting hours on the French radio. In contrast to the majority of jazz programs, which aired late at night, *Panorama du jazz américain* was broadcast on Saturdays at midday, when most people were off work and at home. His youngest listeners had just enough time to run home from their compulsory Saturday school lessons to hear the program start at 12:18 or 12:20. And thanks to the hour and day, Copans's listening audience also included those listeners whose relationship to the music was more casual, distracted, or even openly antagonistic.[30] Journalist Bernard Demory recalled listening to Copans on the family radio set, hoping to catch the strains of Louis Armstrong or Duke Ellington "in the midst of the shouts of my father, who ordered me to stop listening to this *musique de nègres*."[31] For these listeners, his programs were integrated into everyday life. In 1978, novelist Georges Perec catalogued his youthful postwar memories: "I remember the holes in the metro tickets," "I remember May 68," and no. 190: "I remember the jazz broadcasts of Sim Copans."[32] Like those that precede and follow it, this memory is stated simply and offered without explanation or assessment. Copans's radio programs were just one of the many "small fragments of everyday life," one of "the things that in this or that year, every one of the same age saw, experienced, and shared," part of the ephemera of daily life.[33]

In addition to its more quotidian importance to French listeners, *Panorama* also attracted a cadre of faithful adherents. This included the many young listeners afflicted with tuberculosis, who listened to his programs with particular fidelity. When in 1948 Copans promised to dedicate his Christmas Day *Panorama* program to a group of students in a sanatorium in Neufmoutiers-en-Brie, the students described the "great joy" this news had created, promising that "on this day, everyone will be listening to Paris Inter."[34] Writing from the Sanatorium de Belligneux in Hauteville in 1953, J. Jean Mornet thanked Copans for the many "happy moments" his programs had provided for him and his classmates before asking if he might send some records that they might in turn microbroadcast to the other 2,500 tuberculosis patients in residence. The signatures of twenty students at the bottom of the letter must have charmed Copans, who sent them a dozen recordings by Duke Ellington, Sidney Bechet, Don Byas, and Django Reinhardt.[35] In 1948, Copans opened his studio to his young listeners, who were invited to bring in their favorite jazz records to the show. That way, Copans observed, "from one week to the next, the listener judges for himself, and not according to my choice."[36] This programmatic decision in turn helped to cultivate a new generation of jazz critics. Among Copans's young guests were future radio and television producers like André Clergeat, Jean-Christophe Averty, and Yann Gillot, as well as future jazz radio host Daniel Filipacchi, who came twice to present some "splendid Duke Ellingtons" from his father's collection (see figure 5.1).[37] For future blues critic Jacques Demêtre, Copans's radio programs were like "oxygen."[38] For jazz photographer Jean-Pierre Leloir, Copans's programs were "the one reason for wanting to be alive on Saturdays." After classes finished, he ran from his *lycée* across the street to the local branch of the Hot Club, where he listened to *Panorama* while completing his physics and chemistry homework. Leloir recalled: "We didn't have many jazz records then," and the recordings they did have were mostly of "local musicians interpreting what they had heard on records." By contrast, "Copans gave us the original records, and explained the genealogy of every band." Even after several hours of classroom instruction on Saturday mornings, Leloir cherished this opportunity to hear different musicians, genres, and band formations given meaning and value within a kind of jazz "genealogy."[39]

In addition to the program's content, Leloir and others were especially drawn to Copans's voice, which was described as sober and composed, yet still seemed open and friendly.[40] Leloir found that Copans's "American accent made him very kind," affirming his own sense that "we could trust him on American jazz." He trusted Copans because he was American, for "he had been there," where he had presumably gained direct access to African American life and culture.[41] Copans thus appeared to serve as a means of maintaining fidelity to African American music while reinforcing his own primacy to this encounter. Also important was the fact that his voice moved effortlessly between French and English. Ever sympathetic to his audience's difficulty in understanding the accents and allusions in songs and titles, Copans translated the lyrics, titles, references, and musicians' names with precision and authority. While easily comprehensible in French, when he would "announce the name of the U.S. jazz record he is about to play," his American identity was clear.[42] Bernard Vincent, who went on to direct the French Association for American Studies, contrasted

FIGURE 5.1. Sim Copans with some of his young listeners, who came to the studio with their favorite records. Photo courtesy of the Copans Family Archive.

the kindness, warmth, and slight American accent in Copans's voice with the harshness of German voices.[43] Moreover, Copans did not sound like most RTF announcers, who employed a formal tone and didactic style. Although he was erudite and intelligent, he nonetheless sounded friendly, enthusiastic, and young. One listener was reportedly horrified on learning that Copans was a middle-aged man "with a pronounced tendency to baldness," rather than the twenty-five-year-old he had imagined.[44]

As these recollections reveal, his listeners were imagining Copans's body even as they listened to his musical selections. While he was driven to translate—literally and figuratively—this material for his French audiences, listeners were still conscious of his physical and racial presence. Copans's racial identity would never have been announced on the radio, but his assumed white identity still shaped the listening experience, for it enabled listeners to listen to African American music without being near—sonically or physically—African Americans.[45] In these listener experiences are echoes of Jennifer Stoever's "sonic color line," wherein the "listening ear" functions as "an organ of racial discernment, categorization, and resistance."[46] Likewise, his audience discerned in

Copans an authoritative (and white) voice who explained and in many ways cultivated the experience of hearing Black musicians.

The *Negro Spirituals* program, though considerably shorter, was also renowned for Copans's musical choices and presentation. Described as "sober, direct, and very likeable," the program featured what Copans considered to be the primary sources of African American music, including recordings made in churches and by the New Deal's Works Progress Administration (WPA) field recorders in addition to better-known records of gospel and formal spiritual choirs.[47] As Copans wrote later, he considered the spiritual to be the root of jazz, one of "the depositories of the African elements that gave birth to this powerful and varied folklore."[48] In a typical program in March 1949, Copans introduced recordings by two vocal groups whose performance style was traditionally considered to be gospel: the Golden Gate Quartet, with performances of "The Rocks and the Mountain" and "There Is a Light Shining," and the Delta River Boys, with the recording "Scandalize My Name."[49] He then played two pieces that represented the classical spiritual tradition. The first was Marian Anderson's "Fix Me Jesus," followed by Paul Robeson's "Sometimes I Feel like a Motherless Child."[50]

While these recordings encompassed a wide range of African American spiritual music, Copans grouped them under the category of "Negro spiritual," which was common on the French radio. Most French enthusiasts did not understand the lyrics; one French Negro spirituals choir leader claimed that one could "simply say 'Mm' and it's very pretty."[51] Like his contemporary Louis Achille, Copans valued the accuracy of language, always translating the titles and lyrics for his listeners, and tied it to the experience of African Americans. In Copans's programs, the spiritual appeared not as undifferentiated sound but instead as an articulation of hope, sadness, pain, and suffering.[52] A later report by the Office de la Radiodiffusion et Télévision Française (ORTF) attributed the success of the long-running program to its "simplicity" and its "high standards." It further reported that Copans had a "lot of ease at the microphone" and that he commented on the recordings "with intelligence," offering helpful information and "a succinct translation of each song."[53] The lone dissenter was the Catholic newspaper *La Croix,* which reviewed the program in 1952 and found it "uninteresting" and rather "breathless."[54]

By the early 1950s, as new technologies and networks expanded the radio listening audience, Copans's programs were heard by an increasingly large number of people throughout metropolitan France. Though its reach was initially limited to the Parisian region, by 1952 Paris Inter had become a national presence and, moreover, one of the most popular stations in the RTF network.[55]

In 1953, roughly 90 percent of the population had a radio set, up from less than half in the interwar period, and the average French adult listened to two hours of radio per day.[56] Within this growing audience, Copans continued to bring in large numbers of listeners, prompting RTF director Wladmir Porché in 1952 to comment on his "considerable French audience" and Artistic Director Paul Gilson to characterize Copans's programs as having "uninterrupted success."[57] When Paris Inter's director, Jean-Vincent Brechnigac, wrote Copans directly to express his satisfaction, he cited ratings from a recent French listening study, which had found that the *Negro Spirituals* program brought in nine hundred thousand regular listeners, that *L'Amérique et sa musique* had 1.2 million, and that *Panorama du jazz américain* drew in approximately 1.5 million listeners per week. Furthermore, the report speculated that the audience for Copans's other musical and variety program, *Tour du monde autour d'une table* (*World Tour around a Table*), was likely 2.5 million listeners, a figure enabled by its slot just before the Sunday evening news.[58]

Throughout this period of growing popularity, Copans was employed by the US government, first at the State Department and then at the United States Information Agency (USIA), where information and propaganda activities were transferred in 1953.[59] However, on January 15, 1954, within a year of the French listening study, Copans officially resigned from the USIA. He did so in a period of tremendous political pressure and restructuring for State Department employees, whose political views, sexuality, and allegiances were questioned surreptitiously or openly in interviews and hearings.[60] Although Copans had previously identified with leftist politics, he had not only avoided any political party or demonstrations since at the State Department but had himself also regularly participated in its monitoring of the communist press. Despite this participation in anticommunist work, Copans's commitment to African American culture put him in a more precarious place.

While some State Department officials had begun to value African American music as a means of cultural diplomacy, others regarded Copans's interest in jazz, along with an attachment to French culture, as evidence of communist tendencies. Copans later recounted being "summoned to an office at the American Embassy," where he was accused of "dishonouring the United States by playing folk music and jazz."[61] He also recalled the concern of US government officials that he was "too closely attached to the French radio."[62] This ambivalence would soon change, for in crafting a positive image of American society, US officials faced growing international concern regarding the treatment of African Americans in the United States. This political crisis built on decades of activism by African Americans, who had long enlisted global networks and transnational institutions to fight racism and imperialism.[63] However, the end of World War II marked a new era of "Cold War civil rights," within which policy-makers, politicians, and activists advocated or resisted social change on a global stage.[64] In response to this shifting terrain, US State Department officials based in France began to feature African Americans—and African American music—in their publications intended for French audiences.[65] In addition to local campaigns, the Voice of America would later broadcast jazz programs by Willis Conover, whose English-language *Music U.S.A.* program reiterated that the love of American jazz was synonymous with loving freedom and that it corrected the "fiction that America is racist."[66]

In the early 1950s, however, this particular Cold War campaign was still nascent and Copans's situation more precarious.[67] With an established life in France, where he lived with his French wife and two children, Copans potentially feared the possible repercussions, including reappointment, termination, or the forced return to the United States. Even though it meant leaving a post with substantial economic and political benefits, Copans sought greater personal freedom and job security. Moreover, by leaving, Copans gained the "rather peculiar advantage of being an ex-official" in the US Information Service (USIS), free to begin "free-lancing in a dozen fields."[68] He was no longer "subject to following directives from any official source" and therefore had time to experiment with new forms of radio and television programming, whose reach into the provinces and empire continued to grow. While Copans's departure was officially attributed to his desire to return to academic work, within a few months of leaving Copans reappeared on Paris Inter with the same programs, albeit with different titles: *L'Amérique et sa musique* had become *Regards sur la musique américaine* (*A Look at American Music*), *Panorama du jazz américain* had become *Jazz en liberté* (*Jazz at Large* or *Jazz on the Loose*), and *Negro Spirituals* had been renamed *Fleuve profond* (*Deep River*). Now introduced as the *former* delegate of the Voice of America, Copans hosted his regular weekly programs as well as a biweekly program, *Actualités du disque aux États-Unis* (*Recording News from the United States*), on the new *modulation de fréquence* (FM) station Haute Fidelité (later France IV, then France Musique), created in 1954 specifically to broadcast music. In addition, Copans hosted the rebroadcast of US festivals and programs, including the Newport Jazz Festival, as well as local concerts and regional festivals in France (see figure 5.2).

Critical to this broader reach was the commercialization of the transistor radio in the mid- to late 1950s, which meant that Copans's audiences were no longer tethered to a console radio that was typically placed in the living room. With a small, portable device, they could listen to the radio while preparing

FIGURE 5.2. Sim Copans backstage at the 1958 Festival de Jazz de Cannes, where he would introduce trumpeter Roy Eldridge (seated) and saxophonist Coleman Hawkins (standing). Photo courtesy of the Copans Family Archive.

dinner, while driving, or in the privacy of the bedroom. This new device also diversified his listening audience. Between 1957 and 1959, Copans received at least five hundred listener letters, which reveal that his audience included housewives, children, teachers, marketing consultants, priests, business owners, musicians, record shop owners, restaurant and hotel owners, doctors, bankers, and archivists.[69] Many wrote to express their admiration for *Fleuve profond* and to pose specific questions: the name of a singer, a track name, or where to buy a record. Roughly one-third of the letters were from women or girls, indicating a diversity of listeners not always acknowledged by the male world of French jazz criticism.[70] Only one-fifth of the letters were from the Paris region, suggesting that the majority of listeners lived in the provinces, in overseas France, and even in neighboring countries.

Copans's overseas transistor audience included some of the 2 million French soldiers deployed in North Africa during the course of the Algerian War (1954–62). Many of these soldiers were especially captivated by *Fleuve profond*. In 1957, Copans received a letter from Sous-lieutenant Leurquin, who was "struck" by the "poetic realism" of a funeral song sung by Harry Belafonte.[71] Sergeant Fernand Villette, an "avid listener" of his programs, wrote to find out the name of a particular record.[72] One corporal described how, when listening to *Fleuve profond*, he was "literally captivated by the musical beauty and the spiritual profundity of the 'Negro Spirituals.'" Because he was "currently in the service of the AFN [in this case, Afrique Française du Nord]," the radiophonic transmission was scrambled and he couldn't catch the titles or singers.[73] While the corporal's account offers few details, it is clear that Copans's programs were part of the everyday life of military service in the Algerian War, accompanying the conflict's violent and routine existence.[74] Copans later claimed that his program was also popular among the combatants in the Front de Libération Nationale (FLN), who gathered to collectively listen to *Fleuve profond* "because that gave us enough courage to last into the week."[75] In these accounts, we see the conflicting legacy of Copans's voice. On one hand, it accompanied the sounds of African American music, which was interpreted as a form of spiritual power and sustenance by combatants on both sides. On the other hand, it was the sound of Cold War power, the "voice of the occupier," as Frantz Fanon argued more broadly in his analysis of colonial radio in Algeria.[76] However, while Radio Alger was a technology of dehumanization and humiliation, Copans's programs broadcast a liberatory soundscape that nevertheless intimated the reach of a new world power.

Building on this larger reach, in 1954, Copans expanded his repertoire to include the history of African American music. That same year, he made several appearances on the radio program *Jeunesse magazine* (*Youth Magazine*) to present short segments on jazz history in Chicago and New Orleans.[77] Hoping to establish its cultural value, he first identified the influence of French composers like Claude Debussy and Darius Milhaud. But Copans also explored its "sources," including marches, Creole quadrilles, and "most of all," he said, "its black musical heritage."[78] Several years later, Copans partnered with producer Jean-Christophe Averty, one of the young record collectors who had first visited his studio in the late 1940s, to create *Jazz Memories*, the first jazz television program for the RTF.[79] Each episode took up a theme—"Way down the Mississippi," Scott Joplin, or Prohibition—to explore the history of jazz but began with footage of young people dancing at the Caveau de la Huchette in Paris to the sounds of Maxim Saury's band. The camera then turned to Copans, whose voice narrated that week's musical history, which was then illustrated by historical images intercut with footage of Saury's white band, the dancers, and photographs of Black musicians, who all sometimes appeared simultaneously on screen. A 1959 episode, which was broadcast "live from the Club Saint-Germain," featured jazz musicians living in Paris, including Bud Powell,

FIGURE 5.3. Sim Copans with trumpeter Bill Coleman on the set of the television program *Jazz Memories,* which was directed by Jean-Christophe Averty, 1959. Photo courtesy of Getty.

Kenny Clarke, and Bill Coleman (see figure 5.3). As on the radio, Copans mediated the imagined relationship between his audience and African American communities; now televised, his body *and* voice demonstrated his authority.[80]

Rooting Jazz

Building on these televised jazz histories, Copans began to give public lectures on the history of African American music with USIA support. While he had resigned from the agency in 1954, he had maintained good relations with many of his former USIA colleagues, who helped arrange nearly two hundred public lectures between 1954 and 1960. In this period, Copans lectured throughout France, at tuberculosis sanatoriums, town halls, schools, libraries, military hospitals, and municipal cultural centers, where his audiences ranged in size from intimate gatherings of fifty people to large lecture halls of fifteen hundred. While Copans occasionally lectured on folk music, the vast majority of his presentations charted the "origins of jazz from the Slave Coast to New Orleans" ("Les origines du jazz; de la côte des esclaves à la Nouvelle Orléans"). In this format, Copans was able to assume a more explicitly pedagogical approach to explain the evolution and cultivation of jazz, which he defined as a historical and sociocultural form created by the movement of people, culture, and commodities in the Atlantic world.

Copans's first major lecture tour was in December 1955 in the Burgundy region. As would be the case with most of his tours, it was initiated by USIS officials based in the regional office in Lyon and the cultural division in Paris. These offices, part of the larger USIA network, were charged with promoting American culture and politics abroad. In France, the USIS had established *centres culturels américains* (American Cultural Centers) in major provincial cities, including Lyon, Bordeaux, Lille, Strasbourg, Marseille, Tunis, and Algiers. In addition to providing meeting spaces, book and record libraries, regular exhibitions and lectures, and film screenings, these cultural centers frequently sponsored jazz-related content, including concerts, music lectures, and jazz listening clubs.[81] While these USIS regional offices organized, monitored, and promoted Copans's provincial tours, he nonetheless relied on the financial support and resources of local organizations and civic associations. As diplomatic historians have argued, these forms of mediation and negotiation were key dimensions of cultural diplomacy in this period.[82] For the 1955 Burgundy tour, for example, the USIS Lyon office worked closely with the Association Bourguignonne Culturelle (Burgundy Cultural Association) in Dijon.[83] In fact, while the USIS had initially requested that Copans lecture on American folklore, the association had insisted on jazz.[84] For this tour, Copans's ten-thousand-franc lecture fee was paid by the Lyon regional office, while his transportation and per diem costs were paid by USIS Paris. This would end soon after, in 1956, when the local sponsoring organizations paid the lecture fees themselves.

As Copans wrote the local organizer in Dijon, his goal in the lecture was "to show, with numerous musical illustrations," that American jazz "can be understood by the persistent African influence on the folkloric music of southern black Americans."[85] This decision was based in his deepening knowledge of the slave trade and his understanding that most enslaved people in North and South America were from West Africa. Copans grounded the history of jazz in African and African American musical traditions, frequently playing traditional African music alongside African American folk songs, and incorporating the latest academic research on Atlantic cultural exchange into his remarks. Though he retained the pedagogical tone, language, and institutional support of the French radio, Copans was quite unlike French jazz critics.[86] He was, however, similar to his contemporary Marshall Stearns, who was likewise known to be erudite and articulate, a "savant without being a pedant," and would also be engaged by the State Department in international performance tours.[87] As white men, Stearns and Copans enjoyed largely unquestioned authority with their audiences and patrons, while Black writers and musicians—like Stearns's collaborator, musician Randy Weston—did not experience the same immediate respect.[88]

Rather than focusing on jazz in France or the significance of French critics to jazz, Copans focused on the links among European, African, and African American cultures. To demonstrate the contours of this transatlantic exchange at the root of jazz history, Copans built his lectures around musical recordings played on long-playing and 78 rpm records with his three-speed *pick-up* (record player).[89] In fact, in the course of his lectures, Copans typically played forty to fifty musical excerpts culled from his own collection, which comprised nearly 60 percent of his two-hour lecture. He created a kind of living liner note, adding value and meaning to the musical selections but also, by asking his audience to listen collectively to these "sonic documents," creating the conditions for the audience itself to "draw the connections together" without necessarily making "definitive conclusions."[90] Copans again struck an ostensibly democratic tone, though one that did not threaten his own academic authority. After introducing the material, Copans opened his lecture with the sounds of a men's choir accompanied by drums. He then played songs from Brazil, Haiti, and Cuba, many of which were recorded by Melville Herskovits in the 1940s, and all of which prominently featured polyrhythmic drumming.[91] Indeed, Copans was clearly influenced by this approach to music, but as he lacked training in ethnomusicology, he preferred to showcase rather than explain the sonic connections.[92] He argued that "the musical and cultural distance between Nigeria and the United States was larger than between Nigeria and Brazil, Haiti, and Cuba," but "even in the United States, one finds survivals." To show this, Copans paired "Bara-Sanabo-Bara" with a 1950 musical excerpt of Rosie Hibler and her family in Alabama, "My Name Has Been Written Down," included in the same edited collection, and noted that "the clapping of hands has replaced the drums."[93] He emphasized the responsive singing, rhythmic punctuation, falsetto voice, and humming style, all of which, he argued, demonstrated the reach of West African musical and rhythmic traditions into the American South.[94] Copans told the audience, "It is clear that there are differences among these songs that you have just heard. What is extraordinary is that there are so few."[95]

Moving next to the *folklore noir* of the US South, Copans continued to place these recordings next to recordings from West Africa, crossing the Atlantic many times over in the course of his presentation. After underscoring again that he hoped his audience would "make the connections" themselves, Copans played recordings of Mano children in Liberia and children in Alabama—including "I'm Goin' Up North" and "Little Sallie Walker"—and drew attention to the call-and-response and handclapping featured in each.[96] He next played blues songs, work songs recorded in Liberia, Alabama, and

Texas, and then spiritual music, comparing recordings made in Côte d'Ivoire to Rosie Hibler's "Move Members Move" and then to spirituals recorded with congregations in New York, Alabama, Los Angeles, and Washington, DC. Copans next led his audience to the birth of jazz in New Orleans by drawing together these musical roots: blues, spirituals, work songs, and children's songs, the "first material of jazz." He then introduced several early recordings made in New Orleans, including "High Society" by King Oliver and the Creole Jazz Band, a spiritual by George Lewis's band, a recording of "Les oignons" by Albert Nicholas, and "Perdido Street Blues" by Johnny Dodds.[97] If time permitted, he ended by quickly sketching the development of jazz from 1920 to the present, illustrated with recordings by Duke Ellington, Count Basie, Mahalia Jackson, and Big Bill Broonzy. He apologized for not spending more time on contemporary jazz, but pointed out that "jazz is very much a living thing." Instead, he ended by noting that, after centuries of movement across the Atlantic, jazz rhythms "had once again remade the tour of the world."[98] By ending his account in the 1920s, Copans skirted the questions that would emerge as jazz moved into the commercial sphere and recorded sound to maintain his focus on the Afro-Atlantic world.

This first major lecture tour in Burgundy was a resounding success, drawing nearly three hundred people in Mâcon and sixty in the tiny town of Avallon, which was considered an impressive feat on a rainy Sunday night.[99] Local newspapers praised Copans for being erudite, professional, and thorough in his presentation. The local paper in Mâcon reported on the audience's thrilling travels through "three centuries of jazz in two hours." It noted that the origins of jazz could be traced to the seventeenth century, when French slave ships from Bordeaux, La Rochelle, and Nantes bought slaves cheaply on the coast of West Africa. It lauded Copans's comparative structure, praising his use of contemporary recordings from Alabama alongside those from "the AOF [French West Africa] and AEF [French Equatorial Africa]."[100] Embedded in this account were references not only to French slavery, and its implementation in the French Antilles, but also to contemporary colonial federations. Following his successful tour, the organizer in Mâcon thanked Copans again for the "masterful way in which you presented jazz to our young compatriots," which guaranteed a large audience for Sidney Bechet's concert there just a month later.[101] The organizer in Mâcon invited Copans to return in the fall of 1956 to give a lecture on nineteenth-century poet and politician Alphonse de Lamartine. Copans reported this invitation to the sponsoring USIS official, noting with pride that this invitation "proves that jazz opens all doors."[102] Copans's jazz lectures were soon opening doors across France with the continued partnership with

USIS regional offices and the organization France-États-Unis, which operated its own cultural centers throughout hexagonal France.[103] There were reports of local libraries "filled to capacity" and of crowds that "overflowed into the corridors" in Strasbourg. In November 1958, Copans, "always a crowd-puller," brought in 775 people in Rouen and St. Omer, where he lectured on Negro spirituals and the origins of jazz.[104] In 1958, one official lauded Copans's "particular knack for drawing in the public, in spite of the political atmosphere"—an allusion to the specter of the Algerian War.[105]

While USIS's own political interest was critical to the lecture tours, its success depended on the agency's partnership with the established networks of civic associations and national organizations that frequently sponsored Copans's tours. In October 1955, for example, while the request for a four-day lecture tour in the Lyon region originated with the USIS regional office, it was local organizations that ensured the audience and helped determine the lecture content. In Vienne, Copans was sponsored by the Cercle Artistique et Littéraire (Artistic and Literary Circle), who "insisted on opening" their season with Copans "because they felt that it would assure the success of their succeeding programs." They were thrilled when his lecture on the origins of American jazz drew in eighty audience members, many "already addicted to his radio broadcasts."[106] Lectures were frequently cosponsored by youth organizations, including the Hot Club de France, but also other youth organizations that were not organized around jazz fandom.[107] This included the Maisons des Jeunes et de la Culture (MJC), which comprised a large network of youth clubs and "cultural leisure centers" throughout France and its overseas departments and territories, and the Jeunesses Musicales de France (JMF), a state-sponsored youth music organization with over two hundred thousand members in metropolitan and overseas France.[108] The Hot Club could guarantee an enthusiastic crowd, as in Nîmes, whose local lecture hall was filled with "a very large audience, formed mostly of young people driven 'mad' by jazz and rhythm."[109] Although the JMF was a youth-oriented organization, it had until the mid-1950s eschewed jazz in its programs and concerts, limiting its activities to European classical music.[110] Beginning in 1955, the JMF began sponsoring African American music, including a national tour of jump blues pianist Sammy Price and one by the Fisk Jubilee Singers. Hoping to include an article on the history of jazz in its newsletter in preparation for Price, a JMF chapter in Poitiers had found that their usual musicologist was not up to the task. Instead, they asked Copans, who had previously delivered a lecture in Poitiers on American folklore.[111] While Copans declined an invitation in October 1956 to visit local JMF branches in North African cities—likely reluctant to travel in the midst of Algerian War hostilities—he frequently lectured before young people confined to military hospitals as they recovered from injuries sustained in the Algerian War.[112] Doctors could care for their physical treatment, the organizer indicated, but he believed that Copans might give them spiritual relief.[113]

Just as radio listeners were taken by in by Copans's voice, reports suggested that the positive response of these diverse lecture audiences was linked to his familiarity with French language and culture. Indeed, Copans's "flawless French" was noted in almost all reports.[114] One newspaper claimed that Copans "expresses himself so well in our language . . . that one has difficulty imagining that he is a foreigner."[115] Many also noted his academic training, finding that it was a "pleasure" to hear this "former student at the Sorbonne," who speaks "with great erudition," but without the "pomposity" that characterized some academics.[116] Other reports noted with interest the "exceptional documentary wealth assembled by the speaker" and the "sonic anthology that crackled on the *pick-up* thanks to the engraved wax . . . those black suns."[117] One reviewer praised the fact that Copans did not "meticulously dissect the evolution of jazz" but, rather, stayed in the background, facilitating "an easy coming and going between Africa and America."[118] Because Copans played different records alongside one another, the audience heard a "sonic parallel between the recordings of the rhythms of little-evolved tribes of the Congo and those by folk singers in Cuba."[119] Within these musical interludes, the audience saw Copans standing next to the record player, a visual confirmation that while these racialized sounds echoed in "civilized" spaces, they had been safely ferried into them by a cultured, white, and erudite intermediary. In fact, many reports contrasted the lecture's subject and the lecture hall itself, noting, in one case, that jazz had entered the conservatory "on the run and by the back door."[120] One report described how the Mozart room had become "for two hours the temple of jazz and one of the contrasts of our time," and another pointed out that for the first time, "the Rameau Hall had resounded with the notes of Louis Armstrong and Duke Ellington."[121]

When Copans lectured in March 1958 in Marseille at the municipal opera, reports noted with surprise that the lecture by this "excellent jazz teacher" had failed to result in a fistfight. Though it noted the presence of "agitated young people in black duffle-coats," Copans had nonetheless helped jazz acquire its "titles of nobility in breaching the Opera" and showed that jazz had no connection to "broken chairs," a clear reference to Bechet's infamous concert.[122] In January 1956, when Copans lectured before "two hundred future jurists" in Paris, reports described audience members who had taken the available chairs "by storm" but had done so "very peacefully." In all of these cases, Copans was perceived to have established the cultural credentials of jazz. It was no longer the province of young people—perhaps best embodied by Copans himself, who was evidently middle-aged—but instead appeared to be a legitimate cultural tradition that had "henceforth gained the right of citizenship." Moreover, many noted how jazz itself had "evolved" as it "crossed the Atlantic" and been further "refined" and "civilized" by its movement and the "constant infusions of European music."[123] These references to evolution, refinement, and civilization underscore a key point: Copans had not just presented jazz but had, in the eyes of his audience, literally civilized it. In this, Copans spoke to a broader preoccupation in this period with the civilizing process at home, the vanguard of a cultural model that would be institutionalized within the next few years, reimagining and reordering the borders of white French cultural supremacy beyond the metropole.

Locating the African Origins of Jazz

Amid this success, in December 1959 Copans began to decline invitations to give lectures outside Paris. This was due in large part to his family commitments and his involvement with the creation of the first Institute for American Studies (Institut d'Études Américaines) in France.[124] However, he made one exception to this rule. Since the 1950s, Copans had grown increasingly interested in presenting his lecture on jazz history to African and Antillean students. In 1958, one African student in Paris wrote of his delight in seeing Copans give a lecture and his disappointment that it was so short.[125] In 1959, at the Centre Culturel Américain in Paris, Copans's lecture on jazz history was sponsored by the MJC and an organization that a USIS official referred to as the Maisons des Jeunes d'Afrique Noire.[126] In 1962, the Union des Étudiants Catholiques Africains in Paris sponsored a lecture by Copans that would link West African musical traditions to the Negro spiritual. The organizer, Père Desobry, had approached Copans after some of his students had attended another of Copans's lectures on "African music and its negro-American survivals." They were "so enthusiastic that they would like the other members of a group of Catholic African students in Paris to benefit."[127] As these students had all been educated within a system that was predicated on the French *mission civilisatrice* and were therefore likely very aware of the possible repercussions of identifying with a cultural form deemed uncivilized or unevolved, this request indicates the extent of Copans's success in "civilizing" jazz before French audiences. While his duties at the institute grew, Copans was inspired by the enthusiastic response of African students and eager to see firsthand what he believed was the source of jazz. He was also responding to work by African American musicians and writers, including the poet Langston Hughes. In 1962, Copans wrote an introduction to the French translation of Hughes's own introduction to jazz, in which Copans highlighted the "return to sources" in modern jazz. He had been particularly struck by Art Blakey's statement, in a November 1959 interview by Copans, that jazz originated in Africa.[128]

With a growing interest in the African continent, in December 1963 Copans made what would be the first of many trips there, where he gave lectures on the "African influences on the origins of Negro spirituals and jazz" ("influences Africaines sur les origines des négro spirituals et du jazz") in Dakar (Senegal), Conakry (Guinea), Abidjan (Côte d'Ivoire), Douala (Cameroon), Brazzaville (Republic of the Congo), Léopoldville, now Kinshasa (Democratic Republic of the Congo), Bangui (Central African Republic), and Fort-Lamy, now N'Djamena (Chad). During this tour, he participated in eighteen radio programs and four television programs, and made contacts with local *lycées*, *écoles supérieures*, record labels, radio stations, and musicians. Once again, the USIS played a direct role in organizing, financing, and assessing his tours in Africa. While Copans relied on the USIS infrastructure for financial and logistical support and often presented at the local American cultural center, he sometimes struck out on his own, pursuing an independent intellectual agenda. In almost every town he visited, Copans visited local record stores, bars, and bookstores, took in local music, and met with African students, musicians, specialists, radio personalities, and intellectuals. However, as his son, Jean Copans, has noted elsewhere, when Sim Copans traveled to African cities, he still largely inhabited a European colonial world.[129]

Similar to those in metropolitan France, Copans's African audiences were already familiar with his voice by virtue of the retransmission of French radio programs through postcolonial radio networks in Francophone Africa. Just as it had transformed listening practices in the metropole, the transistor radio was distributed widely by governmental and nongovernmental entities throughout France's overseas departments and territories in the Caribbean and Africa, where his listening audience continued to expand.[130] Until the transistor's popularization, radio listening had been, by virtue of the expense of radio receivers and batteries as well as the vagaries of infrastructure and climate, limited to either wealthy urban residents or to white French colonial families. By contrast, running on low-voltage and inexpensive batteries, the transistor was a boon to villages and remote hamlets, where a single radio set frequently served ten to twenty listeners.[131] In 1954, overseas radio stations were transferred to the authority of the Ministry of Overseas France, which maintained its own radio department.[132] This was the first in a succession of new overseas radio networks, all of which sought to secure for France the predominant radio position before and after the end of empire.

As early as 1958, Copans had secured contracts to broadcast both *Fleuve profond* and *Jazz en liberté* in the overseas departments and territories, first on the Société de Radiodiffusion de la France d'Outre-mer (SORAFOM) and then, in 1956, through the Office de Coopération Radiophonique (OCORA), which advised the new national radio networks in postcolonial Africa, including Radio Nationale Centrafricaine, Radio Côte d'Ivoire, Radio Dakar, Radio Mali, Radio Bangui, Radio Tchad, Radio Gabon, and Radio Congo.[133] In the first four years of independence, each of these postcolonial radio stations prominently featured two programs by Copans: *Jazz en liberté* and *Fleuve profond*. The *Fleuve profond* program was particularly well distributed. It appeared weekly on nearly every Francophone national radio station in Central and West Africa, including Senegal, Gabon, Guinea, Côte d'Ivoire, Cameroon, the Central African Republic, the former French Congo (Republic of the Congo), and Chad.[134] It was typically broadcast in the evening or on Sunday mornings, providing an ecumenical interlude between Catholic and Protestant religious programs.

As was the case in metropolitan France, Copans's radio popularity drew in large numbers of young people to his lectures, eager to hear jazz and to finally see Copans in person (see figures 5.4, 5.5, and 5.6). In Léopoldville, for example, Copans gave three lectures: one for the students at the Jesuit Université Lovanium, another for the students at the École Nationale de Droit et de l'Administration, and one at a final event for the Association Congo-Amérique. At the Université Lovanium, more than three hundred students reportedly attended his lecture. Though they had initially been concerned about attracting an audience, one USIS official remarked that Copans was already "something of a celebrity" among young people due to his popular radio shows. Other USIS officials in Léopoldville reported that his *Fleuve profond* program was a "regular feature" on the Brazza radio network.[135] And according to the newspaper reports of the lectures in Léopoldville, Copans was once again a huge success. The local newspaper reported that "one sees the smiles appear on the faces of a large number of listeners when the lecturer played several examples of black American folkloric music—the 'Negro spirituals'—which clearly betrayed their African origins."[136] Reports also noted that Copans met with a local singing group that specialized in the performance of Negro spirituals, having translated them into several Bantu languages (Lingala and Kikongo). Other reports noted how the students "reacted to Copans's humor, tapped their feet with the music, and registered satisfied recognition when African elements in American music came through clearly." These reports of tapping feet and smiling faces

FIGURE 5.4. Sim Copans gives a lecture to students in Senegal, either in Saint-Louis or Ziguinchor, during his 1967 tour. Photo courtesy of the Copans Family Archive.

were not incidental to USIS organizers, who were actively seeking audiences for American cultural programming. Apparently, his stay in Léopoldville "gave a substantial lift to the post's cultural and youth programs, providing an excellent opportunity for meaningful contact" with "prime target audiences."[137]

Despite the similarities to his activities in metropolitan France—the USIS support, the presence of young people, and his radio popularity—there were slight but meaningful shifts evident in the creation and reception of Copans's lectures in Africa. As one official noted, Copans was a "thoroughly professional performer" who did a "masterful job of adapting his talks to each audience." In addition, as evidenced by his own writing, Copans had become increasingly interested in the African influence on jazz. As he indicated in a 1963 interview in Abidjan, he had become even more "convinced that the true and first source of the folkloric music of black Americans was the rhythm of Africans who crossed the Atlantic."[138] While the lectures in provincial France had provided audiences a way to understand a foreign music in the context of decolonization, Copans's lectures in postcolonial Africa had a different effect. By

FIGURE 5.5. Sim Copans gives a lecture at the Centre Culturel Américain in Fort Lamy (later N'Djamena), Chad, in 1964. Photo courtesy of the Copans Family Archive.

affirming the importance of Africa to the history of jazz, he underscored the centrality of Africa to diasporic cultural formations, both past and present. In both European and African settings, Copans presented his lectures in fluent French, which immediately affirmed his credentials yet likely had a profoundly different effect on his audiences. Speaking in the language of a fallen empire with the accent of an emerging one, Copans signaled the emergence of a new postcolonial soundscape.

In the coming years, Copans continued to tour in West and North Africa, where his lectures attracted large numbers of young people. In Algiers in 1965, he reportedly told his audience that "jazz was the manifestation of the courage of man, who in searching to create an identity gave birth to one of the most beautiful forms

FIGURE 5.6. Sim Copans talking with two students after a lecture in Dakar, Senegal, during his 1967 tour. Photo courtesy of the Copans Family Archive.

of music. Jazz is the manifestation of a grand fraternity among all cultures."[139] A report the following day noted the "resonance" of these words among young people in Bône, where Copans was subjected to a "barrage of questions."[140] As a reporter at *El Moudjahid* noted: "With talent, but also with simplicity and with warmth, Sim Copans has shown the human side of jazz which somehow reconstitutes the tragic epic of millions of Africans."[141] Yet even as Copans's words created a new discursive space for understanding jazz in relation to slavery, colonialism, and empire, they were preserved through the careful observations and monitoring of the assigned Public Affairs Officer (PAO) and the US embassy in Algiers, which paid for expenses and travel and offered an honorarium for his efforts. As PAO Arthur Lee noted after the tours, it was "pleasant to note" that the Algerian press "gave spontaneous credit and praise to the American Cultural Center for bringing Sim Copans to Algeria." Lee was especially delighted, as this was the Center's "first major venture into cultural programming for the general public in Algeria," where US influence was tenuous at best.[142] Indeed, just two years later, Algeria would cut off diplomatic ties with the United States in the course of the Arab-Israeli War. In the interim, however, Copans had created new inroads for US diplomatic efforts, and his success, from the perspective of US officials, was rooted in his capacity to do so undetected.

In this regard, whether as the Voice of America's official delegate or as a free agent, Copans embodied the work of Cold War cultural diplomacy, which depended on local networks, social relationships, and an "intensive process of negotiation and engagement."[143] Furthermore, as Danielle Fosler-Lussier has shown, the State Department welcomed critiques of US power and racism, which it incorporated into a progressive, liberal narrative of social change in its cultural programming.[144] In this way, too, Copans fit the bill, as he rooted jazz in a history of slavery and oppression, yet also located in jazz a mode of transcendence and transformation. Finally, Copans's own elevation as a white expert within the field of African American music heralded later forms of Cold War jazz diplomacy, which, as Penny Von Eschen argues, depended on the same racist ideologies of authority and authenticity, and was likewise resistant to recognizing African American musicians' own authority on the subject.[145]

However, while they were indebted to the Cold War infrastructure, Copans's lectures and radio programs also troubled some of the same hierarchical structures that existed in France and the French empire. By affirming the African roots of African American music in a colonial language—and, indeed, the language of a colonial power that was still unable and unwilling to conceive of a modern, Black subject—Copans underscored the modernity and cosmopolitanism of his African audiences. On his radio programs, which stretched across the imperial nation-state and its postcolonial territories, Copans's interventions were simpler—the translation of a title here and a quick explanation of an allusion there—but still made possible those moments of diasporic recognition and discovery. By defining jazz as modern, African, and Atlantic, he offered his audiences alternate visions of national and racial meaning at the end of colonialism and beginning of independence. Like Achille, he was a *passeur* of African American music, someone who ferried ideas, goods, or people through space in the language of empire but with the voice of America. Within this aural framework, African American music gained distinct and sometimes contradictory forms of political, cultural, and spiritual value. Whether one was listening in a rural town in provincial France, fighting on behalf of the French military in Algeria, or fighting for independence on behalf of the FLN, Copans's voice gave a distinct resonance to the encounter. Broadcast into a crumbling French empire, the *voix de l'Amérique* simultaneously consoled, emboldened, and unnerved its listeners.

6

LIBERATION REVISITED

African American Music and the Postcolonial Soundscape

————

The narrator of Moussa Sene Absa's 1993 film *Ça twiste à Popenguine* is a young boy, Bacc, who observes everyday life in the seaside village of Popenguine, Senegal, in December 1964.[1] In between running errands and delivering notes between love-struck teenagers, Bacc recites seventeenth-century poetry in a French school, listens to stories by his grandmother, and watches in awe as the village gathers around a television for the first time, stopping only for evening prayers. Even in the mundane act of mail delivery, we see how life in Popenguine is linked to a changing world: the pension check that awaits a veteran of World War II, the letter home from those now living in the "big city," or the long-awaited delivery of a copy of the French variety magazine *Salut les copains*. It is the realm of popular culture that particularly fascinates Bacc, who quickly introduces the viewer to Popenguine's two rival clubs. The first are the Inséparables, or "Ins," a group of young men devoted to French pop stars like Sylvia Vartan, Johnny Hallyday, and Eddie Mitchell. When not in school, the Ins wear shirts adorned with the images of their idols. The rival club, the Kings, adore American soul and R&B. Fishermen by day, by late afternoon they change clothes (into bellbottoms and sunglasses) and listen to music in their own clubhouse, which is plastered with images of Otis Redding, Ray Charles, and James Brown and graffiti lifted from African American culture: "Freedom," "Harlem City," "Black Panthers," and the lyrics to "Hit the Road, Jack."

Besides class and taste, the two groups are also critically differentiated by their access to technology. While the Ins own no record player, the Kings have a Teppaz portable electrophone, through which they can listen to African American music. After Bacc negotiates the short-term rental of the record player for the Ins' first *surprise-partie* at their own clubhouse—at which the "surprise" is the cost of entry—the Ins and Kings fight over the final accounting, resulting in the destruction of the building, and their records, in a fiery blaze. The film concludes after the Ins assemble and host a new party, where the sounds of a French cover of Chubby Checker's "Let's Twist Again" give way to James Brown's "It's a Man's Man's Man's World." Whether transmitted from the electrophone in the film's plot or as the soundtrack, the sounds of French pop and American R&B animate the film, which includes Otis Redding's "(Sitting on) The Dock of the Bay" (1967), Percy Sledge's "When a Man Loves a Woman" (1966), and two recordings by Brown, "Sex Machine" (1971) and the aforementioned "Man's World" (1971). While the film is ostensibly set in 1964, the music extends into the early 1970s, reclaiming a wider range of popular music in its depiction of the postcolonial era. Wrestling with Islamic traditions, the town's elders, and the French language, the film's young people claim authority through their acquisition and personification of both French and African American popular cultures. But within the contested sphere that pits French pop stars against R&B icons, it is clear that African American music sounds the promise of liberation. Visible in the clubhouse graffiti and audible in the final strains of James Brown over the film's end, African American music signals a new kind of posture in the world.

This chapter clarifies the material conditions for this new relationship to African American music in postcolonial Francophone Africa, where the economic, political, and cultural value ascribed to African American music was transformed by its incorporation into postcolonial spaces of political and cultural expression. The chapter is, on the one hand, the culmination of the book's analytical frameworks, particularly insofar as it considers the convergence of mediating networks that had defined the soundscapes of liberation to this point. These same networks were now refracted in the postcolonial moment, when distinct material conditions facilitated new kinds of aural fantasies and liberatory visions. Although the chapter builds on this book's study of the material history of African American music in France, this inquiry into the postcolonial era also constitutes a significant point of departure. Put simply, the meaning ascribed to African American music by African listeners requires a different kind of critical lens. While intermediaries sought to maintain influence and power in defining African American music, their intentions were in many ways "outrun" by the liberatory potential that Francophone African listeners invested in this musical tradition.[2] Rather than simply tracing these networks throughout the postcolonial period, this chapter explores the specific ambivalences and contradictions that were constructed within these same networks, leading to their transformation in a new setting. As sophisticated consumers of African American music, African audiences sifted through the layers of its politicization and commercialization, seeking out its potential value in forming postcolonial societies.[3]

At the center of this inquiry are the archival and material remnants of this history in Senegal and Algeria, both of which, as scholar Tsitsi Jaji writes, "produced potent iconographies of Africa writ large that far exceed their territorial reach."[4] While the chapter examines well-known festivals that defined culture in the 1960s and early 1970s—including the First World Festival of Negro Arts (1966), the First Pan-African Cultural Festival (1969), and the Zaire 74 music festival (1974)—it looks beyond the main stages to consider, first, how these festivals facilitated unexpected and unforeseen encounters among African-descended people, and, second, how these experiences were shaped by decades of aural and visual encounters with African American musical traditions. These more quotidian histories rarely appear in official archives but are critical to understanding what African American music meant to African listeners in the postcolonial period. Within these spaces, African American music became a tangible and audible way to define, reshape, and sometimes defy postcolonial power. It was by no means the only aural site of creativity and contestation: it should be considered alongside other forms of popular music, including Afro-Cuban rumba and West African highlife. But the particular political and economic investment of both France and the United States in African American music made it a potent site of struggle in the postcolonial period. While African American music might have sounded like liberation and Black power, its revolutionary potential was nevertheless tied to transatlantic networks of power and profit that were resistant to those same principles.

In early December 1960, France's ambassador to Cameroon and Togo, Henri-Francis Mazoyer, sent a memorandum to Paris detailing several alarming developments.[5] While France had busied itself conducting economic studies and instituting training programs throughout postcolonial Africa, an entirely new form of Cold War diplomacy had been launched by its rivals. Earlier that same week, the municipal stadium in the Togolese capital of Lomé had hosted not only a Soviet-sponsored football match but also a concert by trumpeter Louis Armstrong, whose nine-week tour of various African nations was organized by the US State Department.[6] The tours epitomized the paradoxical politics of Cold War cultural diplomacy, in which African American jazz musicians were asked to embody the universalist claims of a rising global power and to stage American exceptionalism, for even jazz's improvisational structure was purported to parallel American-style democracy.[7]

Despite its efforts, however, the US State Department could not anticipate or control the range of responses of those involved. For African American musicians, the opportunity to tour under the aegis of the State Department proved a mixed blessing. Although it required representing a government that had consistently excluded African Americans from full citizenship, it was for many the first opportunity to travel to Africa and was thus perceived as a kind of homecoming. The tour prompted Armstrong himself to proclaim in Ghana, "Now I know this is my country too."[8] For African audiences, the experience was equally complex. Some audiences might have seen African American musicians as a new variation on the menace of American empire, especially as these concerts often coincided with regime changes. It is also possible that the sight of those like Armstrong conveyed on a red *tipoye*—as he was in Léopoldville in 1960—signified Black power and potential in a postcolonial world, particularly as African leaders struggled to fend off neo-imperial claims to natural resources and influence on the continent.[9]

At least one observer had his doubts about the efficacy of this new form of cultural exchange. While Ambassador Mazoyer initially imagined that Armstrong's claims to "African origins" would have resonated among the gathered crowd, he reported that the Togolese audience was "unmoved, uncomprehending of this music that they had [just] been told was representative of their own genius."[10] It was, Mazoyer noted, the white and mixed-race bourgeoisie who applauded most loudly and shouted with approval and recognition, thus belying the American presumption that jazz could serve as a lingua franca among African-descended people. The apparent sangfroid of the African audience was even more striking, Mazoyer wrote, given that the organizer had endorsed the event with the words of French jazz critic Hugues Panassié himself, one of the "most fanatical admirers" of jazz in "the white race."[11] Mazoyer's report not only racially encoded the responses of the African, white, and *métis* audiences but also reinforced the continued mediating power of Panassié's own words in developing a proper understanding of jazz. It was still white French people, Mazoyer claimed, who had the keenest ear to hear and interpret the genius of African American music.

This disquieting interpretation introduces yet another complication into a thorny historical moment, one whose contours are well defined by historians of the US State Department and US foreign relations.[12] The Cold War witnessed a range of cultural diplomacy programs in Africa, which were sustained by military and intelligence agencies' interventions in African politics and economies and a sustained effort to control the "information" that reached the non-aligned world. This interest was particularly focused in Dakar, where in 1950 the US State Department opened its first American embassy in French West Africa, and in 1958 the US Information Service (USIS) opened the first Centre Culturel Américain, where young people could attend lectures, concerts, and exhibitions.[13] By the late 1950s, the State Department had inaugurated its jazz ambassador program, through which musicians like Louis Armstrong, Randy Weston, Benny Goodman, Dave Brubeck, and Dizzy Gillespie traveled throughout the decolonizing world with stops in Southeast Asia, South America, the Middle East, and Africa. Extending the reach of these performances, the State Department also sponsored jazz lectures—like those by Sim Copans—as well as radio programs like Willis Conover's *Music U.S.A.* (including a "Jazz Hour"), which debuted on the Voice of America (VOA) in 1955. One of his listeners was future producer Jacques Muyal, who recalled Conover's programs as well as the jazz programs broadcast on Radio Tanger and Radio Africa. Immersed in a rich—if crowded—soundscape, Muyal soon became a radio host himself, first on the Voice of America and then on Radio Tanger International, where he took over André Francis's "Le Club de Jazz" in 1956.[14]

While Conover's programs were a worldwide phenomenon, Francophone listeners were especially interested in the soul and rhythm-and-blues broadcasts of Georges Collinet, who joined the roster of radio hosts at VOA in 1964. His program, *Bonjour l'Afrique*, which attracted listeners throughout Francophone Africa to Collinet, or "Le Maxi Voum Voum," and his collection of American soul music, including James Brown, Otis Redding, and Wilson Pickett, as well as popular music from Latin America and the African continent (see figure 6.1).[15] Collinet was born in Cameroon in 1940, the son of a white French father and a Cameroonian mother. In 1947, he left for France, where he was educated in the Auvergne region under the supervision of his French grandparents. From an early age, Collinet described the ways in which he was "caught between these two worlds," the grandson of a Cameroonian village chieftain yet also the child of a white industrialist. In France, he was seen as a curiosity, objectified by classmates and neighbors due to his mixed race. Perhaps due to this sense of estrangement, he was drawn to African American music, including rock 'n' roll and jazz, which he listened to in Parisian jazz clubs whenever possible. In 1959, Collinet left for the United States. He found work in New York at the French Cultural Center, where he was recorded reading French literature for language courses, and then at the Voice of America broadcasting

agency, which sought qualified French speakers. Uninterested in returning to France—where he would have been enlisted into military service—he left for Washington, DC, in 1961. Like Louis Achille, who had moved to DC thirty years before, Collinet was fearful of moving to a racially segregated city, but he soon found companionship among an international community of friends and colleagues. In the next few years, he learned the radio trade—from production to delivery—and was offered his own program in 1964. As the "only black host at VOA," he imagined his job was to "put some color in [the] broadcasts."

From the beginning, *Bonjour l'Afrique* was promoted as a "breakfast show," a two-hour program that began at 6:00 a.m. GMT, when it might accompany his listeners as they began their days and went off to work. Its format included news, music, and informal conversation.[16] The program was recorded in Washington and then transmitted through VOA short-wave networks to a relay station in Monrovia, Liberia, from which it reached transistor radios throughout the continent.[17] In developing his program, Collinet consciously drew on the model of local deejays in Washington, DC, where radio hosts like "Petey" Greene not only played the latest in soul music—including Wilson Pickett and James Brown—but also employed an intimate, informal style in talking to their audiences and introduced energetic and explosive noises into their programs' sound environment. As Collinet recalled, the twenty-minute segments of music on *Bonjour l'Afrique* were the first in the agency's history to include rhythm and blues, which he could only find at Tower Records, as these records were absent from VOA's own record library. Through them, Collinet created his own American "voice," even though he was presenting in French. While he greatly admired Willis Conover, Collinet described his own program as the "opposite" of Conover's (he noted, too, that he was paid considerably less). Collinet's distinct voice and program were extraordinarily popular among Francophone African audiences.[18] While some US embassies rejected his style, he nevertheless recalled receiving a large number of fan letters from listeners. In Abidjan, the African All Stars cited Collinet by name in their song "Les Champions," believing his name alone would "influence record sales."[19] In the late 1960s, the VOA sent Collinet on promotional tours, which included stops in the cities of Conakry, Dakar, Kinshasa, and Bamako, where he was mobbed by fans at airports (see figure 6.2).

FIGURE 6.2. Collinet with fans in Bamako, Mali. Photo courtesy of Georges Collinet.

In his life and radio programming, Collinet shared key characteristics with the intermediaries who preceded him, particularly Copans. Fluent in both French and English, and familiar with African American culture, he offered his African listeners a unique entry point into African American spaces and life. While he looked to African American cultural forms and discourses in his self-presentation, Collinet did not present himself as African American. Instead, he underscored the ways in which he offered a link or connection to these social and political worlds, mediated through his own voice as well as the music itself. Though pleased by his popularity, Collinet nevertheless mourned the fact that all of the local bands he saw on his goodwill tours now "sounded like James Brown": he wondered, "What have I done?" While lamenting the displacement of local traditions, Collinet nevertheless delighted in the sounds of soul that he carried, sharing with the world his own admiration for African American music.

While the US State Department was particularly invested in using African American music to uphold global power, it was not alone in seeing jazz as a key to maintaining influence in Africa. In fact—notwithstanding the doubts of Ambassador Mazoyer in 1960—the French government explicitly borrowed from the American example to promote French jazz in Africa. Beginning in 1963, the French Ministry of Cooperation sponsored its own jazz tours by Maxim Saury throughout the continent, including stops in Cameroon and Togo.[20] But while the French may have borrowed from the American model, the transmission of African American music through Francophone networks of production and dissemination explicitly refuted American claims to exceptionalism. The French state's own efforts in West and Central Africa were first supported by its own cultural centers, which were seen as an "extension of metropolitan plans both to provide and control the usage of leisure time."[21] Between 1954 and 1957, France opened 170 West African cultural centers, which they imagined could serve as "a place to diffuse potentially damaging political views which were most often articulated by *évolués* [evolved people]."[22] The centers provided French material, including magazines like *Paris Match* and *Bingo*, which were intended to "bind Africans" to French culture and to offer opportunities for "African cultural expression within the context of French culture, not as a separate entity." Soon young people pushed back, asking that the same centers be renamed "Maisons des Jeunes et de la Culture" (Houses of Youth and Culture), as they were known in the metropole. In 1956, the first of these newly renamed centers opened in Dakar.[23] While these centers focused on French cultural programming, they nevertheless became venues for jazz fandom, just as they had in metropolitan France, by sponsoring local Hot

Clubs or by facilitating music listening in their own *discothèques*. In 1963, the Centre d'Échanges Culturels de Langue Française in Dakar created its own jazz club, where local musicians gathered to play and fans joined weekly listening sessions.[24]

Building on its long-standing broadcasting networks within Africa, the French state also broadcast African American music to Francophone radio listeners, first through the Société de Radiodiffusion de la France d'Outre-mer (SORAFOM) and then through the Office de Coopération Radiophonique (OCORA), which advised new national radio networks in postcolonial Africa, including Radio Nationale Centrafricaine, Radio Côte d'Ivoire, Radio Dakar, Radio Mali, Radio Bangui, Radio Tchad, Radio Gabon, and Radio Congo.[25] But by 1962, French radio officials were competing for listeners on an increasingly crowded radio spectrum. In addition to regional broadcasts out of Senegal and Mali, African listeners with short-wave radios could hear transmissions from the British Broadcasting Corporation, the Vatican Radio, Radio Moscow, Radio Peking, and the Voice of America.

In the competition for aural power in postcolonial Africa, however, the French had some distinct advantages. French authorities maintained their influence by providing 80 percent of all African radio journalists, producers, technicians, and station managers with training in radio broadcasting in a yearlong program at the Studio École de Maisons Laffitte outside Paris. Among their courses in reporting, writing, editing, speaking, and technical support, all students beginning in 1962 could take a yearlong, weekly course on the history and evolution of jazz.[26] As the course instructor André Clergeat recalled years later, the jazz course was particularly popular among students hoping to locate the roots of jazz in Africa, even though, by virtue of its context, pedagogical format, and content, it reinforced French cultural authority. In addition, OCORA distributed French-produced programs to the newly formed national radio stations. With limited resources and the pressing need to attract widely dispersed populations, these national stations sometimes supplemented their own programming through the relay and transmission of French-produced programs.

It was through this postcolonial network that the French radio's new *bureau du jazz,* or "jazz office," began in 1961 to relay the nightly program *Jazz dans la nuit* (*Jazz at night*) throughout Francophone Africa. This new initiative grouped all jazz programs, including those by Sim Copans and André Francis, under one coherent heading. It was led by Lucien Malson, who, even among a distinguished cohort of jazz critics, most clearly embodied French cultural and intellectual authority. Under Malson's leadership, listeners throughout France (and now Francophone Africa) heard *Jazz dans la nuit* broadcast nightly, beginning with opening strains of Ray Charles's 1959 "Jumpin' in the Morning." This choice reveals the producers' intent to educate their listening public, who might initially think Charles's music was simply a form of "variety" but would soon learn that it was rooted in the jazz tradition.[27] While many in the jazz community shared this pedagogical principle, no one else had the power or resources to implement it on such a large scale. For in addition to nightly broadcasts on France Inter and France Musique, archival radio program schedules for the national radio stations in Gabon, Chad, Cameroon, the Côte d'Ivoire, and the Central African Republic all list regular rebroadcasts of *Jazz dans la nuit* throughout the early 1960s.[28]

Likewise, commercial networks challenged American authority on the meaning and value of African American music. The international recording industry had focused on the African continent since the early twentieth century. By the interwar period, African consumers were buying, sharing, and listening to the vernacular phonograph records that circulated throughout the colonial world, in what Michael Denning describes as a "soundscape of working class daily life in an archipelago of colonial ports."[29] Radio proved also a critical technology in diffusing both local and international music. By the end of the 1950s, a growing number of listeners in Francophone Africa had private or communal access to radio. The advent of the low-energy transistor radio dramatically shifted access as the decade progressed. While radio broadcasts were not all emitting from the metropole—as witnessed by the emergence of local radio stations—the recording industry was organized around European ownership and profit.[30] Listeners could buy records from HMV/Zonophone, which released 8 million records in West Africa in the early 1930s, and after World War II they could find records released by Decca and Pathé-Marconi, which had offices in Nigeria, Kenya, and South Africa.[31] Beyond radio and recordings, there were also performances, including those by US servicemen who performed at Dakar's Place Protêt and inspired the creation of new bands, like Les Déménageurs.[32] Just as it had in 1944 Normandy, the US military's infrastructure created new spaces of jazz fandom in Francophone Africa.

By virtue of France's own imperial networks, radio listeners and record consumers included white *colons* (colonists), particularly those in the department of Algeria. However, new sound technologies were most transformative for African youth in cities like Dakar and Brazzaville.[33] The 1950s marked the emergence of African *melomanes* (music lovers), whose consumption—and production—of popular music made African American music central to the colonial and later postcolonial soundscape. They listened to music on Radio Brazzaville and read about African American musicians and new recordings in popular magazines like *Bingo*, which was launched in 1953 to reach readers across France and Francophone Africa. In these outlets, young people encountered media personalities, consumer goods, and visions of "black cosmopolitanism" that required new kinds of literacy—what Jaji calls "sheen reading"—to navigate.[34] For young people in Leopoldville in the 1950s, jazz became part of modernity's vernacular. The Congolese musical group O.K. Jazz, for instance, drew inspiration from two sides: "O.K." conjured the "swagger and panache of the American Westerns that delighted youthful audiences at the *cité*'s open-air cinemas," while "Jazz" suggested the "hip sophistication of black America, Louis Armstrong and Duke Ellington."[35] Simultaneously, African listeners were drawn to Afro-Cuban music, which had emerged in the late 1940s. An "act of cultural resistance" and "aural sign of liberation," it proffered access to diasporic connection without the same racial hierarchies instituted by either Cold War or colonial powers.[36]

In Dakar, music fans gathered in record stores and *comptoirs commerciaux* (colonial trading posts) owned by Lebanese and French merchants, like Radio Standard, Radio Africaine, Disco Parade, and Disco Club, that sold recordings alongside the necessary hardware.[37] While they first specialized in 78 rpm records, in the 1960s, these same stores introduced vinyl records, so that fans might purchase 45 and 33 rpm records for five hundred and fifteen hundred francs, respectively, in addition to three-speed record players. A 1963 article on a local hi-fi club in Abidjan reveled in the ways in which the blues had "entwined" its listeners, transporting them to "other horizons."[38] By 1961, Gallo and then Barclay Records began distributing Atlantic Records' recordings in West Africa.[39] By the mid-1960s, flight attendants also began bringing in records from Europe and the United States, especially after Air Afrique began service to the United States in 1965.[40] Record producer Ibrahima Sylla recalled years later that these *stewards* sometimes succeeded in beating the speed of the "pirates" by conveying records through Air Afrique.[41]

Whether they found African American music through US State Department propaganda, French radio, or local stores, young listeners integrated American music into the burgeoning youth cultures in cities like Dakar, Abidjan, and Brazzaville. With records in hand, young people formed their own *clubs des quarters*, *grins*, or *associations*, where they danced "the jerk" to James Brown alongside Georges Collinet's program; listened to *Salut les copains*, broadcast on Senegal's Chaine Inter; or read magazines featuring their favorite musicians. Malian writer and filmmaker Manthia Diawara recalled this world with particular fondness, citing Bamako's *grins* (clubs) as venues for self-expression and liberation.[42] One listener, Alioune Diop, remembered that radio producers often played records brought to the studio by friends, whose status or personal connections in the United States might have given them access to new music.[43] As Diop recalled, it was not a "professional" or paid arrangement but instead something that occurred "between friends," a personal debt that was acknowledged on air by radio hosts. Moving between fan and producer, the music was transformed into a means of collaboration among friends.

Festival Circuits

While the circulation of records had shifted listening habits, and likewise altered the kinds of political, aesthetic, and racial meanings ascribed to African American music, the first World Festival of Negro Arts in April 1966 in Dakar drew on a different set of assumptions about the political power and racial meaning of African American culture.[44] By all accounts, the festival was an extraordinary gathering. Reporting for *Ebony* later that summer, Hoyt Fuller declared that there had "never been anything quite like it," bearing witness to the "thousands of people with some claim to an African heritage" who gathered in Senegal.[45] Though reportedly sixty thousand visitors from thirty-seven countries came for the event, the racial makeup of the festival crowds became a subject of much discussion as tension emerged between what appeared to be a "manufactured Negritude state" and the neighborhoods inhabited by Senegalese citizens.[46] The festival opened officially on March 30 with the Colloque International sur les Arts Nègres. It remained open for three weeks in April, allowing attendees to visit art exhibitions and lectures, hear concerts and speeches, and attend plays and film screenings, all of which were "designed to illustrate the genius, the culture and the glory of Africa."[47] The festival was also broadcast on Radio Senegal to listeners throughout West Africa by Joseph Zobel—the same writer whose criticism had especially displeased Boris Vian—who began coordinating cultural programming for the station in the 1950s.[48]

The festival was officially cosponsored by the Senegalese government, the United Nations Educational, Scientific, and Cultural Organization (UNESCO), and the Société Africaine de Culture (SAC), a cultural and educational organization that had been formed after the 1956 Congress of Black Writers and Artists in Paris. All of the sponsors were allies during a period in which revolutionary Pan-Africanist politics had become increasingly disconcerting for US and French officials. The Senegalese government was led by former *négritude* poet Léopold Sédar Senghor, who was more favorably oriented toward the United States and Europe than were Guinean president Sékou Touré and

Ghanaian president Kwame Nkrumah, both of whom advanced a more radical vision of Pan-Africanism.[49] By contrast, the festival itself constituted a very specific expression of Pan-Africanism.[50] Throughout the planning process, Senghor reiterated the possibilities of solidarity through culture, which appeared to some of his political contemporaries as a means of accommodating capitalist incursions into Africa.

The SAC held particular authority at this event by virtue of its American counterpart, the American Society of African Culture (AMSAC), which was criticized by many for its close ties to the US State Department and suspected—rightly so—of accepting CIA funding.[51] In 1961, AMSAC had funded a two-day festival on African and American Negro art celebrating a new exchange program and cultural center in Lagos, Nigeria, that featured Lionel Hampton, Duke Ellington, Odetta Holmes, Brother John Sellers, Randy Weston, and Nina Simone.[52] AMSAC's president, John A. Davis, helped run the US coordinating committee for the festival, which secured funding from the US State Department and the US Information Agency (USIA), as well as from private donors, foundations, and corporations. Through the sponsoring committee, the United States intended to send one hundred performers and writers as well as a traveling exhibition of African American art. By sponsoring AMSAC and the committee's selected delegates, State Department officials hoped to disengage from overt politics, particularly to shift international focus away from the 1966 coup in Ghana that had ousted Nkrumah. Indeed, the State Department's involvement in the festival launched a "cultural blitz" in Africa in 1966 and 1967 to promote culture as a basis for African nationalism.[53]

Despite these political claims, the 1966 festival also proved an opportunity for African Americans to forge new relationships within the African diaspora.[54] In his 1966 documentary of the festival, filmmaker William Greaves highlighted the diasporic routes of this "historic occasion," which revealed the "important contributions the black man has made, and is making, to world civilization."[55] This trip was Greaves's first to the African continent; it would become a critical moment for him in creating a cinematic representation of both the universal dimensions of Black culture and the diasporic links among Black people. Others were frustrated by the American organizing committee's financial limitations and political affiliations, as well as Senghor's own vision for the festival, in which *négritude* was seemingly entwined with accommodationist politics. When Virginia Inness-Brown, a white woman, assumed chairmanship of the committee, it confirmed the suspicions of many that the festival was never intended to facilitate any real development of pan-African culture or politics. Boycotts were led by prominent African American intellectuals and artists, including James Baldwin,

Harry Belafonte, Ralph Ellison, Ossie Davis, and Sidney Poitier.[56] And a number of artists, including Romare Bearden, Hale Woodruff, and Jacob Lawrence, officially withdrew their work from the travelling exhibition just weeks before the festival, citing disputes with the US committee regarding the transfer of "original budgetary commitments" to the performing arts.[57]

In the end, the delegation featured a range of performing artists, including jazz bandleader Duke Ellington, choreographer Alvin Ailey, soprano Martina Arroyo, concert pianist Armenta Adams, composer Leonard du Paur, and gospel singer Marion Williams, as well as public presentations by Katherine Dunham and Langton Hughes. These choices were questioned by some of the festival attendees, who wondered why modern jazz icons like Miles Davis or Thelonious Monk did not fit within this tableau of African American artistic achievement. While Duke Ellington's orchestra and the Alvin Ailey dancers were praised, some thought that the classical performers in particular were "inappropriate" in a festival "dedicated to the glorification of Negro arts." Fuller even reported one American as saying, "There's nothing particularly 'Negro' about a black woman playing Chopin etudes"—an observation that underscored the challenges facing African American classical performers.[58] By contrast, State Department officials were relieved by these representatives, believing they were in line with US liberal agendas but also hoping that their participation would confine "the compatibility of African and African American peoples to the realm of culture rather than politics."[59] The US government did not, however, anticipate that these same artists might bring their own cultural and political agendas to the festival. As Von Eschen writes, in many cases, the "assertions of black cultural solidarity" that occurred in Dakar "far exceeded the cultural politics and vision of American officialdom."[60]

One such example was Duke Ellington, whose band performed before packed venues in Dakar (see figure 6.3). In these concerts, and in interviews, the composer and bandleader spoke frequently about his affinity for African culture. As he later recounted in his memoir, Ellington was thrilled to be in Dakar, finally able to present his music to African people "after writing African music for thirty years."[61] Describing his performance in the stadium, Ellington noted that they received "the usual diplomatic applause from the diplomatic corps down front" but also added, "The cats in the bleachers really dig it. You can see them rocking back there while we play. When we are finished, they shout approval and dash for backstage, where they hug and embrace us, some of them with tears in their eyes. It is acceptance at the highest level, and it gives us a once-in-a-lifetime feeling of having truly broken through to our brothers."[62] He described a conversation with an artist named Papa Tall, who inspired Elling-

FIGURE 6.3. Duke Ellington performing during the First World Festival of Negro Arts in Dakar, Senegal, 1966. Photograph courtesy of the Mercer Cook Papers, Moorland-Spingarn Research Center, Howard University.

ton's own comparison of jazz to a sturdy tree with a "kind of translucent bark, which might appear on first glance to be labeled *Made in Japan*." However, while jazz was branded within global commercial networks, Ellington found that "its very blue-blooded roots are permanently married to, and firmly ensconced in, the rich black earth of beautiful Black Africa."[63] In addition to beginning work on his planned "Senegalese Suites" (eventually becoming the composition "La Plus Belle Africaine") en route to the festival, Ellington affirmed jazz's musical roots in Africa. When asked about the "meaning" of his coming to Dakar, he noted that the festival had provided an opportunity for artists to "observe what the other Negro artists around the world are doing," which would "contribute tremendously to the adjustment or readjustment of their perspective artistically." Asked about his fellow musicians, Ellington reiterated that they, too, "wanted to get here to see what was happening at the original point." This commitment to underscoring jazz's African origins was deepened by Ellington's assertion, "After all, we have accepted the fact that jazz is an African export."[64] In a decidedly diplomatic fashion, Ellington had inverted the logic of cultural diplomacy. Jazz was not America's to export but instead was African.

African American music also featured in the sound and light show, the *Spectacle féerique*, which was displayed every evening on the beach at the Île de Gorée, transforming one of the largest slave-trading centers in West Africa into a space of national and diasporic celebration. The nightly program included the music of the Fisk Jubilee Singers, whose voices accompanied a narrative history of the 1878 yellow fever epidemic. Drawing perhaps on the Jubilee Singers' own international prominence, their inclusion helped to reinforce the "tragic realism" of the program.[65] Likewise, a live recording of gospel songs by the Back Home Choir was chosen to mark the celebration of the "heroes of Negritude." The program noted that their singing was a "moving illustration if ever there were one, of the contribution of Negritude to universal civilization."[66] A brochure from the program specifically noted that use of the recordings was made possible by the "friendly support of the Centres Culturels Américains" in Paris and Dakar.[67] While African American spiritual music proved critical to the success of the nightly show, its centrality was made possible through the same political networks that had long propagated African American music as a means of generating support in the Cold War.

Even in the festival's lectures and discussions, African American music loomed large. Both Senghor and the French minister of culture, André Malraux, cited African American music in their opening speeches of the festival, and Malraux enumerated two kinds of African American music: spirituals and jazz.[68] Within the broader context of his speech, which focused on improving partner relations between France and Africa and offering a cultural companion to the model of economic relations known as *Françafrique*, Malraux contended that Africa had "rediscovered its soul" through jazz, although, he added, the form was rooted in its "European or American melodic elements." Extending the "civilizing mission" beyond the end of empire, Malraux's words underscore his paternalistic belief that Europeans were critical to crafting the African future and, as Tsitsi Jaji notes, the importance of jazz as a powerful "signifier" in the state's effort to define French culture.[69] As Jaji further contends, the festival illustrated the contours of Senghor's "Negritude musicology," which was informed by Senghor's own embeddedness in diasporic spaces in the interwar period and his encounters with African American art. Senghor's positioning shaped his perspective on jazz, which he considered exemplary of *négritude*, and enabled him to "articulate parallels between African vernacular oral art forms and jazz as commensurable modern black forms."[70]

Moreover, African American music was central to the Colloque International sur les Arts Nègres, which opened the festival on March 30, 1966. The colloquium featured over thirty presenters, each of whom spoke at length on the topic "Function and Significance of African Negro Art in the Life of the People and for the People."[71] While the colloquium highlighted African presenters, including radio broadcaster Francis Bebey and filmmaker Paulin Soumanou Vieyra, it was dominated by well-known American and European specialists, such as filmmaker Jean Rouch, anthropologist Michel Leiris, art historian James A. Porter, sociologist St. Clair Drake, and choreographer Katherine Dunham. Among the presenters were Sim Copans and Louis T. Achille, both of whom were invited to give papers on African American music. While these subjects might have been taken up by African or African American scholars, the extended invitations instead ran through French cultural networks, which further illustrated the continued importance of these same links in defining expertise on these subjects.

When invited to present on jazz, Copans was happy to contribute, asking only that he be allowed to situate this genre within the longer history of African American music.[72] He ultimately gave a presentation titled "The African Heritage in the Music of the American Negro," which advanced a more indepth and academically grounded account of African American music than Copans typically presented in his lecture tours. In short, Copans aimed to show that American folk music, including the spiritual, work songs, the blues, and children's songs, were "strongly shaped by the music of Africa" and were thus central to the development of jazz, albeit "indirectly." He drew on work by Melville Herskovits, E. Franklin Frazier, Marshall Stearns, W. E. B. Du Bois, James Weldon Johnson, and Leroi Jones (later Amiri Baraka), as well as his own interviews with the drummers Art Blakey, Max Roach, and Kenny Clarke, all of whom had insisted on the importance of African drumming in jazz's development.[73] Copans further remarked on the American jazz musicians' investment in African independence, referencing John Coltrane's *Africa/Brass* (1961) and Max Roach's *We Insist!* (1960). He ended by emphasizing how "history has come full swing," for while African rhythms had contributed to the "birth of Afro-American folk songs," now "American Negro jazz musicians turn toward the music and rhythms of Africa," discovering in them "a fresh source renewing this music of the twentieth century."[74] Whereas Copans had previously sought to "civilize" jazz for his French audiences, he now defined it as a form of African diasporic cosmopolitanism.

Achille too had been invited to attend and happily accepted, only to discover immediately before the festival that his own Park Glee Club had been invited to perform before Martin Luther King, Jr. at the Bourse du Travail in Lyon on March 29. While torn between his respective commitments to US civil rights and *négritude*, Achille decided to honor his long friendship with

Senghor by attending the festival and presenting on the meaning and history of "Negro spirituals." In many respects, Achille's paper extended the formality and precision that characterized his presentation in Paris at the Congress of Black Writers and Artists in 1956. While his 1956 presentation attempted to reconcile Black cultural debates under colonialism, however, the political conditions in Dakar allowed for a different kind of political reconciliation. Clarifying its parameters, Achille first situated his study within the colloquium's own aims, casting a "backward glance over the valiant and painful past which cradled these songs" and finding there a rich cultural realm open for research.[75] He praised Senghor and the search for a shared cultural heritage among Black people but also celebrated the fact that it had been done on "their ancestral soil."[76] Achille then turned to the history of the spiritual. In clarifying its religious, expressive, civic, cultural, and sociological value, he returned repeatedly to its roots in collective expression and reiterated his belief in the spiritual's participatory nature. By virtue of this "collective" dimension, Achille claimed, the Negro spiritual had become the preeminent "broadcaster of Negritude" in the world, "the most effective 'public relations' agents of the black race." While Achille's formulation echoed the US State Department's interpretation of African American music as a democratic model, his aims were distinct. His central goal in highlighting the participatory nature of the spiritual was to further his own argument, for to "know Negro spirituals and Negro dances in their fullest reality, it is not enough to look at them." Instead, he argued, "you must *participate* with your voice, your feelings and your limbs." In his view, "execution brings to exterior knowledge an interior revelation, both physiological and spiritual."[77] Uncertain as to the revelations that might result, Achille nevertheless sought to bind the Negro spirituals to Africa, "that ancient motherland of the Blacks of the entire world."[78]

In her own colloquium speech, Katherine Dunham noted the presence of Achille: "I see Louis Achille here and am carried back to Martinique where his father took over from Price-Mars and acquainted me with the tiny island and what was left of song, ritual, and dance."[79] While Dunham was carried back to the Caribbean, Achille had found himself in Africa, seeking answers to questions that had preoccupied him for several decades. Both Achille and Copans were in a very new context yet on familiar terms, as their own expertise—based in large part on their distance from the source material—remained unquestioned. Beyond speaking in Dakar, both Achille and Copans served on the *jury des disques,* which reviewed musical albums and selected winners in several categories: "Artistes noirs (classique)," "Artistes noirs (populaires)," "Classical Music Composed by Black People," "Jazz (Big Band)," "Jazz Soloists," "Negro

Spirituals (Ensemble)," and "Negro Gospels (Soloists)." In correspondence between the American embassy in Dakar and festival organizers, it was clear that
individual countries submitted their own suggestions, ranging from traditional
to popular music, including Manu Dibango and O.K. Jazz. The US committee
had sent the recordings of a number of contestants, including Leontyne Price,
Harry Belafonte, Duke Ellington, Ray Charles, Charles Mingus, the Leonard
De Paur Chorus, Mahalia Jackson, and Louis Armstrong (some of whom performed in Dakar and some of whom had declined to attend).[80] The winners
were then adjudicated by the cultural attachés of the embassies in Dakar. In the
end, the prize did not recognize the changing musical tastes of young people
in Francophone Africa and beyond. While the Motown Record Company had
submitted its own set of records to the festival for consideration—a musical
collection, they wrote, that was "much imitated in America and in the rest of
the world" by white performers—in the end, state officials' tastes dictated the
selection of the winners.[81]

In his review of the festival in *Liberator*, South African poet and African
National Congress activist Keorapetse Kgositsile began by noting that he had
"nothing against festivals—not even negro ones."[82] He acknowledged that he
had enjoyed himself immensely in Dakar, reveling in the "Black magic" that
filled the Daniel Sorano Theater and stadium, the sounds of "the Duke Ellington band splitting the skies to awaken the sleeping guardian gods," and the
"blues, spirituals and the Alvin Ailey dancers portraying a historical experience" that "America would rather die than take a quick glance at." But while
"electrified" by the performances, Kgositsile nevertheless had a sinking sensa-
tion that "the past and future of my culture was being played around with." Emphasizing his own claims to Black culture, he noted that the "predominantly
white" audience surrounding him appeared to be waiting for Black culture to
be made "illustrious" and hence deserving of white patronage. Kgositsile could
not ignore the fences that contained the slums of Dakar, maintaining the strict
class and racial divides in this moment of purported unity.[83] He was likewise
frustrated by the ways in which this festival, which was purported to defend
and illustrate *négritude*, appeared disconnected from the same Black people it
claimed to represent. He further argued that "to omit rhythm-and-blues at any
festival or carnival where contemporary art in Black America is supposed to be
represented is as questionable as the omission of Nkrumah's ideas in any serious discussion on the dangers of neo-colonialism." Punctuating his argument,
Kgositsile demanded, "Where was James Brown!"[84]

While absent from the festival proceedings, the sounds of James Brown had
begun to be integrated into the postcolonial soundscape. Extending the same

commercial networks that had been introduced in the early 1960s, African American music—and soul in particular—had found an audience throughout Francophone Africa. In 1969, Eddie Barclay was reported to be in Dakar for a four-day sales meeting—attended by Léopold Sédar Senghor—to create a new record company that would serve West Africa.[85] They anticipated that the company's foray into the continent would begin with a study, conducted with the cooperation of the ministries of culture, ministries of youth, and ministries of industrial planning in Mali, Guinea, Mauritania, and Senegal. Several years later, Barclay executives continued to work in French-speaking Africa, which they saw as a "natural market for expansion."[86] In 1968, the USIA recruited Junior Wells to tour West Africa (including stops in Abidjan in Côte d'Ivoire, Bamako in Mali, and Lomé in Togo). Having heard his music on Voice of America's own shortwave broadcasts, on Radio Mali (which broadcast Voice of America tapes), and through OCORA's networks, audiences filled the stadium in Bamako. For Wells and his audience, it was an extraordinary encounter. Reporting on the tour in *Ebony*, journalist David Llorens observed that "the rhythms amid their 12 bar blues were by no means foreign to the emotions of the brothers and sisters that side of the Middle Passage." Llorens also noted that Wells was stunned by the experience. When he got off the plane and "saw all them beautiful black folks," he knew: "I was home."[87] Wells's audiences were likewise thrilled. Those who could not enter listened to the speakers set up outside the stadium, so that "the huge throng that could not get inside could hear his performances."[88]

In fact, writer and filmmaker Manthia Diawara attended the same concert by Wells and his All Stars at the Omniport in Bamako. By this point, Diawara had already formed his own club, the Rockers, who gathered around a turntable "with piles of rock and R&B records: James Brown, Wilson Pickett, Otis Redding, Jimi Hendrix, Howlin' Wolf, Aretha Franklin, Nina Simone, Ike and Tina Turner, Sly and the Family Stone, B. B. King, Buddy Miles, and Albert King."[89] While the show itself was "electrifying," Diawara was particularly thrilled by the opportunity to meet the band after the show. Initially, a "white guy from the United States Information Agency" acted as translator, but soon Diawara asked to speak directly to the musicians in English, thrilling his friends and himself.[90] Like Kgosoitsile, Diawara was already familiar with what African American music could mean, having purchased his own records and likely interpreted the lyrics for himself. While US State Department officials attempted to control the encounter—and booked Junior Wells to attract young listeners—Diawara wanted direct contact, without mediation. In accessing African American music and musicians for themselves, even in the context of a state-sanctioned event, Diawara and his friends enacted a new form of Black consciousness that resisted extant models and evaluations in postcolonial Africa.

"Jazz Is an African Music"

Such shared encounters, and the desire to circumvent control, were critical to the planning of the July 1969 Pan-African Cultural Festival in Algiers, which appeared to many observers to be a direct refutation of the festival in Dakar.[91] While the Dakar festival had attracted "the most well-known artists and entertainers, the Duke Ellingtons and the like," the festival in Algiers had brought in a more "militant" generation.[92] Reporting in the first issue of *Black Scholar*, Nathan Hare noted that the debates over *négritude* continued but that now, in the adopted country of Frantz Fanon, *négritude* was positioned as a dialectical stage in the advance of a global revolution.[93] As Hare observed, this Fanon-inspired view loomed large in Algiers, as did the presence of Stokely Carmichael (later Kwame Ture) and Eldridge Cleaver, who were exiled, respectively, in Guinea and Algeria. Hare wrote, "We soon learned to say 'pouvoir noir' (black power) to taxi-drivers, who could tell, from our skin color and French, that we were black Americans. Thus we could avoid otherwise frequent over-charging, or even obtain a long free ride."[94] In Algiers, Hare reported seeing ample evidence of the resistance to "the re-entry of the French and American imperialists," which included revolutionary graffiti on "buildings, walls and fences, and the old pre-revolutionary symbol of resistance, the haik (or veil), worn by so many of the women." While Hare noted the presence of African American musicians Archie Shepp and Nina Simone, he suggested that Algerian leaders were particularly concerned with the "pitfalls of cultural attachment on the part of oppressed people." According to Hare, they criticized the "ultra-devolution of many black intellectuals to jazz music and black art," linking these to a reactionary understanding of *négritude*.[95]

Hare's own view, however, is challenged by other accounts of the festival, which advanced a different interpretation of African American music. In the days leading up to the festival, the Algerian newspaper *El Moudjahid* featured musicians like Simone and Shepp, framing them in revolutionary terms. Simone was already defined in the newspaper as a "militant star" who has "never dissociated her art from the daily struggle against all forms of oppression," and the review of her performance suggested that it was a means of dramatizing the struggle of African Americans.[96] Another review noted that she showed, "in her particular style, the drama of Blacks in the United States." Veering between apparent impassivity and barely contained aggression toward the piano, she succeeded in communicating to the spectators the meaning of "Soul," and in the meantime "split their souls in half." While the crowd was likely already prepared to enjoy "Revolution" (a "word Algerians were already greatly enthusiastic about"), when performed by Simone, its effect became "unilateral."[97] The newspaper also featured a French translation of Ted Joans's poem "The Black Jazz Smile," which would be published several years later in English.[98] When the "black man smiles in jazz," the poem advises, "look for the sadness in his eyes." In the poem, Joans uses a first-person narration to depict the perspective of a Black jazz musician and to critique the ways in which music is reframed and revalued by white critics. While the jazz musician seeks to "blow [his] soul through the white man's machine," the white critic retains the authority to tell the musician if it was "Right (white) or wrong (black song!)." After revealing himself to the world, "millions of whites" now "steal from" him without offering "compensation, celebration, or fair explanation." This was, Joans wrote, the "Western world's way: EXPLOITATION." In this world, to be a jazz musician—which Joans frames in masculinist terms—is "to be putdown, face the frowns, & be starved by white power's clowns." After citing Joans's poem, the article contended that jazz could not be dissociated from those who made it. The author once again quoted Joans's poem: "because the original, it is us."

While these reports suggest for some observers that African American music had already exceeded the limits placed on it by officials, the performances themselves were also revealing. Most were captured in William Klein's 1969 film *The Pan-African Festival of Algiers*, a stunning montage of archival newsreels, photographs, and posters, along with footage from the festival itself, including concerts, rehearsals, and speeches.[99] In it, Klein managed to capture the sensory emporium of the festival: the gun salutes, the drums, and the sounds of different voices, speaking in French, English, Arabic, Yoruba, and Swahili. He also recorded numerous performances, including Nina Simone, Miriam Makeba, and the electrifying concert of Marion Williams, who brought her rendition of "When the Saints Go Marching In" into the aisles of an ecstatic audience.

Klein was present backstage on July 29 during the remarkable late-night performance by Archie Shepp, who was joined onstage by musicians Clifford Thornton, Grachan Moncur, Dave Burrell, Alan Silva, and Sunny Murray, poets Don Lee and Ted Joans, and, finally, a large ensemble of Algerian and Tuareg musicians (see figures 6.4 and 6.5).[100] Influenced by Coltrane's use of Western concert and African instrumental music, Shepp had hoped in his first visit to Africa to create a kind of musical "reunion," not just a way for jazz to

FIGURE 6.4. Archie Shepp and Ted Joans at the Pan-African Cultural Festival in Algiers, 1969. Photo by Guy Le Querrec. Photo courtesy of Magnum Photos.

FIGURE 6.5. Archie Shepp performing with an ensemble of Algerian and Tuareg musicians, Algiers, 1969. Photo by Guy Le Querrec. Photo courtesy of Magnum Photos.

incorporate traditional sounds.[101] In many ways, Shepp's thinking fits within a longer history of African Americans' relationship to Africa, which was seen not as a distant or foreign land but instead as an ancestral home. While rooted in late nineteenth-century Pan-African thinking, this view had become more widespread among jazz musicians involved in the Black Arts Movement.[102] It also echoed a newer phenomenon: the transnational encounters between jazz musicians, which, as Robin D. G. Kelley describes, in turn "figured into the formation of modern African identity."[103] Earlier in the trip, Shepp had rehearsed an improvisational performance with the Algerian musicians in a schoolyard in Algiers.[104] Klein recorded Shepp's final instructions to the musicians: "C'est une experience d'improvisation. C'est le jazz" (It's an experience of improvisation. It's jazz), after which he began to play, soon followed by Joans's own poetic recitation, which alternated between French and English:

> Nous sommes revenus. Nous sommes les noirs Américains. Les Afro-Américains. Les Africains des Etats-Unis. We have returned. We are Black Americans, Afro-Americans, Africans from the United States.
> Mais la première chose, nous sommes Africains. But first, we are Africans.
> We are still Black and we have come back. Nous sommes revenus. We have returned.
> We have come back, brought back to our land, Africa, the music of Africa.
> Jazz is a Black power. Jazz is a Black power. Jazz is an African power.
> Jazz is an African music. Jazz is an African music. We have come back.

Joans continued, marking their return—"From Watts, From Chicago, From Alabama, From Kentucky, we have returned"—the momentum in his voice punctuated in Klein's film by visual representations of these foreign spaces. The performance's polyrhythmic sounds were exhilarating, as were Joans's words, a direct statement that reclaimed jazz as African and as a form of Black power.

The capacity crowd, which included the Algerian president Houari Boumediane, was invigorated and astonished. The Algerian poet Rachid Boudjedra recalled that Shepp had "electrified the Algerian crowd that had never heard jazz before."[105] The French anthropologist Michel Leiris described the concert as an "enormous collective improvisation" and "fabulous kind of happening." Even with its "cacophony" and "dissonance," he recalled, "they managed to keep all of this together." It was, Leiris said, "one of the most beautiful things I've ever seen or heard."[106] Shepp himself reflected on the event in an interview for *El Moudjahid*: "In my opinion, jazz is the music of all the long-lost Africans in America. So, I am happy to be here in Algeria: it is a return to Africa after 500 years of estrangement. I see the Tuareg and I sense they are close to me, that was a revelation."[107] For Shepp and Joans, it was also an opportunity to speak directly to African musicians and audiences. While brought together by political and cultural networks that extended beyond Algeria, in this moment Joans and Shepp embodied the connection between jazz and Africa and found themselves with no need of intermediaries or translators.

The power of the performance was primed by several features on Shepp in the publicity materials that appeared in the months before the festival. In a May 1969 newsletter, one writer defined African American musicians as members of what Amiri Baraka had called "blues people."[108] These musicians had not only retained the music's "African dimension," they argued, but had also made out of the experience of oppression an opportunity to create, for the jazzman's "cries" were "the cries from the ghettos, from Watts, from Harlem, from the South Side of Chicago." The article asserted further that "the *Noir* could not become *Blanc* and that is his strength," and this "resistance to assimilation" was the root of his liberation. This sense of jazz "power" and "strength" may have pulled directly from Amiri Baraka's 1962 *Blues People*, but more likely it cited the 1968 French translation, which would transform French jazz criticism.[109] Inspired by Baraka, as well as the presence of free jazz at the Sorbonne in May 1968 and the arrival of musicians like Frank Wright, Anthony Braxton, Don Cherry, Ornette Coleman, and Albert Ayler in Paris, French critics like Philippe Carles and Jean-Louis Comolli embraced free jazz as an articulation of Black nationalism.[110] While their aesthetic positions were a direct refutation of the previous generation of French critics—who had rejected the notion that jazz had a "politics"—this new generation was still frustrated by the seemingly unbridgeable distance between themselves and Black performers.

For their part, African American free jazz performers had come to Paris in the late 1960s seeking out new audiences, with the hopes that a new "planetary approach" might lead to greater professional stability.[111] Beginning in the late 1960s, members of the Art Ensemble of Chicago, including Malachi Favors, Joseph Jarman, Famoudou Don Moye, and Lester Bowie, performed regularly in clubs like the Vieux Colombier (where Bechet had long performed) and at the American Center for Students and Artists, a "kind of networking area" that offered ample studios and rehearsal space.[112] In 1970, the French cultural ministry organized concerts by the Art Ensemble at different Maisons de la Culture, regional cultural centers established in the 1960s in provincial capitals such as Le Havre, Rennes, Amiens, and Grenoble.[113] In these spaces, they confronted not only the continued legacy of primitivism but also the increasing pressure to now embody the political movements associated with Black power. Most French critics saw them as the "musical avatars of an imminent black nationalist rebellion."[114] While less primitivist in its orientation, *Présence Africaine* still proclaimed free jazz to be "today at the vanguard of a people in full revolution."[115]

Moye had first encountered members of the Association for the Advancement of Creative Musicians (AACM) in Chicago, but he began playing with the Art Ensemble on his arrival in Paris in 1969. There he met poets, writers, and musicians, but he was particularly drawn to the opportunity to perform with a transnational community of percussionists from throughout West Africa, including Guinea, Côte d'Ivoire, Mali, and Senegal.[116] It was, Moye recalled, "a Pan African pool" into which he gladly dove. In addition to musical encounters, Moye also met African workers at social centers in the Parisian neighborhood of Barbès, and he raised funds for African garbage workers through various concerts. France was, he recalled, not exceptional in its treatment of Black musicians but nevertheless offered a unique crossroads of connection in the pan-African world.[117]

While Moye forged these political and creative connections in Paris, the festival in Algiers offered an opportunity to build those diasporic relationships on the African continent. In 1968, the festival's newsletters drew a direct connection to free-jazz performance, particularly Shepp. Another newsletter piece leading up to the festival asked whether jazz did in fact interest African audiences. To answer the question, the author drew on the work of scholars and cited Louis Armstrong and Dizzy Gillespie's tours of Ghana, but declared that the "best proof that jazz interests Africans is that Sim Copans successfully presented almost everywhere in Africa. . . . [Africans] recognize very well that it is the song of hope for the unhappy children exiled from Africa."[118] Several years later, Guinean scholar Ibrahima Baba Kaké cited Shepp as one of the many African American composers and musicians who had "returned to seek out a new inspiration in Africa." He then stated: "We say, with Simon Copans, that 'history has closed the loop.' From Africa came the musical elements present and immortalized in the African American songs; and thereby survived the essential factors that contained the germ of instrumental jazz created around 1890." He continued, describing how "a half-century later, black American jazzmen, returning to the songs and ancestral rhythms of Africa, discover there the fresh sources to enrich, and to a large extent, to renew the music of the twentieth century."[119] Likely citing Copans's own lectures on African American music, Kaké underscored the vitality and historicity of jazz and the continued relevance of Africa to the music's contemporary resonance.

Both quotations bring into relief a set of questions that had been simmering in this period: What exactly did African American music represent, both at this festival and beyond? Was it a mechanism of American power, or evidence of an accommodationist alliance with French colonial authority, or the articulation of a revolutionary form of politics? And if it did represent all of these intentions and influences at once, what effect did those forces and influences have on the musicians and the music itself? The contradictions that encircled African American music in postcolonial Francophone Africa are perhaps most clearly seen in the ambiguous role of Sim Copans, the unlikely American expatriate who so clearly embodied the conflicting structures of power in postwar France and postcolonial Africa. But those contradictions were also evident in the performances themselves: the music, the gestures, the asides, and Joans's verbal urgings in French and English, using colonial languages to reject the imposition of imperial power. They were evident in the ways in which these performances and performance spaces were supported and financed. They were evident in the audiences themselves, which were composed of Africans as well as European tourists and American officials, who kept a watchful eye on the proceedings. The contradictions manifested in the networks of distribution, whether through BYG/Actuel's sales of the recordings of Shepp's concert or the postcolonial radio and television networks set up by France, the United States, and the USSR to reach Francophone African listeners.[120] While these networks sought to define African American music's meaning and power in Francophone Africa, the performance of African American music—and the borders and barriers that surrounded it—would change the music's meaning and potential power.

Say It Loud: James Brown in Africa

In late September 1974, a crowd of seventy thousand people crowded into the Stade du 20 Mai in Kinshasa, Zaire, to attend a music festival of unprecedented proportions: Zaire 74.[121] The festival had originally been scheduled to accompany a boxing match between Muhammad Ali and George Foreman, known in the United States as the "Rumble in the Jungle" and in Zaire as the "supercombat du siècle" (Fight of the Century). When organizers were forced to postpone the match, the music festival continued as planned, culminating in a three-day event that featured thirty-one musicians from across the diaspora, including South African singer Miriam Makeba, Cameroonian musician Manu Dibango, the Congolese rumba performers O.K. Jazz Orchestra and Tabu Ley Rochereau, Cuban singer Celia Cruz, and American musicians Bill Withers,

B. B. King, Etta James, the Spinners, and James Brown.[122] Financed by Liberian investors, and given ostensible sponsorship by Mobutu Sese Seko's government, the promoters presented the festival as a celebration of Black Power and Pan-African solidarity.[123] According to one report, it represented a "spiritual commitment by Blacks from all over the world ... bringing together two cultures linked by a similar heritage and joined in a celebration of life, a rededication through music."[124] No stranger to hyperbole, promoter Don King defined it as the "greatest musical event in the history of the world," a recognition of shared "roots and heritage" by people "who have had their beginnings in swamps and ghettos."

While it was many fans' first opportunity to see James Brown in person, it was not Brown's first visit to the African continent or even to this particular stadium. Brown first traveled to Africa in 1968 for a private concert, but in 1970 he returned with a twenty-two-piece band to Lagos, Nigeria, where thousands of fans waited to greet him at the airport. He and the other band members learned that there were more copies of "Say It Loud" in Nigeria than turntables to play the discs.[125] Brown and the other musicians recalled that the fans "clutched their copies like prizes."[126] Brown returned in 1972, this time to Kinshasa, where he once again remembered the "thousands of people just waiting to see and touch me" (see figure 6.6). He recalled that their "respect was like reverence, it was like they were looking up to me like a god."[127] Brown gave a matinee performance at the Theatre de Verdure at Mount Ngaliema (Stanley) before a crowd of "pop-boys" and "pop-girls," who "couldn't believe their eyes." To see "James Brown in Kinshasa, and above all in front of them, made them crazy." The evening's second show was also a hit, leading to additional performances in Lubumbashi, the second-largest city in the Congo.[128]

In his memoir, Brown described being "overwhelmed" by seeing "kids walking around in the streets, wherever I went, with James Brown albums under their arms—four, five, six different ones." He learned that they didn't have record players—that these albums cost them a huge amount of money, and as a result they had to use a "communal phonograph." Brown wrote later that he would have preferred to stay on the African continent, where he "felt the strong pull of my ancestors." Rather than simply reading about their history, now he "was walking in it." He continued, "Here I was, in Africa, where Black meant something other than 'Hey, you' or 'You're not welcome here.'"[129] In another account, there were twenty-five thousand people in attendance at a concert at a cricket field in Kinshasa. In Brown's view, the African response was rooted in his ability to succeed in a "country controlled completely by whites." To these observers, he was "not a normal man ... abnormal even."[130] Likewise, Maceo Parker—who traveled with Brown to Nigeria in 1968—recalled being moved

FIGURE 6.6. James Brown in Africa, unknown date and location. Photo courtesy of Getty Images.

by the chanting of his own name. The "fact that his own name, overheard on a record, could infiltrate a place's language" demonstrated "just how much influence James Brown had, not only in America but all over the world."[131]

Brown returned to Africa in 1975, this time to Senegal, where he performed in both planned and unscheduled concerts. Some of his visit was captured on film by Ricardo Niasse, a DJ who introduced soul music to dance parties in Dakar in the 1970s. While Niasse's first DJing opportunities were as a child—when he was required to turn the handle of the *Voix de sa maître* phonograph player, bringing the sounds of Edith Piaf and Jacques Brel to his parents' parties—his professional DJing career began in 1968 in Dakar, when he spun records at Le Baobab, the Gamma Club, Soumbedioune, Cabo, and Sahel.[132] Having met Brown's manager at one of these parties, he invited Brown to perform, taking photographs of the soul singer among the Dakar youth, who crowded the stage to see him. The visit was also filmed by a foreign crew, led by director Adrian Maben, who eventually completed a documentary film intended for French television.[133] The film opens at the Dakar airport, where a crowd has gathered in anticipation of Brown's arrival, shouting his name. A French narration weaves together interviews of Brown with footage of his time in Senegal, including his concerts. When asked about his relationship to Africa, Brown says that he believes he is "something of a hero" in Africa and sees himself as a "model man for [his] brothers and sisters of Africa."

While Brown's reflections suggest a kind of reverent distance between himself and his audience, the concert footage tells a different story. Indeed, it captures Brown's unique way of physically and vocally engaging his audience, whose own responses suggest the intimacy of the performance space in Dakar. Trombonist Fred Wesley Jr. recalled later, "[Audiences] loved us to the point of hysteria," which prompted local police to set up a fence around the stage (Brown himself promptly jumped off that fence to join the throngs).[134] During the remarkable instrumental opening of "It's a Man's Man's Man's World," Brown asks the audience "Can I scream?" Responding to the crowd's urgings, Brown lets out a "yeah," which is soon transformed into an "extended melismatic invention." He repeats "Senegal" dozens of times before transitioning to a vocalization that, as R. J. Smith has noted, sounds like the muezzin's call to prayer, and then again to the urgent repetition of "Senegal."[135] This particular performance recalls the brilliant insights of James Snead, who argued that "the cut"—the continued return to the start, that "abrupt, seemingly unmotivated break"—was a critical dimension of African American music.[136] While Jacques Attali saw repetition as a manifestation of mass production and standardization, "stockpiled until it loses its meaning," Snead argued instead that the practice of repetition did not, in fact, disrupt the rhythm but strengthened it, allowing its meaning to circulate, "there for you to pick it up when you come back to get it."[137] For Snead and many of his listeners, James Brown and his continued exhortations—"Hit me" and "Take it to the bridge"—exemplified this kind of musical power. By repeating the word "Senegal," Brown seemed to reclaim its power, strengthening his and his audience's connection to one another.

The film ends by documenting Brown and his band's visit to the Île de Gorée and their tour of the Maison des Esclaves (House of Slaves). In visiting the site and encountering the remnants of the Atlantic slave trade, the band is led by a Senegalese tour guide, who explains in English the history that sits before them. Reflecting on this experience, Maceo Parker recalled a "strange mix of sadness and pride" but said that, overall, being in the "motherland" had given him a "great sense of fulfilment." He recalled in particular the trip to Gorée, "where slaves were housed until they were ready to be shipped off to the New World." They walked through the "giant buildings, that reminded" him of the "tobacco warehouses in Kinston [North Carolina]." Parker thought of "all of the people who'd been there, shackled," and "to this day," he wrote, he could not "find the words to describe it other than to say that it was a powerful experience." He continued, "Black Americans were reestablishing ties to Africa—the idea of black power was taking hold, and I was proud of being part of that bridge back to the motherland."[138] The film follows Brown and the band as they leave the island by boat, with children hanging on to the sides, and the narration concludes: "Soul music has become a code that can be understood by Blacks on the other side of the Atlantic. James Brown is the one who deciphered this code."

Manthia Diawara has contended that there is something critical to be gained in thinking about postcolonial history through the frame of rock 'n' roll and Black Power. And for Diawara, it was James Brown in particular who embodied this period, as he combined the "ethos of black pride with the energy of rock and roll."[139] In his view, Brown and "other diaspora aestheticians from North America" were able to somehow elude the association of American culture with imperialism and capitalist exploitation. He later recalled, "For me and for many of my friends, to be liberated was to be exposed to more R&B songs and to be up on the latest news."[140] They were not "stuck" or defined only by ethnicity, religion, tradition, or home, but instead were finding themselves through this foreign culture, which united Black youth "through a common habitus of black pride, civil rights, and self-determination."[141] And Brown, "a figure mediated through civil rights and worldwide decolonization," had become for Diawara the "link between the new freedom and an African identity that had been repressed" by colonialism.

From Diawara's perspective, the "storehouse of African cultural and spiritual practices," which had been "forced into silence and rendered invisible by colonialism and Islam," was reignited when young people encountered James Brown.[142] He furthermore suggested that Brown himself connected Bamako's youth to a "pre–Atlantic slavery energy," which in turn "enabled them to master the language of independence and modernity and to express the return of Africanism to Africa through black aesthetics."[143] Though he draws on his own memories of the era, Diawara also points to Malick Sidibé's photographs of youth culture in mid-1960s Bamako, which captured the texture of the moment and the centrality of individual records.[144] (See figure 6.7.) Diawara underscores the importance of Sidibé himself in "shaping and expanding" youth culture, comparing his work to that of barbers and tailors, who "became artists by first pleasing their customers, by providing them with the best hairstyles, dresses, and photographs." Admonished by their elders, who misrecognized their representations as mimicry, young people had in fact rejected the older systems, "collapsed the walls of binary opposition between colonizer and colonized, and made connections beyond national frontiers with the diaspora and international youth

Piique-Nique. a la Chaussée. 1976   Malick sidibe ____ 2002

FIGURE 6.7. Malick Sidibé, *Pique-nique à la chausée 1976* (*Picnic at the Beach, 1976*). Photo courtesy of the artist and Jack Shainman Gallery, New York.

movements."[145] They found in consumer culture—and the consumption of soul music and R&B in particular—a new language for defining African independence, an "alternative source of cultural capital" in the postcolonial era.[146]

In a particularly striking photograph by Sidibé, two young women hold between them a 1968 James Brown album, *Live at the Apollo*, vol. 2 (see figure 6.8). Originally released by King Records in the United States, the album was distributed by the German label Polydor (which acquired Brown's back catalogue in 1971) in France and beyond. This particular album may have come directly to these fans from the United States, distributed through unofficial circuits of airline stewards and students, or it might have been distributed through the more official networks of distribution. Absent this information, we can only

FIGURE 6.8. Malick Sidibé, *Fans de James Brown, 1965* (*James Brown Fans, 1965*). Photo courtesy of the artist and Jack Shainman Gallery, New York.

imagine how it arrived at this moment and in this location. The women are posed as if dancing, and the album is centered between them, underscoring its important place in the composition of the photograph.

While Brown appears in this photograph as a commodity, his performances created new kinds of meaning and urgency, punctuated by his riffs on his own surroundings and his direct calls to his audience. Likewise, while a range of African American musicians brought to the continent their own expectations—seeking a spiritual or mythical homeland—the experiences of the tours were transformative. The audiences before them, who might have otherwise seemed like lost ancestors, were now real and contemporary peers who responded verbally and physically to their own musical creations. In Dakar, Algiers, and Kinshasa, African American music, in the moments during and around its performance, had created new conditions for the comprehension and valuation of African American culture. While linked to those that came before it, this soundscape of liberation was pan-African, a critical new space of inquiry, connection, and transformation.

EPILOGUE

Sounding like a Revolution

———

In May 1944, the Martiniquan writer René Ménil contributed a short essay
on poetry, jazz, and freedom to *Tropiques*, a surrealist journal published in
Fort-de-France, Martinique.[1] The journal was founded in 1941 by Aimé and
Suzanne Césaire, who sought new ways of freeing the mind from racism and
colonialism by investigating the "domain of the strange, the marvelous and the
fantastic."[2] Deemed subversive by Vichy officials, *Tropiques* was forced to pass
as a "journal of West Indian folklore" until 1943, when Free French forces removed the Vichy regime from Martinique.[3] By 1944, while less constrained
by state officials, the journal was still defined by the long-standing systems of
patronage and authority that had supported *négritude*, with poetry by Aimé
Césaire appearing alongside an essay by white surrealist André Breton extolling
his genius. In his own essay, Ménil examined the state of contemporary Antillean poetry, which appeared to him to be a dying art form. By contrast, Ménil
found new aesthetic power in the immediacy of jazz performance, whose value,
he argued, was rooted in its improvisational nature and its capacity to "create
beauty as one goes along." For Ménil, jazz's improvisational quality provided
a new set of aesthetic possibilities. He found in jazz a kind of freedom, for
neither the content nor the structure was "concretely preconceived," so that
it might re-create in the performer and audience "the sense of the instant and
the sense of transition." Ménil further suggested that the capacity of jazz to

"simultaneously resurrect the past while remaining in the moment" was based on its dialectical synthesis of old traditions and new forms, the "simultaneous living negation and living consummation of old cultural forms."

In many ways, Ménil's essay is an artifact of the liberation era, when African American music became a means through which the war's end and a postwar future were imagined. His views were certainly distinct from those of his white French contemporaries, but Ménil's belief that American jazz would reinvigorate an otherwise moribund culture was part and parcel of a much longer tradition of French jazz criticism.[4] Although Ménil's words are very clearly embedded in and bear witness to a specific historical moment, they nevertheless resist the same temporality that historical sources typically require. Looking around him, Ménil saw a world that had been "poisoned," robbed of the possibility of change and burdened by the knowledge of what came before and was likely to come next. In response, Ménil's essay located in jazz a future liberated from the weight of the past. Rejecting the inevitability of a desiccated landscape, Ménil envisioned instead a soundscape that was freed by virtue of jazz performance, which itself might radically transform Black consciousness. In a sense, Ménil found in jazz performance a way to refuse the colonization of time and space: to remove the preconditions and presuppositions that frame the future, to reject the limits of time in securing liberation, and ultimately to reclaim the radical potential in African American music.[5]

Moving from Ménil's argument, which defines jazz as a liberatory force that exceeds temporal limits, I want to return to the historical stakes of this book, which has illuminated the labor involved in defining the meaning, value, and power of African American music. Beginning with the liberation of France and the US military's role in redefining jazz, the book has looked closely at the different networks of dissemination that followed: the circuits of postwar print culture, the commercial record industry, Cold War political propaganda, and postwar Black internationalism. It has foregrounded the critical work of intermediaries, who were powerful arbiters in framing—and restraining—the racial meaning and political power of jazz, spirituals, and blues. And it has linked the postwar and the postcolonial soundscapes, tracing the networks of musical production and circulation from France to Francophone Africa. Whether in the work of Louis Achille and Sim Copans, or the growing reach of the recording and publishing industries, or the expanded interests of US and French officials in shaping the encounter with jazz, the same networks that defined the return of African American music at the end of World War II were critical to its continued power in the postcolonial period. Just as US officials worked within French networks in the postliberation period, French officials took advantage of colonial radio networks that were already embedded in West and Central Africa to broadcast French-produced jazz and Negro spirituals programs to African audiences after the formal end of colonialism. Likewise, French record companies invested in the expansion of the record industry in West Africa, where they might find both new performers and a generation of consumers for rhythm and blues, jazz, and gospel. And finally, leaders like Léopold Sédar Senghor continued to draw on old relationships and networks in defining the value of African American culture for postcolonial Africa.

Though these networks were clearly conduits for the consolidation of power throughout the postwar period, they also created new venues in which that same power was contested. In some cases, the efforts of intermediaries to define African American music were revised and challenged by African diasporic musicians, artists, and intellectuals, who employed a range of strategic essentialisms and issued direct challenges to critical authority to ensure that they also benefited from these new systems of valuation for African American expressive culture.[6] Whether in Joseph Zobel's scathing critiques of Boris Vian's attempts to write Black identity, Marge Singleton's use of Mezz Mezzrow's public image to secure fair payment, Sidney Bechet's strategic moves to profit from his own symbolic value for Vogue, or Frantz Fanon's decision to use jazz criticism as a metaphor for French colonialism, it is clear that African diasporic musicians, writers, and producers worked within these networks to lay claim to the African American musical tradition. Likewise, Francophone African listeners critiqued the underlying message of these modes of dissemination as well as the very possibility that any form of culture might in itself be a liberatory agent.

In many respects, the possibility of innovation within existing structures resembles the contingency in musical performance itself, which created unexpected intrusions and responses. Transformative change could come from the musicians, who might alter or annotate a scheduled set, or from the audiences, whose responses were sometimes predictable but were never predetermined. But as this book documents, the "venue" far exceeded one night's performance in a club or concert hall. Rather, it was a global arena, whose large-scale systems of production and distribution were matched by the amplified power of a much larger potential audience. This shared experience of "listening in," to borrow Tsitsi Jaji's phrasing, opened up a range of possibilities for African American music, which would, in the years to come, expand to include new genres and media.[7] As Shana Redmond has demonstrated, Black anthems in particular have served as an instrument of global liberation and a "method of rebellion, revolution, and future visions that disrupt and challenge the manufactured differences used to dismiss, detain, and destroy communities."[8]

Likewise, Michael Denning has suggested that interwar encounters with record commodities were critical to the "decolonization of the ear," which "preceded and made possible the subsequent decolonization of legislatures and literatures, schools and armies."[9] This history—in which music became "anticipatory, prophetic, utopian"—echoes Ménil, who saw jazz as a way to resist the very temporality that power seeks to define and delimit.[10]

Black people, however, were not the only ones listening in, nor were they the only ones to benefit from the global circulation of African American music. The liberatory potential of African American music was deployed, revised, and sold in contradictory ways throughout the postwar period by institutions and figures who traded in visions of African American liberation, emancipation, and defiance, thus transforming the conditions in which African American and African diasporic cultural producers could articulate their own emancipatory interpretation of this tradition. The continued presence of these intermediaries complicates a deceptively simple question that has trailed the global circulation of African American culture in the twentieth century: Why is African American culture so valued when Black lives are not? The answer is, in part, found in the rich scholarly work on African American music in the United States, which has revealed how seemingly contradictory desires flourished in the same physical and symbolic landscapes.[11] While the global framework complicates the terms—and, indeed, underlines the real and persistent confusion about what exactly "Black culture" means—it too makes clear that the celebration of African American culture is closely linked to contemporaneous systems of racism and exclusion outside the United States.[12] In some ways, these links are epistemological: just as racism is a system of knowledge that has changed over time, adapting to new economic conditions and policies while conveying ideologies regarding hierarchy, superiority, and debasement, so too is celebration a projection of knowledge.[13] While less immediately threatening, celebration nevertheless relies on social fictions: the presumption of intimacy and access, the implicit assumptions regarding who assesses and evaluates, and the belief that a cultural artifact could represent the breadth and fullness of African American culture.

In the case of postwar France, I find that the *same* historical and material conditions facilitated both phenomena, enabling a persistent belief in the universal liberatory capacity of African American music even as political forces mobilized to curtail the freedom of African and African-descended people. Whether in the military infrastructure that promoted jazz and arrested African American soldiers, the magazines where Black people's voices were denigrated while white men claimed jazz expertise, the radio networks that silenced the violence of imperialism at the same time that they broadcast African American spirituals, or the physical space of the Palais des Sports, where the sounds of Ray Charles drowned out the cries of North Algerian detainees, the French interest in African American music was sustained by the same infrastructures that perpetuated racist domination and white supremacy during and after the end of empire. It is not enough to simply juxtapose the resounding French silence on race and empire with the unprecedented production and propagation of African American music in France. Instead, we must look at the archives of these twinned aural histories, whose correspondences and connections were preserved in state records, books, magazines, radio broadcasts, concert recordings, scrapbooks, albums, and the ephemera of everyday life. There we find not only the technologies, intermediaries, and networks that helped to produce African American music in postwar France but also the cultural logic that facilitated the broad appeal of African American culture while quelling the claims of African and African-descended people to self-determination and dignity in France and beyond.

Notes

INTRODUCTION: MAKING SOUNDWAVES

1. For a full account of this concert series, and the disparate histories that converged at the Palais des Sports, see Moore, "Ray Charles in Paris."

2. See House and MacMaster, *Paris 1961*, 161–79; Cole, "Remembering the Battle of Paris."

3. Ritz and Charles, *Brother Ray*, 278. Leroy Cooper quoted in Mike Evans, *Ray Charles*, 146–47.

4. Catherine Pierre, "Ray Charles a fait salle comble," *Le Monde*, October 23, 1961.

5. Two concerts were recorded for André Francis's *Jazz sur scène* program on RTF: "Ray Charles au Palais des Sports," *Jazz sur scène* (Paris Inter, October 22, 1961), INA. The recordings are also available in *Ray Charles: Live in Paris 20–21 Octobre 1961/17–18–20–21 Mai 1962* (Paris: Fremeaux & Assoc., 2014).

6. "Des étudiants algériens accusent," *L'Étudiant algérien* (November 1961), reproduced in *Partisans* 3 (February 1962): 119–24.

7. On the analytical possibilities in soundscapes, see especially Thompson, *Soundscape of Modernity*; Schafer, *Soundscape*; Samuels, Meintjes, Ochoa, and Porcello, "Soundscapes."

8. Attali, *Noise*, 4.

9. In thinking through sound, media, and listening practices, I draw on David Suisman and Susan Strasser, *Sound in the Age of Mechanical Reproduction*; Stoever, *Sonic Color Line*; Larkin, *Signal and Noise*; Bronfman, *Isles of Noise*; Hirschkind, *Ethical Soundscape*; Sterne, *Audible Past*; Ochoa Gautier, *Aurality*; Kun, *Audiotopia*; Suisman, *Selling Sounds*; Vaillant, "Sounds of Whiteness."

10. On the "listening ear," see Stoever, *Sonic Color Line*.

11. To define this mediating role, I draw from a range of work that has identified the importance of cultural gatekeepers, critics, and tastemakers in the twentieth century. See especially Gennari, *Blowin' Hot and Cool*; Green, *Selling the Race*; Frank, *Conquest of Cool*. I also guided by work on the mediating work of recording studios, including Meintjes, *Sound of Africa!*; Veal, *Dub*.

12. On the historical precedents of intermediaries and the work of mediation in the Atlantic world, see Berlin, *Many Thousands Gone*. On the Black Atlantic, see Gilroy, *Black Atlantic*; Weheliye, *Phonographies*; Dubois, *Banjo*.

13. On misreading and mistranslation in Black diasporic and internationalist cultural production, see Edwards, *Practice of Diaspora*. This work also echoes what Vèvè A. Clark has described as "diaspora literacy," which "implied an ease and intimacy with more than one language, with interdisciplinary relations among history, ethnology, and the folklore of regional expression" within the African diaspora. See Clark, "Developing Diaspora Literacy."

14. Holt, "Marking."

15. See Blake, *Le tumulte noir*; Archer-Straw, *Negrophilia*.

16. I am mindful that the concept of "agency" can sometimes reproduce the logic of white supremacy, which is itself premised on the belief that African-descended people do not have agency or humanity. On this, see Johnson, "On Agency."

17. For work that places African and African diasporic populations, as well as Black cultural production, at the center of sound studies and the global flows of media, technology, and culture, see in particular Weheliye, *Phonographies*; Jaji, *Africa in Stereo*; Stoever, *Sonic Color Line*; Chude-Sokei, *Sound of Culture*; Stadler, "On Whiteness and Sound Studies."

18. As Richard Iton recounted in the US context, the "engagement with and interpellation of black life via cultural representations by (white) American citizens historically has been quite compatible with the marginalization and disenfranchisement of African Americans as political subjects and political members of the republic community." Iton, *In Search of the Black Fantastic*, 12.

19. Hazel Scott, "What Paris Means to Me," *Negro Digest*, November 1961, 61.

20. In thinking through Scott's experiences as a woman in the jazz world, I am indebted to the tradition of Black feminist scholarship on music-making, criticism, and collection. See in particular Brooks, *Liner Notes for the Revolution*; Griffin, *If You Can't Be Free*; G. Wald, *Shout, Sister, Shout!*; Rustin and Tucker, *Big Ears*; Mahon, *Black Diamond Queens*.

21. W. G. Smith, *Return to Black America*, 59–60.

22. W. G. Smith, *Return to Black America*, 61. On Dixon, see R. Jones, *Dean Dixon*.

23. On this history, see especially Germain, *Decolonizing the Republic*; Childers, *Seeking Imperialism's Embrace*; Marker, "Obscuring Race."

24. Wright quoted in Fabre, *From Harlem to Paris*, 260.

25. Simone and Cleary, *I Put a Spell on You*, 165.

26. Famoudou Don Moye, telephone interview with the author, March 12, 2020. On Moye and the Art Ensemble's experiences in France, see also Drott, *Music and the Elusive Revolution*; Lewis, *Power Stronger Than Itself*; Steinbeck, *Message to Our Folks*.

27. "Along the Rue Bechet," *Time*, September 20, 1954, 85. Bechet's financial and business records are held in the Fonds Charles Delaunay (FCD), Département de l'audiovisuel, Bibliothèque nationale de France (BnF), Paris.

28. On this concert, see Fry, "Remembrance of Jazz Past."

29. Bechet, *Treat It Gentle*, 45.

30. Ehrlich, "Old Man with a Horn."

31. On African American musicians' literary and textual interventions, see especially Porter, *What Is This Thing?*; Edwards, *Epistrophies*.

32. In thinking about emblematic and affective power of African Americans, I am indebted to a range of work, including Quashie, *Sovereignty of Quiet*; Hartman, *Scenes of Subjection*; Morrison, "Sound(s) of Subjection"; Campt, *Other Germans*; Layne, *White Rebels in Black*.

33. On the global mobility of racialized commodities and ideas, see especially Auslander and Holt, "Sambo in Paris." On the production of African American culture—and its intersections with global capitalism—see Rose, *Black Noise*; Levine, *Black Culture and Black Consciousness*; Suisman, "Co-workers in the Kingdom"; S. E. Smith, *Dancing in the Street*; Green, *Selling the Race*; Tate, *Everything but the Burden*; Chude-Sokei, *Last "Darky."*

34. Hall, "What Is This 'Black'?," 108, 110.

35. Cannonball Adderley and His Quintet, *En concert avec EUROPE1, Salle Pleyel, 27 Mars 1969* (Paris: RTE, 1992), emphasis mine.

36. On the experiences of African Americans in Paris, see especially Stovall, *Paris Noir*; Fabre, *From Harlem to Paris*; Sharpley-Whiting, *Bricktop's Paris*; Fabre and Williams, *Street Guide*; Broschke Davis, *Paris without Regret*.

37. Stovall, *Paris Noir*, xv.

38. On Paris as a site of memory for Black Americans, see Bruce, "New Negro in Paris."

39. This occlusion has been thoughtfully explored in a range of scholarship, including Keaton and Sharpley-Whiting, *Black France/France Noire*; Hine, Keaton, and Small, *Black Europe*; Archer-Straw, *Negrophilia*; Blake, *Tumulte noir*; Boittin, *Colonial Metropolis*. It has also been interrogated within work on the French Atlantic and Francophone world, see C. L. Miller, *French Atlantic Triangle*; Higginson, *Scoring Race*; Hill, *Black Soundscapes White Stages*; Braddock and Eburne, *Paris, Capital of the Black Atlantic*.

40. See Stovall, "The Fire This Time," 189.

41. The field is too rich to fully capture here, but my own thinking draws in particular on West and Martin, *From Toussaint to Tupac*; Kelley, "But a Local Phase"; Makalani, *In the Cause of Freedom*; Von Eschen, *Race against Empire*; Guridy, *Forging Diaspora*; Blain, *Set the World on Fire*; McDuffie, *Sojourning for Freedom*; Putnam, *Radical Moves*; Byrd, *Black Republic*.

42. On the continued significance (yet silencing) of race and racism in France, see Ndiaye, *La condition noire*; C. M. Fleming, *Resurrecting Slavery*; Mitchell, *Vénus noire*; Balibar, *Race, Nation, Class*; Peabody and Stovall, *Color of Liberty*; Silverman, *Deconstructing the Nation*; Chapman and Laura Frader, *Race in France*; Davidson, *Only Muslim*.

43. James Baldwin, "Encounter on the Seine" (1950), in J. Baldwin, *Collected Essays*, 87.

44. McKay, *Circular Breathing*; Atkins, *Blue Nippon*; A. F. Jones, *Yellow Music*; Poiger, *Jazz, Rock, and Rebels*; Ansell, *Soweto Blues*. While it focuses on a different genre and time period, Kira Thurman's work is especially instructive on the racialization of music in Europe. See Thurman, "Singing the Civilizing Mission."

45. See especially Lane, *Jazz and Machine-Age Imperialism*; A. Fry, *Paris Blues*; Drott, "Free Jazz and the French Critic."

46. See Tournès, *New Orleans sur Seine*. On the interwar period, see Shack, *Harlem in Montmartre*; Martin and Roueff, *La France du jazz*; J. H. Jackson, *Making Jazz French*; Jordan, *Le jazz*; Lane, *Jazz and Machine-Age Imperialism*; Kenney, "Assimilation of Jazz in France"; Stovall, "Music and Modernity."

47. On the postwar period, see Fry, *Paris Blues*; Perchard, *After Django*; Braggs, *Jazz Diasporas*; McGregor, *Jazz and Postwar French Identity*; Nettelbeck, *Dancing with De Beauvoir*. On free jazz in particular, see Lehman, "I Love You"; Drott, "Free Jazz"; Cotro and Levallet, *Chants libres*. On music and globalization in postwar France, see J. Briggs, *Sounds French*.

48. See McGregor, *Jazz and Postwar French Identity*; Perchard, *After Django*; Braggs, *Jazz Diasporas*. For work focused on African Americans' own experiences and perspectives, see also Broschke Davis, *Paris without Regret*; Broschke Davis, "Art Simmons in Paris"; Haggerty, "Under Paris Skies."

49. On musicians' critiques of the limits of jazz in particular, see Porter, *What Is This Thing?* For more on genre, see K. H. Miller, *Segregating Sound*; E. Wald, *How the Beatles Destroyed Rock*; C. L. Hughes, *Country Soul*.

50. On African American music and the public sphere, see Neal, *What the Music Said*; G. P. Ramsey, *Race Music*; Ward, *Just My Soul Responding*; Lordi, *Meaning of Soul*. Placing the creation of jazz within economic and social histories also departs from the canonization of jazz as an anticommercial art form. See DeVeaux, "Constructing the Jazz Tradition."

51. On racial consciousness and music, see in particular Radano and Bohlman, *Music and the Racial Imagination*; Kun, *Audiotopia*; Werner, *Change Is Gonna Come*; G. P. Ramsey, *Race Music*; Baraka, *Blues People*; Neal, *What the Music Said*; Monson, *Freedom Sounds*; Weheliye, *Phonographies*; E. Wald, *How the Beatles Destroyed Rock*; Hamilton, *Just around Midnight*; Saul, *Freedom Is, Freedom Ain't*; Hughes, *Country Soul*; Pecknold, *Hidden in the Mix*. On race and sound, see Eidsheim, *Race of Sound*; Stoever, *Sonic Color Line*.

52. On the temporal and spatial dimensions of decolonization, see Getachew, *World-making after Empire*; Cooper, *Citizenship between Empire and Nation*; Wilder, *Freedom Time*.

53. See Joseph-Gabriel, *Reimagining Liberation*, 7. On race, decolonization, and liberation movements in the UK and Europe, see Perry, *London Is the Place*; Matera, *Black London*; Pennybacker, *From Scottsboro to Munich*; Adi, *West Africans in Britain*; Florvil, *Mobilizing Black Germany*.

54. This moment is thus part of what Michael Denning describes as the "age of three worlds," which was dominated by "cultural industries and ideological state apparatuses." Denning, *Culture in the Age*, 3. On US power and decolonization in postwar France, see especially Ross, *Fast Cars, Clean Bodies*; Lebovics, *Bringing the Empire Back Home*; Shepard, *Invention of Decolonization*; Kuisel, *Seducing the French*; Pells, *Not Like Us*; De Grazia, *Irresistible Empire*.

55. See Von Eschen, *Satchmo Blows Up the World*; Von Eschen, *Race against Empire*.

56. See, for example Fosler-Lussier, *Music in America's Cold War*; Gienow-Hecht, "What Bandwagon?"; Blower, *Becoming Americans in Paris*; Schwartz, *It's So French!*

57. I want to thank Sandhya Shukla for sharpening my thinking on this point. In making sense of race and transnational histories of the twentieth century, and in particular the history of US imperialism, I draw on Kramer, *Blood of Government*; Renda, *Taking Haiti*; Singh, *Black Is a Country*; L. Briggs, *Reproducing Empire*; Man, *Soldiering through Empire*; Miller-Davenport, *Gateway State*; Singh, *Race and America's Long War*, Vitalis, *White World Order*; Kramer, "Power and Connection."

58. Radano and Olaniyan, *Audible Empire*, 7. On the transnational production of Black music, see especially Denning, *Noise Uprising*; Dubois, *Banjo*; Monson, *Freedom Sounds*; Von Eschen, *Satchmo Blows Up the World*; Redmond, *Anthem*; Jaji, *Africa in Stereo*; Garcia, *Listening for Africa*; Kelley, *Africa Speaks, America Answers*; Charry, *Hip Hop Africa*; Rollefson, *Flip the Script*; Putnam, *Radical Moves*; Veal, *Dub*; Chude-Sokei, *Last "Darky"*; Aidi, *Rebel Music*.

59. See Weheliye, *Phonographies*; Redmond, *Anthem*; Gilroy, *Black Atlantic*.

CHAPTER 1. JAZZ EN LIBERTÉ

1. Chesnel, *Le jazz en quarantaine*, 47.

2. Chesnel, *Le jazz en quarantaine*, 57–58.

3. On the violence of the liberation, see Hitchcock, *Bitter Road to Freedom*; Wieviorka, *Normandy*; Footitt, *War and Liberation in France*.

4. On anti-Black racism and rape accusations during the liberation, see especially Roberts, *What Soldiers Do*; Kaplan, *Interpreter*.

5. On Louis and World War II, see Sklaroff, "Constructing G.I. Joe Louis." See also Erenberg, *Greatest Fight of Our Generation*.

6. On Europe's band and the African American experience in World War I, see Badger, *Life in Ragtime*; Williams, *Torchbearers of Democracy*.

7. Williams, *Torchbearers of Democracy*, 165.

8. On the interwar period, see Sharpley-Whiting, *Bricktop's Paris*; Archer-Straw, *Negrophilia*; Blake, *Le Tumulte noir*; Boittin, *Colonial Metropolis*; Ezra, *Colonial Unconscious*.

9. See Jules-Rosette, *Josephine Baker in Art*. As Matthew Pratt Guterl argues, Baker was engaged in an entirely new kind of racial and cultural project by the 1940s. Guterl, *Josephine Baker*.

10. On *négritude*, see Edwards, *Practice of Diaspora*; Sharpley-Whiting, *Negritude Women*; Kesteloot, *Black Writers in French*; Wilder, *French Imperial Nation-State*.

11. Fry, *Paris Blues*, 118. On some of these same questions of authenticity and creative ownership among jazz critics in the United States, see Gennari, *Blowin' Hot and Cool*.

12. Ledos, "Un demi-siècle de jazz," 29, 31. For more on interwar radio, see Scales, *Radio and the Politics of Sound*; Méadel, *Histoire de la radio*; Brochand, *Histoire générale de la radio*; Neulander, *Programming National Identity*; Hill, *Black Soundscapes White Stages*.

13. On the origins of the Hot Club, see Legrand, *Charles Delaunay et le jazz*; Conte, "Les origines du Hot Club."

14. On Vichy, see Pollard, *Reign of Virtue*; Rousso, *Vichy Syndrome*. On the restructuring of French society through racial classification in this same period, see Camiscioli, *Reproducing the French Race*; Lebovics, *True France*.

15. Tournès, *New Orleans sur Seine*, 74.

16. Letter from the Director of Programs and Artistic Services at the Radiodiffusion Nationale (RN), December 2, 1941, Application de la législation antisémite aux artistes musiciens, 1941–1947, Radiodiffusion-Télévision Française, F43/170, Archives Nationales de France (ANF), Paris.

17. Beevor and Cooper, *Paris after the Liberation*, 171. See also Shack, *Harlem in Montmartre*, 119. On zoot suiters, see R. D. G. Kelley, *Race Rebels*, 163; Peiss, *Zoot Suit*.

18. See Régnier, *Jazz et société sous l'Occupation*, 185–86. I have chosen to leave *nègre* in the original French. On the history of this racial terminology, see C. L. Miller, *Blank Darkness*.

19. On jazz during World War II, see Régnier, *Jazz et société*; Fry, *Paris Blues*. On the persistence of this myth, see Tournès, *New Orleans sur Seine*, 84.

20. Some American musicians left voluntarily, while others, including Harry Cooper and Arthur Briggs, were captured and sent to labor camps. See Legrand, *Charles Delaunay*, 156. Vichy's Radiodiffusion Nationale (RN) featured several jazz programs, including *Jazz symphonique*, *Swing*, *Le grand cabaret*, *Vive le jazz*, and *L'orchestre de jazz*.

21. On the creation of new chapters, see *Jazz hot*, October 1945. See also Tournès, *New Orleans sur Seine*, 76–77.

22. Régnier, *Jazz et société*, 183.

23. On Reinhardt, see Dregni, *Gypsy Jazz*; Givan, *Music of Django Reinhardt*; Lie, "Genre, Ethnoracial Alterity."

24. For a discussion of Delaunay's intentions, whether sincere, subversive, or satirical see Lane, *Jazz and Machine-Age Imperialism*, 142–43; Tournès, *New Orleans sur Seine*, 82–84; Legrand, *Charles Delaunay*, 136–46; Fry, *Paris Blues*.

25. See "Causeries illustrés sur le jazz par Charles Delaunay," box 72, Fonds Charles Delaunay (FCD), Bibliothèque nationale de France, Paris (BnF). He suggested later that, given the Nazi respect for French culture, he chose to reiterate in articles and interviews that jazz had its roots in French Creole music.

26. See Tournès, *New Orleans sur Seine*; Legrand, *Charles Delaunay*.

27. Panassié contributed two articles for the right-wing *L'Insurgé*, in which he contrasted the authenticity and vitality of jazz with the decadence of the modern, commercial age, all of which, of course, drew on anti-Semitic tropes. On this, see Tournès, *New Orleans sur Seine*, 55–57, 176–77. On Panassié's wartime writing, see Lane, *Jazz and Machine-Age Imperialism*, chap. 4; Perchard, *After Django*, chap. 2.

28. Lane, *Jazz and Machine-Age Imperialism*, chap. 5.

29. The history of these musicians is not widely documented outside of the liner notes of *Swing caraïbe* at the Médiathèque Caraïbe in Basse-Terre, Guadeloupe. Material was first accessed August 18, 2011, on its website, www.lameca.org.

30. On the mass conscription of soldiers and laborers during World War I from throughout the African diaspora, see Williams, *Torchbearers of Democracy*; Stovall, "Color-Blind France?"; Echenberg, *Colonial Conscripts*.

31. On the experiences of veterans, see Mann, *Native Sons*.

32. See *Swing caraïbe: Premiers jazzmen antillais à Paris, 1929–1946*, CD (Vincennes: Frémeaux, 1997). In English in the original.

33. Letter from Abel Beauregard to Radiodiffusion Nationale, June 19, 1943, Organisation des services des programmes, 1940–49, Direction générale de la radio-diffusion, Office de la radiodiffusion et télévision française (ORTF), 950218/23, Centre des archives contemporaines (CAC), Fontainebleau. See also Régnier, *Jazz et société*, 188–89.

34. On this same surreptitious move, see Robin D. G. Kelley's discussion of *Tropiques*, whose radical surrealism was camouflaged in its promotion as a "journal of West Indian folklore." R. D. G. Kelley, "Poetics of Anticolonialism," 14.

35. Circulaire no. 1, Hot Club de France, January 1944, box 72, FCD, BnF.

36. See *Swing caraïbe*.

37. Circulaire, Hot Club de France, December 1943, box 72, FCD, BnF.

38. Circulaire, Hot Club de France, January 1944, box 72, FCD, BnF.

39. Ollie Stewart, "Normandy, Land of Plenty despite War, Stewart Says," *Baltimore Afro-American*, July 22, 1944; Ollie Stewart, "Our Soldiers Busy in France," *Baltimore Afro-American*, June 24, 1944; Ollie Stewart, "Sowing and Reaping," *Baltimore Afro-American*, December 21, 1940.

40. Ollie Stewart, "53 Motor Transport Units under 1 Leader in France," *Baltimore Afro-American*, August 5, 1944.

41. See Allan Morrison, "Negro Troops to Form 10.4% of US Army of Occupation," *Stars and Stripes*, June 14, 1945. Tyler Stovall estimates seven hundred thousand black troops: see Stovall, *Paris Noir*, 153. On African American GIs, see Ulysses Lee, *Employment of Negro Troops*; Thomas A. Guglielmo, "Martial Freedom Movement."

42. Bruce Wright cited in Fabre, *From Harlem to Paris*, 163.

43. Claud Collin, "J'étais un officier noir dans l'armée américaine pendant la Deuxième Guerre mondiale [interview with Thomas Russell Jones]," *Guerres mondiales et conflits contemporains* 204 (October–December 2001): 141–48.

44. On the global vision and politics of African Americans during World War II, see especially Von Eschen, *Race against Empire*; Plummer, *Rising Wind*.

45. R. B. Lovett, Report to Adjutant General, War Department on "Participation of Negro Troops in the Post-war Military Establishment, 1945, Classified General Correspondence, Adjutant General's Administration Branch, United States Army (World War II), European Theater of Operations, box 365, Record Group (RG) 338, National Archives and Records Administration, College Park, MD (hereafter cited as NARA-CP).

46. Jones quoted in Collin, "Interview with Thomas Russell Jones."

47. Letter from Joseph O. Curtis, August 9, 1945, folder 13, box 10, Simons Family Collection, Library of Congress (LOC).

48. Moore, *To Serve My Country*, 120.

49. The complaints were overwhelmingly focused on American troops, who were billeted in the region in greater numbers. Rapports des commissaires régionaux de la Republique, October 1944–January 1946, Relations avec les pays alliés, F1a/3304, ANF.

50. Ollie Stewart, "Disemboweled Stock Sign of Fierce Fight," *Baltimore Afro-American*, August 12, 1944.

51. Cited in Footitt, *War and Liberation in France*, 91.

52. Footitt, *War and Liberation in France*, 85.

53. The Judge Advocate General found that fifty-five of the seventy men executed by court-martial in the ETO between 1943 and 1946 were African American. Kaplan, *Interpreter*, 7. See also Lilly, *Taken by Force*, 81–94; Roberts, *What Soldiers Do*, 195–96.

54. Lilly, *Taken by Force*, 87. On the zones of contact, see Fehrenbach, "Learning from America," 108–9.

55. As Mary Louise Roberts has argued, these conditions were critical to the circulation of rumor regarding rape in rural Normandy. Roberts, *What Soldiers Do*.

56. Obituary of Richard Copans, March 19, 1956, in Copans Family Archives (CFA), Paris. Other family information found in Sim Copans's papers, the Fonds Sim Copans (FSC), Bibliothèque municipale, Souillac.

57. "8 Scholarships Given for Study in Europe," *New York Times*, May 4, 1931.

58. On his recruitment, see interview with George de Caunes, "De la radio mobile en Normandie à la creation de 'Ce soir in France,'" *Cahiers d'histoire de la radiodiffusion* 42 (September–November 1994): 196–99. Information on Copans's political views is from Richard Copans, interview with the author, April 21, 2010, Paris.

59. See letter granting Copans leave from February 1 to June 30, 1944, "for work with the Office of War Information." Letter from Columbia University to Sim Copans, February 11, 1944, CFA.

60. Vaillant, *Across the Waves*, 68. On the Voice of America, see Pirsein, *Voice of America*. On music and the Office of War Information, see Fauser, *Sounds of War*.

61. Memorandum from Helene Feller to George Barnes, March 17, 1944, Office of the Director, 1942–45, Records of the Office of the Director and Predecessor Agencies, Office of War Information (OWI), box 6, RG 208, NARA-CP.

62. See "Report on Radio Operations," February 7, 1943, Subject File, 1941–46, Records of the Historian, OWI, box 14, RG 208, NARA-CP.

63. Pirsein, *Voice of America*, 82. See also Office of War Information, *OWI in the ETO*. For the history of radio and foreign policy see Vaillant, *Across the Waves*; Horten, *Radio Goes to War*; Rawnsley, *Radio Diplomacy and Propaganda*; Savage, *Broadcasting Freedom*.

64. Letter from Edward W. Barrett, OWI, to Copans, March 2, 1944, CFA.

65. See January 1944 report on the Psychological Warfare Branch (precursor to PWD) describing its task as the "propaganda of liberation." "Report by Allied Force Headquarters," January 6, 1944, Information and Censorship Section, Psychological Warfare Branch, OWI, box 1, RG 208, NARA-CP.

66. Letter to Lucienne Copans, June 27, 1944, CFA.

67. "Robb-Hollander Report," 17, n.d., Historian's Records of the Psychological Warfare Branch, 1942–45, OWI, box 2, RG 208, NARA-CP.

68. "Robb-Hollander Report," 17–18.

69. "Popular Man on French Radio," *Stars and Stripes*, October 28, 1958, in Clippings, FSC.

70. Oriano, "Sim Copans, ambassadeur." Copans later claimed to have played jazz from V-Disc records for the GIs who asked to hear them. "Souvenirs et rencontres," n.d., Manuscripts, FSC.

71. "Sim le sage," *Jazz hot*, March 1965, 19–21.

72. The V-Disc he played was V-Disc 1B. This record was also one of the first V-Discs published in 1943 by the US government. Gillot, "Sim Copans."

73. Stowe, *Swing Changes*, 13, 153.

74. On the recording ban, see DeVeaux, "Bebop and the Recording Industry."

75. Stowe, *Swing Changes*, 153.

76. On the V-Disc, see Kendall, "Music for the Armed Services"; Sears, *V-Discs*; Anne Legrand, "La petite histoire des V-Discs," *Chroniques de la Bibliothèque nationale de France* 19 (July–September 2002). See also the V-Disc collection (The Richard Sherwood Sears Collection), Glenn Miller Archives, American Music Research Center, University of Colorado, Boulder.

77. Stowe, *Swing Changes*, 154.

78. Magee, "Irving Berlin's 'Blue Skies.'"

79. On *The Jazz Singer*, see Rogin, *Blackface, White Noise*. See also Melnick, *Right to Sing the Blues*.

80. Undated manuscript, "En juin 1944," FSC. See also Kaiser, *Veteran Recall*, 82.

81. De Caunes, "De la radio mobile," *Cahiers d'histoire de la radiodiffusion*, 196–99.

82. Corbin, *Village Bells*, x, 158.

83. Vaillant, "Occupied Listeners," 141–58.

84. On "signal" and "noise" as opposing or competing social forces in media circulation, see Larkin, *Signal and Noise*.

85. See "Incidents et délits causés par les troupes alliés," F1a/3305, ANF.

86. *Jazz hot*, October 1945, 16.

87. "Disques," *Jazz hot*, April 1946, 13.

88. On the circulation of nearly 123 million copies of the Armed Services Editions books, see J. Y. Cole, *Books in Action*. The largest distribution of ASE books to combat troops was in the "marshaling areas" of southern England immediately before the invasion of France. John Jamieson, a staff member of the War Department's library section, used official records and interviews to write *Books for the Army*. Jamieson, *Books for the Army*, 26.

89. P. E. Miller, *Esquire's Jazz Book*, 75. See also "GI Bookshelf," *Stars and Stripes Magazine*, October 7, 1945, 7; Jamieson, *Books for the Army*, 27; A. J. Liebling, "Cross-Chanel Trip I," *New Yorker*, July 1, 1944; Goffin, *Jazz*; P. E. Miller, *Esquire's 1945 Jazz Book*; P. E. Miller, *Esquire's Jazz Book*; Ramsey and Smith, *Jazzmen*.

90. Legrand, *Charles Delaunay*, 167.

91. From September 1944 to August 1946, roughly 3.6 million servicemen were stationed at the Le Havre camp. Bergère, "Français et Américains en Basse-Seine." See also Hillel, *Vie et mœurs des G.I.'s*; Hitchcock, *The Bitter Road to Freedom*, 50.

92. Bergère, "Français et Américains en Basse-Seine," 207.

93. Hennessey, *Klook*, 53–55. Clarke and Lewis were featured in the June 1945 United Service Organizations (USO) tour of "Jive's a poppin," "Entertainment in Paris," *Stars and Stripes*, June 14, 1945; "Le jazz à Paris," *Jazz hot*, October 1945, 23.

94. Regnier, *Jazz au Havre and Caux,* 39.

95. "L'activité des hot clubs régionaux," *Bulletin du Hot Club* 3 (1945), 16.

96. "L'activité des hot clubs régionaux." *Jazz hot* reported in December 1945 that American musicians had begun leaving. "Le jazz à Marseille," *Jazz hot*, December 1945.

97. "Hugues Panassié à Marseille, nouvelle capitale du jazz," *Jazz hot*, October 1945.

98. See Max Johnson, "Army Pollutes Marseilles with Dixie Jim Crow," *Baltimore Afro-American*, December 9, 1944. See also Shack, *Harlem in Montmartre*, 159.

99. "GI's in First Waxing Session," *Baltimore Afro-American*, October 27, 1945. The musicians included Arthur Hampton (alto saxophone), Eddie Williams (alto saxophone), Pette Proctor (tenor saxophone), Louis Williams (bass), Rogers Williams (piano), Earl Belcher (drums), Horatico McFarrin (trumpet), William Morris (trumpet), James Roberson (trombone), Charlie McCray (vocals), and Sporty Johnson (vocals).

100. Arma and Arma, *Mémoires à deux voix*.

101. Arma and Arma, *Mémoires à deux voix*, 356–57.

102. Review of concert in *Arts*, July 25, 1945, cited in Arma and Arma, *Mémoires à deux voix*, 357. The Armas claimed that the recordings were later released by Pathé-Marconi in 1951.

103. Reviews cited in Arma and Arma, *Mémoires à deux voix*, 92.

104. "Swing Returns to Free Paris," *Stars and Stripes,* September 2, 1944. On Briggs, see Atria, *Better Days Will Come Again*.

105. Legrand, *Charles Delaunay*, 156.

106. Rudolph Dunbar, "Paris Blossoms Again with Negro Music as the Theme," *Chicago Defender*, November 11, 1944. See *Jazz hot,* November 1945, 24, which includes advertisements for a "jam session" on Sunday, November 18, at 2:30 at L'École Normale de Musique and a concert by the army jazz orchestra under the direction of Tony Proteau.

107. Ollie Stewart, "Nazi Free Paris Swaying to Swing," *Baltimore Afro-American*, September 9, 1944, 8.

108. Roi Ottley, "Artists, GIs Mold Goodwill Overseas," *Pittsburgh Courier*, April 7, 1945; Allan Morrison, "Free Jazz: Zasou Is All Hepped Up about It, but the Artist Questions Its Vitality," *Stars and Stripes Magazine*, September 2, 1945, 10.

109. Stewart, "Nazi Free Paris Swaying."

110. "Harlem à Paris," *Bulletin du Hot Club*, June 1945, 2.

111. See Morley, "*This Is the American Forces Network*." AFN France was dismantled in 1967.

112. Clipping, *Stars and Stripes*, January 9, 1945, in Manuscripts and Research Notes, FSC. AFN broadcast weekly program of Duke Ellington on Mondays at 8:00 p.m., "A travers les ondes," *Jazz hot*, October 1945, 10. AFN hosted a "jam-session franco-américaine" with vibraphonist Jack Conner, "Le jazz à Paris," *Jazz hot*, October 1945, 23.

113. Sklaroff, *Black Culture*, 160.

114. Sklaroff, *Black Culture*, 178.

115. "AFN Station in Paris to Close for Good on New Year's Eve," *New York Herald Tribune*, December 27, 1946.

116. Legrand, *Charles Delaunay*, 160. Following the removal of AFN, Delaunay stayed on the RDF with "Musique de danse" on Sundays at 11:30 p.m.

117. See "Django et l'A.T.C.," *Jazz hot*, November 1945, 2; "Django Reinhardt et l'A.T.C. Band à Pleyel," *Jazz hot*, December 1945, 2.

118. "Django Reinhardt et l'A.T.C. Band à Pleyel," *Jazz hot*, December 1945, 2.

119. Claude Briac, "Jazz américain," *Radio revue*, August 11, 1945.

120. On "distracted" listening, see Goodman, "Distracted Listening," 15–46.

121. Yann Gillot, interview with the author, April 8, 2011, Vernouillet, France; Gillot, "Le Jazz dans la peau."

122. Yann Gillot, "Sim Copans, le parcours d'un ambassadeur du jazz," Fonds Festival du Jazz, Souillac.

123. On the transformation of the French radio after Vichy, see Cowans, "Political Culture and Cultural Politics," 145; Vaillant, *Across the Waves*.

124. Of Imbs, Alice B. Toklas remarked: "We liked Bravig, even though as Gertrude Stein said, his aim was to please." "Radio: Death of Darling," *Time*, June 10, 1946, 62–64.

125. See October 28, 1944 Report, Records of the Historian, Area File, OWI, box 1, RG 208, NARA-CP.

126. By October 1944, Copans had been transferred from his assignment with the PWD's Allied Information Service Group to join Imbs in the radio section in the new Paris office of the OWI. Memorandum from SHAEF, October 20, 1944, box 107, Decimal Files, 1944–45, Allied Information Service Group, Psychological Warfare Division, Records of Allied Operational and Occupation Headquarters, World War II, RG 331, NARA-CP. For more on this history of broadcasting exchange, see Vaillant, *Across the Waves*, 79–101.

127. "American Music and Culture Beamed to Europe by OWI," *Christian Science Monitor*, May 26, 1945, Radio Program Bureau, OWI, RG 208, NARA-CP.

128. Martin Gansberg, "OWI's Cultural Formula: Picture of Musical Life in America Is Beamed to Nations of the World," *New York Times*, April 1, 1945.

129. "33 Tours . . . et puis s'en vont," *Radio 47*, January 26–February 1, 1947, Newspaper clippings, FSC.

130. Christian-Jacques Stan, "L'envers du micro: La 'Voix' de l'Amérique," *Cité-Soir*, August 6, 1946; see also "Le début de la Voix de l'Amérique," Manuscripts, FSC.

131. For more on these records, see "33 Tours . . . et puis s'en vont," *Radio 47*.

132. See Report, Courier et notes relatifs au service des échanges internationaux, 1947–54," Archives de la Direction Générale de la Radiodiffusion, 950218/22, CAC. There was only one national radio station until February 1945, when a second was added, making the first the "Programme National" and the second "Programme Parisien." The radio would become known as Radiodiffusion Française on March 23, 1945, with the passage of an ordinance nationalizing French radio and ending private radio broadcasting.

133. "Radio: Death of Darling," *Time*, June 10, 1946. Jean-Claude Correge recalled hearing Imbs on Saturdays around midday. Jean Claude-Correge, "Souvenirs d'auditeur," *Cahiers d'histoire de la radiodiffusion* 75 (January–March 2003); *Ce soir en France*, May 10, 1945, Collection René Marchand, Institut national de l'audiovisuel (INA).

134. "Editorial," *Jazz hot*, October 1945, 1–2.

135. "Editorial," *Jazz hot*, 2.

136. Georges Brisson, "A travers les ondes," *Jazz hot*, October 1945, 13.

137. Brisson, "A travers les ondes."

138. Jean Michaux, "Initiation . . . à M. Bravig Imbs," *Jazz hot*, October 1945, 16, 21.

139. Michaux, "Initiation . . . à M. Bravig Imbs."

140. Charles Delaunay, "Jazz 44," *Radio 44*, December 30, 1944, 13.

141. "La Radio inaugure une quatrième chaîne," *L'étoile du soir*, January 4, 1947.

142. Letter from Copans to Horatio Smith, August 27, 1947, Correspondence, 1945–53, FSC. In September 1946, Copans replaced Imbs when director of artistic programming Paul Gilson created *Tour du monde autour d'une table*, and began adding musical subjects (added from VOA discotheque) to *Ici New York* and *Tour* because the short-wave transmission from the United States provided poor quality; see also "Simon Copans nous parle," *La semaine radiophonique*, July 29, 1951.

143. Nathalie Moffat, "Nuits sans importance," *Les temps modernes* 3 (December 1945): 471–94. On Nathalie (Sorokine) Moffat's relationship to Sartre and Beauvoir, see Rowley, *Tête-à-Tête*.

144. Moffat, "Nuits sans importance," 7. On this terminology, see Roberts, *What Soldiers Do*, 153.

145. Ollie Stewart, "War Need Over, French Reveal Basic Prejudices," *Baltimore Afro-American*, April 6, 1946.

146. Edward B. Toles, "US Jim Crow Invades France, GIs Discover," *Chicago Defender*, June 30, 1945.

147. "Paris Cries for Tan American Entertainment as Season Opens," *Baltimore Afro-American*, September 21, 1946.

CHAPTER 2. WRITING BLACK, TALKING BACK

1. Mezzrow and Wolfe, *Really the Blues*, 203–4.

2. Mezzrow and Wolfe, *Really the Blues*, 204. Mezzrow and Wolfe define this term as slang for "white person." Mezzrow and Wolfe, *Really the Blues*, 377.

3. While "voluntary Negro" is an evocative phrase, Mezzrow and Wolfe did not invent it. See Levering Lewis, "Parallels and Divergences."

4. On the history of passing, and the social and familial loss that accompanied this decision, see Hobbs, *Chosen Exile*. As Hobbs argues, the momentary delight in prevailing over the Jim Crow racial regime was nevertheless tempered by "the agony of losing one's sense of self and one's family" (176). On literature and passing, see G. Wald, *Crossing the Line*; Ginsberg, *Passing and the Fictions*; Dreisinger, *Near Black*. By the end of World War II, some hoped that the social practice of racial passing might "pass out." See, for example, "Why 'Passing' Is Passing Out," *Jet*, July 17, 1952, 12–16.

5. Mezzrow and Wolfe, *La rage de vivre*. In 1950, the same year as the book's publication, a new edition was published by Editions Corrêa in Paris.

6. Vian, *J'irai cracher sur vos tombes*.

7. Passing may have been recognizable in France, where systems of racial and religious categorization for Jewish communities had profound implications for survival. Moreover, its connection to ideas of racial miscegenation and mixing would have been familiar to those with ties to the French empire, in which in-between racial identities had emerged at the borders of race and citizenship. On this, see Saada, *Empire's Children*; Jean-Baptiste, "Miss Euroafrica."

8. There is important extant scholarship on both texts by literary theorists and race scholars. On Mezzrow's literary Blackness, see G. Wald, *Crossing the Line*; Monson,

"Problem with White Hipness; Melnick, *Right to Sing the Blues*; Gubar, *Racechanges*. On Vian and the Vernon Sullivan novels, see Arnaud, *Le dossier de l'affaire*; Lapprand, *Boris Vian, la vie contre*; Pierrot, "Chester Himes, Boris Vian"; Campbell, *Paris Interzone*; Higginson, *Scoring Race*, 73–82; Braggs, *Jazz Diasporas*.

9. On the Série noire, see Eburne, "Transatlantic Mysteries of Paris." Himes's work was translated by Yves Malartic, whose novel *Au pays du bon dieu* detailed the experiences of a Black GI in France. Fabre, *From Harlem to Paris*, 217.

10. For biographical information on Vian, see Cismaru, *Boris Vian*; Lapprand, *Boris Vian, la vie contre*; Arnaud, *Les vies parallèles*.

11. Michelle Vian altered the novel's title, which was initially to be titled "I Will Dance on Your Graves" (J'irai danser sur vos tombes). Hoping to make it more provocative and "revolutionary" without betraying its non-American roots, she suggested a title that was drawn from the Jewish Hassidic folktale tradition. See Grégoire Leménager, "Ma vie avec Boris Vian (par Michelle Vian)," *Le nouvel observateur*, April 25, 2013.

12. Michelle Vian's vital role as an intermediary was largely unacknowledged. Later recounting the gendered dimensions of these characterizations, she described herself as a kind of "hyphen" (*un trait d'union*) and as "a flower who speaks" (*une fleur qui parle*). Michelle Vian, interview with the author, June 2012, Paris.

13. Delaunay, *Delaunay's dilemma*, 203.

14. On the mythologies surrounding this neighborhood, see especially Dussault, *Le mythe de la bohème*. On the mystifications of key cultural moments in French history, see Ross, *May '68 and Its Afterlives*.

15. "Introduction: Le jazz est la musique de notre époque," *Jazz 47: America* (1947).

16. See Vian and Arnaud, *Manuel de Saint-Germain-des-Prés*.

17. "Passers," *Time*, August 12, 1946, Articles in American Press, Articles recueillis par Boris Vian de 1943 à 1958, Archives Cohérie Boris Vian (ACBV), Paris.

18. On Sartre and Wright, see Fabre, "Richard Wright and the." On the journal, see Boschetti, *Intellectual Enterprise*, 184–223.

19. Jean-Paul Sartre, "Présentation," *Les Temps modernes* 1 (October 1945): 1–21; St. Clair Drake and Horace R. Cayton, "À travers la ligne de démarcation des races," trans. Catherine Le Guet, *Les Temps modernes* 11–12 (August–September 1946): 523–42.

20. Boris Vian, "Impressions d'Amérique," in Vian and Arnaud, *Chroniques du menteur*, 85–86, 93.

21. Brandon, *Surreal Lives*, 429, 431. Breton was part of a cohort of French intellectuals who spent the war in New York. On this, see Loyer, *Paris à New York*; Loyer, "À la croisée des chemins transatlantiques," 237–54.

22. On Césaire and surrealism, see R. D. G. Kelley, "Poetics of Anticolonialism,"; R. D. G. Kelley, *Freedom*.

23. Jean-Paul Sartre, "Orphée Noir," in Senghor, *Anthologie de la nouvelle poésie*, ix–xliv. Sartre's preface was eventually published as Jean-Paul Sartre, *Black Orpheus*, trans. S. W. Allen (Paris: Présence Africaine, 1963). See also Diawara, *In Search of Africa*, 1–11.

24. Vian, *I Spit on Your Graves*, 65–69. The original publication was Vernon Sullivan [Boris Vian], *J'irai cracher sur vos tombes* (Paris: Éditions du Scorpion, 1946). All English-language citations from Vian, *I Spit on Your Graves*.

25. Vian, *I Spit on Your Graves*, 69, 139.

26. On this, see Sollors, *Neither Black nor White*, 271.

27. Vian, *I Spit on Your Graves*, 17, 34.

28. Vian, *I Spit on Your Graves*, 94–95.

29. Vian, *I Spit on Your Graves*, 95.

30. Vian, *I Spit on Your Graves*, 85.

31. Vian, *I Spit on Your Graves*, 36.

32. Vian, *I Spit on Your Graves*, 177.

33. Vian, *I Spit on Your Graves*, 5.

34. Review in *Gazette des lettres,* January 4, 1947, cited in Arnaud, *Le dossier*, 19.

35. Preface to Vian, *I Spit on Your Graves*, xii.

36. Vian, *I Spit on Your Graves*, xiii.

37. Vian, *I Spit on Your Graves*, xi.

38. Vian, *I Spit on Your Graves*, xiii.

39. Vian, *I Spit on Your Graves*, xi.

40. Robert Kanters, "Traduit de l'américain," *Spectateur*, November 26, 1946.

41. "Avec 'J'irai' un nouveau romancier noir américain dépassera-t-il le 'scandaleux' Miller?," *Samedi soir*, December 7, 1946, in Articles sur J'irai cracher sur vos tombes, Le Roman, de 1946 à 1949, ACBV.

42. "Watch and Word in Paris," *Newsweek*, February 24, 1947, 104.

43. "L'editeur de 'J'irai cracher sur vos tombes' de défend d'avoir publié un roman pornographique," *Samedi soir,* February 8, 1947, ACBV.

44. J. Lermachan, "J'irai cracher sur vos tombes," *Combat*, April 25, 1948.

45. Article in *Afrique Magazine* cited in Arnaud, *Le dossier*, 27–28.

46. This edition was also published by Éditions du Scorpion, which printed 950 copies on July 18, 1947. For information on printing, see reference copy at Beinecke Rare Book and Manuscript Library, Yale University, New Haven, CT.

47. Arnaud, *Le dossier*, 27–28. See also Pierrot, *Black Avenger in Atlantic Culture*.

48. Jacques Howlett, "Présence Africaine, 1947–1958," *Journal of Negro History* 43, no. 2 (1958): 142.

49. Jacques Howlett, "Revue de revues," *Présence Africaine* 1 (November–December 1947): 165–66.

50. Howlett, "Revue de revues."

51. Madeleine Gautier, "Un romancier de la race noire," *Présence Africaine* 1 (November–December 1947): 163–65.

52. On Zobel and his relationship to *négritude*, see Hardwick, *Joseph Zobel*.

53. Joseph Zobel, "Les nègres et l'obscénité en littérature," *Les Lettres françaises*, July 25, 1947, 4.

54. According to Ivy's later account, Vian wrote back immediately to claim authorship, sparking a long correspondence between the two men. James Ivy to Boris Vian, April 26, 1948, 5, Courier Jazz, Anglais, ACBV.

55. Vian, *Dead All Have the Same Skin*, 116. This novel presents another protagonist who passed for white; this time, the protagonist, after murdering several people to hide his racial identity, discovers he is not Black after all.

56. "Contrairement à Boris Vian, Raphaël Tardon fait violer des noires par des blancs," *Samedi soir*, May 15, 1948. The novel was later reviewed by Mercer Cook, who also underscored the question of representation. Cook, "Review of *Starkenfirst*."

57. Raphaël Tardon, "Richard Wright Tells Us: The White Problem in the United States," *Action*, October 24, 1946, 10–11, in Kinnamon and Fabre, *Conversations with Richard Wright*, 99–105.

58. Rosenthal was working at UNESCO in the Division of Cultural Development and had published a letter "from a demobilized American" in *Les Temps modernes*. Milton Rosenthal, "Lettre d'un Américain demobilize," *Les Temps modernes* 11–12 (1946): 460–63. According to Michelle Vian, after meeting Rosenthal at the Centre Culturel Américain, she introduced him to Boris Vian. Michelle Vian, interview with the author, June 2012, Paris. Notably, that same year, Boris Vian worked with American journalist Ned Brandt to produce jazz radio programs for broadcast on WNEW in New York. See Vian and Pestureau, *Jazz in Paris*. The collaboration was confirmed by Brandt. See Ned Brandt, interview with the author, July 23, 2010, Midland, MI.

59. "Le nègre de soi," *Opéra*, December 15, 1948, 71.

60. On the double meaning of *nègre* as both Black person and ghostwriter, see C. L. Miller, *Blank Darkness*, 225.

61. Duhamel, *Raconte pas ta vie*, 555.

62. Baldwin, *Devil Finds Work*, 38. On Vian and Baldwin, see Braggs, *Jazz Diasporas*.

63. Baldwin, *The Devil Finds Work*, 39. Italicized in the original.

64. The novel would also be the basis for future condemnations of French racism. In 1959, the novel was adapted for the screen by the filmmaker Michel Gast as a condemnation of the Algerian War. *J'irai cracher sur vos tombes*, directed by Michel Gast (1959; Boulogne-Billancourt: Gaumont Columbia Tristar, 2006), DVD. In 2000, the French hip-hop artist Disiz la Peste borrowed the novel's title for a song that issued a "plague on both of your houses," condemning the racial logic that made his own *métis* identity undesirable. Disiz la Peste, *Le poisson rouge*.

65. Vian (under pseudonym of Hugo Hachebuisson), "Le jazz et ses gestes," *Jazz hot*, November 1947, reproduced in Vian and Remeil, *Autres écrits sur le jazz*, 1:47.

66. "Les noirs ont forcement raison quand il s'agit de jazz," cited in Ténot, *Boris Vian*, 8.

67. Vian, "Faut-il zigouiller les Blancs," *Combat*, April 1948, reproduced in Vian and Remeil, *Autres écrits sur le jazz*, 1:262.

68. Article cited in Hennessey, *Klook*, 81.

69. Panassié, "Les réactionnaires du jazz," *La revue du jazz* (January 31, 1949), 32.

70. For a corrective to this reading, see DeVeaux, *Birth of Bebop*, 17.

71. Delaunay attributed his own appreciation of Charlie Parker and Dizzy Gillespie to living among the musicians themselves, and having "vibrated on the same frequency." Charles Delaunay, interview by François Postif, transcript, Manuscripts, box 48, ACBV.

72. See Jaji, *Africa in Stereo*.

73. Hugues Panassié, "Revue des revues," *Jeune Afrique*, October 1948.

74. Joseph Zobel, manuscript, 117, 8, Fonds Hugues Panassié (FHP), Mediathèque muncipale, Villefranche-de-Rouergue.

75. Though many of Mezzrow's exploits remain unverified, his early incarceration at Pontiac Reformatory was reported in the *Chicago Daily Tribune* on December 31, 1916, in a story about the "auto kleptomania" sweeping Chicago: "Seventeen-year-old Milton Mesirow was sentenced to from one to ten years at Pontiac for the theft of an automobile," cited in "Aids of Hoyne Push Fight on Auto Thieves," *Chicago Daily Tribune*, December 31, 1916, 3. On Mezzrow and the Austin High Gang, see Kenney, *Chicago Jazz*.

76. Neither a master of the New Orleans style nor an innovator of new forms, Mezzrow was regarded by most critics and musicians as possessing minimal musical talents. Nat Hentoff once wrote that Mezzrow was "so consistently out of tune that he may have invented a new scale system." Nat Hentoff, "Counterpoint," *Down Beat*, February 11, 1953, 5. Pops Foster wrote, "Any little boy can play the clarinet or sax as good as Mezz can. He just stands up there and goes toot-toot-toot. . . . I like him, but man he can't play no jazz." P. Foster, Stoddard, Russell, and Rust, *Pops Foster*, 166–67.

77. According to John Hammond, Mezzrow introduced Armstrong to marijuana in the mid-1920s. Hammond and Townsend, *John Hammond on Record*, 106. Mezzrow's arrest in 1941 was covered by the jazz press. "'Weed' Lands Milt Mesirow in N.Y. Cell," *Down Beat*, June 15, 1941.

78. On the session, see Condon and O'Neal, *Eddie Condon Scrapbook of Jazz*.

79. On the debates between the "moldy figs" and modernists, see Gendron, *Between Montmartre and the Mudd Club*, 125.

80. On his business interests, see "Case History of an Ex-White Man," *Ebony*, December 1946, 11.

81. White jazz musicians were especially critical. Bob Wilber contended that Mezzrow "loved to be thought of as a black man," noting his acquisition of a "rich southern drawl" as well as his paternalism: "the Great White Father looking after his slaves." Wilber and Webster, *Music Was Not Enough*, 40. Eddie Condon wrote, "There was nothing you could do about Mezz, who was from the west side of Chicago; when he fell through the Mason-Dixon Line he just kept going." Condon and Sugrue, *We Called It Music*, 192.

82. Biographical information comes from his curriculum vitae and its addendum, box 606, Bernard Wolfe Papers (BWP), Yale Collection of American Literature, Beinecke Rare Book and Manuscript Library, Yale University, New Haven, CT, as well as Geduld, *Bernard Wolfe*. See also Burt A. Folkart, "One-Time Pornographer and Aide to Trotsky Comedic Novelist Bernard Wolfe, 70," *Los Angeles Times*, October 30, 1985. Wolfe detailed his career in his *Memoirs of a Not Altogether Shy Pornographer*. On Wolfe and the "New York intellectuals," see A. M. Wald, *New York Intellectuals*, 133–35.

83. See Wolfe, Report on recent research, box 606, BWP.

84. Ralph Ellison, in reviewing Myrdal's work, would critique this formulation. Ellison, "*An American Dilemma*: A Review."

85. Draft of "Nausea in Blackface," box 606, BWP.

86. Mezzrow and Wolfe, *Really the Blues*, 333–35.

87. Wolfe, afterword to Mezzrow and Wolfe, *Really the Blues*, 389–90.

88. Legal Agreement, April 23, 1945, between Milton Mezzrow, 596 Edgecombe Avenue, and Bernard Wolfe, 10 Monroe Street, box 606, BWP. On Wolfe's role in the creation of *Really the Blues*, see Saul, *Freedom Is, Freedom Ain't*, 49–51.

89. In a later interview, Mezzrow claimed that while Wolfe had "good ideas," he "had to wrap them in my language." See Yannick Bruynoghe, "Mezzrow Talks about the Old Jim Crow," *Melody Maker and Rhythm*, November 17, 1951, 9. Wolfe contended that if there was any literary "value" in the text, "it is there in spite of my collaborator and not because of him." He maintained that he "had to make the thing into a popular-market work against Mezzrow's constant, line-by-line opposition." Wolfe to Don Congden, an employee of Mezzrow and Wolfe's literary agent, October 13, 1954, box 606, BWP. In a letter from March 11, 1946, Random House editor Robert Linscott urged Wolfe to change the ending of the book; Linscott referred to his attempts to change Mezzrow's mind and appealed to Wolfe to come up with a substitute. Linscott to Wolfe, box 606, BWP. In other published essays by Mezzrow in the mid-1940s, his writing employed a southern Black vernacular rather than hipster jive. See, for example, Mezzrow, "In the Idiom," 28, 32.

90. Mezzrow and Wolfe, *Really the Blues*, 340.

91. Mezzrow and Wolfe, *Really the Blues*, 66.

92. Mezzrow and Wolfe, *Really the Blues*, 305.

93. Mezzrow and Wolfe, *Really the Blues*, 311–12.

94. Mezzrow and Wolfe, *Really the Blues*, 324.

95. Mezzrow and Wolfe, *Really the Blues*, 221–22.

96. Mezzrow and Wolfe, *Really the Blues*, 225, 227.

97. Mezzrow and Wolfe, *Really the Blues*, 221.

98. Mezzrow and Wolfe, *Really the Blues*, 357. The glossary included definitions for "moo-mop" ("modern corruption of jazz built up around mechanical riffs"), "hipster" ("man who's in the know, grasps everything, is alert"), "beat" ("exhausted, broke"), and "ofay" ("a white person"), 371. The book references both Cab Calloway's 1944 *Hepster's Dictionary* and *Dan Burley's Original Handbook of Harlem Jive* (1944), with particular attention to Calloway's definition of "mezz" as "anything supreme, genuine." Cab Calloway, "The New Cab Calloway Hepster's Dictionary: Language of Jive (1944)," in A. Clark, *Riffs and Choruses*, 351–56. Henry Louis Gates Jr. describes Mezzrow's definition of "signifying" as "perceptive and subtle" and further contends that "Mezzrow was one of the first commentators to recognize that Signifyin(g) as a structure of performance could apply equally to verbal texts and musical texts." Gates, *Signifying Monkey*, 69.

99. See advertisement in *Publishers Weekly*, box 606, BWP.

100. Bucklin Moon, "The Real Thing," *New Republic*, November 4, 1946, 605. For other reviews, see Paul Speegle, "Really the Blues (Book Review)," *San Francisco Chronicle*, December 22, 1946; Will Davidson, "Mezz's Story of Marijuana, Misery, Music," *Chicago Daily Tribune*, November 3, 1946; Billy Rose, "Life Set to Music Is the Story of Mezz," *Chicago Sun*, October 28, 1946; "Vipers, Tea and Jazz," *Newsweek*, October 28, 1946, 88; John McNulty, "Hot Music and Hopheads," *New York Herald Tribune*, October 27, 1946; Richard B. Gehman, "Poppa Mezz," *Saturday Review of Literature*, November 16, 1946; Luther Noss, "Really the Blues," *Notes* 4, no. 1 (1946): 71–72; Willis James, "Really the Blues," *Phylon* 8, no. 4 (1947): 377–78; S. I. Hayakawa, "Second Thoughts: Really the Blues," *Chicago Defender*, November 30, 1946.

101. "Really the Blues," *Negro Digest*, November 1946, 102–13.

102. "Case History of an Ex-White Man," *Ebony*, December 1946, 11–16.

103. These observations are present throughout the series. See "L'Amérique au jour le jour," *Les Temps modernes* 29 (February 1948): 1462; Beauvoir, "L'Amérique au jour le jour," *Les Temps modernes* 27 (December 1947): 979; Beauvoir, "L'Amérique au jour le jour," *Les Temps modernes* 30 (March 1948): 1655. The account was later published as Beauvoir, *L'Amérique au jour le jour*. On Beauvoir in this era, and her relationship to American culture, see especially Coffin, "Historicizing the Second Sex."

104. Beauvoir, "L'Amérique au jour le jour," *Les Temps modernes* 27 (December 1947): 988.

105. *Jazz hot*, September–October 1946, 6.

106. In November 1946, the same month that *Really the Blues* was published, the union of musicians had signaled the alarm about the growing number of foreign musicians and bands in Paris. *Jazz hot,* November 1946, 20.

107. Charles Delaunay, "La querelle du jazz: le point de vie du Hot Club de France," *Jazz hot*, December 1946, 25.

108. Frank Ténot, "Quand les blancs jouent hot," *Jazz hot*, January 1947, 5.

109. On their close working relationship, and the critical role of Gautier in Panassié's career, see Christian Senn, *Hugues Panassié, 1912–1974* (self-published manuscript, 1996), 282, in FHP. See also Tailhefer, "Louis et Hugues Panassié."

110. Fallet, *Carnets de jeunesse*, 40–41, 45, 297.

111. "Constellation 48 : Le premier festival international de jazz à Nice," *Chaîne Nationale*, February 22, 1948, Institut national de l'audiovisuel (INA). Similar descriptions are in "Mezz Mezzrow et Sidney Bechet," *Jazz 48*, July 10, 1948 and Jean Poliac, *Nice-Matin*, February 20, 1948, in Pierre Merlin Scrapbooks, private collection of Philiippe Baudoin, Paris.

112. *Jazz hot,* February 1948, 17.

113. Hugues Panassié, "Le mal blanc," *Présence Africaine* 1 (November 1947): 146–48.

114. Panassié, "Le mal blanc."

115. Robert Linscott, Random House, to Wolfe, June 6, 1946, box 606, BWP.

116. D. Ungemac-Benedicte to Wolfe, October 9, 1946, box 606, BWP.

117. Duhamel, *Raconte pas ta vie*, 501.

118. See Richard Wright, "Jeunesse Noire," *Les Temps modernes* 16–21 (January–June 1947), which was also published by Albin Michel in 1947. Duhamel was also the translator for *Native Son*, which was published as *Les enfants de l'Oncle Tom*, trans. Marcel Duhamel (Paris: Albin Michel, 1946), and other translations that appeared in newspapers, including *Samedi soir* and the underground newspaper *L'Arbalète*, and in the inaugural issue of *Les Temps modernes*. Richard Wright, "Le feu dans la nuée," trans. Marcel Duhamel, *Les Temps modernes* 1 (October 1945): 22–47. On this, see Duhamel, *Raconte pas ta vie*, 511–13.

119. Duhamel, *Raconte pas ta vie*, 475.

120. See Gwendolyn Brooks, "La complainte de Pearl May Lee," trans. Madeleine Gautier, *Présence Africaine* 1 (November–December 1947): 111–19. See her translations of poetry in *Jazz hot*, December 1945, January–February 1946, May–June 1946, and July–August 1946. In December 1946, Panassié wrote to Boris Vian, noting that

Gautier was a "specialist in this genre of translation." Panassié to Vian, December 29, 1946, Correspondence, folder 3, ACBV. See also a 1955 letter from Gautier regarding her translations, in which she also contended that Mezzrow was the real author of *Really the Blues*. Gautier to Roselyn Germon, May 10, 1955, Correspondence, folder 47, ACBV.

121. On publication plans in France, see Marcel Duhamel to Bernard Wolfe, May 7, 1947, box 606, BWP. Excerpts of the memoir were first published as Mezz Mezzrow and Bernard Wolfe, "La rage de vivre (fragment)," trans. Madeleine Gautier and Marcel Duhamel, *Les Temps modernes* 56 (June 1950): 2175–2211.

122. Bernard Wolfe, "L'Oncle Rémus et son lapin," trans. René Guyonnet, *Les temps modernes* 43 (May 1949): 888–915. The essay was originally published as "Uncle Remus and the Malevolent Rabbit," in *Commentary* 8 (July 1949).

123. Wolfe, "L'Oncle Rémus et son lapin," 888.

124. In "Revue des revues," *Présence Africaine* 7 (1949): 331–32.

125. Fanon, *Black Skin, White Masks*, 32, 151. Later in the text he quoted from *J'irai cracher sur vos tombes* to illustrate the ambivalence of sexual attraction and phobia. Fanon, *Black Skin, White Masks*, 159.

126. Bernard Wolfe, "Extase en noir: Le noir comme danseur et chanteur," in *Les Temps modernes* 59 (September 1950): 385–401. No translator was listed. The essay was originally published as "Ecstatic in Blackface," *Modern Review*, January 1950. Most critical citations of Wolfe refer to the essay as it was published in the appendixes of *Really the Blues*, which differs from the original published version in *Modern Review*, a short-lived socialist publication.

127. Wolfe, "Ecstatic in Blackface."

128. Preface to Mezzrow and Wolfe, *La rage de vivre*. Correspondence from Miller, as well as Wolfe's role in securing the author's endorsement, in 1948 can be found in in Wolfe's papers. See Wolfe, Correspondence with Henry Miller, box 606, BWP.

129. Mezzrow and Wolfe, *La rage de vivre*, 16, 27, and 242.

130. Mezzrow and Wolfe, *La rage de vivre*, 256.

131. "Parution de livres sur le jazz," 1950, INA.

132. Duhamel, postface to Mezzrow and Wolfe, *La rage de vivre*, 418, 414.

133. Duhamel, postface to Mezzrow and Wolfe, *La rage de vivre*, 415.

134. Duhamel, postface to Mezzrow and Wolfe, *La Rage de vivre*, 415.

135. Duhamel, postface to Mezzrow and Wolfe, *La rage de vivre*, 416.

136. M. Pierre Drouin's review in *Le Monde* (July 26, 1950) cited in "Revue de la presse," *Bulletin du Hot Club*, 1950, 15.

137. M. Claude Roy's review in *Action* cited in "Revue de la presse," *Bulletin du Hot Club*, 1950, 15.

138. Marcel Peju's review in *Franc-Tireur* (July 6, 1950) cited in "Revue de la presse," *Bulletin du Hot Club*, 1950, 15.

139. Jacques Howlett, review in "Notes de lecture," *Présence Africaine* 10/11 (1951): 202–4.

140. Mudimbe, *Surreptitious Speech*, xvii. The publishing house began publishing poetry, novels, and studies in 1949. Kesteloot, *Black Writers in French*, 295. Jacques Howlett

identified the first few years as the "heroic era." Howlett, *Présence Africaine, 1947–1958,* 140. See also Hassan, "Inaugural Issues," 215.

141. Jules-Rosette, "Conjugating Cultural Realities," 30.

142. Edwards, *Practice of Diaspora,* 4–5.

143. See Fanon, *Wretched of the Earth,* 176. Fanon's book was originally published as *Les damnés de la terre* in 1961.

CHAPTER 3. SPINNING RACE

1. Marge Creath Singleton, "The Truth about Mezz Mezzrow," box 57, Fonds Charles Delaunay (FCD), Bibliothèque nationale de France, Paris (BnF).

2. On November 15, 1951, they recorded "Boogie Parisien," "Clarinet Marmalade," "If I Could Be with You," "Struttin' with Some Barbecue," and "The Sheik of Araby" (Vogue 4145–49). On November 16, 1951, they recorded "Blues Jam," "Revolutionary Blues No. 2," "Blues No One Dug," "Mezzerola Blues," "Drum Face," and "Blues in the Twenties," which were released by Vogue as Mezz Mezzrow, *Jazz Concert,* feat. Lee Collins and Zutty Singleton (Vogue LD 037).

3. L. Collins and M. S. Collins, *Oh, Didn't He Ramble,* 125.

4. According to the AFM, a judgment was made against Mezzrow "by default." "Mezzrow expelled from the AFM," September 6, 1952, box 28, Articles in American Press, Archives Cohérie Boris Vian (ACBV). On systemic racism and segregation in various locals of American Federation of Musicians, see Monson, *Freedom Sounds.*

5. Singleton, "The Truth about Mezz Mezzrow."

6. When a friend commented on Bechet's physical strength at the end of his life, Bechet allegedly remarked: "I just tell myself that I'm chasing Mezzrow for the money he owes me." Chilton, *Sidney Bechet,* 286.

7. On the political economy of African American music, see Horne, *Jazz and Justice;* N. Kelley, *R&B, Rhythm and Business;* Kofsky, *Black Nationalism and the Revolution;* Spellman, *Four Lives in the Bebop Business;* Radano, "On Ownership and Value"; George, *Death of Rhythm & Blues;* Gilbert, *Product of Our Souls;* K. H. Miller, *Segregating Sound;* Suisman, "Co-workers in the Kingdom of Culture."

8. On copyright and music, see Stahl, *Unfree Masters;* Chanan, *Repeated Takes.*

9. The role of women in brokering business arrangements and attending to the financial (and physical) well-being of jazz musicians remains understudied. On gender and jazz, see Rustin and Tucker, *Big Ears.*

10. While French law had dictated that all musical formations be at a minimum ninety percent French since 1933, this regulation was not actively enforced until 1965. See "Musicians' Job Crisis Attacked," *Billboard,* December 11, 1965, 1, 24. On the effect on American jazz musicians, see "Negro Musicians' Jobs Threatened in Paris," *Jet,* December 30, 1965, 59.

11. Coleman cited in Spellman, *Four Lives,* 129.

12. Tournès, *New Orleans sur Seine,* 44. See also Delaunay, *Delaunay's Dilemma,* 256.

13. On the transition from shellac to plastic, see Devine, *Decomposed.*

14. Delaunay, *Delaunay's Dilemma,* 226.

15. Delaunay, *Hot discographie.*

16. On the anthropological side of interwar jazz fandom, see Jordan, "Amphibiologie: Ethnographic Surrealism in French Discourse on Jazz." See also Martin, "De l'excursion à Harlem"; Edwards, "Ethnics of Surrealism."

17. Servin, "La maison de disques Vogue," 44.

18. Tournès, *New Orleans sur Seine,* 107.

19. "Application for Nonimmigrant Visa," July 8, 1946, box 48, FCD. See also Servin, "La maison de disques Vogue," 24. As a letter to Keynote's Eric Bernay suggests, Delaunay was interested in acquiring masters (of the "good jazz" that "seems to have grown up with the private record companies in the States") to be manufactured and distributed in Europe. Delaunay to Bernay, n.d., box 1, FCD. On the potential of a Swing affiliate in the United States, see Delaunay to Stephen Sholes at RCA, December 20, 1946, box 1, FCD.

20. On the history of Disques Barclay, see especially Chasseguet, *Barclay.*

21. Mike Hennessey, "The Barclay Story," *Billboard,* May 30, 1970, 49. On Cooper, see Glass, *Americans in Paris.*

22. Allan Morrison obituary, *Jet,* June 6, 1968, 51–52.

23. Jerry Mengo and Arthur Briggs had also been interned in German work camps. On these recording sessions, see Ruppli and Lubin, *Blue Star.*

24. See DeVeaux, *Birth of Bebop,* 322.

25. See Delaunay's letter to Don Byas regarding four tracks, December 16, 1946, from Pathé-Marconi (R. Courtonne), FCD. Hugues Panassié, "Session Don Byas," *Hot Club Magazine* 21, November 1, 1947, 11. See also Legrand, *Charles Delaunay,* 198–99. While Delaunay and Panassié remained artistic directors of Swing, Panassié and Madeleine Gautier had decamped in 1941 to his villa Montauban in the southwest of France. Panassié continued to share in Swing's profits as artistic director until 1945.

26. See letter from Delaunay to M. Dougnac, Pathé-Marconi, September 26, 1947, and letter from Delaunay to MM. Maget, Capstick, Dougnac at Pathé-Marconi regarding visit by M. Ruault (Eddie Barclay), box 16, FCD. See also Hugues Panassié, "Dernière heure," *Bulletin Panassié,* September 25, 1947, 7; "Les bonds Disques parus en France," *Bulletin Panassié,* September 3, 1947, 2. On the financial issues between Panassié and Delaunay, see Tournès, *New Orleans sur Seine,* 107.

27. Panassié in circular cited by Delaunay, letter to Dougnac, box 16, FCD.

28. Chatou had stayed open during the war and was directly associated with Pathé. See Servin, "La maison de disques Vogue," 25.

29. Servin, "La maison de disques Vogue," 28.

30. Chilton, Sidney Bechet, 250. Letter from Sidney Bechet, [November 16, 1948?], box 16, FCD.

31. "The Barclay Story," *Billboard,* May 30, 1970.

32. See Delaunay, *Delaunay's Dilemma,* 221. Legrand, *Charles Delaunay,* 200. On the Parker records, see Komara, *Dial Recordings of Charlie Parker,* 42.

33. "Notre directeur Eddie Barclay à New York," *Jazz news,* October 1949, 9.

34. "Notre directeur Eddie Barclay à New York," *Jazz news,* 9.

35. "Eddie Barclay à New-York" and advertisement, *Jazz news,* November 1949, 7, 20. See also *Jazz news,* January 1949.

36. Catalogue Général, 1949, Disques Blue Star, 29, Courier "échanges jazz," ACBV. Eddie Barclay later wrote, "I was first and foremost crazy for jazz. I had a tendency to compartmentalize the genres and Blue Star, it was only for jazz." Barclay, *Que la fête continue*, 46.

37. "Pond Hop Eyed by Granz Jazz Troupe, Disks," *Billboard*, April 16, 1949; "French Disk Owner Inks Mercury Pact," *Billboard*, June 21, 1952.

38. "French Diskery, Atlantic in Swap," *Billboard*, September 17 and September 10, 1949; "Music as Written," *Billboard*, March 19, 1949; "Mercury Pitches Int'l Disk Deal, Longhair Power," *Billboard*, April 1, 1950.

39. On the Swing venture, see box 1, FCD.

40. See box 48, FCD. See also Legrand, *Charles Delaunay*; AFCDJ, dossier no. 18294-P, Préfecture de Police de Paris, Bureau des Associations, cited in Servin, "La maison de disques Vogue," 25.

41. Ruppli, *Vogue*. Registered as Jazz Sélection on December 1, 1948, au register du commerce de la Seine, no. 344.602B, Registre du tribunal, cited in Servin, "La maison de disques Vogue," 26. See also Delaunay, *Delaunay's Dilemma*, 255.

42. Servin, "La maison de disques Vogue," 51.

43. "Nice Jumps," *Time*, March 8, 1948, 42.

44. See *Jazz news*, April 1949, 22. On Clarke's participation, see Hennessey, *Klook*, 78–79.

45. Chilton, *Sidney Bechet*, 215.

46. Hadlock quoted in Chilton, *Sidney Bechet*, 233.

47. Servin, "La maison de disques Vogue," 45.

48. Fry, "Remembrance of Jazz Past," 315.

49. Servin, "La maison de disques Vogue," 30–31.

50. Chilton, *Sidney Bechet*, 220.

51. See correspondence between Delaunay and Paul Gilson, 1951, Relations avec la direction des services artistiques, Direction des services artistiques, Archives de la Direction Générale de la Radiodiffusion, ORTF, 950218/24, Centre des archives contemporaines (CAC), Fontainebleau.

52. Charles Delaunay, "Pourquoi le salon du jazz?," Official Program, box 63, FCD.

53. Tournès, *New Orleans sur Seine*, 129; "Avec son premier Salon le jazz fête son jubilé," *Paris-Presse*, December 2, 1950, 4; "Le premier Salon du Jazz a pris un bon départ," *Paris-Presse*, December 3–4, 1950, 7; "Le premier Salon du Jazz," *Le Monde*, December 2, 1950, 12; Charles Delaunay, interview by Maurice Cullaz, "Ouverture du premier salon du jazz," Centre Marcelin Berthelot, Institut national de l'audiovisuel (INA).

54. See Program, box 63, FCD.

55. See report on Salon du Jazz in *Jazz hot*, January 1951, 10.

56. See Program, box 63, FCD.

57. Tournès, *New Orleans sur Seine*, 132.

58. In thinking through the commodification of images of enslavement and anti-Black violence, I draw on Johnson, *Soul by Soul*; Hartman, *Scenes of Subjection*; Mitchell, *Vénus noire*; Goldsby, *Spectacular Secret*.

59. DeVeaux, *Birth of Bebop*; Chanan, *Repeated Takes*.

60. On the creation of race records and "hillbilly music," see especially K. H. Miller, *Segregating Sound*.

61. These technological transformations were accompanied by the reorganization of labor. On this history, see Cowie, *Capital Moves*.

62. "It's Longhair, 2 to 1 over Prewar Days, in France; Ask Polydor's Meyerstein," *Billboard*, July 2, 1949. In 1951, Barclay moved from 54 rue Pergolese to 6 rue Chambiges, the new offices of Productions Phonographiques Françaises (PPF).

63. Barclay, *Que la fête continue*, 33, 39–40.

64. Perrin Ludovic, "Eddie Barclay, la fête est finie," *Libération*, May 14, 2005.

65. Pierre Cressant, "Les premiers Disques de longue durée publiés en France," *Jazz hot*, September 1951, 25. Now manufacturers had to create machines for LPs and 78s, requiring three or four speeds (78 rpm, 45 rpm, 33 1/3 rpm, and sometimes 16 rpm).

66. Bernard Demory, *Au temps des cataplasmes* 406.

67. "The Barclay Story," *Billboard*, May 30, 1970.

68. Delaunay had obtained permission from Pathé to take Swing under the Vogue label. Like Barclay, it had vacated its one-room studio for bigger office, first at 54 de la rue Hauteville, then on the rue des Petites-Écuries, and finally to suburban Villetaneuse. Servin, "La maison de disques Vogue," 26; Delaunay, *Delaunay's Dilemma*, 257.

69. Delaunay, *Delaunay's Dilemma*, 255–57.

70. On Broonzy's life, see especially Riesman, *I Feel So Good*. On the blues in France, see Springer, "Blues in France"; Sauret, "Et la France découvrit"; Prévos, "Four Decades of French Blues." On the blues in Europe in the 1950s and 1960s, see Adelt, "Germany Gets the Blues."

71. Panassié, *Revue du jazz*, cited in Riesman, *I Feel So Good*, 158.

72. Riesman, *I Feel So Good*, 157; Vasset, *Black Brother*, 20.

73. Riesman, *I Feel So Good*, 159; Madeleine Gautier to Joe Glaser, September 7, 1951, Fonds Hugues Panassié (FHP), Médiathèque municipale, Villefranche-de-Rouergue.

74. Madeleine Gautier to Joe Glaser, April 21, 1952, folder 14, classeur 2, Correspondence établie entre Joe Glaser et Hugues Panassié, 1950–1964, FHP. In English in the original.

75. Riesman, *I Feel So Good*, 162–63.

76. See Horne, *Paul Robeson*.

77. The interview with Broonzy by Alan Lomax on May 13, 1952, in Paris is available through the Association for Cultural Equity. http://research.culturalequity.org. Lomax was in Paris working at the Musée de l'Homme to find music for Columbia Records' world library of folk and primitive music series.

78. Riesman, *I Feel So Good*, 207–8, 189–90. See Broonzy, *Big Bill*.

79. Riesman, *I Feel So Good*, 179.

80. Riesman, *I Feel So Good*, 162. On "the folk," see R. D. G. Kelley, "Notes on Deconstructing 'The Folk.'"

81. Servin, "La maison de disques Vogue," 46–47.

82. Goreau, *Just Mahalia, Baby*, 125.

83. Delaunay, *Delaunay's Dilemma*, 228; Charles Delaunay, interview with Michael Haggerty, August 14, 1982, Private Collection of Michael Haggerty, Mirabeau, France.

84. Advertisement in author's collection.

85. Delaunay to Mingus, folder 7, box 57, Charles Mingus Collection, Music Division, Library of Congress (LOC).

86. See Pierre Merlin Scrapbook, private collection of Philippe Baudoin, Paris.

87. On the changing face of Banania, see Berliner, *Ambivalent Desire*, chap. 1. In thinking about Merlin's particular mimetic work, I draw on Auslander and Holt, "Sambo in Paris," 163.

88. Michel Dorigné, "Après le salon du jazz," *La Gazette du jazz* (December 1950).

89. Daver, *Jazz Album Covers*, 68–79.

90. "La semaine du jazz au Marigny," *Bulletin du Hot Club de France*, 1948, 1.

91. Pierre Cressant, "Les premiers Disques de longue durée publiés en France," *Jazz hot*, September 1951.

92. The Merlin covers discussed in this chapter are held in the Pierre Merlin collection of the Médiathèque musicale de Paris. They are also featured in Daver, *Jazz Album Covers*.

93. On this gaze, and its absence, see Homi Bhabha, "Of Mimicry and Man"; Campt, *Listening to Images*.

94. Servin, "La maison de disques Vogue," 51.

95. Delaunay, *Delaunay's Dilemma*, 47–48.

96. Riesman, *I Feel So Good*, 170.

97. Special issue celebrating thirty years of Vogue, *Show Magazine*, February 1978.

98. Servin, "La maison de disques Vogue," 26.

99. Chilton, *Sidney Bechet*, 277.

100. See box 57bis, FCD. The tour went through numerous personnel changes due to military conscription. See Chilton, *Sidney Bechet*, 273.

101. Chilton, *Sidney Bechet*, 266.

102. Bechet, *Treat It Gentle*, 194.

103. "Les 'fans' de Paris sacrifient à leur dieu Bechet en saccageant un music-hall," *Paris Match*, October 29, 1955, box 29, FCD.

104. Jacqueline Cartier, "Le concert Sydney [*sic*] Bechet dégénère en émeute," *L'Aurore*, n.d., box 29, FCD. See also the November 4, 1955, bill from the Société d'Exploitation et de Réalisations Artistiques, box 26, FCD.

105. Cartier, "Le concert Sydney [*sic*] Bechet dégénère en émeute."

106. Michelle Vian served as *secrétaire* during Bechet's tour in Algeria and noted that the audience was entirely white European. Michelle Vian, interview with the author, June 2012, Paris.

107. "Sydney [*sic*] Bechet: 'La jeunesse d'Alger est formidable': Les gendarmes ont dû faire évacuer la salle," *Écho d'Alger*, October 18, 1957. See also J. D. Roob, "Un excellent Sydney [*sic*] Bechet," *L'écho d'Oran*, October 21, 1957, box 26, FCD.

108. "Sidney Bechet Millionaire," *Jazz hot*, November 1955, 38.

109. On youth culture and music in this period, see J. Briggs, *Sounds French*.

110. Tournès, *New Orleans sur Seine*, annexe IV, 465–67. See also Fry, "Remembrance of Jazz Past," 23.

111. Ollie Stewart, "Count Basie 'Moves' Europe's Jazz Fans," *Baltimore Afro-American*, April 17, 1954.

112. On African and Caribbean students in France in this period, see Germain, *Decolonizing the Republic*; Guimont, *Les étudiants africains en France*.

113. Winders, *Paris Africain*, 13–14. The album included reissued recordings from 1949 to 1950.

114. Germain, *Decolonizing the Republic*, 10.

115. See Tournès, *New Orleans sur Seine*, particularly chap. 5.

116. The Delta Rhythm Boys relocated to Paris in 1956 and were featured on Music Hall Parade in 1957. "Music Hall Parade: Emission du 23 Janvier 1957," Music Hall Parade, canal 1, January 23, 1957, INA.

117. See, for example, Sharpley-Whiting, *Bricktop's Paris*.

118. See Val Wilmer, "Days and Nights in the Interzone," *The Wire*, May 2014, 26–33.

119. "Memphis Slim: La vie est bonne," *Ebony*, June 1966, 56–62.

120. Favors quoted in Beauchamp, *Art Ensemble of Chicago*, 28.

121. On Scott, see Mack, "Hazel Scott."

122. Though their public description of their lives in France differed, both Scott and Memphis Slim joined other writers and musicians in August 1963 in a march to the US embassy in solidarity with the March on Washington. Dudziak, *Cold War Civil Rights*, 191.

123. On surveillance of the jazz community, see Broschke Davis, "Art Simmons in Paris."

124. McCloy, *Negro in France*, 230.

125. "Jazz note," *Bulletin du Hot-Club de Lyon*, January–February and August 1953.

126. On Armstrong, see "Satchmo Finds Europe 'Just like New Orleans,'" *Jet*, November 27, 1952, 60. Information related to Broonzy tour in Oran, Algeria in Riesman, *I Feel So Good*, 193. Buck Clayton recalled the trip to North Africa with Mezz Mezzrow, though he had hoped instead to "see what is called black Africa." Clayton, *Buck Clayton's Jazz World*, 202–3. On Hampton's tour, see Correspondence between Joe Glaser and Panassié, FHP.

127. Ollie Stewart, "Tan Entertainers Mean Cash in European Clubs, Theatres," *Afro-American*, April 7, 1956.

128. Stewart, "Tan Entertainers."

129. Servin, "La maison de disques Vogue," 58. As Cabat said in 1978, "To tell the truth, it was jazz that launched everything." *Show*, February 1978.

130. "The Barclay Story," *Billboard*, May 30, 1970, 68. The label had also combined as Compagnie Phonographique Française (CFP) Barclay in 1953, bringing Blue Star, Rivieria, and Classic under one label.

131. See liner notes by Alain-Guy Aknin and Philippe Crocq for *Pour ceux qui aiment le jazz: Le programme de l'émission radiophonique culte des années soixante* (Paris: Warner, 2003), 12–13.

132. "The Barclay Story," *Billboard*, May 30, 1970.

133. Barclay, *Que la fête continue*, 31–32.

134. Art Simmons, "Paris Scratchpad," *Jet*, February 20, 1969, 55. See Jane Bundy, "R&R to Get Gallic Accent via Barclay," *Billboard*, March 17, 1956, 17, 48.

135. See Bundy, "R&R to Get Gallic Accent via Barclay," 17.

136. Like his contemporaries in France, Lehner discovered jazz through military radio broadcasts. Chasseguet, *Barclay*, 12, 16.

137. On Leonard's photography, see Pinson, *Jazz Image*. See also Leonard and Carles, *Eye of Jazz*, 17.

138. Dan Burley, "Back Door Stuff: A Free Ghana and Those Lazy White Folks," *New York Amsterdam News*, March 16, 1957.

139. "New York Beat," *Jet*, September 13, 1962, 63

140. See "The Last Days of Richard Wright" in Harrington, *Why I Left America*, 17.

141. Edgar A. Wiggins, "Negroes in Paris Form Inner Circle," *Amsterdam News*, August 13, 1960.

142. Wheatley's notes on a 1954 Miles Davis record liner suggest that she might have assisted in both administrative and aesthetic decision-making. A photograph of the record liner is reproduced in Chasseguet, *Barclay*, 62. On Wheatley, see also Art Simmons, "Paris Sketchpad," *Jet*, February 29, 1969, 55.

143. Margolies, *Several Lives of Chester Himes*, 122.

144. See "The Last Days of Richard Wright" in Harrington, *Why I Left America, and Other Essays*, 17.

145. September 23, 1960 letter from Wright cited in Fabre, *Unfinished Quest of Richard Wright*, 623.

146. Fabre and Williams, *Street Guide*, 166.

147. Fabre, *Unfinished Quest*, 515–17.

148. Letter from Wright on October 8, 1960, cited in Fabre, *Unfinished Quest*, 623.

149. Fabre, *Unfinished Quest*, 623.

150. See Ruppli and Rubin, *Blue Star*.

151. Gavin, *Deep in a Dream*, 121.

152. Letter from Sim Copans in December 1954 about Mary Lou Williams, who was in France to record with Blue Star and Vogue. Correspondence, Fonds Sim Copans (FSC), Bibliothèque municipale, Souillac.

153. Dahl, *Morning Glory*.

154. Q. Jones, *Q*, 121.

155. See Tucker, "Nadia," cited in Q. Jones, *Q*, 121.

156. Tucker, cited in Q. Jones, *Q*, 122.

157. Tucker, cited in Q. Jones, *Q*, 121.

158. Q. Jones and Gibson, *Q: On Producing*, 45.

159. Q. Jones, *Q*, 125–26, 128.

160. Q. Jones, *Q*, 129.

161. Hennessey, *Klook*, 73, 132.

162. Hennessey, *Klook*, 195.

163. Haggerty, "Under Paris Skies," 209.

164. Hennessey, *Klook*, 141.

165. Hennessey, *Klook*, 87.

166. Haggerty, "Under Paris Skies," 210.

167. Russell, *Bird Lives*, 272.

168. Dizzy Gillespie, interview with Ursula Borschke Davis, May 31, 1981, Pittsburgh, in Broschke Davis, *Paris without Regret*, 55.

169. See liner notes to Donald Byrd Quintet, *Byrd in Paris*, 2 vols. (Brunswick 87 903, 1958).

170. Broschke Davis, *Paris without Regret*, 109.

171. Gilroy, *Black Atlantic*, 18.

172. Gilroy, *Black Atlantic*, 107.

CHAPTER 4. SPEAKING IN TONGUES

1. Mercer Cook, interview by Ruth S. Njiri, June 24, 1981, Silver Spring, MD, transcript, Phelps-Stoke Fund's Oral History Project on former Black Chiefs of Mission, Writings by Mercer Cook, box 157-5, folder 6, Will Mercer Cook Papers (WMCP), Manuscript Division, Moorland-Spingarn Research Center, Howard University.

2. Cook, "Negro Spiritual Goes to France."

3. Cook, "Negro Spiritual Goes to France," 43.

4. Cook, "Negro Spiritual Goes to France," 44.

5. On secularization in postwar France and its intersection with the end of empire, see especially Davidson, *Only Muslim*; E. Foster, *African Catholic*; Ross, *Fast Cars, Clean Bodies*.

6. On this occlusion, see Edwards, *Practice of Diaspora*, 4.

7. On Achille's family and its connection to the Nardal family, see Church, "In Search of Seven Sisters." On Paulette Nardal, see Joseph-Gabriel, *Reimagining Liberation*, chap. 2.

8. Robeson, "Black Paris, II," 10. Robeson wrote this description after she and her husband, Paul Robeson, met the Nardal sisters. On Robeson, see Ransby, *Eslanda*.

9. On the experiences of African and Caribbean students at Louis-le-Grand, see J. G. Vaillant, *Black, French, and African*, 67–86.

10. See Cook's discussion of Achille and Senghor's friendship. "Afro-Americans in Senghor's Poetry [ca. 1970s]," Writings by Mercer Cook, folder 27, WMCP.

11. Interview by Emmanuel Payen, Radio Fourviere, Lyon, January 19, 1974, Achille Family Archives (AFA), Caen.

12. On this dynamic, see Wilder, *French Imperial Nation-State*; Conklin, *Mission to Civilize*; Betts, *Assimilation and Association*.

13. J. G. Vaillant, *Black, French, and African*, 86.

14. On African and Caribbean migration to Paris in this period, see in particular Boittin, *Colonial Metropolis*; Gary Wilder, *French Imperial Nation-State*.

15. Paynter, *Fifty Years After*, 63–64. The apartment was at 51 rue Geoffrey St. Hilaire.

16. See Edwards, *Practice of Diaspora*; Sharpley-Whiting, *Negritude Women*; Boittin, *Colonial Metropolis*; R. P. Smith, "Black like That."

17. Interview by Emmanuel Payen, Radio Fourvière, 1974, AFA.

18. Achille, preface to *La revue du monde noir*, xv.

19. Achille, preface to *La revue du monde noir*, xv.

20. Senghor recalled that Achille introduced him to the "Négro-Renaissance" and poets like Langston Hughes and Countee Cullen. See Senghor and Aziza, *La poésie de*

l'action, 59. Senghor's copy of the first issue of *La revue du monde noir* was inscribed "De la part de Louis Achille" (from Louis Achille). Sirinelli, "Deux étudiants 'coloniaux' à Paris," 82.

21. On the distinct yet connected ways of engaging diasporic and imperial identities, and the impact on *négritude*, see Wilder, *French Imperial Nation-State*; Edwards, *Practice of Diaspora*.

22. "Our Aim," *La Revue du monde noir*, no. 1 (1931): 2.

23. Achille, "L'art et les noirs."

24. On the Colonial Exposition, see Blanchard and Lemaire, *Culture impériale*; Blanchard, *Human Zoos*; Morton, *Hybrid Modernities*.

25. Achille, "L'art et les noirs," 56.

26. See Sablé, *Mémoires d'un foyalais*, 63.

27. The Compagnons led French and German young people on walking pilgrimages like St. Francis of Assisi. On the Compagnons, see Mabille, *Les catholiques et la paix*.

28. Louis Achille, "Chant l'esprit, chant le negro spiritual," 1990, 128, Manuscripts, AFA.

29. R. P. Smith Jr., "Black like That," 60–61. Paulette Nardal later created a choir specializing in Negro spirituals in Martinique. André, *Fort-de-France*, 270–72.

30. His thesis, "Life and Poetical Works of Paul Lawrence Dunbar," was noted in *The Crisis*, November 1933, 258.

31. Payen interview, AFA.

32. Achille to his mother, Marguerite Achille, January 25, 1932, Correspondence, AFA. He wrote that he was staying at 1915 New Hampshire Ave. NW, on the edge of the U Street corridor, with Mrs. Plumb.

33. Payen Interview, AFA.

34. Achille to Marguerite Achille, December 1935, Correspondence, AFA.

35. Achille to Marguerite Achille, May 4, 1932, Correspondence, AFA.

36. Achille letters to Marguerite Achille, February 13, 1933; March 24, 1933; February 11, 1936; October 10, 1936; March 18, 1937, AFA.

37. See Howard University Annual Report, College of Liberal Arts, Howard University Archives. While there, Achille tried to initiate an academic exchange between Howard and his former school in Fort-de-France.

38. "International House Holds Birthday Party Tonight," *Washington Post*, July 18, 1941, Clippings, Vertical File for Louis Achille, Howard University Archives.

39. Letters to his mother in this period document these friendships. Correspondence, passim, AFA. Jones, who taught in Howard's Fine Arts Department in the late 1930s, encouraged Achille to begin painting. In the summer of 1941, he participated in an "artist colony" sponsored by Jones in Martha's Vineyard, where he completed several paintings and sketches. "Washington Social Notes," *Chicago Defender*, October 25, 1941. On Jones's relationship to Africa, see VanDiver, *Designing a New Tradition*.

40. On Atlanta University's summer school in French, see Moore, "'Every Wide-Awake Negro Teacher,'" 25–40. On Mercer Cook and his role in Black French Studies, see Germain, "Mercer Cook and the Origins."

41. Achille to Marguerite Achille, August 1, 1939, Correspondence, AFA.

42. Achille to Marguerite Achille, June 16, 1936, Correspondence, AFA.

43. Achille to Marguerite Achille, June 16, 1936, Correspondence, AFA.

44. Achille to Marguerite Achille, June 16, 1936, Correspondence, AFA.

45. Logan, *Howard University*, 281. The choir's performances were frequently covered in the *Washington Bee* in this period. See also performance program on May 31, 1927, Howard University Glee Club, Evans-Tibbs Collection, Anacostia Community Museum, Smithsonian Institution. The Glee Club performed for the Colored Social Settlement of Washington, DC, in December 1913 alongside lectures by Alain Locke, cited in *The Crisis*, February 1913, 168.

46. On the history of the spiritual, see Lovell, *Black Song*; Cone, *Spirituals and the Blues*; Floyd *Power of Black Music*.

47. See Best, *Passionately Human, No Less Divine*; D. L. Baldwin, *Chicago's New Negroes*; J. A. Jackson, *Singing in My Soul*.

48. Lovell, *Black Song*, 416.

49. Hurston, "Spirituals and Neo-spirituals."

50. See "Negro Spirituals" in Locke, *New Negro*, 199–213. Alain Locke's own views should be considered alongside his colleague Sterling A. Brown, whose courses at Howard introduced students to African American vernacular culture, including poetry, music, and folklore. See Hutchinson, *Harlem Renaissance in Black and White*.

51. Langston Hughes, "The Negro Artist and the Racial Mountain," *Nation*, June 23, 1926.

52. A 1931 radio program on WMAL featured Howard's Glee Club performing "two spirituals" and the Alma Mater. "H.U. Glee Club in Broadcast over WMAL," *Baltimore Afro-American*, May 16, 1931. One article featured a photograph of the tuxedoed choir, "35 Men in Howard University's 1935 Men's Glee Club," *Baltimore Afro-American*, February 2, 1935. Annual concert at Rankin Memorial Chapel reported in "Howard University Men's Glee Club Observes Silver Anniversary," *Baltimore Afro-American*, May 8, 1937.

53. Schenbeck, "Representing America, Instructing Europe."

54. Payan interview, AFA.

55. Payan interview, AFA.

56. Douglass, *Narrative of the Life*, 14; W. E. B. Du Bois, *Souls of Black Folk*, 250. On the spiritual power of this musical genre, see Radano, "Denoting Difference."

57. The recording was released in 1997 by Frémeaux and Associates as *Swing caraïbe: Premiers jazzmen antillais à Paris*, a collection of recordings by Antillean jazz musicians from 1929 to 1946.

58. Correspondence, AFA.

59. In addition to publishing short essays in *The Crisis* and the *Washington Post*, Achille also presented his research on interracialism and religion at academic conferences. See Vertical File for Louis Achille, Howard University Archives.

60. Achille, "Catholic Approach to Interracialism."

61. Louis T. Achille, "Loyal French Writer Opposes 'Sale' of Isles in West Indies," *Washington Post*, May 26, 1940, AFA.

62. Payen interview, AFA.

63. Untitled article, *Cleveland Gazette*, July 20, 1940, AFA.

64. Payen interview, AFA.

65. Louis T. Achille to Dr. Patterson, May 23, 1943, from 1st Co., Fort Benning, Georgia, AFA; italics here indicate underscoring in the original.

66. Payen interview, AFA.

67. Payen interview, AFA.

68. Payen interview, AFA.

69. Gutton, *Histoire de Lyon*, 112.

70. Payen interview, AFA.

71. Payen nterview, AFA.

72. Citations from the thirtieth-anniversary tour of Martinique, published as *Trentenaire du Park Glee Club*, November 26, 1978, Lycée du Parc, Lyon, AFA. As a devout Catholic in a rapidly secularizing country wherein the classroom was a flashpoint for debates, Achille was wary of wearing his devotion on his sleeve.

73. Achille, *Trentenaire*, 1.

74. Achille, *Trentenaire*, 1.

75. Cook, "Negro Spiritual Goes to France," 44. Achille was concerned that the choir's composition "gave the false impression that negro spirituals were not for women's voices," and admitted that the "historic masculinity of the Lycée du Parc imprinted on the Park Glee Club a vigorous, even muscular style, even a bit martial, that is perhaps an expression of the national *temperament*." Photographs of choir in the mid- to late 1960s suggest a different racial makeup than the earlier days. Photographs, AFA.

76. Cook, "Negro Spiritual Goes to France," 44. On Bunche's 1951 trip to France, see Urquhart, *Ralph Bunche*, chap. 17.

77. Macey, *Frantz Fanon*, 119.

78. Fanon, *Black Skin, White Masks*, 14.

79. Fanon also cited from an article that Achille had contributed in 1949 to the Christian missionary publication *Rythmes du Monde* in which he described the "spontaneity of religious expression" in African American spirituals: "From Our Representatives," in *African Music Society Newsletter* 1 (March 1949): 14. Fanon, *Black Skin, White Masks*, 52–53.

80. Louis T. Achille, "Amérique du Nord," in "Le monde noir," special issue, *Présence Africaine* 8/9 (1950): 357–82. *Esprit* was part of "new Left" alternatives to the communist press in postwar France and had by the late 1940s begun to openly critique French colonialism. On *Esprit*, see Armus, "The Eternal Enemy." On Catholicism and African and Caribbean students, see Daily, "Race, Citizenship"; E. A. Foster, *African Catholic*.

81. *Esprit* was connected to Éditions du Seuil, a small publishing house that published *Peau noire, masques blancs* in 1952. Its editor Francis Jeanson had also contributed essays on "le monde noir" to *Présence Africaine*.

82. On this opening line, and its relationship to the lived experience of race, see Holt, "Marking."

83. Achille, "Negro Spirituals," 707–8.

84. Achille, "Negro Spirituals," 707.

85. Achille's devotion to its original status is, of course, complicated by how this musical tradition was sung, "lined out," transcribed, notated, and preserved over time. Whereas it had once served as a way for those not literate in English (including those slaves who knew African or Creole languages) to engage in religious practice, to accompany long hours of work, to form coded plans of escape or insurrection, or simply to share pain, sorrow, hope, fear, and joy, the spiritual was later transmitted through a range of media. On the early transcription of the spiritual, see Cruz, *Culture on the Margins*, 3.

86. Achille, "Negro Spirituals," 707. Cook thought Achille was "stumped by the simplicity and directness of 'Steal away to Jesus,' which he rendered in two lines: "Comme se cache le voleur, Je cherche refuge auprès de Jésus (As the thief goes into hiding, I seek refuge in Jesus)." Cook, "Negro Spiritual Goes to France." Reviewing the essay in *Présence Africaine*, Alioune Diop proclaimed Achille to be the most qualified person to bring an anthology of Negro spirituals to Francophone readers. Alioune Diop, "Plainte du noir," *Présence Africaine* 12 (1951): 252.

87. In this same period, Achille was also publishing on African American religious life. See Achille, "Organisation de la vie religieuse."

88. Achille's son Dominique Achille compared it to the way in which "Take the A Train" opened Duke Ellington's concerts. Dominique Achille, interview with the author, April 26, 2012, Caen.

89. J. W. Johnson, *Second Book of Negro Spirituals*. The first edition, *The Book of American Negro Spirituals*, was also published in 1926.

90. Dominique Achille, interview with the author.

91. Ad Lucem invited the Park Glee Club in order to help raise money for scholarships for Congolese students. Payen Interview, AFA.

92. Payen interview, AFA.

93. *Trentenaire*, AFA.

94. *Trentenaire*, AFA.

95. Payen interview, AFA. In 1972, musicologist John Lovell cited Achille on the relationship of the soloist to the choir. Lovell, *Black Song*, 199.

96. *Trentenaire*, AFA.

97. Jacques Joyard, interview with the author, June 17, 2014, Grenoble, France.

98. *Trentenaire*, AFA.

99. See Gaunt, *Games Black Girls Play*, 3.

100. In thinking of how African American culture has been admired, appropriated, borrowed, and stolen, I am especially indebted to Lott, *Love and Theft*; Tate, *Everything but the Burden*; Hamilton, *Just around Midnight*; L. M. Jackson, *White Negroes*; E. P. Johnson, *Appropriating Blackness*.

101. See Gaunt, *Games Black Girls Play*, 3. On pedagogy and performance, see also E. P. Johnson, *Appropriating Blackness*.

102. Redmond, *Anthem*, 11, 13.

103. E. P. Johnson, *Appropriating Blackness*, 201.

104. In February 1950, there was a "Negro spirituals" program on Programme Parisien, Programming, ORTF, 950218/3, Centre des archives contemporaines (CAC), Fontainebleau. See also April 1950, "Rhapsodies noires: Negro Spirituals" on the Programme

Parisien, Dossiers W. Porché, Service des échanges internationaux, 1947–50, Direction des Services Artistiques, ORTF, 950218/22, CAC.

105. James Kirkup, "Obituary: John Littleton," *The Independent*, September 2, 1998.

106. "Going to Shout All Over God's Heaven" (1938), Louis Armstrong and his orchestra, *The Complete Decca Sessions, 1935–46*. For archives of the television program, see *À la recherche du jazz*, RTF Télévision, 1956–57, Institut national de l'audiovisuel (INA).

107. See Heath, *Deep Are the Roots*.

108. Letter from Heath to parents, June 22, 1947, folder 41, box 4, series 2, Gordon Heath Papers (GHP), Special Collections and University Archives, University of Massachusetts Amherst.

109. Nesta Roberts," The Exiles" (unknown publication), June 14, 1973, folder 9, box 2, series 1, Heath Papers, GHP.

110. Interview, folder 14, box 2, series 1, Heath Papers, GHP.

111. Heath, *Deep Are the Roots*, 156.

112. Heath, untitled manuscript, folder 9, box 2, series 1, GHP.

113. "An American in Paris," *Réalités*, 1951, folder 1643, box 12, series 5, GHP.

114. Cook, "Negro Spiritual Goes to France," 42, 44, 48.

115. "Un remarquable récital des Golden Jubaleers," *L'Écho républicain*, May 11–12, 1957, Clippings, Fonds Sim Copans (FSC), Bibliothèque municipale, Souillac. Publicity materials and news coverage refer to the group forming at the Dreux-Senonches airbase.

116. Manuscript entitled "Les Golden Jubaleers," Conférences, FSC.

117. "Une excellent soirée de negro-spirituals avec les Golden Jubileers," *La Republique du Centre*, May 11/12, 1957, Conférences, FSC.

118. Louis T. Achille, "Chanter avec dieu, danser avec lui: *Fleuve Profond, Sombre Rivière*," *Présence Africaine* 54 (1965): 128.

119. Louis T. Achille, "Amérique du Nord," *Présence Africaine* 8/9, *Le monde noir* (1950): 357–82.

120. On *Présence Africaine* in the 1950s, see Jules-Rosette, *Black Paris*; Mudimbe, *Surreptitious Speech*; Hassan, "Inaugural Issues."

121. The entire proceedings were published in *Présence Africaine* 8–10 (June–November 1956). A translation of the proceedings was published separately as a special issue: "The First International Conference of Negro Writers and Artists," *Présence Africaine* 8–10 (June–November 1956). It was first advertised in the August–September 1955 issue of *Présence Africaine,* in a letter signed by African, Antillean, and American intellectuals and artists, including Louis Armstrong, Josephine Baker, and Richard Wright.

122. James Baldwin, "Princes and Power: Letter from Paris," *Encounter*, January 1957, 52. Later reprinted in J. Baldwin, *Nobody Knows My Name: More Notes of a Native Son*.

123. Du Bois was barred from leaving the United States by the State Department, which had itself briefed the US delegation prior to the meeting. As one official wrote: "It is possible that communist elements known to be associated with the Congress or planning to attend will endeavor to divert the meeting from cultural into political discussions and resolutions," box 72, Bureau of Public Affairs, 1946–1962, General Records of the Department of State, Record Group (RG) 59, National Archives and Records Administration, College Park, MD (NARA-CP).

124. On the press, see Jacques Howlett, "Le premier congrès des écrivains et artistes noirs et la presse internationale," *Présence Africaine* 20 (June–July 1958): 111–17.

125. J. Baldwin, "Princes and Power," 52.

126. Alioune Diop, "Discours d'ouverture," *Présence Africaine* 8–10 (June–November 1956): 11. While there were no female delegates, a "group of black women" called attention to women's contributions as educators and activists.

127. Diop, "Discours d'ouverture," 16.

128. On the American Society of African Culture and Cold War liberalism, see R. D. G. Kelley, *Africa Speaks, America Answers*; Plummer, *In Search of Power*; Gaines, *American Africans in Ghana*.

129. "Débats, 19 septembre à 21h," *Présence Africaine* 8–10 (June–November 1956): 67, original in English.

130. "Débats, 19 septembre à 21h," 74.

131. "Débats, 20 septembre à 21h," *Présence Africaine* 8–10 (June–November 1956): 213–14.

132. Ollie Stewart, "Artists, Writers in Paris; Dubois Sends Message," *Baltimore Afro-American,* October 6, 1956.

133. J. Baldwin, "Princes and Power," 55.

134. See Julien, "Terrains de Rencontre."

135. E. A. Foster, *African Catholic*, 186.

136. "Débats, 20 septembre à 21h," *Présence Africaine*, 217, original in English.

137. "Débats, 20 septembre à 21h," 209.

138. Louis T. Achille, "Les Negro-spirituals et l'expansion de la culture noire," *Présence Africaine* 8–10 (June–November 1956), 227–37. Achille's presentation was on September 21, 1956, at ten o'clock in the morning.

139. Achille, "Les Negro-spirituals," 227.

140. Achille, "Les Negro-spirituals," 227–28.

141. Achille, "Les Negro-spirituals," 229.

142. Achille, "Les Negro-spirituals," 227.

143. Achille, "Les Negro-spirituals," 231.

144. Achille, "Les Negro-spirituals," 231, 234. On the later incorporation of African-American music into Catholic liturgy, see Ludovic Tournès, "La culture de masse à l'église? L'introduction avortée de la musique noire américaine dans la liturgie catholique française (1960–1970)," in Quéniart, *Le chant, acteur de l'Histoire*, 265–78.

145. Achille, "Les Negro-spirituals," 232.

146. Achille, "Les Negro-spirituals," 232.

147. Achille, "Les Negro-spirituals," 233.

148. Original in English. "Conférence de Louis Thomas Achille au congrès des écrivains et artistes noirs," Fonds OCORA, INA. This recording was preserved in the Institut Nationale de l'Audiovisuel in Paris, which maintains the audiovisual records of the French national radio and broadcasting networks. This recording was filed under the Office de Coopération Radiophonique (OCORA), which succeeded the Société de Radiodiffusion de la France d'Outre-mer (SORAFOM) in 1962 to manage radio and television broadcasts in the French empire and the postcolonial Francophone world.

149. Achille, "Les Negro-spirituals," 233.

150. Achille, "Les Negro-spirituals," 235–36.

151. Achille, "Les Negro-spirituals," 236.

152. As noted in the introduction, this same space served as a temporary prison for North Africans during the Algerian War, as well as a venue for a Ray Charles concert series. On this convergence, see Moore, "Ray Charles in Paris."

153. Ollie Stewart, "Report from Europe," *Baltimore Afro-American*, April 16, 1966.

154. "US Barred Ambassador from Rally," *New York Amsterdam News*, April 9, 1966. In turn, the organizing committee "issued a statement disassociating itself from King's stand on Vietnam." On the concert, see "Europeans Give Generously to Dr. King's Rights Fund," *Chicago Defender*, April 6, 1966; "Viet Nam Stand Splits King's Paris Backers; $50,000 Raised at Rally," *Baltimore Afro-American*, April 9, 1966. In the months leading up to the tour, King had become increasingly vocal in opposing the war, revealing a "Third World" consciousness that infused his thinking in his last years. See Cone, "Martin Luther King, Jr."

155. "Giant King Benefits Set in France, Norway," *Jet*, March 24, 1966, 59.

CHAPTER 5. THE VOICE OF AMERICA

1. Jean-Claude Martini, "Au Centre Culturel, 'Avec moi le Jazz entre à l'Académie Française,'" *Le Méridional–La France*, Hyères edition, February 6, 1958, Conférences, Fonds Sim Copans (FSC), Bibliothèque municipale, Souillac.

2. Martini, "Au Centre Culturel," *Le Méridional-La France*, Conférences, FSC.

3. Daniel Behrman, "Doctor Copans and Monsieur Jazz," *Réalités*, February 1965, 51.

4. Ollie Stewart, "He Just Keeps Playing Our Music to the French," *Rhode Islander*, May 7, 1961, 20–21, Clippings, FSC.

5. Obituary of Richard Copans, March 19, 1956, in Copans Family Archives (CFA), Paris. Other family information found in Biography, FSC.

6. "8 Scholarships Given for Study in Europe," *New York Times*, May 4, 1931.

7. On his recruitment to the OWI, see interview with George de Caunes, "De la radio mobile en Normandie à la création de 'Ce soir en France,'" *Cahiers d'histoire de la radiodiffusion* 42 (September–November 1994): 196–99. On Copans's political views, Richard Copans, interview with the author, April 21, 2010, Paris.

8. On the history of the Voice of America, see Pirsein, *Voice of America*.

9. Pianist Art Simmons, for example, alerted fellow expatriates of State Department surveillance and aided them in navigating the pressures of Cold War travel. While Simmons reluctantly played this role in the 1960s, he later resisted this insidious form of power. In 1971, Simmons was asked by the State Department to lead a jazz group tour in Algeria. He soon realized that the tour was a pretense for locating Eldridge Cleaver, who had been in exile since 1968 and was being protected by Algerian musicians. After this experience, Simmons decided to return home to West Virginia. On this, see Broschke Davis, "Art Simmons in Paris." On these Cold War constraints, see especially Dudziak, *Cold War Civil Rights*; Von Eschen, *Satchmo Blows Up the World*; Singh,

Black Is a Country; Plummer, *Rising Wind*; C. Anderson, *Eyes off the Prize*; Horne, *Black and Red*.

10. See De Grazia, *Irresistible Empire*; McKenzie, *Remaking France*; Kuisel, *Seducing the French*; Pells, *Not like Us*; Kroes, *If You've Seen One*; Schwartz, *It's So French!*

11. See Job Description, 1946, US Information Service (USIS) files, FSC. See also Memorandum to Secretary of State, October 16, 1947, box 2, , Paris Embassy, France, General and Classified Subject Files of the USIA Office, Records of the Foreign Service Posts of the Department of State, Record Group (RG) 84, National Archives and Records Administration, College Park, MD (NARA-CP).

12. "La radio inaugure une quatrième chaîne," *L'étoile du soir*, January 4, 1947, Clippings, FSC. Wladmir Porché, the new director general of the RDF, wrote to the American ambassador to thank him for their collaboration with the RDF and the "représentants du Signal Corps des États Unis d'Amérique" for the use of the American transmitter at Reuil-Malmaison. Porché to Jefferson Caffery, January 4, 1947, Direction Générale de la Radiodiffusion Française, Office de la Radiodiffusion-Télévision Française (ORTF), 950218/22, Centre des archives contemporaines (CAC), Fontainebleau.

13. Paris Inter was known to be chatty and informal, especially when compared to the Programme National, which broadcast news and national cultural programming, and the Programme Parisien, which offered more "recreational" programs. See Wladimir Proché, Report, September 29, 1948, 2, Organisation des Service Artistiques, F41/2247, Archives nationales de France (ANF). Paris Inter's range was initially limited to Paris and its surrounding suburbs, for its long-wave transmitter in the suburbs operated only at 1 kw power. Eventually, all three stations transmitted programs over medium wave (AM radio). See Direction générale de la RDF, 950218/3, CAC.

14. "Plan des émissions des Chaines Nationale, Parisienne, et Paris-Inter à partir du 5 octobre 1947," F41/2247, ANF.

15. See program transcript, "L'Amérique et sa musique," Radio Manuscripts, FSC.

16. Plan des émissions, Direction des services artistiques, Service des Echanges Internationaux, ORTF, 950218/22, CAC. See also Sim Copans, "Les productions radiophoniques assurés depuis le 1er octobre, 1957," RTF Manuscripts, FSC.

17. This was eventually released commercially in 1955 by the Westminster label (WN 18080).

18. There were also jazz programs on peripheral stations like Radio Andorre, Radio Suisse, Radio Luxembourg, Radio Monte Carlo, Radio Strasbourg, Radio Alger, and Radio Tunis, as well as other programs on RDF national and regional stations. This included regular programs by Jean-Marie Masse, who in 1947 began a hosting regular program out of Limoges with a broadcasting range that found listeners in Algeria. Jean-Marie Masse, interview with the author, November 2010, Limoges. An issue of *Radio revue* in September 1947 listed the following for its listeners: the three stations of Radiodiffusion Française, regional stations, stations of the "Union Française," and then a long list of peripheral stations, including those in Luxembourg, Monte-Carlo, Germany, Poland, Sweden, Switzerland, Italy, Belgium, the Netherlands, and the United Kingdom.

19. "Tableau d'Honneur," February 15, 1947, Special Emissions, FSC.

20. "La radio," *Jazz hot*, May–June 1947, 19.

21. Robert Lovett, Secretary of State, December 3, 1948, in *Foreign Relations of the United States 1948*, vol. 3, *Western Europe* (Washington, DC: GPO, 1948), cited in Wall, *United States and the Making*, 144.

22. The Voice of America had no legal status until January 1948 with the passage of the United States Information and Educational Exchange Act, which expanded the Fulbright program to include countries not specified in the original lend-lease agreements and added new cultural centers. The State Department was responsible for VOA programming and distribution while the ECA's Mission France maintained its own information officer, radio, exhibits, and visual media. See Pirsein, *Voice of America*, 110–35.

23. "L'Amérique telle qu'elle n'est pas," *Humanité*, November 15, 1950.

24. "Au Congrès des Journalistes M. Barnier déclare: 'La radiodiffusion n'est plus française, mais . . . Américaine. Il faut la libérer,'" *Ce soir*, February 21, 1950.

25. "Le pick-up américain," *Radio revue*, July 4–10, 1948.

26. "Vive la radio quand même!," *Radio revue*, April 17, 1949.

27. Pierre Drouin, "Les tendances du jazz aux U.S.A.," *Le Monde*, August 29, 1951.

28. Roland de Serbois, "Le jazz n'excuse pas tout," *Reforme-Paris*, March 10, 1951.

29. "Qui? Pourquoi? Comment?," *Opéra*, March 21, 1951.

30. Though the start time varied slightly, *Panorama* kept its Saturday midday hour for many years, always on Paris Inter, lasting forty-five minutes to an hour. In 1948, the start time was 12:18 p.m. See Memorandum from Copans, September 13, 1948, FSC and *Jazz hot* for broadcast times.

31. Bernard Demory, *Au temps des cataplasmes*, 408.

32. Perec, *Je me souviens*, 53. Perec described Copans as a "man who knew jazz," who first introduced him to Clifford Brown, Lester Young, and Charlie Parker.

33. Perec, *Je me souviens*, back cover.

34. Letter from J. Boileau de Castelneau, October 1948, Correspondence, FSC.

35. Copans dedicated his December 25, 1948 program for the students on the "Negro-Spiritual et le jazz." Jean Mornet to Copans, March–June 1953, Correspondence, FSC.

36. "Échos des ondes," *Jazz hot*, April 1948, 10.

37. "L'hospitalité du Panorama du Jazz," Manuscripts, FSC.

38. Jacques Demêtre, interview with the author, April 19, 2012, Paris.

39. These citations from Leloir are from Daniel Behrman's 1965 feature on Copans, which appeared in English in *Réalités*. Thus, the citations from Leloir were already translated, featuring select French words in the original. Behrman, "Doctor Copans and Monsieur Jazz," 51.

40. See, for example, Bernard Vincent, interview with the author, April 10, 2012, Paris. See also "Jazz Radio," *Jazz hot*, October 1952, 19.

41. Leloir, cited in Behrman, "Doctor Copans and Monsieur Jazz," 51.

42. Don Walter, "Popular Man on French Radio," *Stars and Stripes*, October 28, 1958.

43. Bernard Vincent, interview with the author, April 10, 2012, Paris.

44. Behrman, "Doctor Copans and Monsieur Jazz," 51.

45. As Barbara Savage has described in the US context, the radio rendered the "black world held harmless under the reassuring surveillance of unseen listeners," an insight that

is complicated within this global context of listening. Savage, *Broadcasting Freedom*, 7. On race and radio, see also D. W. Vaillant, "Sounds of Whiteness"; Ely, *Adventures of Amos 'n' Andy*; Barlow, *Voice Over*; Hilmes, *Radio Voices*.

46. Stoever, *Sonic Color Line*, 4. My thinking here is also indebted to the work of Eidsheim, *Race of Sound*.

47. This description is from 1961. "Syntheses de serie des émissions inscrites au programme de France I," February 1961, Service du Contrôle Artistique des Émissions, 1943–61, Direction Générale et Inspection Générale, Direction Générale, ORTF, 950218/6, CAC.

48. Copans, "Quelques réflexions sur les negro-spirituals," n.d., Manuscripts, FSC.

49. Both vocal groups would eventually relocate to France in the mid- to late 1950s. The Golden Gate Quartet was also popular in West and Central Africa; see Von Eschen, *Satchmo Blows Up the World*, 78.

50. *Negro Spirituals*, Paris Inter, March 1, 1949, Institut national de l'audiovisuel (INA).

51. "Negro Spirituals Français," *Ainsi va le monde*, Chaine Parisienne, April 28, 1950, INA.

52. Copans also described the spiritual's latest incarnation in the "protest songs of millions of black Americans who are demonstrating for their right to be considered full citizens." Copans, "Le Negro Spiritual," n.d., Manuscripts, FSC.

53. "Syntheses de serie des émissions inscrites au programme de France I," February 1961, Service du Contrôle artistique des émissions, 1943–61, Direction Générale et Inspection Générale, ORTF, 950218/6, CAC.

54. "La critique: Negro spirituals," *La Croix*, June 20, 1952, 16.

55. Thanks to its retransmission out of the colonial station's transmitter in Allouis, the reach of Paris Inter grew to include listeners throughout France. By 1951, it was regularly transmitted on short wave (during the day) and medium wave (at night) out of a new transmitter in Villebon. "Rapport: Éléments d'appréciation sur les émissions artistiques de la R.T.F., 1951," Dossiers de W. Porché, Services artistiques, 1950–51, Direction Générale de la Radiodiffusion, ORTF, 950218/3, CAC. By 1952, it could be heard "in almost the totality of the French territory" by "a much-increased number of listeners." Brochand, *Histoire générale de la radio*, 522.

56. Specifically, Raymond Kuhn estimates that it was 118 minutes per day in this period. Kuhn, *Media in France*, 79. On radio listening, see Cowans, "Political Culture and Cultural Politics," 162.

57. Gilson to Copans, June 23, 1952, Relations avec la direction des services artistiques, 1950–52, Direction des services artistiques, 19950218/24, CAC.

58. "Letter from French Radio Official concerning Local Broadcasts of Radio Officers," January 16, 1953, Manuscripts, FSC; Memorandum from Charles Moffly (PAO), citing Jean-Vincent Brechnigac, Director of Paris Inter, RTF Correspondence, FSC.

59. Letter from Copans to R. Douglas Smith, Personnel Officer, January 15, 1954, USIS Files, FSC. Copans was employed by the State Department until 1953, when its information activities fell under the purview of USIS, the overseas name of the USIA. On this agency, see Cull, *Cold War and the United States*.

60. See Sim Copans's file at the Federal Bureau of Investigation (FBI), which includes records of the US State Department's investigation of Copans before he was hired. Neighbors were interviewed regarding his religious and political views. On the investigation of US State Department employees in this period, see D. K. Johnson, *Lavender Scare*; Schrecker, *Many Are the Crimes*.

61. Behrman, "Doctor Copans and Monsieur Jazz," 51.

62. Michel Oriano, "Sim Copans, ambassadeur," 9.

63. On the global history of the Black freedom struggle, see especially Singh, *Black Is a Country*; R. D. G. Kelley, "But a Local Phase"; Von Eschen, *Race against Empire*; Makalani, *In the Cause of Freedom*; Blain, *Set the World on Fire*.

64. On Cold War civil rights, see especially Dudziak, *Cold War Civil Rights*; Von Eschen, *Race against Empire*; Borstelmann, *Cold War and the Color Line*; Slate, *Colored Cosmopolitanism*; Plummer, *Rising Wind*; Plummer, *In Search of Power*; C. Anderson, *Eyes off the Prize*; C. Anderson, *Bourgeois Radicals*.

65. In response to Washington's call for more programs, the French office argued that an "overly-aggressive campaign on this subject" might make them appear defensive and prolong a debate "which is not necessarily to our advantage." Instead, they argued that the "best approach" was to "continue to present the colored American and his achievements as part of the broad and varied fabric of American life and not as a special 'problem' which we are trying to solve." Memorandum from William E. Tyler, PAO, American Embassy, Paris, to Department of State, February 20, 1952, folder "Negro Question," box 44, General and Classified Subject Files of the USIA Office, Paris Embassy, France, Records of the Foreign Service Posts of the Department of State, RG 84, NARA-CP.

66. Conover cited in Von Eschen, *Satchmo Blows Up the World*, 17. Conover's program began broadcasting in January 1955, relayed through Tangiers in the evenings at nine o'clock, *Jazz hot*, January 1956, 6. In contrast to Conover's more overtly propagandistic portrayal of jazz, Copans was renowned for more subtle insinuations of US authority. Copans's fan mail also revealed an "extensive following behind the Iron Curtain among listeners able to tune in the French radio." Don Walter, "Popular Man on French Radio," *Stars and Stripes*, October 28, 1958. Notably, in this same period, Copans also created programs that were translated and broadcast through the US-sponsored and CIA-funded Radio Free Europe (RFE) network in Eastern Europe. See Radio Free Europe Files, FSC. On RFE, see Puddington, *Broadcasting Freedom*.

67. Other work suggests that this uncertainty within the USIS persisted into the late 1950s. See Krenn, "'Unfinished Business.'"

68. Letter from Copans to Laurence Wylie, May 30, 1966, Correspondence, FSC.

69. See Listener Letters, FSC.

70. In this, I see a slightly different audience than what is defined in McGregor, *Jazz and Postwar French Identity*.

71. Letter 33, September 21, 1957, Listener Correspondence, FSC.

72. Sgt. Fernard Villette, June 17, 1958, Listener Correspondence, FSC.

73. Letter 360, AFN, Listener Correspondence, FSC.

74. On radio during the Algerian War, see Méadel, Ulmann-Mauriat, and Bussierre, *Radios et télévision au temps*. On the Algerian War's effect on French politics and culture,

see especially Le Sueur, *Uncivil War*; Ross, *Fast Cars, Clean Bodies*; Lyons, *Civilizing Mission in the Metropole*; Shepard, *Invention of Decolonization*; Stora, *La gangrène et l'oubli*.

75. Hilary Kaiser interview with Copans, 1991, private collection.

76. Fanon, "This Is the Voice," 94–96.

77. *Jeunesse magazine*, Chaîne Nationale, 1954.

78. Copans, "La petite histoire du jazz," Manuscripts, FSC.

79. *Jazz memories*, RTF Télévision, 1959–60, INA. In 1954 only 1 percent of homes had a television set, but by 1962 televisions could be found in a quarter of all residences in hexagonal France, with just one station until 1963; both RTF stations broadcast in black-and-white until 1967. Television did not reach the overseas departments of Guadeloupe and Martinique until 1964 and did not become widespread in West Africa until the late 1960s and early 1970s. Kuhn, *Media in France*, 92.

80. On the embodied practice of mass media, see Chaplin, *Turning On the Mind*.

81. In Algiers, the center sponsored weekly jazz listening events on Thursday afternoons for young people, and regular movie screenings, including the 1956 film *Homme de la Nouvelle Orléans: La vie de Kid Ory*. Along with the local MJC chapter, the American center in Toulouse sponsored in February 1960 a lecture on "negro-spirituals." *Bulletin of Toulouse Cultural Center*, February 1960.

82. Fosler-Lussier, *Music in America's Cold War Diplomacy*. On music and cultural diplomacy, see also Von Eschen, *Satchmo Blows Up the World*; Monson, *Freedom Sounds*; Gienow-Hecht, *Sound Diplomacy*. See also "Special Forum: Musical Diplomacy." On other forms of cultural diplomacy in the Cold War, see especially Barnhisel, *Cold War Modernists*; Croft, *Dancers as Diplomats*.

83. For more on the ABC, see Pulh, *Au fil du jazz*.

84. Once the lecture topic was determined, the ABC coordinated with a local representative who booked a hotel, arranged the lecture hall, met Copans at the train station, and coordinated the technical requirements: a *pick-up*, speakers, and microphone. See M. Bon (Amical Laïque Chagny) to Copans, December 12, 1955, Conférences, FSC.

85. Copans to A. Lhuiller, Association Bourguignonne Culturelle, November 28, 1955, Conférences, FSC. This was also a marked difference from his earlier lectures, when his preparatory notes read: "I am American, I like jazz, and I've heard a lot of jazz." See 1948, Association France-USA, Conférences, FSC. For coverage of the event, see Henri Chpindel, "Le jazz américain," *France-USA*, May 1948, Manuscripts, FSC.

86. On French jazz critics in this period, see Tournès, *New Orleans sur Seine*, particularly chap. 7. For a discussion of contemporary debates in jazz criticism in both East and West Germany, see "Jazz and German Respectability" in Poiger, *Jazz, Rock, and Rebels*, 137–67.

87. Copans likely drew from Stearns's own published work on the history of jazz, which was published in full a few years after Copans developed his own lectures. See Stearns, *Story of Jazz*. On Stearns, see Gennari, *Blowin' Hot and Cool*, 147–50.

88. R. D. G. Kelley, *Africa Speaks, America Answers*, 80. See also Von Eschen, *Satchmo Blows Up the World*, 171–77.

89. Copans to M. A. Lhuillier, ABC, November 28, 1955, Correspondence, FSC. See also January 17, 1958, letter from Copans to John Hedges, Directeur, Centre Culturel Américain, Correspondence, FSC.

90. Copans, "Le Jazz: de la Nigéria à la Nouvelle Orléans," Manuscripts, Conférences, FSC.

91. See Harold Courlander and Dick Waterman, liner notes to *Folk Music of Africa and America* (New York: Folkways Records, 1951).

92. On the relationship of Africa to jazz, see Garcia, *Listening for Africa*. In addition to its temporal limits, Copans's account also obscured the impact of Caribbean and Latin American musicians and audiences on the formation of jazz. On this, see especially Washburne, *Latin Jazz*; Fernandez, *From Afro-Cuban*; Putnam, *Radical Moves*; Seigel, *Uneven Encounters*.

93. Copans, "Le Jazz: de la Nigéria à la Nouvelle Orléans," FSC.

94. Copans also played recordings made by Arthur Alberts, who archived popular, sacred, children's, and work songs in West Africa in 1949. See Arthur Alberts, ed., *The Arthur S. Alberts Collection: More Tribal, Folk, and Café Music of West Africa* (Washington, DC: Mickey Hart Collection, 1998).

95. Copans, "Le Jazz: de la Nigéria à la Nouvelle Orléans," FSC.

96. Copans, "Le Jazz: de la Nigéria à la Nouvelle Orléans," FSC. These selections include "I'm Goin' Up North" by the children of the East York School in East York, Alabama, as well as "Little Sallie Walker" and "See See Rider" by children at Lilly's Chapel School in Lilly's Chapel, Alabama. For these recordings, see *Negro Folk Music of Alabama*, vol. 1: *Secular Music*, ed. Harold Courlander (Smithsonian Folkways Recordings, 1951).

97. Copans to John Hedges, Centre Culturel Américain, January 17, 1958, Conférences, FSC.

98. Copans, "Le Jazz: De la Nigéria à la Nouvelle Orléans," FSC.

99. Copans to Stephen Carney, December 17, 1955, Conférences, FSC.

100. "Excellente preparation au concert Sidney Bechet," undated newspaper article in Mâcon, Conférences, FSC.

101. Marcel Vitte to Copans, December 24, 1955, Conférences, FSC.

102. Copans to Stephen Carney, USIS, Lyon, December 17, 1955, Conférences, FSC. This echoes Danielle Fosler-Lussier's account of musical diplomacy, which had a "special power to open doors." Fosler-Lussier, *Music in America's Cold War*, 12.

103. PAO Report from Lilles, May 1958, Conférences, FSC.

104. PAO report from Lille to PAO Paris, November 1958, Conférences, FSC.

105. PAO Report from Tours, May 1958, Conférences, FSC.

106. Stephen Carney, USIS Lyon, to Copans, October 10, 1955, and October 29, 1955, Conférences, FSC.

107. On youth in postwar France, see Jobs, *Riding the New Wave*; Marker, "African Youth on the Move"; Bantigny, *Le plus bel âge?*; Weiner, *Enfants Terribles*; Sohn, *Age tendre*.

108. Bertha Potts, PAO Lyon Report to PAO Paris, October 1957, Conférences, FSC. On the Maisons des Jeunes et de la Culture, see Richard Jobs, *Riding the New Wave*, 105. By 1958, there were two hundred houses throughout greater France, as well as one in Guadeloupe by 1960. Local MJC centers hosted Copans's lectures, and in turn drew in both "jazz fans and regulars." See "Les Conférences: L'histoire du jazz et Sim Copans," *La Dépêche du Midi*, Carcassonne edition, February 14, 1958, Conférences, FSC.

109. "Sous l'égide de 'Connaissance des États-Unis,' le professeur Sim Copans a révélé à très nombreux 'fans' la véritable histoire du jazz," *Le Provençal,* Nîmes edition, February 12, 1958, Conférences, FSC.

110. Alec Strahan, "Les jeunesses musicales de France," *Musical Times,* February 1950, 68. Tournès cites two hundred thousand members in 1957 in Tournès, *New Orleans sur Seine,* 136. On the JMF's cautious embrace of jazz, see "Tournée en France de l'orchestre de Sammy Price," *Rendez-vous à cinq heures,* Paris Inter, January 3, 1956, INA.

111. Jean Michon (JMF) to Copans, December 11, 1955, Correspondence and Manuscripts, Articles, FSC.

112. Donald Davies to Copans, December 28, 1956, Correspondence, FSC.

113. Copans to René Pat, Journal Parlé, Radiodiffusion-Télévision Française, January 1957, Correspondence, FSC. Copans gave his lectures in various military hospitals around Paris, including Val de Grâce in Paris and the Institution des Invalides in Puylobier.

114. PAO Report, April 1958, Conférences, FSC.

115. Paul Roghi, "La jeunesse hyéroise avait envahi la Musée pour entendre M. Sim Copans raconter la merveilleuse histoire du jazz," *La République de Toulon,* February 6, 1958, Conférences, FSC.

116. Max Guizot, "Une causerie de M. Sim Copans sur l'histoire du jazz," *Le Méridional-la France,* February 8, 1958, Conférences, FSC; "Des nombreux auditeurs ont vécu avec Sim Copans l'histoire du jazz," *L'Indépendant,* Carcassonne édition, February 14, 1958, Conférences, FSC. On his accessibility, see "L'histoire illustrée du jazz présenté par Sim Copans, a enthousiasmé un jeune auditoire," *Midi Libre* (Narbonne), February 9, 1958, Conférences, FSC.

117. "Quand le jazz survolte l'Opéra . . . ," *Marseilles Magazine,* March 1958, Conférences, FSC.

118. "Pélérinage aux sources du jazz avec Simon Copans," n.d, Conférences, FSC. See also Stephen Carney, USIS Lyon to Copans, October 10, 1955, Conférences, FSC.

119. Raoul Noilletas, "Naissance et vie du jazz vues par M. Sim Copans," *La République de Toulon,* February 5, 1958, Conférences, FSC.

120. "Passionnante causerie de Sim Copans sur les origines du jazz," *Le Courier Picard,* May 9, 1958, Conférences, FSC.

121. "Quand M. Sim Copans nous fait revivre l'Histoire du jazz, " *La République de Toulon,* February 4, 1958, Conférences, FSC. On the Rameau Hall, see "Jazz au Conservatoire," *Midi-Libre,* Perpignan edition, February 12, 1958, Conférences, FSC.

122. Pierre Bompar, "Sim Copans à Marseille: Le célèbre critique radiophonique donnera une causerie avec disques, samedi 8 février 1958 à l'Opéra," *Le Soir,* February 4, 1958, Conférences, FSC; "Quand le jazz survolte l'Opéra . . . ," *Marseille Magazine,* March 1958.

123. Viviane Bost, "À la Salle Miramar, L'histoire du jazz," *Nice-Matin,* April 22, 1959, Conférences, FSC.

124. Copans to Association Générale des Etudiants de Lyon, December 16, 1959, Correspondence, FSC.

125. Daniel Zwarndé to Copans, March 29, 1958, Joinville-le-Point, Seine, Correspondence, FSC.

126. Stephen V. C. Morris to Copans, Deput Cultural Officer at USIS, Correspondence, FSC. I cannot find a record of this organization. Morris may have been refer-

ring to the Fédération des Étudiants d'Afrique noire en France, whose anticolonial politics would either have made them an appealing or concerning audience for US officials. On African student organizations in this period, see Germain, *Decolonizing the Republic.*

127. Père Desobry to Copans, February 3, 1962; Copans to Desobry, December 2, 1961, Conférences, FSC. The lecture took place on February 24 or March 4, 1962, at 8:30 p.m. in Paris, at the Union des Étudiants Catholiques Africain. On September 14, 1965, Father Desobry wrote again asking for Copans to present to the Club International in Lille on "Les origines du jazz."

128. See Copans's introduction to Hughes, *Une introduction au jazz.*

129. Jean Copans, "Les voyages africains de Sim (Copans) ou l'homme qui revenait du chaud (1963–1967)" (unpublished manuscript, 2020), in the author's possession.

130. On colonial radio, see Bebey, *La radiodiffusion en Afrique Noire*; Brochand, *Histoire générale*, 2:336; Tudesq, *Journaux et radios en Afrique.*

131. Beno Sternberg-Sarel, "La radio en Afrique noire," 108.

132. Brochand, *Histoire générale*, 2:264.

133. Don Walter, "Popular Man on French Radio," *Stars and Stripes*, October 28, 1958. Brochand, *Histoire générale*, 2:264. In 1969, OCORA was absorbed into the overseas broadcasts of the ORTF. It was reformulated in 1974 and then again in 1982 under Radio-diffusion et Télévision Française pour l'Outre-mer (RFO).

134. A study of weekly radio programs for radio stations in Gabon, Cameroon, and the Côte d'Ivoire between 1962 and 1967 demonstrates his reach. Copans's *Fleuve profond* and *Jazz en liberté* could be heard weekly in each country. OCORA, ORTF, 20090288/3948, CAC.

135. PAO Report in Léopoldville-Kinshasa, January 16, 1964, Conférences, FSC.

136. "La jeunesse kinoise a réservé un accueil chaleureux au Dr. Copans," *Étoile du Congo*, January 9, 1964, Conférences, FSC.

137. PAO Report, January 16, 1964, Conférences, FSC.

138. "M. Copans Simon est l'hôte d'Abidjan depuis hier soir," *Bulletin Quotidien d'Information de Agence Ivoirienne de Presse*, December 23, 1963, Conférences, FSC.

139. "M. Simon Copans à Alger, Conférence sur le jazz," *Coopération Hebdo*, October 15, 1965, Conférences, FSC. This publication was sponsored by the French embassy, which may have been particularly invested in identifying this manifestation of *fraternité.*

140. "La semaine culturelle," *El Moudjahid*, October 16, 1965, Conférences, FSC.

141. This tour came just a few months after *El Moudjahid* was reclaimed by the FLN as a state organ of information. "La semaine culturelle," *El Moudjahid*, October 16, 1965.

142. PAO Arthur R. Lee, "Lecture Tour by Paris-Based U.S. Jazz Specialist, Sim Copans," November 16, 1965, Conférences, FSC. On the Algerian War, the Cold War, and decolonization, see Connelly, *Diplomatic Revolution*; Byrne, *Mecca of Revolution.*

143. Fosler-Lussier, *Music in America's Cold War*, 6.

144. Fosler-Lussier, *Music in America's Cold War*, 20–21.

145. Von Eschen, *Satchmo Blows Up the World.*

1. *Ça twiste à Popenguine*, directed by Moussa Sene Absa (1993; San Francisco: California Newsreel, 1994), DVD. On this film, see also Jaji, *Africa in Stereo*. On African film, literature, and jazz, and the relationship of African writers to the "racialized universe" of jazz writing, see also Higginson, *Scoring Race*.

2. On the transatlantic circulation and revision of liberatory ideas, see in particular Dubois, *Colony of Citizens*; Scott, *Common Wind*.

3. Anthropological and historical studies of popular culture and African audiences clarify how new media transformed the audiences' listening experience. Barber, "Preliminary Notes on Audiences," 356. On popular music in colonial and postcolonial Francophone Africa, see especially Stewart, *Rumba on the River*; Jaji, *Africa in Stereo*; Shain, *Roots in Reverse*; Skinner, *Bamako Sounds*; T. Fleming, *Opposing Apartheid on Stage*.

4. Jaji, *Africa in Stereo*, 4–5.

5. Memorandum from the Secrétaire d'État aux Relations avec les États de la Communauté, January 9, 1961, forwarding a letter from the ambassador of France, Henri-Francis Mazoyer, to the Premier Ministre de la République Française, Relations Cameroun-Togo, December 5, 1960, Office des étudiants d'outre-mer, 19780596/42, Centre des Archives Contemporaines (CAC).

6. The first segment of the tour was October 24 to December 4, 1960, and the second was from January 9 to 30, 1961.

7. On the tours, see Von Eschen, *Satchmo Blows Up the World*; Monson, *Freedom Sounds*; Fosler-Lussier, *Music in America's Cold War*. For a detailed tour schedule, see Monson, *Freedom Sounds*, 127. The tours are also surveyed by Lisa E. Davenport, who identifies the contradictions at stake but puzzlingly concludes that these tours transcended Cold War politics. Davenport, *Jazz Diplomacy*.

8. Cited in Von Eschen, *Satchmo Blows Up the World*, 61.

9. Higginson, *Scoring Race*, 9.

10. Mazoyer to the Premier Ministre de la République Française, December 5, 1960, 19780596/42, CAC.

11. Mazoyer to the Premier Ministre de la République Française, December 5, 1960.

12. See Von Eschen, *Race against Empire*; Plummer, *In Search of Power*; Meriwether, *Proudly We Can Be Africans*; Jalloh and Falola, *United States and West Africa*; C. Anderson, "Cold War in the Atlantic World."

13. On the Centre, see Maack, *Libraries in Senegal*, 162–63. On the embassy in Dakar, see Rice, "Cowboys and Communists."

14. Jacques Muyal, telephone interview with the author, September 23, 2019. Muyal would go on to collaborate with a number of African American jazz musicians, including Randy Weston and Dizzy Gillespie. See also Hisham Aidi, "Tangier's Jazzmen—and Their Phantom Producer," *Africa Is a Country* (blog), October 2017, https://africasacountry.com/2017/10/tangiers-jazzmen-and-their-phantom-producer.

15. Georges Collinet, telephone interview with the author, September 9 and 16, 2019.

16. Barber, *History of African Popular Culture*, 138.

17. On Voice of America radio broadcasting in Africa, see Head, *Broadcasting in Africa*.

18. Luchs, *Diplomatic Tales*, 83–84.

19. Stewart, *Rumba on the River*, 248–49.

20. In 1963, the Ministry of Cooperation sponsored a jazz tour by French musician Maxim Saury, "following the American example," in Togo, Côte d'Ivoire, Dahomey, and Cameroon. Jean-Louis Ginibre, "Maxim, ambassadeur itinérant," *Jazz Magazine,* April 1963, 19.

21. Rice, "Cowboys and Communists,"8.

22. Rice, "Cowboys and Communists," 9.

23. Photograph in *The Crisis*, April 1958, 43.

24. "Jazz à Dakar," *Bingo*, April 1963.

25. Brochand, *Histoire générale de la radio*, 264. In 1969, OCORA was absorbed into the overseas broadcasts of the Office de la Radiodiffusion-Télévision Française (ORTF). On the history of radio in Francophone Africa, see especially Bebey, *La radiodiffusion en Afrique Noire*; Sternberg-Sarel, "La radio en Afrique noire"; Scales, *Radio and the Politics of Sound*; Bourgault, *Mass Media in Sub-Saharan Africa*; Asseraf, *Electric News in Colonial Algeria*; Tidiane, *Histoire de la télévision*, 29.

26. André Clergeat, interview with the author, February 20 and July 19, 2012, Paris. On the Studio École, see Tidiane, *Histoire de la télévision,* 29.

27. October 14, 1963, memorandum from Malson to program officials, Fonds Sim Copans (FSC), Souillac, France.

28. Information related to the relay of these programs found in Programmes des Émissions OCORA (Tchad, Gabon, Côte d'Ivoire, Cameroun), 1962–67, OCORA, 200902881/3948 and Émissions vers les DOM et TOM, 1967, OCORA, 20100204/1137, CAC.

29. Denning, *Noise Uprising*, 6.

30. Stewart, *Rumba on the River*, 108.

31. Collins, *Highlife Time*, 245–46.

32. Benga, "Air of the City Makes Free, 76.

33. Shain, *Roots in Reverse*, 43.

34. Jaji, *Africa in Stereo*, 137.

35. Stewart, *Rumba on the River*, 57.

36. Shain, *Roots in Reverse*, 48–49.

37. Information on record stores from interview with Moustafa Sene, who worked at Radio Standard. Moustafa Sene, interview with the author, March 15, 2017, Dakar, Senegal. See also Shain, *Roots in Reverse*.

38. Ousmane Keit, "Beaucoup d'animation pour réveillon à Abidjan," December 26, 1963, publication unknown, FSC.

39. "African Boom in Disk Sales despite Congo," *Billboard*, October 3, 1960; "Audio Fidelity Handled in France and Belgium by Barclay Records," *Billboard*, June 19, 1961.

40. Ricardo Niasse, interview with the author, March 18, 2017, Thies, Senegal. Pan-Am also expanded its service to Africa in 1965. "Pan Am Expands Africa Flights; Three New Services Scheduled," *New York Times*, April 18, 1965.

41. "Trois questions à Ibrahima Sylla," *Jeune Afrique*, August 25, 2003, 46.

42. Diawara, "1960s in Bamako."

43. Alioune Diop, interview with the author, March 17, 2017, Dakar.

44. Murphy, *First World Festival of Negro Arts*; Ratcliff, "When Negritude Was in Vogue."

45. Hoyt Fuller, "World Festival of Negro Arts: Senegal Fete Illustrates Philosophy of 'Negritude,'" *Ebony*, July 1966, 96–106. Fuller had promoted the festival since 1965. See Hoyt Fuller, "The First World Festival of Negro Arts," *Negro Digest*, August 1965, 64. Several years later, Fuller's account of the 1966 festival took on a different tenor. In addition to critiquing ways in which the French remained "omnipresent and omnipotent" in Senegal, even though political independence had come five years before, Fuller laid bare the role of the American intelligence community in organizing the festival, claiming that its true accounting would dishonor those "esteemed Black Americans who lent their prestige to the effort to hold to the barest minimum the political impact" of the event. Fuller, *Journey to Africa*, 87, 92. See also Hoyt W. Fuller, "Festival Postscript: Assessments and Questions," *Negro Digest*, June 1966, 82. On Fuller, see Fenderson, *Building the Black Arts Movement*.

46. Fenderson, *Building the Black Arts Movement*, 100.

47. Fuller, "World Festival of Negro Arts," 97.

48. Hardwick, *Joseph Zobel*, 26.

49. Fuller, "World Festival of Negro Arts," 101. Fuller noted the organizers' desire to "stave off economic collapse" and political disaster and to stimulate tourism by white Europeans and African Americans, who "have a deep longing to visit Africa." He noted, "They might be encouraged to combine this spiritual pilgrimage with a vacation if the price is right" (102).

50. David Murphy, introduction to *The First World Festival of Negro Arts, Dakar 1966*, 16. On these terms, see Edwards, "Uses of Diaspora"; Kelley and Patterson, "Unfinished Migrations." See also George Shepperson, "African Abroad."

51. On AMSAC and jazz, see R. D. G. Kelley, *Africa Speaks, America Answers*.

52. Morris Kaplan, "U.S. Negro Artists Go to Africa to Join in Cultural Exchange," *New York Times*, December 14, 1961.

53. Von Eschen, *Satchmo Blows Up the World*, 151.

54. See, for example, R. D. G. Kelley, *Freedom Dreams*.

55. William Greaves, "The First World Festival of Negro Arts: An Afro-American View," *The Crisis*, June–July 1966, 309–14, 332.

56. Von Eschen, *Satchmo Blows Up the World*, 157.

57. "10 Negro Artists Snub a Festival," *New York Times* (International Division), March 11, 1966.

58. Fuller, "World Festival of Negro Arts," 102.

59. Gaines, *American Africans in Ghana*, 253.

60. Von Eschen, *Satchmo Blows Up the World*, 151.

61. Ellington, *Music Is My Mistress*, 337.

62. Ellington, *Music Is My Mistress*, 337–38.

63. Ellington, *Music Is My Mistress*, 339.

64. "Duke Ellington arrivée à Dakar," *Festival des Arts Nègres*, April 2, 1966, OCORA, INA. "Duke Ellington: Ses impressions sur le festival intégrale," *Festival des Arts Nègres*, April 1966, OCORA, Institut national de l'audiovisuel (INA).

65. Program Notes, *Spectacle féérique de Gorée* (Paris: A. Rousseau, 1966), 21.

66. Program Notes, *Spectacle féérique de Gorée*, 25. While the program referred to the "Baptist Church of New York," the Back Home Choir was, in fact, based at the Greater Harvest Baptist Church in Newark, New Jersey.

67. Program Notes, *Spectacle féérique de Gorée*, 27.

68. Malraux, "Discours de M. André Malraux à l'ouverture du colloque," *L'unité africaine* 196 (April 1966): 1, cited in Jaji, *Africa in Stereo*, 89.

69. Jaji, *Africa in Stereo*, 90.

70. Jaji, *Africa in Stereo*, 66.

71. This was the official English translation of the colloquium, which was titled "Colloque international sur les arts nègres: Leur rôle dans la vie Africaine, leur influence dans le monde, leurs perspectives d'avenir." The conference proceedings from the colloquium were published later by Présence Africaine in French and English, as well as in *Connaissance de l'Afrique* 34 (June 1970).

72. See Correspondence, FSC.

73. Simon J. Copans, "The African Heritage in the Music of the American Negro," in *Colloquium*, 369–95.

74. Copans, "African Heritage in the Music of the American Negro," 394.

75. Louis T. Achille, "Negro Spirituals," in *Colloquium*, 351.

76. Achille, "Negro Spirituals," 353.

77. Achille, "Negro Spirituals," 353.

78. Achille, "Negro Spirituals," 364–65.

79. Dunham, "Address Delivered at the Dakar Festival," 414.

80. Ted Tanen, Centre Culturel Americain, to Suzanne Diop, March 10 and March 15, 1966, FMA013, Fonds festival Mondial des arts nègres (FESMAN), Archives nationales du Sénégal (ANS).

81. Letter from George Schiffer, Attorney to Virginia Inness-Brown, March 9, 1966, First World Festival of Negro Arts, United States Committee, box 1, MG220, Schomburg Center for Research in Black Culture, New York Public Library.

82. K. William Kgosoitsile, "I Have Had Enough! Report on Dakar Festival of Negro Arts," *Liberator*, July 1966, 10.

83. The University of Dakar was closed during the festival, thus undercutting growing student unrest. Murphy, *First World Festival*, 24.

84. Kgosoitsile, "I Have Had Enough! Report on Dakar Festival of Negro Arts," 10.

85. "Barclay May Set Up Firm for OERS," *Billboard*, May 24, 1969.

86. "Barclay Makes South, Central American Shifts," *Billboard*, February 24, 1973.

87. David Llorens, "Big City Bluesman: Junior Wells Is Boss," *Ebony*, June 1968, 138.

88. Robert Baker, "The Junior Wells Chicago Blues Band in Bamako, Mali," *American Diplomacy*, 2013, accessed August 5, 2017, *Academic OneFile*.

89. Diawara, *In Search of Africa*, 99.

90. Diawara, "1960s in Bamako," 103.

91. On the festival, see Meghelli, "'Weapon in Our Struggle'"; S. D. Anderson, "'Negritude Is Dead.'"

92. While these are the words of Nathan Hare, he claims to be paraphrasing Hoyt Fuller, who attended both the 1966 and 1969 festivals. Hare, "Algiers 1969," 3.

93. This recalls Sartre's own dialectical reading of *négritude* in *Orphée Noir*. For the translation, see Sartre, *Black Orpheus*.

94. Hare, "Algiers 1969," 7.

95. Hare, "Algiers 1969," 4.

96. "Une artiste engagée à Alger: Nina Simone," *El Moudjahid*, July 30, 1969.

97. Al-Rachid, "Sacres monstres et monstres sacres!," *El Moudjahid*, August 1, 1969. Oscar Peterson took a different position, arguing that "the Black Americans are Black Americans. And the Africans are Africans. They can have similar problems but because of geographical conditions, the problems are a bit different. I think that the roots are the same but the trees are different." Hamid Bouchakdji, "Le pianiste Oscar Peterson: 'La culture est une chose saine,'" *El Moudjahid*, July 31, 1969.

98. "Quand le jazz se veut arme de combat," *El Moudjahid*, July 18, 1969. Translations in the text are mine and therefore slightly different than the version published in English. See Joans, *Teducation*. This particular poem is also discussed in Val Wilmer's powerful exploration of gender and free jazz. See Wilmer, *As Serious as Your Life*, chap. 12.

99. Klein, *Pan-African Festival of Algiers*. On Klein and the film, see Olivier Hadouchi, "'African Culture Will Be Revolutionary.'"

100. The recording was eventually released as *Live at the Panafrican Festival* by BYG/ Actuel in 1971 (BYG 203). It was produced by Jean Georgakarakos and Jean-Luc Young, with executive production by Jacques Bisceglia and engineered by Barney Wilen.

101. Archie Shepp, interview with the author, March 14, 2012, Ivry-sur-Seine, France. He indicated that he was inspired by recordings by John Coltrane at the Olatunji Center of African Culture.

102. On earlier iterations of pan-Africanism, see especially J. Jones, *In Search of Brightest Africa*. On jazz and Africa, see I. Anderson, *This Is Our Music*; Monson, *Freedom Sounds*; R. D. G. Kelley, *Africa Speaks*. See also Val Wilmer's profile of Randy Weston in "Back to the African Heartbeat," in Wilmer, *Jazz People*, 77–89.

103. R. D. G. Kelley, *Africa Speaks*, 5.

104. Shepp, interview with the author.

105. DVD booklet, *The Pan-African Festival of Algiers*.

106. Michel Leiris, "Jazz (An Interview with Michael Haggerty)." The interview, edited and translated by Michael Haggerty, originally appeared in *Jazz Magazine* in 1984.

107. H. Bouchkadji, "Deux jazzmen nous parlent de la musique (Archie Shepp et Grachan Moncur)," *El Moudjahid*, August 3–4, 1969, 5. For these citations, I am indebted to Meghelli, "'Weapon in Our Struggle for Liberation.'"

108. "La nouvelle musique et les chemins de la revolte," *Bulletin d'information* 3 (May 1969): 22–26.

109. Baraka, *Le peuple du blue*. On its impact on French jazz criticism, see Drott, "Free Jazz and the French"; Lehman, "I Love You"

110. Carles and Comolli, *Free Jazz/Black Power*. The book was originally published in French in 1971. On these kinds of associations with jazz, see Monson, *Freedom Sounds*; Porter, *What Is This Thing?* On May 1968, see also Steve Potts, interview with the author, April 22, 2012, Paris, and Bobby Few, interview with the author, May 13, 2012, Paris.

111. Lewis, *Power Stronger Than Itself*, 217.

112. Steinbeck, *Message to Our Folks*, 135. See also Famoudou Don Moye, telephone interview with the author, March 12, 2020.

113. Steinbeck, *Message to Our Folks*, 141. On the Maisons de la Culture, see Lebovics, *Mona Lisa's Escort*.

114. Steinbeck, *Message to Our Folks*, 71.

115. E. Boundzéki Dongala, "Le 'new jazz': Une interprétation," *Presence Africaine*, n.s., 68 (1968): 141–48. Dongala particularly cited the Sun Ra Arkestra, whose performance in Paris in 1974 at Les Halles almost led to a riot in the street. For more on this and Sun Ra's dealings with French promoters, including Michel Salou, see the Alton Abraham Collection of Sun Ra, University of Chicago Special Collections, Chicago.

116. Steinbeck, *Message to Our Folks*, 135.

117. Famoudou Don Moye, telephone interview with the author, March 12, 2020.

118. "Le jazz: Retour au pays natal," *Bulletin d'information* 3 (May 1969): 30–34. The piece was translated in an English publication from the festival.

119. Kaké, *Les noirs de la diaspora*, 153.

120. The recordings in the summer of 1969 were overseen by Claude Delcloo, who "invited artists participating in the First Pan-African Festival in Algiers at the end of July to stop over in Paris on their way back to the United States and cut records for the label." Drott, *Music and the Elusive Revolution*, 112.

121. Estimates of the total number of attendees is inconsistent, ranging from fifty thousand to one hundred thousand. This citation is from Stewart, *Rumba on the River*, 207. Thomas A. Johnson, "100,000 Cheers Greet Mobutu 'Gift,' a Rebuilt Stadium," *New York Times*, September 23, 1974. See also James P. Murray, "Promoters Organize a Dream Weekend . . . Which May Not Survive," *New York Amsterdam News*, September 21, 1974.

122. Stewart, *Rumba on the River*, 207.

123. *Soul Power*, directed by Jeffrey Levy-Hinte (New York: Antidote Films, 2009), DVD.

124. "Super Bowl of Music World to Precede Foreman-Ali Fight," *New Pittsburgh Courier*, August 17, 1974.

125. R. J. Smith, *The One*, 247.

126. R. J. Smith, *The One*, 247.

127. M. Cordell Thompson, "James Brown Treated like a God in Africa," *Black Stars* (October 1972):10, cited in R. J. Smith, *The One*, 300.

128. Stewart, *Rumba on the River*, 174.

129. Brown, *I Feel Good*, 146–47.

130. M. Cordell Thompson, "James Brown Treated like a God in Africa," *Black Stars* (October 1972): 10.

131. Maceo Parker, *98% Funky Stuff*, 98.

132. Ricardo Niasse, interview with the author, March 18, 2017, Thies, Senegal.

133. *Soul Brother Number 1*, dir. Adrian Maben (Munich: R. M. Productions, 1978). On Maben and the production, which included filming in Mexico City and Augusta, Georgia, see Rhodes, *Say It Loud!*, 91.

134. Wesley, *Hit Me, Fred*, 174.

135. I am indebted to R. J. Smith's biography of Brown, in which he describes this documentary film, as well as his own reading of Brown's voice. R. J. Smith, *The One,* 303.

136. Snead, "On Repetition in Black Culture," 150. See also Rose, *Black Noise.*

137. Attali, *Noise,* 5; Snead, "On Repetition in Black Culture," 150.

138. Parker, *98% Funky Stuff,* 110.

139. Diawara, "The 1960s in Bamako," 252.

140. Diawara, *In Search of Africa,* 103.

141. Diawara, "The 1960s in Bamako," 253–54.

142. Diawara, "The 1960s in Bamako," 254.

143. Diawara, "The 1960s in Bamako," 255.

144. Magnin, *Malick Sidibé.*

145. Diawara, "1960s in Bamako," 246. On African mimicry in particular, see Ferguson, "Of Mimicry and Membership."

146. Diawara, *In Search of Africa,* 103.

EPILOGUE: SOUNDING LIKE A REVOLUTION

1. René Ménil, "Poetry, Jazz, and Freedom," 83. The essay was originally published in *Tropiques* 11 (May 1944): 127–33.

2. Suzanne Césaire cited in R. D. G. Kelley, "Poetics of Anticolonialism," 15.

3. R. D. G. Kelley, "Poetics of Anticolonialism," 14. On Vichy in the Antilles, see Jennings, *Vichy in the Tropics*; Blanchard and Boëtsch, "Races et propagande coloniale." On Ménil's wartime writing, see Lane, *Jazz and Machine-Age Imperialism.*

4. Lane, *Jazz and Machine-Age Imperialism,* particularly chap. 5.

5. In considering how diasporic consciousness was audible in these echoes and reverberations, which projected Black sounds into an unknown future, I am indebted to scholarly work on reggae and sound systems. See especially Veal, *Dub*; Chude-Sokei, *Sound of Culture.*

6. On strategic essentialisms, see Stuart Hall, "Cultural Identity and Diaspora."

7. See, for example, Charry, *Hip Hop Africa*; Rollefson, *Flip the Script*; Aidi, *Rebel Music.*

8. Redmond, *Anthem,* 1.

9. Denning, *Noise Uprising,* 30.

10. Denning, *Noise Uprising,* 15.

11. In the US context, see, for example, Lott, *Love and Theft*; Iton, *In Search of the Black*; Tate, *Everything but the Burden*; Rose, *Black Noise.*

12. Hall, "What Is This 'Black'?"

13. On the reproduction of race and racism, see Holt, *Problem of Race*; Balibar, *Race, Nation, Class*; Stuart Hall, "Race, Articulation, and Societies."

Sources

ARCHIVES AND MANUSCRIPT COLLECTIONS

France

Achille Family Archives, Caen (AFA)
Archives Cohérie Boris Vian, Paris (ACBV)
Archives nationales de France, Paris (ANF)
    Radiodiffusion et Télévision, F/43
    Cabinet du ministre de l'intérieur du gouvernement de Vichy, Relations avec les pays
    alliés, F/1a/3304–5
Bibliothèque municipale, Souillac
    Fonds Festival du jazz
    Fonds Sim Copans (FSC)
Bibliothèque Nationale de France, Département de l'Audiovisuel, Paris
    Fonds Charles Delaunay (FCD)
Centre des archives contemporaines, Fontainebleau (CAC)
    Office de la radiodiffusion-télévision Française (ORTF), Mission d'Aide et de Coopéra-
    tion, 19880085; Bureau du jazz, 19910122; Direction Générale de la Radiodiffusion,
    19950218 ; Émissions vers les DOM et TOM, 20100204; Département de la musique,
    20090288
    Office de Coopération Radiophonique, 20090288
Copans Family Archives, Paris (CFA)
Institut national de l'Audiovisuel, Paris (INA)
Médiathèque Muncipale, Villefranche-de-Rouergue
    Fonds Hugues Panassié (FHP)
Médiathèque Musicale de Paris, Paris
Private Collection of Daniel Richard, Paris
Private Collection of Michael Haggerty, Mirabeau
Private Collection of Philippe Baudoin, Paris

Senegal

Archives nationales du Sénégal, Dakar (ANS)
  Fonds festival mondial des arts nègres (FESMAN)
Archives de la Radiodiffusion Télévision Sénégalaise, Dakar (ARTS)

United States

Beinecke Rare Book and Manuscript Library, Yale University, New Haven, CT
  Bernard Wolfe Papers (BWP)
Library of Congress, Washington, DC (LOC)
  Charles Mingus Collection
  Simons Family Collection
Moorland-Spingarn Research Center, Howard University, Washington, DC
  Howard University Archives
  Will Mercer Cook Papers (WMCP)
National Archives and Record Administration, College Park, MD (NARA-CP)
  Record Group 59: General Records of the Department of State
  Record Group 84: Records of the Foreign Service Posts of the Department of State
  Record Group 208: Office of War Information
  Record Group 331: Records of Allied Operational and Occupation Headquarters, World War II
  Record Group 338: Records of U.S. Army, World War II, European Theater of Operations
Schomburg Center for Research in Black Culture, New York Public Library, New York
  First World Festival of Negro Arts, United States Committee
University of Chicago Special Collections, Chicago
  Alton Abraham Collection of Sun Ra
University of Massachusetts Amherst, W. E. B. Du Bois Library, Special Collections and University Archives, Amherst, MA
  Gordon Heath Papers (GHP)

INTERVIEWS

All interview transcripts and recordings in possession of the author.
Dominique Achille, interview with the author, April 26, 2012, Caen
Ned Brandt, interview with the author, July 23, 2010, Midland, MI
Philippe Carles, interview with the author, July 30, 2016, Paris
André Clergeat, interview with the author, February 20 and July 19, 2012, Paris
Georges Collinet, telephone interview with the author, September 9 and 16, 2019
Richard Copans, interview with the author, April 21, 2010, Paris
Charles Delaunay, interview with Michael Haggerty, August 14, 1982, Paris
Jacques Demêtre, interview with the author, April 19, 2012, Paris
Alioune Diop, interview with the author, March 17, 2017, Dakar
Cheikh Amala Doucouré, interview with the author, March 16, 2017, Dakar
Bobby Few, interview with the author May 14, 2012, Paris

Yann Gillot, interview with the author, April 8, 2011, Saint-Germain-en-Laye
Jacques Joyard, interview with the author, June 17, 2014, Grenoble
Jean-Marie Masse, interview with the author, December 15, 2010, Limoges
Famoudou Don Moye, telephone interview with the author March 12, 2020
Jacques Muyal, telephone interview with the author, September 23, 2019
Ricardo Niasse, interview with the author, March 18, 2017, Thies
Steve Potts, interview with the author, April 20, 2012, Paris
Moustafa Sene, interview with the author, March 15, 2017, Dakar
Archie Shepp, interview with the author, March 14, 2012, Ivry-sur-Seine
Michelle Vian, interviews with the author, June 2012, Paris
Bernard Vincent, interview with the author, April 10, 2012, Paris
Val Wilmer, interview with the author, August 2, 2016, London

NEWSPAPERS AND PERIODICALS

Amsterdam News
Baltimore Afro-American
Billboard
Bingo
Bulletin du Hot Club
Bulletin of the Centre Culturel Américain
Cahiers d'histoire de la radiodiffusion
Chicago Daily Tribune
Chicago Defender
Combat
Commentary
The Crisis
Dakar Matin
Down Beat
Ebony
El Moudjahid
Esprit
Informations et documents
Jazz hot
Jazz Magazine
Jazz, mensuel d'information du Sud-Est
Jazz news
Jet
Jeune Afrique
La gazette du jazz
Le Monde
Les lettres françaises
Melody Maker
Negro Digest

New York Amsterdam News
New York Times
New Yorker
Pittsburgh Courier
Présence Africaine
Radio revue
Réalités
La Revue du jazz
La Revue du monde noir
Stars and Stripes
Les Temps modernes
Time

COMPACT DISCS, RECORDS, AND FILMS

Alberts, Arthur, ed. *The Arthur S. Alberts Collection: More Tribal, Folk, and Café Music of West Africa*. Mickey Hart Collection, 1998.

Broonzy, Big Bill. *Blues Singer*. Vols. 1–2. Vogue, LD 030 and LD 072, 1952.

Brown, James. *Live at the Apollo*, vol. 2. Polydor 2669005, 1971.

Bud Powell Trio. *Bud Powell Trio*. Vogue, LD 10, 1952.

Cannonball Adderley and His Quintet. *En Concert avec EUROPE1, Salle Pleyel, 27 Mars 1969*. Paris: RTE, 1992.

Charles Ray. *Ray Charles: Live in Paris 20–21 Octobre 1961 / 17–18–20–21 Mai 1962*. Frémeaux & Associates FA 5466, 2014.

Coleman Hawkins and his Orchestra. *Coleman Hawkins*. Vogue, LD 005, 1951.

Disiz la Peste. *Le poisson rouge*. Barclay, 2000.

Donald Byrd Quintet. *Byrd in Paris*. Vols. 1–2. Brunswick 87 903, 1958.

Dorsey, Tommy. "Blue Skies." V-Disc 001-B, 1943.

Folk Music of Africa and America, eds. Harold Courlander and Dick Waterman. Folkways Records (Smithsonian Folkways), 1951.

Gast, Michel, dir. *J'irai cracher sur vos tombes*. 1959; Boulogne-Billancourt: Gaumont Columbia Tristar, 2006. DVD.

Hines, Earl. *Encores*. Vogue, LD 053, c. 1952.

Jackson, Mahalia. *Queen of Gospel Singers*. Vogue LD 097, 1952.

Klein, William, dir. *The Pan-African Festival of Algiers*. 1969; Paris: Arté Editions, 2012. DVD.

Levy-Hinte, Jeffrey, dir. *Soul Power*. 2008; New York: Antidote Films, 2009. DVD.

Mabel, Adrian, dir. *Soul Brother Number 1*. Munich: R. M. Productions, 1978.

Mezzrow, Mezz. *Jazz Concert*, feat. Lee Collins and Zutty Singleton. Vogue LD 037, 1951.

Negro Folk Music of Alabama. Vol. 1, *Secular Music*. Edited by Harold Courlander. Folkways Records (Smithsonian Folkways), 1951.

Pour ceux qui aiment le jazz: Le programme de l'émission radiophonique culte des années soixante. Warner, 2003.

Sene Absa, Moussa, dir. *Ça twiste à Popenguine*. 1993; San Francisco: California Newsreel, 1994. DVD.

Shepp, Archie. *Live at the Panafrican Festival*. BYG/ACTUEL 203, 1971.

Swing caraïbe: Premiers jazzmen antillais à Paris, 1929–1946. Frémeaux and Associates, 1997.

BOOKS, ARTICLES, AND DISSERTATIONS

Achille, Louis T. "L'art et les noirs/The Negroes and Art." *La Revue du monde noir*, no. 1 (1931): 53–56.

Achille, Louis T. "The Catholic Approach to Interracialism in France." *American Catholic Sociological Review* 3 (March 1942): 22–27.

Achille, Louis T. "Negro Spirituals." *Esprit* 179 (May 1951): 707–16.

Achille, Louis T. "Organisation de la vie religieuse chez les noirs des États-Unis." *Chronique sociale de France* 5–6 (1952): 478–84.

Achille, Louis T. "Preface." In *La revue du monde noir / The Review of the Black World*, vols. 1–6. Paris: Jean-Michel Place, 1992.

Adelt, Ulrich. "Germany Gets the Blues: Negotiations of 'Race' and Nation at the American Folk Blues Festival." *American Quarterly* 60, no. 4 (December 2008): 951–74.

Adi, Hakim. *West Africans in Britain 1900–1960: Nationalism, Pan-Africanism and Communism*. London: Lawrence and Wishart, 1998.

Aidi, Hisham. *Rebel Music: Race, Empire, and the New Muslim Youth Culture*. New York: Pantheon Books, 2014.

Anderson, Carol. *Bourgeois Radicals: The NAACP and the Struggle for Colonial Liberation, 1941–1960*. Cambridge: Cambridge University Press, 2014.

Anderson, Carol. "The Cold War in the Atlantic World: African Decolonization and U.S. Foreign Policy." In *The Atlantic World, 1450–2000*, edited by Toyin Falola and Kevin Roberts, 294–314. Bloomington: Indiana University Press, 2008.

Anderson, Carol. *Eyes off the Prize: The United Nations and the African American Struggle for Human Rights, 1944–1955*. Cambridge: Cambridge University Press, 2003.

Anderson, Iain. *This Is Our Music: Free Jazz, the Sixties, and American Culture*. Philadelphia: University of Pennsylvania Press, 2007.

Anderson, Samuel D. "'Negritude Is Dead': Performing the African Revolution at the First Pan-African Cultural Festival (Algiers, 1969)." In *The First World Festival of Negro Arts, Dakar 1966: Contexts and Legacies*, edited by David Murphy. Liverpool: Liverpool University Press, 2016.

André, Marie-Eugénie. *Fort-de-France: Les hommes d'hier dans nos rues d'aujourd'hui*. Fort-de-France, Martinique: Éditions Femmes Actuelles, 1986.

Ansell, Gwen. *Soweto Blues: Jazz, Popular Music, and Politics in South Africa*. New York: Continuum, 2004.

Archer-Straw, Petrine. *Negrophilia: Avant-Garde Paris and Black Culture in the 1920s*. London: Thames & Hudson, 2000.

Arma, Paul, and Edmée Arma. *Mémoires à deux voix: Témoignages de mouvement dans le mouvement.* Vol. 1, *1945–1957.* n.p.: P. Arma, 1986.

Armus, Seth D. "The Eternal Enemy: Emmanuel Mounier's Esprit and French Anti-Americanism." *French Historical Studies* 24, no. 2 (2001): 271–304.

Arnaud, Noël. *Le dossier de l'affaire "J'irai cracher sur vos tombes."* Paris: C. Bourgois, 1974.

Arnaud, Noël. *Les vies parallèles de Boris Vian.* Paris: Union Générale d'Édition, 1970.

Asseraf, Arthur. *Electric News in Colonial Algeria.* New York: Oxford University Press, 2019.

Atkins, E. Taylor. *Blue Nippon: Authenticating Jazz in Japan.* Durham, NC: Duke University Press, 2001.

Atria, Travis. *Better Days Will Come Again: The Life of Arthur Briggs, Jazz Genius of Harlem, Paris, and a Nazi Prison Camp.* Chicago: Chicago Review Press, 2020.

Attali, Jacques. *Noise: The Political Economy of Music.* Translated by Brian Massumi. Minneapolis: University of Minnesota Press, 1985.

Auslander, Leora, and Thomas C. Holt. "Sambo in Paris." In *The Color of Liberty: Histories of Race in France,* edited by Tyler Edward Stovall and Sue Peabody, 147–84. Durham, NC: Duke University Press, 2003.

Badger, Reid. *A Life in Ragtime: A Biography of James Reese Europe.* New York: Oxford University Press, 1995.

Baldwin, Davarian L. *Chicago's New Negroes: Modernity, the Great Migration, and Black Urban Life.* Chapel Hill: University of North Carolina Press, 2009.

Baldwin, James. *Collected Essays.* New York: Library of America, 1998.

Baldwin, James. *The Devil Finds Work: An Essay.* New York: Dial, 1976.

Baldwin, James. "Princes and Power." In *Nobody Knows My Name: More Notes of a Native Son.* New York: Dial, 1961.

Balibar, Étienne. *Race, Nation, Class: Ambiguous Identities.* New York: Verso, 1991.

Bantigny, Ludivine. *Le plus bel âge? Jeunes et jeunesse en France de l'aube des "Trente Glorieuses" à la guerre d'Algérie.* Paris: Fayard, 2007.

Baraka, Amiri. *Blues People: Negro Music in White America.* New York: William Morrow, 1999.

Baraka, Amiri. *Le peuple du blues: La musique noire dans l'Amérique blanche.* Translated by Jacqueline Bernard. Paris: Gallimard, 1968.

Barber, Karin. *A History of African Popular Culture.* New York: Cambridge University Press, 2018.

Barber, Karin. "Preliminary Notes on Audiences in Africa." *Africa* 67, no. 3 (1997): 347–62.

Barclay, Eddie. *Que la fête continue.* Paris: R. Laffont, 1988.

Barlow, William. *Voice Over: The Making of Black Radio.* Philadelphia: Temple University Press, 1999.

Barnhisel, Greg. *Cold War Modernists: Art, Literature, and American Cultural Diplomacy.* New York: Columbia University Press, 2015.

Beauchamp, Lincoln T. *Art Ensemble of Chicago: Great Black Music, Ancient to the Future.* Chicago: Art Ensemble of Chicago, 1998.

Beauvoir, Simone de. *L'Amérique au jour le jour*. Paris: Gallimard, 1956.

Bebey, Francis. *La radiodiffusion en Afrique noire*. Issy-les-Moulineaux: Saint-Paul, 1963.

Bechet, Sidney. *Treat It Gentle*. New York: Hill and Wang, 1960.

Beevor, Antony, and Artemis Cooper. *Paris after the Liberation, 1944–1949*. New York: Doubleday, 1994.

Benga, Ndiouga Adrien. "The Air of the City Makes Free: Urban Music from the 1950s to the 1990s in Senegal." In *Playing with Identities in Contemporary Music in Africa*, 75–85. Stockholm: Nordiska Afrikainstitutet, 2002.

Bergère, Marc. "Français et américains en Basse-Seine à la liberation (1944–1946): Des relations ambivalentes." *Annales de Bretagne et des pays de l'Ouest* 109, no. 4 (2002): 203–15.

Bergeret-Cassagne, Axelle. *Les bases américaines en France: Impacts matériels et culturels 1950–1967. Au seuil d'un nouveau monde*. Paris: Harmattan, 2008.

Berlin, Ira. *Many Thousands Gone: The First Two Centuries of Slavery in North America*. Cambridge, MA: Harvard University Press, 1998.

Berliner, Brett A. *Ambivalent Desire: The Exotic Black Other in Jazz-Age France*. Amherst: University of Massachusetts Press, 2002.

Best, Wallace D. *Passionately Human, No Less Divine: Religion and Culture in Black Chicago, 1915–1952*. Princeton, NJ: Princeton University Press, 2005.

Betts, Raymond F. *Assimilation and Association in French Colonial Theory: 1890–1914*. Lincoln: University of Nebraska Press, 2005.

Bhabha, Homi. "Of Mimicry and Man: The Ambivalence of Colonial Discourse." In *Tensions of Empire: Colonial Cultures in a Bourgeois World*, edited by Ann Stoler and Frederick Cooper, 152–60. Berkeley: University of California Press, 1997.

Blain, Keisha N. *Set the World on Fire: Black Nationalist Women and the Global Struggle for Freedom*. Philadelphia: University of Pennsylvania Press, 2018.

Blake, Jody. *Le tumulte noir: Modernist Art and Popular Entertainment in Jazz-Age Paris, 1900–1930*. University Park: Pennsylvania State University Press, 1999.

Blanchard, Pascal. *Human Zoos: Science and Spectacle in the Age of Colonial Empires*. Liverpool: Liverpool University Press, 2008.

Blanchard, Pascal, and Gilles Boëtsch. "Races et propagande coloniale sous le régime de Vichy, 1940–1944." *Africa* 49, no. 4 (1994): 531–61.

Blanchard, Pascal, and Sandrine Lemaire. *Culture impériale: Les colonies au coeur de la République, 1931–1961*. Paris: Autrement, 2004.

Bleich, Erik. "Anti-racism without Races: Politics and Policy in a Color-Blind State." In *Race in France: Interdisciplinary Perspectives on the Politics of Difference*, edited by Herrick Chapman and Laura Levine Frader, 48–74. New York: Berghahn Books, 2004.

Blower, Brooke L. *Becoming Americans in Paris: Transatlantic Politics and Culture between the World Wars*. New York: Oxford University Press, 2012.

Boittin, Jennifer Anne. *Colonial Metropolis: The Urban Grounds of Anti-imperialism and Feminism in Interwar Paris*. Lincoln: University of Nebraska Press, 2010.

Borstelmann, Thomas. *The Cold War and the Color Line: American Race Relations in the Global Arena*. Cambridge, MA: Harvard University Press, 2001.

Boschetti, Anna. *The Intellectual Enterprise: Sartre and* Les temps modernes. Translated by Richard C. McCleary. Evanston, IL: Northwestern University Press, 1988.

Bourgault, Louise Manon. *Mass Media in Sub-Saharan Africa*. Bloomington: Indiana University Press, 1995.

Braddock, Jeremy, and Jonathan P. Eburne. *Paris, Capital of the Black Atlantic: Literature, Modernity, and Diaspora*. Baltimore: Johns Hopkins University Press, 2013.

Braggs, Rashida K. *Jazz Diasporas: Race, Music, and Migration in Post–World War II Paris*. Berkeley: University of California Press, 2016.

Brandon, Ruth. *Surreal Lives: The Surrealists, 1917–1945*. New York: Grove, 1999.

Briggs, Jonathyne. *Sounds French: Globalization, Cultural Communities, and Pop Music*. New York: Oxford University Press, 2015.

Briggs, Laura. *Reproducing Empire: Race, Sex, Science, and U.S. Imperialism in Puerto Rico*. Berkeley: University of California Press, 2003.

Brochand, Christian. *Histoire générale de la radio et de la télévision en France*. Vol. 2, *1944–1974*. Paris: La Documentation Française, 1994.

Bronfman, Alejandra M. *Isles of Noise: Sonic Media in the Caribbean*. Chapel Hill: University of North Carolina Press, 2016.

Brooks, Daphne. *Liner Notes for the Revolution: The Intellectual Life of Black Feminist Sound*. Cambridge, MA: Belknap Press of Harvard University Press, 2021.

Broonzy, William. *Big Bill: Mes blues, ma guitare et moi*. Translated by Yannick Bruynoghe. Brussels: Éditions des artistes, 1955.

Broschke Davis, Ursula. "Art Simmons in Paris." *International Jazz Archives Journal* 1, no. 4 (1996): 9–32.

Broschke Davis, Ursula. *Paris without Regret: James Baldwin, Kenny Clarke, Chester Himes, and Donald Byrd*. Iowa City: University of Iowa Press, 1986.

Brown, James. *I Feel Good: A Memoir of a Life of Soul*. New York: New American Library, 2005.

Bruce, Marcus. "The New Negro in Paris: Booker T. Washington, the New Negro, and the Paris Exposition of 1900." In *Black France / France Noire: The History and Politics of Blackness*, 207–20. Durham, NC: Duke University Press, 2012.

Byrd, Brandon. *The Black Republic: African Americans and the Fate of Haiti*. Philadelphia: University of Pennsylvania Press, 2019.

Byrne, Jeffrey James. *Mecca of Revolution: Algeria, Decolonization, and the Third World Order*. New York: Oxford University Press, 2016.

Camiscioli, Elisa. *Reproducing the French Race: Immigration, Intimacy, and Embodiment in the Early Twentieth Century*. Durham, NC: Duke University Press, 2009.

Campbell, James. *Paris Interzone: Richard Wright, Lolita, Boris Vian and Others on the Left Bank, 1946–60*. London: Secker & Warburg, 1994.

Campt, Tina. *Listening to Images*. Durham, NC: Duke University Press, 2017.

Campt, Tina. *Other Germans: Black Germans and the Politics of Race, Gender, and Memory in the Third Reich*. Ann Arbor: University of Michigan Press, 2005.

Carles, Philippe, and Jean-Louis Comolli. *Free Jazz / Black Power*. Paris: Éditions Champ Libre, 1971. English edition: *Free Jazz / Black Power*. Translated by Gregory Pierrot. Jackson: University Press of Mississippi, 2015.

Chanan, Michael. *Repeated Takes: A Short History of Recording and Its Effects on Music*. New York: Verso, 1995.

Chaplin, Tamara. *Turning On the Mind: French Philosophers on Television*. Chicago: University of Chicago Press, 2007.

Chapman, Herrick, and Laura Levine Frader, eds. *Race in France: Interdisciplinary Perspectives on the Politics of Difference*. New York: Berghahn Books, 2004.

Charry, Eric S. *Hip Hop Africa: New African Music in a Globalizing World*. Bloomington: Indiana University Press, 2012.

Chasseguet, Thérèse. *Barclay: Une histoire de haute fidélité 1945–1984*. Paris: Rieveneuve Editions, 2017.

Chesnel, Jacques. *Le jazz en quarantaine, 1940–1946, occupation/libération*. Paris: Isoète, 1994.

Childers, Kristen. *Seeking Imperialism's Embrace: National Identity, Decolonization, and Assimilation in the French Caribbean*. New York: Oxford University Press, 2016.

Chilton, John. *Sidney Bechet: The Wizard of Jazz*. Cambridge, MA: Da Capo, 1987.

Chude-Sokei, Louis. *The Last "Darky": Bert Williams, Black-on-Black Minstrelsy, and the African Diaspora*. Durham, NC: Duke University Press, 2005.

Chude-Sokei, Louis. *The Sound of Culture: Diaspora and Black Technopoetics*. Middletown, CT: Wesleyan University Press, 2016.

Church, Emily Musil. "In Search of Seven Sisters: A Biography of the Nardal Sisters of Martinique." *Callaloo* 36 (Spring 2013): 375–90.

Cismaru, Alfred. *Boris Vian*. New York: Twayne, 1974.

Clark, Andrew. *Riffs and Choruses: A New Jazz Anthology*. London: Continuum, 2001.

Clark, Vèvè A. "Developing Diaspora Literacy and *Marasa* Consciousness." In *Comparative American Identities: Race, Sex, and Nationality in the Modern Text*, edited by Hortense J. Spillers, 40–61. New York: Routledge, 1991.

Clayton, Buck. *Buck Clayton's Jazz World*. New York: Oxford University Press, 1987.

Coffin, Judith G. "Historicizing the Second Sex." *French Politics, Culture, and Society* 25, no. 3 (2007): 123–48.

Cole, John Y., ed. *Books in Action: The Armed Services Editions*. Washington, DC: Library of Congress, 1984.

Cole, Joshua H. "Remembering the Battle of Paris: 17 October 1961 in French and Algerian Memory." *French Politics, Culture, and Society* 21, no. 3 (Fall 2003): 21–50.

Collin, Claude. "Interview with Thomas Russell Jones, 'J'étais un officier noir dans l'armée américaine pendant la Deuxième Guerre Mondiale.'" *Guerres mondiales et conflits contemporains* 51, no. 204 (2001): 141–48.

Collins, John. *Highlife Time*. Accra: Anansesem, 1996.

Collins, Lee, and Mary Spriggs Collins. *Oh, Didn't He Ramble: The Life Story of Lee Collins*. Urbana: University of Illinois Press, 1989.

Colloquium: Function and Significance of African Negro Art in the Life of the People and for the People, March 30–April 8, 1966, 351–67. Paris: Éditions Présence Africaine, 1968.

Condon, Eddie, and Hank O'Neal. *The Eddie Condon Scrapbook of Jazz*. New York: St. Martin's, 1973.

Condon, Eddie, and Thomas Sugrue. *We Called It Music: A Generation of Jazz*. New York: Da Capo, 1992.

Cone, James H. "Martin Luther King, Jr., and the Third World." *Journal of American History* 74, no. 2 (1987): 455–67.

Cone, James H. *The Spirituals and the Blues: An Interpretation*. New York: Seabury, 1972.

Conklin, Alice L. *A Mission to Civilize: The Republican Idea of Empire in France and West Africa, 1895–1930*. Stanford, CA: Stanford University Press, 1997.

Connelly, Matthew. *A Diplomatic Revolution: Algeria's Fight for Independence and the Origins of the Post–Cold War Era*. New York: Oxford University Press, 2002.

Conte, Gérard. "Les origines du Hot Club de France." *Les cahiers du jazz: Revue musicale* 1 (2001): 223–36.

Cook, Mercer. "The Negro Spiritual Goes to France." *Music Educators Journal* 40 (May 1954): 42–48.

Cook, Mercer. "Review of *Starkenfirst*." *Journal of Negro History* 33, no. 4 (October 1948): 490–91.

Cooper, Frederick. *Citizenship between Empire and Nation: Remaking France and French Africa, 1945–1960*. Princeton, NJ: Princeton University Press, 2014.

Cooper, Frederick. *Colonialism in Question: Theory, Knowledge, History*. Berkeley: University of California Press, 2005.

Corbin, Alain. *Village Bells: Sound and Meaning in the 19th-Century French Countryside*. New York: Columbia University Press, 1998.

Cotro, Vincent, and Didier Levallet. *Chants libres: le free jazz en France, 1960–1975*. Paris: Outre Mesure, 1999.

Cowans, Jon. "Political Culture and Cultural Politics: The Reconstruction of French Radio after the Second World War." *Journal of Contemporary History* 31, no. 1 (1996): 145–70.

Cowie, Jefferson. *Capital Moves: RCA's Seventy-Year Quest for Cheap Labor*. Ithaca, NY: Cornell University Press, 1999.

Croft, Clare. *Dancers as Diplomats: American Choreography in Cultural Exchange*. New York: Oxford University Press, 2015.

Cruz, Jon. *Culture on the Margins: The Black Spiritual and the Rise of American Cultural Interpretation*. Princeton, NJ: Princeton University Press, 1999.

Cull, Nicholas J. *The Cold War and the United States Information Agency: American Propaganda and Public Diplomacy, 1945–1989*. New York: Cambridge University Press, 2008.

Dahl, Linda. *Morning Glory: A Biography of Mary Lou Williams*. New York: Pantheon Books, 1999.

Daily, Andrew M. "Race, Citizenship, and Antillean Student Activism in Postwar France, 1946–1968." *French Historical Studies* 37, no. 2 (2014): 331–57.

Davenport, Lisa E. *Jazz Diplomacy: Promoting America in the Cold War Era*. Jackson: University Press of Mississippi, 2009.

Daver, Manek. *Jazz Album Covers: The Rare and Beautiful*. Tokyo: Graphic-sha, 1994.

Davidson, Naomi. *Only Muslim: Embodying Islam in Twentieth-Century France*. Ithaca, NY: Cornell University Press, 2012.

De Grazia, Victoria. *Irresistible Empire: America's Advance through Twentieth-Century Europe*. Cambridge, MA: Harvard University Press, 2005.

Delanoë, Nelcya. *Le raspail vert: L'American center à Paris, 1934–1994*. Paris: Seghers, 1994.

Delaunay, Charles. *Delaunay's Dilemma: De la peinture au jazz*. Mâcon: Editions W, 1985.

Delaunay, Charles. *Hot discographie*. Paris: Jazz Hot, 1936.

Demory, Bernard. *Au temps des cataplasmes: Document, 1944–1968, la France d'avant la télé*. Boulagne: Ginkgo, 2003.

Denning, Michael. *Culture in the Age of Three Worlds*. New York: Verso, 2004.

Denning, Michael. *Noise Uprising: The Audiopolitics of a World Musical Revolution*. New York: Verso, 2015.

DeVeaux, Scott. "Bebop and the Recording Industry: The 1942 AFM Recording Ban Reconsidered." *Journal of the American Musicological Society* 41, no. 1 (1988): 126–65.

DeVeaux, Scott. *The Birth of Bebop: A Social and Musical History*. Berkeley: University of California Press, 1997.

DeVeaux, Scott. "Constructing the Jazz Tradition: Jazz Historiography." *Black American Literature Forum* 25, no. 3 (1991): 525–60.

Devine, Kyle. *Decomposed: The Political Ecology of Music*. Cambridge, MA: MIT Press, 2019.

Diawara, Manthia. *In Search of Africa*. Cambridge, MA: Harvard University Press, 1998.

Diawara, Manthia. "The 1960s in Bamako: Malick Sidibé and James Brown." In *Black Cultural Traffic: Crossroads in Global Performance and Popular Culture*, edited by Harry J. Elam and Kenneth Jackson, 242–65. Ann Arbor: University of Michigan Press, 2005.

Douglass, Frederick. *Narrative of the Life of Frederick Douglass, an American Slave*. Boston: Anti-Slavery Office, 1845.

Dregni, Michael. *Gypsy Jazz: In Search of Django Reinhardt and the Soul of Gypsy Swing*. New York: Oxford University Press, 2008.

Dreisinger, Baz. *Near Black: White-to-Black Passing in American Culture*. Amherst: University of Massachusetts Press, 2008.

Drott, Eric. "Free Jazz and the French Critic." *Journal of the American Musicological Society* 61, no. 3 (2008): 541–82.

Drott, Eric. *Music and the Elusive Revolution: Cultural Politics and Political Culture in France, 1968–1981*. Berkeley: University of California Press, 2011.

Du Bois, W. E. B. *The Souls of Black Folk*. Chicago: A. C. McClurg, 1903.

Dubois, Laurent. *The Banjo: America's African Instrument*. Cambridge, MA: Harvard University Press, 2016.

Dubois, Laurent. *A Colony of Citizens: Revolution and Slave Emancipation in the French Caribbean, 1787–1804*. Chapel Hill: University of North Carolina Press, 2004.

Dudziak, Mary L. *Cold War Civil Rights: Race and the Image of American Democracy*. Princeton, NJ: Princeton University Press, 2000.

Duhamel, Marcel. *Raconte pas ta vie*. Paris: Mercure de France, 1972.

Dunham, Katherine. "Address Delivered at the Dakar Festival of Negro Arts." In *Kaiso! Writings by and about Katherine Dunham*, edited by Vèvè Clark and Sarah E. Johnson, 412–17. Madison: University of Wisconsin Press, 2005.

Dussault, Eric. *Le mythe de la bohème: L'invention de Saint-Germain-des-Prés*. Paris: Vendémiaire, 2014.

Eburne, Jonathan P. "The Transatlantic Mysteries of Paris: Chester Himes, Surrealism, and the Série Noire." *PMLA* 120, no. 3 (2005): 806–21.

Echenberg, Myron. *Colonial Conscripts: The Tirailleurs Sénégalais in French West Africa, 1857–1960*. Portsmouth, NH: Heinemann, 1991.

Edwards, Brent Hayes. *Epistrophies: Jazz and the Literary Imagination*. Cambridge, MA: Harvard University Press, 2017.

Edwards, Brent Hayes. "The Ethnics of Surrealism." *Transition* 8, no. 78 (1999): 84–135.

Edwards, Brent Hayes. *The Practice of Diaspora: Literature, Translation, and the Rise of Black Internationalism*. Cambridge, MA: Harvard University Press, 2003.

Edwards, Brent Hayes. "The Uses of Diaspora." *Social Text* 19, no. 1 (2001): 45–73.

Ehrlich, Blake. "Old Man with a Horn: Sidney Bechet at Sixty-One, Is America's Most Renowned Expatriate Musician." *Esquire*, July 1958, 95–98.

Eidsheim, Nina Sun. "Marian Anderson and 'Sonic Blackness' in American Opera." *American Quarterly* 63, no. 3 (2011): 641–71.

Eidsheim, Nina Sun. *The Race of Sound: Listening, Timbre, and Vocality in African American Music*. Durham, NC: Duke University Press, 2019.

Ellington, Edward Kennedy. *Music Is My Mistress*. New York: Da Capo, 1973.

Ellison, Ralph. "*An American Dilemma*: A Review." In *Shadow and Act*, 303–17. New York: Random House, 1964.

Ely, Melvin Patrick. *The Adventures of Amos 'n' Andy: A Social History of an American Phenomenon*. Charlottesville: University Press of Virginia, 2001.

Erenberg, Lewis A. *The Greatest Fight of Our Generation: Louis vs. Schmeling*. New York: Oxford University Press, 2006.

Evans, Mike. *Ray Charles: Birth of Soul*. London: Omnibus, 2009.

Ezra, Elizabeth. *The Colonial Unconscious: Race and Culture in Interwar France*. Ithaca, NY: Cornell University Press, 2000.

Fabre, Michel. *From Harlem to Paris: Black American Writers in France, 1840–1980*. Urbana: University of Illinois Press, 1991.

Fabre, Michel. "Richard Wright and the French Existentialists." *MELUS* 5, no. 2 (1978): 39–51.

Fabre, Michel. *The Unfinished Quest of Richard Wright*. Urbana: University of Illinois Press, 1993.

Fabre, Michel, and John A. Williams. *A Street Guide to African Americans in Paris*. Paris: Cercle d'Études Afro-Américaines, 1996.

Fallet, René. *Carnets de jeunesse, inédits, 5 mars–8 août 1947*. Paris: Denoël, 1990.

Fanon, Frantz. *Black Skin, White Masks*. New York: Grove, 1967.

Fanon, Frantz. *Les damnés de la terre*. Paris: François Maspero, 1961.

Fanon, Frantz. *Peau noire, masques blancs*. Paris: Seuil, 1952.

Fanon, Frantz. "This Is the Voice of Algeria." In *A Dying Colonialism*, translated by Haakon Chevalier, 69–98. New York: Grove, 1967.

Fanon, Frantz. *The Wretched of the Earth*. New York: Grove, 2007.

Fauser, Annegret. *Sounds of War: Music in the United States during World War II*. New York: Oxford University Press, 2013.

Fehrenbach, Heide. "Learning from America: Reconstructing 'Race' in Postwar Germany." In *Americanization and Anti-Americanism: The German Encounter with American Culture after 1945*, edited by Alexander Stephan, 107–28. New York: Berghahn Books, 2005.

Fenderson, Jonathan. *Building the Black Arts Movement: Hoyt Fuller and the Cultural Politics of the 1960s*. Urbana: University of Illinois Press, 2019.

Ferguson, James. "Of Mimicry and Membership: Africans and the 'New World Society.'" *Cultural Anthropology* 17, no. 4 (2002): 551–69.

Fernandez, Raul A. *From Afro-Cuban Rhythms to Latin Jazz*. Berkeley: University of California Press, 2006.

Fleming, Crystal Marie. *Resurrecting Slavery: Racial Legacies and White Supremacy in France*. Philadelphia: Temple University Press, 2017.

Fleming, Tyler. *Opposing Apartheid on Stage: King Kong the Musical*. Rochester, NY: University of Rochester Press, 2020.

Florvil, Tiffany N. *Mobilizing Black Germany: Afro-German Women and the Making of a Transnational Movement*. Urbana: University of Illinois Press, 2020.

Floyd, Samuel A., Jr. *The Power of Black Music: Interpreting Its History from Africa to the United States*. New York: Oxford University Press, 1995.

Footitt, Hilary. *War and Liberation in France: Living with the Liberators*. New York: Palgrave Macmillan, 2004.

Forbes, Jill. "The 'Série Noire.'" In *France and the Mass Media*, edited by Brian Rigby and Nicholas Hewitt. London: Macmillan, 1991.

Fosler-Lussier, Danielle. *Music in America's Cold War Diplomacy*. Berkeley: University of California Press, 2015.

Foster, Elizabeth A. *African Catholic: Decolonization and the Transformation of the Church*. Cambridge, MA: Harvard University Press, 2019.

Foster, Pops, Tom Stoddard, Ross Russell, and Brian A. L. Rust. *Pops Foster: The Autobiography of a New Orleans Jazzman as Told to Tom Stoddard*. Berkeley: University of California Press, 1971.

Frank, Thomas. *The Conquest of Cool: Business Culture, Counterculture, and the Rise of Hip Consumerism*. Chicago: University of Chicago Press, 1997.

Fry, Andy. "Beyond Le Boeuf: Interdisciplinary Rereadings of Jazz in France." *Journal of the Royal Musical Association* 128, no. 1 (2003): 137–53.

Fry, Andy. *Paris Blues: African American Music and French Popular Culture, 1920–1960*. Chicago: University of Chicago Press, 2014.

Fry, Andy. "Remembrance of Jazz Past: Sidney Bechet in France." In *The Oxford Handbook of the New Cultural History of Music*, edited by Jane Fulcher, 307–34. New York: Oxford University Press, 2011.

Fuller, Hoyt W. *Journey to Africa*. Chicago: Third World Press, 1971.

Gaines, Kevin K. *American Africans in Ghana: Black Expatriates and the Civil Rights Era*. Chapel Hill: University of North Carolina Press, 2006.

Garcia, David F. *Listening for Africa: Freedom, Modernity, and the Logic of Black Music's African Origins*. Durham, NC: Duke University Press, 2017.

Gates, Henry Louis. *The Signifying Monkey: A Theory of Afro-American Literary Criticism*. New York: Oxford University Press, 1988.

Gaunt, Kyra Danielle. *The Games Black Girls Play: Learning the Ropes from Double Dutch to Hip-Hop*. New York: New York University Press, 2006.

Gavin, James. *Deep in a Dream: The Long Night of Chet Baker*. New York: Knopf, 2002.

Geduld, Carolyn. *Bernard Wolfe*. New York: Twayne, 1972.

Gendron, Bernard. *Between Montmartre and the Mudd Club: Popular Music and the Avant-Garde*. Chicago: University of Chicago Press, 2002.

Gennari, John. *Blowin' Hot and Cool: Jazz and Its Critics*. Chicago: University of Chicago Press, 2006.

George, Nelson. *The Death of Rhythm & Blues*. New York: Pantheon Books, 1998.

Germain, Félix. *Decolonizing the Republic: African and Caribbean Migrants in Postwar Paris, 1946–1974*. East Lansing: Michigan State University Press, 2016.

Germain, Félix. "Mercer Cook and the Origins of Black French Studies." *French Politics, Culture, and Society* 34, no. 1 (2019): 66–85.

Getachew, Adom. *Worldmaking after Empire: The Rise and Fall of Self-Determination*. Princeton, NJ: Princeton University Press, 2019.

Gienow-Hecht, Jessica C. E. *Sound Diplomacy: Music and Emotions in Transatlantic Relations, 1850–1920*. Chicago: University of Chicago Press, 2009.

Gienow-Hecht, Jessica C. E. "What Bandwagon? Diplomatic History Today." *Journal of American History* 95, no. 4 (2009): 1083–86.

Gilbert, David. *The Product of Our Souls: Ragtime, Race, and the Birth of the Manhattan Musical Marketplace*. Chapel Hill: University of North Carolina Press, 2015.

Gillot, Yann. "Le jazz dans la peau, journal d'une passion." Vernouillet: self-published, 1996.

Gilroy, Paul. *The Black Atlantic: Modernity and Double Consciousness*. Cambridge, MA: Harvard University Press, 1993.

Ginsberg, Elaine K. *Passing and the Fictions of Identity*. Durham, NC: Duke University Press, 1996.

Givan, Benjamin. *The Music of Django Reinhardt*. Ann Arbor: University of Michigan Press, 2009.

Glass, Charles. *Americans in Paris: Life and Death under Nazi Occupation*. New York: Penguin, 2010.

Goffin, Robert. *Jazz: From the Congo to the Metropolitan*. Translated by Walter E. Schaap and Leonard Feather. Armed Services Editions 920. New York: Editions for the Armed Services, 1944.

Goldsby, Jacqueline. *A Spectacular Secret: Lynching in American Life and Literature*. Chicago: University of Chicago Press, 2006.

Goodman, David. "Distracted Listening: On Not Making Sound Choices in the 1930s." In *Sound in the Age of Mechanical Reproduction*, edited by David Suisman and Susan Strasser, 15–46. Philadelphia: University of Pennsylvania Press, 2010.

Goreau, Laurraine. *Just Mahalia, Baby*. Waco: Word Books, 1975.

Green, Adam. *Selling the Race: Culture, Community, and Black Chicago, 1940–1955*. Chicago: University of Chicago Press, 2007.

Griffin, Farah Jasmine. *If You Can't Be Free, Be a Mystery: In Search of Billie Holiday*. New York: Free Press, 2001.

Gubar, Susan. *Racechanges: White Skin, Black Face in American Culture*. New York: Oxford University Press, 1997.

Guglielmo, Thomas A. "A Martial Freedom Movement: Black G.I.s' Political Struggles during World War II." *Journal of American History* 104, no. 4 (2018): 879–903.

Guimont, Fabienne. *Les étudiants africains en France, 1950–1965*. Paris: Harmattan, 1997.

Guridy, Frank Andre. *Forging Diaspora: Afro-Cubans and African Americans in a World of Empire and Jim Crow*. Chapel Hill: University of North Carolina Press, 2010.

Guterl, Matthew Pratt. *Josephine Baker and the Rainbow Tribe*. Cambridge, MA: Harvard University Press, 2014.

Gutton, Jean-Pierre. *Histoire de Lyon et du Lyonnais*. Paris: Presses Universitaires de France, 1998.

Hadouchi, Olivier. "'African Culture Will Be Revolutionary or Will Not Be': William Klein's Film of the First Pan-African Festival of Algiers (1969)." *Third Text* 25, no. 1 (2011): 117–28.

Haggerty, Michael. "Under Paris Skies: Conversation with Kenneth ('Kenny') Spearman Clarke." *Black Perspective in Music* 13 (Autumn 1985): 195–221.

Hall, Stuart. "Cultural Identity and Diaspora." In *Colonial Discourse and Post-colonial Theory*, edited by Patrick Williams and Laura Chrisman, 392–401. London: Harvester Wheatsheaf, 1994.

Hall, Stuart. "Race, Articulation, and Societies Structured in Dominance." In *Black British Cultural Studies: A Reader*, edited by Houston A. Baker Jr., Manthia Diawara, and Ruth H. Lindeborg, 16–60. Chicago: University of Chicago Press, 1996.

Hall, Stuart. "What Is This 'Black' in Black Popular Culture?" In *Stuart Hall: Critical Dialogues in Cultural Studies*, edited by David Morley and Kuan-Hsing Chen, 465–75. New York: Routledge, 1996.

Hamilton, Jack. *Just around Midnight: Rock and Roll and the Racial Imagination*. Cambridge, MA: Harvard University Press, 2016.

Hammond, John, and Irving Townsend. *John Hammond on Record: An Autobiography*. New York: Ridge Press, 1977.

Hardwick, Louise. *Joseph Zobel: Négritude and the Novel*. Liverpool: Liverpool University Press, 2018.

Hare, Nathan. "Algiers 1969: A Report on the Pan-African Cultural Festival." *Black Scholar* 1, no. 1 (1969): 2–10.

Harrington, Oliver W. *Why I Left America, and Other Essays*. Jackson: University Press of Mississippi, 1993.

Hartman, Saidiya. *Scenes of Subjection: Terror, Slavery, and Self-Making in Nineteenth-Century America*. New York: Oxford University Press, 1997.

Hassan, Salah D. "Inaugural Issues: The Cultural Politics of the Early *Présence africaine*, 1947–55." *Research in African Literatures* 30, no. 2 (1999): 194–221.

Head, Sydney W., ed. *Broadcasting in Africa: A Continental Survey of Radio and Television*. Philadelphia: Temple University Press, 1974.

Heath, Gordon R. *Deep Are the Roots: Memoirs of a Black Expatriate*. Amherst: University of Massachusetts Press, 1996.

Hennessey, Mike. *Klook: The Story of Kenny Clarke*. Pittsburgh: University of Pittsburgh Press, 1994.

Higginson, Pim. *Scoring Race: Jazz, Fiction, and Francophone Africa*. Suffolk: James Currey, 2017.

Hill, Edwin C. *Black Soundscapes White Stages: The Meaning of Francophone Sound in the Black Atlantic.* Baltimore: Johns Hopkins University Press, 2013.

Hillel, Marc. *Vie et mœurs des G.I's en Europe: 1942–1947.* Paris: Balland, 1981.

Hilmes, Michele. *Radio Voices: American Broadcasting, 1922–1952.* Minneapolis: University of Minnesota Press, 1997.

Hine, Darlene Clark, Tricia Danielle Keaton, and Stephen Smalls, eds. *Black Europe and the African Diaspora.* Urbana: University of Illinois Press, 2009.

Hirschkind, Charles. *The Ethical Soundscape: Cassette Sermons and Islamic Counterpublics.* New York: Columbia University Press, 2009.

History of AFRTS, the First 50 Years. Alexandria, VA: Armed Forces Information Service and Armed Forces Radio and Television Service, 1993.

Hitchcock, William I. *The Bitter Road to Freedom: A New History of the Liberation of Europe.* New York: Free Press, 2008.

Hobbs, Allyson. *A Chosen Exile: A History of Racial Passing.* Cambridge, MA: Harvard University Press, 2014.

Holt, Thomas C. "Marking: Race, Race-Making, and the Writing of History." *American Historical Review* 100, no. 1 (1995): 1–20.

Holt, Thomas C. *The Problem of Race in the Twenty-First Century.* Cambridge, MA: Harvard University Press, 2000.

Horne, Gerald. *Black and Red: W. E. B. Du Bois and the Afro-American Response to the Cold War, 1944–1963.* Albany: State University of New York Press, 1986.

Horne, Gerald. *Jazz and Justice: Racism and the Political Economy of the Music.* New York: New York University Press, 2019.

Horne, Gerald. *Paul Robeson: The Artist as Revolutionary.* London: Pluto, 2016.

Horten, Gerd. *Radio Goes to War: The Cultural Politics of Propaganda during World War II.* Berkeley: University of California Press, 2002.

House, Jim, and Neil MacMaster. *Paris 1961: Algerians, State Terror, and Memory.* New York: Oxford University Press, 2008.

Howlett, Jacques. "*Présence africaine,* 1947–1958." *Journal of Negro History* 43, no. 2 (1958): 140–51.

Hughes, Charles L. *Country Soul: Making Music and Making Race in the American South.* Chapel Hill: University of North Carolina Press, 2015.

Hughes, Langston. *Une introduction au jazz.* Paris: Nouveaux Horizons, 1962.

Hurston, Zora Neale. "Spirituals and Neo-spirituals." In *Voices from the Harlem Renaissance,* edited by Nathan I. Huggins, 344–47. New York: Oxford University Press, 1995.

Hutchinson, George. *The Harlem Renaissance in Black and White.* Cambridge, MA: Harvard University Press, 1995.

Iton, Richard. *In Search of the Black Fantastic: Politics and Popular Culture in the Post–Civil Rights Era.* New York: Oxford University Press, 2008.

Jackson, Jeffrey H. *Making Jazz French: Music and Modern Life in Interwar Paris.* Durham, NC: Duke University Press, 2003.

Jackson, Jerma A. *Singing in My Soul: Black Gospel Music in a Secular Age.* Chapel Hill: University of North Carolina Press, 2004.

Jackson, Lauren Michele. *White Negroes: When Cornrows Were in Vogue and Other Thoughts on Cultural Appropriation*. Boston: Beacon, 2019.

Jaji, Tsitsi Ella. *Africa in Stereo: Modernism, Music, and Pan-African Solidarity*. New York: Oxford University Press, 2014.

Jalloh, Alusine, and Toyin Falola. *The United States and West Africa: Interactions and Relations*. Rochester, NY: Rochester University Press, 2008.

Jamieson, John. *Books for the Army: The Army Library Service in the Second World War*. New York: Columbia University Press, 1950.

Jean-Baptiste, Rachel. "Miss Euroafrica: Men, Women's Sexuality, and Métis Identity in Late Colonial French Africa, 1945–60." *Journal of the History of Sexuality* 20, no. 3 (2011): 568–93.

Jennings, Eric T. *Vichy in the Tropics: Pétain's National Revolution in Madagascar, Guadeloupe, and Indochina, 1940–1944*. Stanford, CA: Stanford University Press, 2001.

Joans, Ted. *Teducation: Selected Poems*. Minneapolis: Coffee House Press, 1999.

Jobs, Richard Ivan. *Riding the New Wave: Youth and the Rejuvenation of France after the Second World War*. Stanford, CA: Stanford University Press, 2007.

Johnson, David K. *The Lavender Scare: The Cold War Persecution of Gays and Lesbians in the Federal Government*. Chicago: University of Chicago Press, 2009.

Johnson, E. Patrick. *Appropriating Blackness: Performance and the Politics of Authenticity*. Durham, NC: Duke University Press, 2003.

Johnson, James Weldon. *The Second Book of Negro Spirituals*. New York: Viking Press, 1926.

Johnson, Walter. "On Agency." *Journal of Social History* 37, no. 1 (2003): 113–24.

Johnson, Walter. *Soul by Soul: Life Inside the Antebellum Slave Market*. Cambridge, MA: Harvard University Press, 2001.

Jones, Andrew F. *Yellow Music: Media Culture and Colonial Modernity in the Chinese Jazz Age*. Durham, NC: Duke University Press, 2001.

Jones, Jeannette. *In Search of Brightest Africa: Reimagining the Dark Continent in American Culture, 1884–1936*. Athens: University of Georgia Press, 2011.

Jones, Quincy. *Q: The Autobiography of Quincy Jones*. New York: Doubleday, 2001.

Jones, Quincy, and Bill Gibson. *Q: On Producing*. Milwaukee: Hal Leonard Books, 2010.

Jones, Rufus, Jr. *Dean Dixon: Negro at Home, Maestro Abroad*. Lanham, MD: Rowman & Littlefield, 2015.

Jordan, Matthew F. "Amphibiologie: Ethnographic Surrealism in French Discourse on Jazz." *Journal of European Studies* 31 (2001): 157–86.

Jordan, Matthew F. *Le jazz: Jazz and French Cultural Identity*. Urbana: University of Illinois Press, 2010.

Joseph-Gabriel, Annette K. *Reimagining Liberation: How Black Women Transformed Citizenship in the French Empire*. Urbana: University of Illinois Press, 2020.

Jules-Rosette, Bennetta. *Black Paris: The African Writers' Landscape*. Urbana: University of Illinois Press, 1998.

Jules-Rosette, Bennetta. "Conjugating Cultural Realities: *Présence Africaine*." In *The Surreptitious Speech: Présence Africaine and the Politics of Otherness, 1947–1987*, edited by V. Y. Mudimbe, 14–44. Chicago: University of Chicago Press, 1992.

Jules-Rosette, Bennetta. *Josephine Baker in Art and Life: The Icon and the Image*. Urbana: University of Illinois Press, 2007.

Julien, Eileen. "Terrains de rencontre: Césaire, Fanon, and Wright on Culture and Decolonization." In "The French Fifties," special issue, *Yale French Studies*, no. 98 (2000): 149–66.

Kaiser, Hilary. *Veteran Recall: Americans in France Remember the War*. Paris: Graphics Group, 1994.

Kaké, Ibrahima Baba. *Les noirs de la diaspora*. Libreville: Lion, 1978.

Kaplan, Alice. *The Interpreter*. New York: Free Press, 2005.

Kaplan, Alice. "Liberation: The View from France." *Contemporary French and Francophone Studies* 8, no. 3 (2004): 239–52.

Keaton, Tricia Danielle, and T. Denean Sharpley-Whiting, eds. *Black France/France Noire: The History and Politics of Blackness*. Durham, NC: Duke University Press, 2012.

Kelley, Norman, ed. R&B, *Rhythm and Business: The Political Economy of Black Music*. New York: Akashic, 2002.

Kelley, Robin D. G. *Africa Speaks, America Answers: Modern Jazz in Revolutionary Times*. Cambridge, MA: Harvard University Press, 2012.

Kelley, Robin D. G. "But a Local Phase of a World Problem: Black History's Global Vision, 1883–1950." *Journal of American History* 86, no. 3 (1999): 1045–77.

Kelley, Robin D. G. *Freedom Dreams: The Black Radical Imagination*. Boston: Beacon, 2003.

Kelley, Robin D. G. "Notes on Deconstructing 'The Folk.'" *American Historical Review* 97, no. 5 (1992): 1400–1408.

Kelley, Robin D. G. "A Poetics of Anticolonialism." In *Discourse on Colonialism*. New York: Monthly Review Press, 2000.

Kelley, Robin D. G. *Race Rebels: Culture, Politics, and the Black Working Class*. New York: Free Press, 1996.

Kelley, Robin D. G., and Tiffany Ruby Patterson. "Unfinished Migrations: Reflections on the African Diaspora and the Making of the Modern World." *African Studies Review* 43, no. 1 (2000): 11–45.

Kendall, Raymond. "Music for the Armed Services." *Musical Quarterly* 31, no. 2 (1945): 141–56.

Kenney, William H. "The Assimilation of Jazz in France, 1917–1940." *American Studies* 15, no. 1 (1984): 5–24.

Kenney, William H. *Chicago Jazz: A Cultural History, 1904–1930*. New York: Oxford University Press, 1993.

Kesteloot, Lilyan. *Black Writers in French: A Literary History of Negritude*. Translated by Ellen Conroy Kennedy. Philadelphia: Temple University Press, 1974.

Kgosoitsile, K. William. "I Have Had Enough! Report on Dakar Festival of Negro Arts." *Liberator*, July 1966, 10–11.

Kinnamon, Keneth, and Michel Fabre, eds. *Conversations with Richard Wright*. Jackson: University Press of Mississippi, 1993.

Kofsky, Frank. *Black Nationalism and the Revolution in Music*. New York: Pathfinder, 1970.

Komara, Edward M. *The Dial Recordings of Charlie Parker: A Discography*. Westport, CT: Greenwood, 1998.

Kramer, Paul A. *The Blood of Government: Race, Empire, the United States, and the Philippines*. Chapel Hill: University of North Carolina Press, 2006.

Kramer, Paul A. "Power and Connection: Imperial Histories of the United States and the World." *American Historical Review* 116, no. 5 (2011): 1348–91.

Krenn, Michael. "'Unfinished Business': Segregation and U.S. Diplomacy at the 1958 World's Fair." *Diplomatic History* 20, no. 4 (1996): 591–612.

Kroes, Rob. *If You've Seen One, You've Seen the Mall: Europeans and American Mass Culture*. Urbana: University of Illinois Press, 1996.

Kuhn, Raymond. *The Media in France*. New York: Routledge, 1995.

Kuisel, Richard F. *Seducing the French: The Dilemma of Americanization*. Berkeley: University of California Press, 1993.

Kun, Josh. *Audiotopia: Race, Music, and America*. Berkeley: University of California Press, 2005.

Lane, Jeremy F. *Jazz and Machine-Age Imperialism: Music, "Race," and Intellectuals in France, 1918–1945*. Ann Arbor: University of Michigan Press, 2013.

Lapprand, Marc. *Boris Vian, la vie contre*. Ottawa: Presses de l'Université d'Ottawa, 1993.

Larkin, Brian. *Signal and Noise: Media, Infrastructure, and Urban Culture in Nigeria*. Durham, NC: Duke University Press, 2008.

Layne, Priscilla. *White Rebels in Black: German Appropriation of Black Popular Culture*. Ann Arbor: University of Michigan Press, 2018.

Lebovics, Herman. *Bringing the Empire Back Home: France in the Global Age*. Durham, NC: Duke University Press, 2004.

Lebovics, Herman. *Mona Lisa's Escort: André Malraux and the Reinvention of French Culture*. Ithaca, NY: Cornell University Press, 1999.

Lebovics, Herman. *True France: The Wars over Cultural Identity, 1900–1945*. Ithaca, NY: Cornell University Press, 1992.

Ledos, Jean-Jacques, ed. "Un demi-siècle de jazz sur les radios francophones." Special issue in *Cahiers d'histoire de la radiodiffusion* 75 (March 2003).

Lee, Ulysses. *The Employment of Negro Troops*. Washington, DC: Office of Military History, 1966.

Legrand, Anne. *Charles Delaunay et le jazz en France dans les années 30 et 40*. Paris: Layeur, 2009.

Lehman, Stephen. "I Love You with an Asterisk: African-American Experimental Music and the French Jazz Press, 1970–1980." *Critical Studies in Improvisation* 1, no. 2 (2005): 38–53.

Leiris, Michel. "Jazz (An Interview with Michael Haggerty)." In "New Translations of Michel Leiris," special issue, *Sulfur* 15 (1986): 97–104.

Leonard, Herman, and Philippe Carles. *The Eye of Jazz: The Jazz Photographs of Herman Leonard*. New York: Viking, 1990.

Lesueur, Daniel. *L'histoire du disque et de l'enregistrement sonore*. Chatou: Carnot, 2004.

Le Sueur, James D. *Uncivil War: Intellectuals and Identity Politics during the Decolonization of Algeria*. Philadelphia: University of Pennsylvania Press, 2001.

Levering Lewis, David. "Parallels and Divergences: Assimilationist Strategies of Afro-American and Jewish Elites from 1910 to the Early 1930s." *Journal of American History* 71, no. 3 (1984): 543–64.

Levine, Lawrence W. *Black Culture and Black Consciousness: Afro-American Folk Thought from Slavery to Freedom.* New York: Oxford University Press, 2007.

Lewis, George E. *A Power Stronger Than Itself: The AACM and American Experimental Music.* Chicago: University of Chicago Press, 2008.

Lie, Siv B. "Genre, Ethnoracial Alterity, and the Genesis of Jazz Manouche." *Journal of the American Musicological Society* 72, no. 3 (2019): 665–718.

Lilly, J. Robert. *Taken by Force: Rape and American GIs in Europe during World War II.* New York: Palgrave Macmillan, 2007.

Locke, Alain. *The New Negro.* New York: Simon and Schuster, 1925.

Logan, Rayford W. *Howard University: The First Hundred Years, 1867–1967.* New York: New York University Press, 1969.

Lott, Eric. *Love and Theft: Blackface Minstrelsy and the American Working Class.* New York: Oxford University Press, 1993.

Lordi, Emily. *The Meaning of Soul: Black Music and Resilience since the 1960s.* Durham, NC: Duke University Press, 2020.

Lovell, John. *Black Song: The Forge and the Flame. The Story of How the Afro-American Spiritual Was Hammered Out.* New York: Macmillan, 1972.

Loyer, Emmanuelle. "A la croisée des chemins transatlantiques: Breton, Lévi-Strauss, Césaire, Fort-de-France, avril 1941." In *L'amitié et les sciences*, edited by Jean-Charles Darmon and Françoise Waquet, 237–54. Paris: Hermann, 2010.

Loyer, Emmanuelle. *Paris à New York: Intellectuels et artistes français en exil, 1940–1947.* Paris: Bernard Grasset, 2005.

Luchs, Lewis Richard. *Diplomatic Tales: Stories from a Foreign Service Career and One Family's Adventures Abroad.* Morrisville, NC: Lulu, 2016.

Lyons, Amelia. *The Civilizing Mission in the Metropole: Algerian Families and the French Welfare State during Decolonization.* Stanford, CA: Stanford University Press, 2013.

Maack, Mary Niles. *Libraries in Senegal: Continuity and Change in an Emerging Nation.* Chicago: American Library Association, 1981.

Mabille, François. *Les catholiques et la paix au temps de la guerre froide.* Paris: Harmattan, 2004.

Macey, David. *Frantz Fanon: A Life.* London: Granta Books, 2000.

Mack, Dwayne. "Hazel Scott: A Career Curtailed." *Journal of African American History* 91, no. 2 (2006): 153–70.

Magee, Jeffrey. "Irving Berlin's 'Blue Skies': Ethnic Affiliations and Musical Transformations." *Musical Quarterly* 84, no. 4 (2000): 537–80.

Magnin, André. *Malick Sidibé.* Zurich: Scalo, 1998.

Mahon, Maureen. *Black Diamond Queens: African American Women and Rock and Roll.* Durham, NC: Duke University Press, 2020.

Maisonneuve, Sophie. *L'invention du disque 1877–1949: Genèse de l'usage des médias musicaux contemporains.* Paris: Archives Contemporaines, 2009.

Makalani, Minkah. *In the Cause of Freedom: Radical Black Internationalism from Harlem to London, 1917–1939*. Chapel Hill: University of North Carolina Press, 2011.

Man, Simeon. *Soldiering through Empire: Race and the Making of the Decolonizing Pacific*. Berkeley: University of California Press, 2018.

Mann, Gregory. *Native Sons: West African Veterans and France in the Twentieth Century*. Durham, NC: Duke University Press, 2006.

Margolies, Edward. *The Several Lives of Chester Himes*. Jackson: University Press of Mississippi, 1997.

Marker, Emily. "African Youth on the Move in Postwar Greater France: Experiential Knowledge and Decolonial Politics at the End of Empire." *KNOW: A Journal on the Formation of Knowledge* 3, no. 2 (2019): 283–303.

Marker, Emily. "Obscuring Race: Franco-African Conversations about Colonial Reform and Racism after World War II and the Making of Colorblind France, 1945–1950." *French Politics, Culture, and Society* 33, no. 3 (2015): 1–23.

Martin, Denis-Constant. "De l'excursion à Harlem au débat sur les 'Noirs': Les terrains absents de la jazzologie française." *L'homme* 158/159 (April/September 2001): 261–77.

Martin, Denis-Constant, and Olivier Roueff. *La France du jazz: Musique, modernité et identité dans la première moitié du XXe siècle*. Marseille: Parenthèses, 2002.

Matera, Marc. *Black London: The Imperial Metropolis and Decolonization in the Twentieth Century*. Berkeley: University of California Press, 2015.

McCloy, Shelby T. *The Negro in France*. Lexington: University of Kentucky Press, 1961.

McDuffie, Erik. *Sojourning for Freedom: Black Women, American Communism, and the Making of Black Left Feminism*. Durham, NC: Duke University Press, 2011.

McGregor, Elizabeth Vihlen. *Jazz and Postwar French Identity: Improvising the Nation*. Lanham, MD: Lexington Books, 2016.

McKay, George. *Circular Breathing: The Cultural Politics of Jazz in Britain*. Durham, NC: Duke University Press, 2005.

McKenzie, Brian Angus. *Remaking France: Americanization, Public Diplomacy, and the Marshall Plan*. New York: Berghahn Books, 2005.

Méadel, Cécile. *Histoire de la radio des années trente: Du sans-filiste à l'auditeur*. Paris: Anthropos, 1994.

Méadel, Cécile, Caroline Ulmann-Mauriat, and Michèle de Bussierre. *Radios et télévisions au temps des "événements d'Algérie," 1954–1962*. Paris: Harmattan, 1999.

Meadows, Eddie S. *Bebop to Cool: Context, Ideology, and Musical Identity*. Westport, CT: Greenwood, 2003.

Meghelli, Samir. "'A Weapon in Our Struggle for Liberation': Black Arts, Black Power, and the 1969 Pan-African Cultural Festival." In *The Global Sixties in Sound and Vision: Media, Counterculture, Revolt*, edited by Timothy Scott Brown and Andrew Lison, 167–84. London: Palgrave Macmillan, 2014.

Meintjes, Louise. *Sound of Africa! Making Music Zulu in a South African Studio*. Durham, NC: Duke University Press, 2003.

Melnick, Jeffrey. *A Right to Sing the Blues: African Americans, Jews, and the American Popular Song*. Cambridge, MA: Harvard University Press, 1999.

Ménil, René. "Poetry, Jazz, and Freedom." In *Surrealism and Its Popular Accomplices*, edited by Franklin Rosemont. San Francisco: City Lights Books, 1980.

Meriwether, James H. *Proudly We Can Be Africans: Black Americans and Africa, 1935–1961*. Chapel Hill: University of North Carolina Press, 2002.

Mezzrow, Mezz. "In the Idiom." In Sinclair Traill, *Concerning Jazz*, 28–32. London: Faber and Faber, 1957.

Mezzrow, Mezz. "Really the Blues." In *Selections from the Gutter: Jazz Portraits from "The Jazz Record,"* edited by Art Hodes and Arthur W. Hansen. Berkeley: University of California Press, 1977.

Mezzrow, Mezz, and Bernard Wolfe. *La rage de vivre*. Translated by Marcel Duhamel and Madeleine Gautier. Paris: Coréa, 1950.

Mezzrow, Mezz, and Bernard Wolfe. *Really the Blues*. New York: Random House, 1946; New York: Citadel Underground, 1990.

Miller, Christopher L. *Blank Darkness: Africanist Discourse in French*. Chicago: University of Chicago Press, 1985.

Miller, Christopher L. *The French Atlantic Triangle: Literature and Culture of the Slave Trade*. Durham, NC: Duke University Press, 2008.

Miller, Karl Hagstrom. *Segregating Sound: Inventing Folk and Pop Music in the Age of Jim Crow*. Durham, NC: Duke University Press, 2010.

Miller, Paul Eduard, ed. *Esquire's Jazz Book*. Armed Services Editions 676 [U list]. New York: Editions for the Armed Services, 1944.

Miller, Paul Eduard, ed. *Esquire's 1945 Jazz Book*. Armed Services Editions 1000. New York: Editions for the Armed Services, 1945.

Miller-Davenport, Sarah. *Gateway State: Hawai'i and the Cultural Transformation of American Empire*. Princeton, NJ: Princeton University Press, 2019.

Mitchell, Robin. *Vénus noire: Black Women and Colonial Fantasies in Nineteenth-Century France*. Athens: University of Georgia Press, 2020.

Monson, Ingrid T. *Freedom Sounds: Civil Rights Call Out to Jazz and Africa*. New York: Oxford University Press, 2007.

Monson, Ingrid T. "The Problem with White Hipness: Race, Gender, and Cultural Conceptions in Jazz Historical Discourse." *Journal of the American Musicological Society* 48, no. 3 (1995): 396–422.

Moore, Brenda L. *To Serve My Country, to Serve My Race: The Story of the Only African American WACs Stationed Overseas during World War II*. New York: New York University Press, 1996.

Moore, Celeste Day. "'Every Wide-Awake Negro Teacher of French Should Know': The Pedagogies of Black Internationalism in the Early Twentieth Century." In *New Perspectives on the Black Intellectual Tradition*. Evanston, IL: Northwestern University Press, 2018.

Moore, Celeste Day. "Ray Charles in Paris: Race, Protest, and the Soundscape of the Algerian War." *American Quarterly* 71, no. 2 (June 2019): 449–72.

Morehouse, Maggi M. *Fighting in the Jim Crow Army: Black Men and Women Remember World War II*. Lanham, MD: Rowman & Littlefield, 2000.

Morley, Patrick. *"This Is the American Forces Network": The Anglo-American Battle of the Air Waves in World War II*. Westport, CT: Praeger, 2003.

Morrison, Matthew. "The Sound(s) of Subjection: Constructing American Popular Music and Racial Identity through Blacksound." *Women and Performance: A Journal of Feminist Theory* 27, no. 1 (2017): 13–24.

Morton, Patricia A. *Hybrid Modernities: Architecture and Representation at the 1931 Colonial Exposition, Paris.* Cambridge, MA: MIT Press, 2003.

Mudimbe, V. Y., ed. *The Surreptitious Speech: Présence Africaine and the Politics of Otherness, 1947–1987.* Chicago: University of Chicago Press, 1992.

Murphy, David, ed. *The First World Festival of Negro Arts, Dakar 1966: Contexts and Legacies.* Liverpool: Liverpool University Press, 2016.

Ndiaye, Pap. *La condition noire: Essai sur une minorité française.* Paris: Calmann-Lévy, 2008.

Neal, Mark Anthony. *What the Music Said: Black Popular Music and Black Public Culture.* New York: Routledge, 1997.

Nettelbeck, Colin W. *Dancing with De Beauvoir: Jazz and the French.* Carlton: Melbourne University Press, 2004.

Neulander, Joelle. *Programming National Identity: The Culture of Radio in 1930s France.* Baton Rouge: Louisiana State University Press, 2009.

Ochoa Gautier, Ana María. *Aurality: Listening and Knowledge in Nineteenth-Century Colombia.* Durham, NC: Duke University Press, 2014.

Office of War Information. *OWI in the ETO: A Report on the Activities of the Office of War Information in the European Theatre of Operations, January 1944–January 1945.* London: US Office of War Information, 1945.

Oriano, Michel. "Sim Copans, ambassadeur de la musique américaine en France [interview conducted in 1997]." In "Play It Again, Sim . . . Hommages à Sim Copans," special issue, *Revue française d'études américaines* (December 2001): 6–15.

Parker, Maceo. *98% Funky Stuff: My Life in Music.* Chicago: Chicago Review Press, 2013.

Paynter, John Henry. *Fifty Years After.* New York: Margent, 1940.

Peabody, Sue, and Tyler Edward Stovall, eds. *The Color of Liberty: Histories of Race in France.* Durham, NC: Duke University Press, 2003.

Pecknold, Diane, ed. *Hidden in the Mix: The African American Presence in Country Music.* Durham, NC: Duke University Press, 2013.

Peiss, Kathy. *Zoot Suit: The Enigmatic Career of an Extreme Style.* Philadelphia: University of Pennsylvania Press, 2014.

Pells, Richard H. *Not like Us: How Europeans Have Loved, Hated, and Transformed American Culture since World War II.* New York: Basic Books, 1997.

Pennybacker, Susan D. *From Scottsboro to Munich: Race and Political Culture in 1930s Britain.* Princeton, NJ: Princeton University Press, 2009.

Perchard, Tom. *After Django: Making Jazz in Postwar France.* Ann Arbor: University of Michigan Press, 2015.

Perec, Georges. *Je me souviens: Les choses communes.* Paris: Hachette, 1978.

Perry, Kennetta Hammond. *London Is the Place for Me: Black Britons, Citizenship, and the Politics of Race.* New York: Oxford University Press, 2016.

Pierrot, Grégory. "Chester Himes, Boris Vian, and the Transatlantic Politics of Racial Representation." *African American Review* 43, no. 2 (2009): 247–62.

Pierrot, Gregory. *The Black Avenger in Atlantic Culture*. Athens: University of Georgia Press, 2019.

Pinson, K. Heather. *The Jazz Image: Seeing Music through Herman Leonard's Photography*. Jackson: University Press of Mississippi, 2010.

Pirsein, Robert William. *The Voice of America: An History of the International Broadcasting Activities of the United States Government, 1940–1962*. New York: Arno, 1979.

Plummer, Brenda Gayle. *In Search of Power: African Americans in the Era of Decolonization, 1956–1974*. Cambridge: Cambridge University Press, 2012.

Plummer, Brenda Gayle. *Rising Wind: Black Americans and U.S. Foreign Affairs, 1935–1960*. Chapel Hill: University of North Carolina Press, 1996.

Poiger, Uta G. *Jazz, Rock, and Rebels: Cold War Politics and American Culture in a Divided Germany*. Berkeley: University of California Press, 2000.

Pollard, Miranda. *Reign of Virtue: Mobilizing Gender in Vichy France*. Chicago: University of Chicago Press, 1998.

Porter, Eric. *What Is This Thing Called Jazz? African American Musicians as Artists, Critics, and Activists*. Berkeley: University of California Press, 2002.

Pottier, Olivier. *Les bases américaines en France: 1950–1967*. Paris: Harmattan, 2003.

Prévos, André J. M. "Four Decades of French Blues Research in Chicago: From the Fifties into the Nineties." *Black Music Research Journal* 12 (Spring 1992): 97–112.

Puddington, Arch. *Broadcasting Freedom: The Cold War Triumph of Radio Free Europe and Radio Liberty*. Lexington: University Press of Kentucky, 2000.

Pulh, Michel. *Au fil du jazz: Bourgogne 1945–1980*. Neuilly-lès-Dijon: Murmure, 2011.

Putnam, Lara. *Radical Moves: Caribbean Migrants and the Politics of Race in the Jazz Age*. Chapel Hill: University of North Carolina Press, 2013.

Quashie, Kevin. *The Sovereignty of Quiet: Beyond Resistance in Black Culture*. New Brunswick, NJ: Rutgers University Press, 2012.

Quéniart, Jean, ed. *Le chant, acteur de l'Histoire, Actes du colloque*. Rennes: Presses Universitaires de Rennes, 1999.

Radano, Ronald M. *Lying up a Nation: Race and Black Music*. Chicago: University of Chicago Press, 2003.

Radano, Ronald M. "On Ownership and Value." *Black Music Research Journal* 30, no. 2 (2010): 363–69.

Radano, Ronald, and Philip V. Bohlman, eds. *Music and the Racial Imagination*. Chicago: University of Chicago Press, 2000.

Radano, Ronald, and Tejumola Olaniyan, eds. *Audible Empire: Music, Global Politics, Critique*. Durham, NC: Duke University Press, 2016.

Ramsey, Fredric, Jr., and Charles Edward Smith, eds. *Jazzmen*. Armed Services Editions 726. New York: Editions for the Armed Services, 1945.

Ramsey, Guthrie P., Jr. *Race Music: Black Cultures from Bebop to Hip-Hop*. Berkeley: University of California Press, 2004.

Ransby, Barbara. *Eslanda: The Large and Unconventional Life of Mrs. Paul Robeson*. New Haven, CT: Yale University Press, 2013.

Ratcliff, Anthony J. "When Negritude Was in Vogue: Critical Reflections of the First World Festival of Negro Arts and Culture in 1966." *Journal of Pan African Studies* 6, no. 7 (February 2014): 167–86.

Rawnsley, Gary D. *Radio Diplomacy and Propaganda: The BBC and VOA in International Politics, 1956–64*. New York: St. Martin's, 1996.

Redmond, Shana. *Anthem: Social Movements and the Sound of Solidarity in the African Diaspora*. New York: New York University Press, 2013.

Regnier, Gérard. *Jazz au Havre and Caux, depuis les années 20 . . . et ça continue*. Luneray: Bertout, 1997.

Regnier, Gérard. *Jazz et société sous l'Occupation*. Paris: Harmattan, 2009.

Renda, Mary A. *Taking Haiti: Military Occupation and the Culture of U.S. Imperialism, 1915–1940*. Chapel Hill: University of North Carolina Press, 2001.

Rhodes, Don. *Say It Loud! My Memories of James Brown, Soul Brother No. 1*. Guilford, CT: Lyons, 2009.

Rice, Louisa. "Cowboys and Communists: Cultural Diplomacy, Decolonization and the Cold War in French West Africa." *Journal of Colonialism and Colonial History* 11, no. 3 (2011): 493–509.

Riesman, Bob. *I Feel So Good: The Life and Times of Big Bill Broonzy*. Chicago: University of Chicago Press, 2011.

Ritz, David, and Ray Charles. *Brother Ray: Ray Charles' Own Story*. Cambridge, MA: Da Capo, 2004.

Roberts, Mary Louise. *What Soldiers Do: Sex and the American GI in World War II France*. Chicago: University of Chicago Press, 2013.

Robeson, Eslanda Goode. "Black Paris, II." *Challenge* 1, no. 5 (1936): 9–12.

Rogin, Michael. *Blackface, White Noise: Jewish Immigrants in the Hollywood Melting Pot*. Berkeley: University of California Press, 1996.

Rollefson, J. Griffith. *Flip the Script: European Hip Hop and the Politics of Postcoloniality*. Chicago: University of Chicago Press, 2017.

Rose, Tricia. *Black Noise: Rap Music and Black Culture in Contemporary America*. Middletown, CT: Wesleyan University Press, 1994.

Rosemont, Franklin, ed. *Surrealism and Its Popular Accomplices*. San Francisco: City Lights Books, 1980.

Ross, Kristin. *Fast Cars, Clean Bodies: Decolonization and the Reordering of French Culture*. Cambridge, MA: MIT Press, 1995.

Ross, Kristin. *May '68 and Its Afterlives*. Chicago: University of Chicago Press, 2002.

Rousso, Henry. *The Vichy Syndrome: History and Memory in France since 1944*. Translated by Arthur Goldhammer. Cambridge, MA: Harvard University Press, 1994.

Rowley, Hazel. *Tête-à-Tête: The Lives and Loves of Simone de Beauvoir and Jean-Paul Sartre*. London: Chatto & Windus, 2006.

Ruppli, Michel. *Vogue*. Paris: AFAS, 1992.

Ruppli, Michel, and Jacques Lubin. *Blue Star*. Paris: AFAS, 1993.

Russell, Ross. *Bird Lives: The High Life and Hard Times of Charlie (Yardbird) Parker*. New York: Da Capo, 1973.

Rustin, Nichole T., and Sherrie Tucker, eds. *Big Ears: Listening for Gender in Jazz Studies*. Durham, NC: Duke University Press, 2008.

Saada, Emmanuelle. *Empire's Children: Race, Filiation, and Citizenship in the French Colonies*. Chicago: University of Chicago Press, 2012.

Sablé, Victor. *Mémoires d'un foyalais: Des îles d'Amérique aux bords de la Seine*. Paris: Maisonneuve et Larose, 1993.

Samuels, David W., Louise Meintjes, Ana María Ochoa, and Thomas Porcello. "Soundscapes: Toward a Sounded Anthropology." *Annual Review of Anthropology* 39 (2010): 329–45.

Sartre, Jean-Paul. *Black Orpheus*. Translated by S. W. Allen. Paris: Présence Africaine, 1963.

Sartre, Jean-Paul. "Orphée Noir." In Léopold Sédar Senghor, *Anthologie de la nouvelle poésie nègre et malgache de langue française*, ix–xliv.

Saul, Scott. *Freedom Is, Freedom Ain't: Jazz and the Making of the Sixties*. Cambridge, MA: Harvard University Press, 2003.

Sauret, Philippe. "Et la France découvrit le blues: 1917 à 1962." Master's thesis, University of Paris 1.

Savage, Barbara Dianne. *Broadcasting Freedom: Radio, War, and the Politics of Race, 1938–1948*. Chapel Hill: University of North Carolina Press, 1999.

Scales, Rebecca P. *Radio and the Politics of Sound in Interwar France*. Cambridge: Cambridge University Press, 2018.

Scales, Rebecca P. "Subversive Sound: Transnational Radio, Arabic Recordings, and the Dangers of Listening in French Colonial Algeria, 1934–1939." *Comparative Studies in Society and History* 52, no. 2 (2010): 384–417.

Schafer, R. Murray. *The Soundscape: Our Sonic Environment and the Tuning of the World*. New York: Knopf, 1977.

Schenbeck, Lawrence. "Representing America, Instructing Europe: The Hampton Choir Tours Europe." *Black Music Research Journal* 25, nos. 1/2 (2005): 3–42.

Schrecker, Ellen. *Many Are the Crimes: McCarthyism in America*. Princeton, NJ: Princeton University Press, 1998.

Schwartz, Vanessa R. *It's So French! Hollywood, Paris, and the Making of Cosmopolitan Film Culture*. Chicago: University of Chicago Press, 2007.

Scott, Julius. *The Common Wind: Afro-American Currents in the Age of the Haitian Revolution*. New York: Verso, 2018.

Sears, Richard S. *V-Discs: A History and Discography*. Westport, CT: Greenwood, 1980.

Seigel, Micol. *Uneven Encounters: Making Race and Nation in Brazil and the United States*. Durham, NC: Duke University Press, 2009.

Senghor, Léopold Sédar. *Anthologie de la nouvelle poésie nègre et malgache de langue française*. Paris: Presses Universitaires de France, 1948.

Senghor, Léopold Sédar, and Mohamed Aziza. *La poésie de l'action*. Paris: Stock, 1980.

Servin, Lucie. "La maison de disques Vogue: De la croissance à la faillite. Analyse artistique et commerciale d'un label français pendant les Trente Glorieuses, 1948–1992." PhD diss., University de Paris VIII, 2010.

Shack, William A. *Harlem in Montmartre: A Paris Jazz Story between the Great Wars*. Berkeley: University of California Press, 2001.

Shain, Richard M. *Roots in Reverse: Senegalese Afro-Cuban Music and Tropical Cosmopolitanism*. Middletown, CT: Wesleyan University Press, 2018.

Sharpley-Whiting, T. Denean. *Bricktop's Paris: African American Women in Paris between the Two World Wars*. Albany: State University of New York Press, 2015.

Sharpley-Whiting, T. Denean. *Negritude Women*. Minneapolis: University of Minnesota Press, 2002.

Shepard, Todd. *The Invention of Decolonization: The Algerian War and the Remaking of France*. Ithaca, NY: Cornell University Press, 2006.

Shepperson, George. "The African Abroad or the African Diaspora." In *Emerging Themes in African History*, edited by Terrence O. Ranger, 152–76. Nairobi: East African Publishing House, 1968.

Silverman, Maxim. *Deconstructing the Nation: Immigration, Racism and Citizenship in Modern France*. London: Routledge, 1992.

Simone, Nina, and Stephen Cleary. *I Put a Spell on You: The Autobiography of Nina Simone*. New York: Pantheon Books, 1991.

Singh, Nikhil Pal. *Black Is a Country: Race and the Unfinished Struggle for Democracy*. Cambridge, MA: Harvard University Press, 2004.

Singh, Nikhil Pal. *Race and America's Long War*. Berkeley: University of California Press, 2019.

Sirinelli, Jean-François. "Deux étudiants 'coloniaux' à Paris à l'Aube des années trente." *Vingtième siècle, revue d'histoire* 18 (April–June 1988): 77–88.

Skinner, Ryan Thomas. *Bamako Sounds: The Afropolitan Ethnics of Malian Music*. Minneapolis: University of Minnesota Press, 2015.

Sklaroff, Lauren Rebecca. *Black Culture and the New Deal: The Quest for Civil Rights in the Roosevelt Era*. Chapel Hill: University of North Carolina Press, 2009.

Sklaroff, Lauren Rebecca. "Constructing G.I. Joe Louis: Cultural Solutions to the 'Negro Problem' during World War II." *Journal of American History* 89, no. 3 (2002): 958–83.

Slate, Nico. *Colored Cosmopolitanism: The Shared Struggle for Freedom in the United States and India*. Cambridge, MA: Harvard University Press, 2012.

Smith, R. J. *The One: The Life and Music of James Brown*. New York: Gotham Books, 2012.

Smith, Robert P., Jr. "Black like That: Paulette Nardal and the Negritude Salon." *CLA Journal* 45, no. 1 (2001): 53–68.

Smith, Suzanne E. *Dancing in the Street: Motown and the Cultural Politics of Detroit*. Cambridge, MA: Harvard University Press, 1999.

Smith, Thelma M., and Ward L. Miner. *Transatlantic Migration: The Contemporary American Novel in France*. Durham, NC: Duke University Press, 1955.

Smith, William Gardner. *Return to Black America*. Englewood Cliffs, NJ: Prentice-Hall, 1970.

Snead, James A. "On Repetition in Black Culture." *Black American Literature Forum* 15, no. 4 (1981): 146–54.

Sohn, Anne-Marie. *Age tendre et tête de bois: Histoire des jeunes des années 1960*. Paris: Hachette Littératures, 2001.

Sollors, Werner. *Neither Black nor White and Yet Both: Thematic Explorations of Interracial Literature*. New York: Oxford University Press, 1997.

"Special Forum: Musical Diplomacy: Strategies, Agendas, Relationships," *Diplomatic History* 36 (2012).

Spellman, A. B. *Four Lives in the Bebop Business*. New York: Pantheon Books, 1966.

Springer, Robert. "The Blues in France." In *Cross the Waters Blues: African American Music in Europe*, edited by Neil Wynn, 235–49. Jackson: University Press of Mississippi, 2007.

Stadler, Gus. "On Whiteness and Sound Studies." *Sounding Out!* (blog), July 6, 2015. https://soundstudiesblog.com/2015/07/06/on-whiteness-and-sound-studies/.

Stahl, Matt. *Unfree Masters: Recording Artists and the Politics of Work*. Durham, NC: Duke University Press, 2013.

Steinbeck, Paul. *Message to Our Folks: The Art Ensemble of Chicago*. Chicago: University of Chicago Press, 2017.

Sternberg-Sarel, Beno. "La radio en Afrique noire d'expression française." *Communications* 1 (1961): 108–26.

Sterne, Jonathan. *The Audible Past: Cultural Origins of Sound Reproduction*. Durham, NC: Duke University Press, 2003.

Stewart, Gary. *Rumba on the River: A History of the Popular Music of the Two Congos*. New York: Verso, 2003.

Stoever, Jennifer Lynn. *The Sonic Color Line: Race and the Cultural Politics of Listening*. New York: New York University Press, 2016.

Stora, Benjamin. *La gangrène et l'oubli: La mémoire de la guerre d'Algérie*. Paris: Découverte, 1998.

Stovall, Tyler. "Color-Blind France? Colonial Workers during the First World War." *Race and Class* 35, no. 2 (1993): 35–55.

Stovall, Tyler. "The Fire This Time: Black American Expatriates and the Algerian War." In "The French Fifties," special issue, *Yale French Studies* 98 (2000): 182–200.

Stovall, Tyler. "Music and Modernity, Tourism and Transgression: Harlem and Montmartre in the Jazz Age." *Intellectual History Newsletter* 22 (2000): 36–48.

Stovall, Tyler. *Paris Noir: African Americans in the City of Light*. Boston: Houghton Mifflin, 1996.

Stowe, David W. *Swing Changes: Big-Band Jazz in New Deal America*. Cambridge, MA: Harvard University Press, 1994.

Suisman, David. "Co-workers in the Kingdom of Culture: Black Swan Records and the Political Economy of African American Music." *Journal of American History* 90, no. 4 (2004): 1295–1324.

Suisman, David. *Selling Sounds: The Commercial Revolution in American Music*. Cambridge, MA: Harvard University Press, 2009.

Suisman, David, and Susan Strasser. *Sound in the Age of Mechanical Reproduction*. Philadelphia: University of Pennsylvania Press, 2009.

Tailhefer, Jacques. "Louis et Hugues Panassié: Des mines du Caucase au *Jazz hot* en passant par le château de Gironde." *Revue du Rouergue* 50 (1997): 309–33.

Tate, Greg. *Everything but the Burden: What White People Are Taking from Black Culture*. New York: Broadway Books, 2003.

Ténot, Frank. *Boris Vian, le jazz et Saint-Germain*. Paris: Du May, 1993.

Thompson, Emily. *The Soundscape of Modernity: Architectural Acoustics and the Culture of Listening in America, 1900–1933*. Cambridge, MA: MIT Press, 2002.

Thurman, Kira. "Singing the Civilizing Mission in the Land of Bach, Beethoven, and Brahms: The Fisk Jubilee Singers in 1870s Germany." *Journal of World History* 27, no. 2 (Fall 2016): 443–71.

Tidiane, Dioh. *Histoire de la télévision en Afrique noire francophone, des origines à nos jours.* Paris: Editions Karthala, 2009.

Tournès, Ludovic. "La culture de masse à l'église? L'introduction avortée de la musique noire américaine dans la liturgie catholique française (1960–1970)." In *Le chant, acteur de l'histoire, actes du colloque*, edited by Jean Quéniart, 265–78. Rennes: Presses Universitaires de Rennes, 1999.

Tournès, Ludovic. "Le Hot Club de France: La métamorphose d'une association d'amateurs de jazz (1932–1974)." In *De l'acculturation du politique au multiculturalisme: Sociabilités musicales contemporaines*, edited by Ludovic Tournès, 111–35. Paris: Honoré Champion, 1999.

Tournès, Ludovic. "Les Hot Clubs: Des sociétés savantes au service de la diffusion de jazz." In *Les sociabilités musicales*, edited by Ludovic Tournès and Loïc Vadelorge, 105–20. Rouen: Publications de l'Université de Rouen, 1997.

Tournès, Ludovic. *New Orleans sur Seine: Histoire du jazz en France.* Paris: Fayard, 1999.

Tudesq, André Jean. *Journaux et radios en Afrique aux XIXe et XXe siècles.* Paris: Groupe de Recherche et d'Echanges Technologiques, 1998.

Tudesq, André Jean. *La radio en Afrique noire.* Paris: A. Pedone, 1983.

Urquhart, Brian. *Ralph Bunche: An American Life.* New York: W. W. Norton & Company, 1998.

Vaillant, Derek W. *Across the Waves: How the United States and France Shaped the International Age of Radio.* Urbana: University of Illinois Press, 2017.

Vaillant, Derek W. "Occupied Listeners: The Legacies of Interwar Radio for France during World War II." In *Sound in the Age of Mechanical Reproduction*, edited by David Suisman and Susan Strasser, 141–58. Philadelphia: University of Pennsylvania Press, 2009.

Vaillant, Derek W. "Sounds of Whiteness: Local Radio, Racial Formation, and Public Culture in Chicago, 1921–1935." *American Quarterly* 54, no. 1 (2002): 25–66.

Vaillant, Janet G. *Black, French, and African: A Life of Léopold Sédar Senghor.* Cambridge, MA: Harvard University Press, 1990.

VanDiver, Rebecca. *Designing a New Tradition: Loïs Mailou Jones and the Aesthetics of Blackness.* University Park: Penn State University Press, 2020.

Vasset, André. *Black Brother: La vie [et] l'oeuvre de Big Bill Broonzy. Chanteur, guitariste et personnalité capitale du monde du blues.* Gerzat: Decombat, 1996.

Veal, Michael E. *Dub: Soundscapes and Shattered Songs in Jamaican Reggae.* Middletown, CT: Wesleyan University Press, 2007.

Vian, Boris, and Claude Remeil. *Autres écrits sur le jazz.* Vol. 1. Paris: Bourgois, 1981.

Vian, Boris. *Blues for a Black Cat and Other Stories.* Translated by Julia Older. Lincoln: University of Nebraska Press, 1992.

Vian, Boris. *The Dead All Have the Same Skin.* Translated by Paul Knobloch. Los Angeles: TamTam Books, 2007.

Vian, Boris. *I Spit on Your Graves*. Translated by Boris Vian and Milton Rosenthal. Paris: Vendôme, 1948; Los Angeles: TamTam Books, 1998.

Vian, Boris. *J'irai cracher sur vos tombes*. Paris: Éditions du Scorpion, 1946.

Vian, Boris, and Noël Arnaud. *Chroniques du menteur*. Paris: C. Bourgois, 1974.

Vian, Boris, and Noël Arnaud. *Manuel de Saint-Germain-des-Prés*. Paris: Pauvert, 1997.

Vian, Boris, and Gilbert Pestureau. *Jazz in Paris: Chroniques de jazz pour la station de Radio WNEW, New York (1948–1949)*. Paris: Pauvert, 1997.

Vitalis, Robert. *White World Order, Black Power Politics: The Birth of American International Relations*. Ithaca, NY: Cornell University Press, 2017.

Von Eschen, Penny M. *Race against Empire: Black Americans and Anticolonialism, 1937–1957*. Ithaca, NY: Cornell University Press, 1997.

Von Eschen, Penny M. *Satchmo Blows Up the World: Jazz Ambassadors Play the Cold War*. Cambridge, MA: Harvard University Press, 2004.

Wald, Alan M. *The New York Intellectuals: The Rise and Decline of the Anti-Stalinist Left from the 1930s to the 1980s*. Chapel Hill: University of North Carolina Press, 1987.

Wald, Elijah. *How the Beatles Destroyed Rock 'n' Roll: An Alternative History of American Popular Music*. New York: Oxford University Press, 2009.

Wald, Gayle. *Crossing the Line: Racial Passing in Twentieth-Century U.S. Literature and Culture*. Durham, NC: Duke University Press, 2000.

Wald, Gayle. *Shout, Sister, Shout! The Untold Story of Rock-and-Roll Trailblazer Sister Rosetta Tharpe*. Boston: Beacon, 2007.

Wall, Irwin M. *The United States and the Making of Postwar France, 1945–1954*. New York: Cambridge University Press, 1991.

Ward, Brian. *Just My Soul Responding: Rhythm and Blues, Black Consciousness, and Race Relations*. Berkeley: University of California Press, 1998.

Washburne, Christopher. *Latin Jazz: The Other Jazz*. New York: Oxford University Press, 2020.

Weheliye, Alexander G. *Phonographies: Grooves in Sonic Afro-Modernity*. Durham, NC: Duke University Press, 2005.

Weiner, Susan. *Enfants Terribles: Youth and Femininity in the Mass Media in France 1945–1968*. Baltimore: Johns Hopkins University Press, 2001.

Werner, Craig. *A Change Is Gonna Come: Music, Race, and the Soul of America*. Ann Arbor: University of Michigan Press, 2001.

Wesley, Fred, Jr., *Hit Me, Fred: Recollections of a Sideman*. Durham, NC: Duke University Press, 2002.

West, Michael O., and William G. Martin, eds. *From Toussaint to Tupac: The Black International since the Age of Revolution*. Chapel Hill: University of North Carolina Press, 2009.

Wieviorka, Olivier. *Normandy: The Landings to the Liberation of Paris*. Cambridge, MA: Harvard University Press, 2010.

Wilber, Bob, and Derek Webster. *Music Was Not Enough*. New York: Oxford University Press, 1988.

Wilder, Gary. *Freedom Time: Negritude, Decolonization, and the Future of the World*. Durham, NC: Duke University Press, 2015.

Wilder, Gary. *The French Imperial Nation-State: Negritude and Colonial Humanism between the Two World Wars*. Chicago: University of Chicago Press, 2005.

Williams, Chad L. *Torchbearers of Democracy: African American Soldiers in the World War I Era*. Chapel Hill: University of North Carolina Press, 2010.

Wilmer, Valerie. *As Serious as Your Life: The Story of the New Jazz*. London: Allison & Busby, 1977.

Wilmer, Valerie. *Jazz People*. London: Allison & Busby, 1977; New York: Da Capo, 1991.

Winders, James A. *Paris Africain: Rhythms of the African Diaspora*. New York: Palgrave Macmillan, 2006.

Wolfe, Bernard. "Ecstatic in Blackface." Originally published in *Modern Review* 3 (January 1950); reprinted in *The Scene before You: A New Approach to American Culture*, edited by Chandler Brossard, 51–70. New York: Rinehart, 1955.

Wolfe, Bernard. *Memoirs of a Not Altogether Shy Pornographer*. Garden City, NY: Doubleday, 1972.

Wolfe, Bernard. "Uncle Remus and the Malevolent Rabbit." *Commentary* 8 (1949): 31–41.

Wynn, Neil A., ed. *Cross the Water Blues: African American Music in Europe*. Jackson: University Press of Mississippi, 2007.

Index

Black power, 163–64, 184, 186, 188, 191
Black Scholar (journal), 181
Black Skin, White Masks (Fanon), 65, 118
Black soldiers, presence in France, 19, 27,
  33–35, 41–42, 73, 207n49
Blakey, Art, 154
Blue Note (club), 98
Blue Note (record label), 83, 86
blues, 85–86
"Blue Skies" (Dorsey), 29
Blues People (Baraka), 185
Blues Singer (Broonzy), *90*
Blue Star (record label), 75–79, 82–84, 96
"Body and Soul" (Hawkins), 35
Bohlen, Charles E., 130
Bonjour l'Afrique (radio program), 165–66
book banning, 52–53
Boudjedra, Rachid, 184
Boulanger, Nadia, 98
Boullet, Jean, 53
Boumediane, Houari, 184
Bowie, Lester, 185
boxing, 17–18, 187
Braggs, Rashida, 10
Braxton, Anthony, 185
Brechnigac, Jean-Vincent, 143
Breton, André, 48–49, 195
Bridgers, Aaron, 93
Briggs, Arthur, 35, 76
British Broadcasting Corporation (BBC), 29
Brooks, Gwendolyn, 65
Broonzy, "Big Bill," 73, 84, 86, 89, 94, 122
Brown, James, 15, 161–62, 165–66, 171, 179–80,
  187–93, *189*
Brown, Sterling A., 229n50
Brubeck, Dave, 165
Brunswick (record label), 100
Bruynoghe, Yannick, 86
Bulletin du Hot Club (journal), 36
Bureau pour la Migration des Départments
  d'Outre-mer (Bumidom), 7
Burke, Edna, *111*
Burrell, Dave, 182
Byas, Don, 76, 140
Byrd, Donald, 99–101

Cabat, Léon, 78, 86, 90
Caldwell, Erskine, 45

Calloway, Cab, 50
caricature, 45, 49
Carles, Philippe, 185
Carmichael, Stokely (Kwame Ture), 181
Cartel de l'Action Social et Morale, 52, 56
Catholicism, 105–6, 113, 126–27, 142, 153
Ça twiste à Popenguine (Absa), 161
Cavanaugh, Inez, 93
Cayton, Horace, 48
Centre d'Échanges Culturels de Langue
  Française, 169
Cercle Artistique et Littéraire, 151
Césaire, Aimé, 49, 105, 124, 195
Césaire, Suzanne, 195
Ce soir (newspaper), 138
Chaîne Parisienne (radio station), 38–39
"Champions, Les" (African All Stars), 167
Charles, Ray, 1–2, 8, 16, 161, 170, 199
Checker, Chubby, 162
Cherry, Don, 185
Chesnel, Jacques, 17–18, 33, 37
Chess (record label), 93
Chevalier, Maurice, 94
Chicago Defender (newspaper), 35, 42
Circle (record label), 77
citizenship, 23, 26
civilization, 64, 108, 112, 130, 152–53, 176
civil rights, 11, 93–94, 125, 130
Clarke, Kenny, 6, 33, 73, 79, 98–99
classical music, 97
Clayton, John, 124
Cleaver, Eldridge, 181
Clef (record label), 88
Clergeat, André, 140, 169
Club Artistique et Musical des Coloniaux, 23
Club Saint-Germain, 47, 98, 146
Cocteau, Jean, 47
Coeuroy, André, 23
Cold War, 3, 11–12, 14, 86, 134, 137, 171,
  204n54, 234n9. *See also* communism;
  McCarthyism
Cold War civil rights, 144
Cold War cultural diplomacy, 14, 41, 135, 143,
  158–59, 163–65
Coleman, Bill, 75, *147*
Coleman, Ornette, 73, 94, 185
Collinet, Georges, 15, 165, *166,* 167, *167,* 168, 171
Collins, Lee, 71–72

Programme National (radio station), 235n13
propaganda, 138, 171, 238n66
Psychological Warfare Division (PWD), 28

Quintette du Hot Club de France, 75

race: and authenticity, 21, 43, 60, 159; and classification, 21, 69, 106, 141, 179; consciousness of, 28, 95, 109–10; and division of labor, 9; embodiment of, 116–17; hierarchies of, 32, 104, 171; objectification of, 165; stereotypes of, 57, 118; and violence, 48; and whitewashing, 41
racial hypodescent policies, 44
racial mimicry, 59–60, 65–66
racial violence, 1–2, 19, 27, 49–50
racism: critiques of, 65, 159; and fantasies, 48; in France, 2, 6–8, 57, 215n64; infrastructures of, 26, 199; opposition to, 143–44, 195; persistence of, 42; reproduction of, 118, 249n13; responses to, 129; as a system of knowledge, 198; tropes of, 24, 50, 64; in the United States, 6–7, 9, 85–86, 100–101, 144. *See also* colorblindness, racial violence
Radano, Ron, 12
radio broadcasting, 4–5, 13, 21, 29, 36–38, 85, 95, 121, 129, 142–44, 166–69. *See also* media
Radio-Cité (radio station), 21
Radiodiffusion-Télévision Française (RTF), 136, 141–42
Radiodiffusion Française (RDF), 38, 79, 129, 136–37
Radiodiffusion Nationale (RN), 23
radio networks: American influence on, 13, 18, 40–41, 136, 196–97; expansion of, 36, 142–44, 154–55; of France, 37, 79, 100, 121, 211n127, 235n13; structure of, 38, 134, 169, 187; and the Vichy regime, 22, 24. *See also* specific stations
Radio revue (magazine), 37, 138, 235
Radio Tanger International, 165
Raelettes, The, 1–2
Random House (publisher), 64
rape accusations, 27
RCA-Victor (record label), 31, 83
Really the Blues (Mezzrow and Wolfe), 13, 43–44, 60–61, 62, 64, 67, 71

record formats, 17, 74, 77, 79, 80, 83–84, 90, 113, 149, 171. *See also* technology
record industry, 13–14, 31, 72, 82, 84, 121, 170, 197. *See also* independent record labels
recording technologies, 2, 5, 13, 34, 36, 74, 113, 182
Redding, Otis, 161, 165
Redman, Don, 76
Redmond, Shana, 12, 121, 197
Réforme-Paris (newspaper), 139
Regards sur la musique américaine (radio program), 144
Reinhardt, Django, 22, 35–36, 140
religion, 119, 121, 126, 162
resistance, 11, 21, 60–61
Rhapsodies noires (radio program), 34
rhythm and blues (R&B), 82, 166, 179
Roach, Max, 177
Robeson, Paul, 6, 86, 135
Rochereau, Tabu Ley, 187
rock 'n' roll, 92, 165, 191
"Role of the Negro in American Popular Culture, The" (Wolfe), 59
Rosenthal, Milton, 56, 215n58
Rostaing, Hubert, 35
Rouch, Jean, 177
rumba, 163, 187

Sajous, Leo, 107
Salle Pleyel (concert hall), 8, 24–25
Salon (International) du Jazz, 79, 80–81, 82, 87
salons, 106–7
Salut les copains (magazine), 161
Salut les copains (radio program), 95, 171
Samedi soir (newspaper), 54
Sartre, Jean-Paul, 41, 47–49, 53, 59, 66
Sasson, Jean-Pierre, 75
satire, 49, 54, 56
Saury, Maxim, 168
Savage, Barbara, 236n45
Savoy (record label), 75
Schaeffner, André, 21
Schmeling, Max, 18
Scorpion (publisher), 45, 51
Scott, Hazel, 6, 86, 93, 135, 202n20
Second Mobile Radio Broadcasting Company, 29
Secret Star, 34

Senghor, Léopold Sédar, 57–58, 124–26, 130, 172, 176, 178, 197
Série noire (publishing imprint), 45, 213n9
78 rpm records, 17, 74, 77, 79, 83, 113, 149, 171
sexuality, 93
Shepp, Archie, 15, 181–82, *183*, 185–87
Sidibé, Malick, 191–93
Silva, Alan, 182
Simmons, Art, 234n9
Simone, Nina, 7, 181–82
Singleton, Marge, 71–72, 197
Singleton, Zutty, 71–73, 86, 90
Siobud, Sylvio, 23
6,888th Central Postal Directory Battalion, 27
Sklaroff, Lauren, 36
slang, 43, 217n98. *See also* language
slavery, 115, 120–21, 150, 158, 190
Slim, Memphis, 6, 93
Smith, Ada "Bricktop," 9
Smith, R. J., 190
Smith, William Gardner, 6
Snead, James, 190
Société Africaine de Culture (SAC), 172
Société de Radiodiffusion de la France d'Outre-mer (SORAFOM), 155, 169, 233
sonic Afro-modernity, 12
sonic color line, 141
soul music, 10–11, 161, 165–68, 180, 189–92
soundscapes: American influence on, 40; and colonialism, 129, 134; as crowded, 165; development of, 3–5, 179–80; evolution of, 134, 157; jazz in, 139; as pan-African, 193; perceptions of, 196; sacredness of, 119; and silence, 29; and social life, 32; and spaces, 152; technologies of, 18
Southern Christian Leadership Conference, 130
Spinners, The, 188
spirituals: authenticity of, 118–19; as compared to jazz, 127; as a contested form, 124; in France, 14; influence of, 2–5, 113, 128–29, 153, 176, 178, 237n52; as markers of difference, 108; as a mode of cultural contact, 119–20; perceptions of, 103–5, 114, 116, 121, 142, 145–46, 177–78; performances of, 119, 121–23, 155; radio broadcasts of, 136, 144–45; style of, 111, 142. *See also* gospel; hymns
"Spirituals to Swing" concert, 85
Starkenfirst (Tardon), 54

Stars and Stripes (newspaper), 35, 37, 75
Stearns, Marshall, 148
Steinbeck, John, 52
Stepter, Merrill, 85
Stewart, Ollie, 25–26, 35, 42, 94, 130
Stewart, Rex, 75
Stoever, Jennifer, 141
Stovall, Tyler, 9
Stowe, David, 30
strategic contestation, 8
Strayhorn, Billy, 137
Studio École de Maisons Laffitte, 169
Sullivan, Vernon, 44, 51–52, 54–56. *See also* Vian, Boris
swing (genre), 30–31, 35–36, 58. *See also* jazz
Swing (record label), 23, 75–76, 78–79, 83–84, 221n25
"Swing Low, Sweet Chariot," 103–4, 113
Sylla, Ibrahima, 171
syncopation, 19, 118

Tardon, Raphaël, 54–55
Taylor, Louis, *111*
technology: access to, 96, 154, 162, 170; and audio quality, 152; development of, 19, 142–44, 223n61; and music formats, 31, *80*, 84 (*See also* record formats); of radio, 37–38, 144–45, 154, 170
television, 146, 161, 239n79. *See also* media
Ténot, Frank, 63, 95, 99
Thibault, Maurice, 23
33 rpm records, *80*, 83–84, 90, 171
"33 tour" format, 38–39
Thompson, Sir Charles, 87
Thornton, Clifford, 182
Tibbs, Roy W., 110
Time (magazine), 48
Toles, Edward, 42
Toujours du jazz (radio program), 38–39
Tour du monde autour d'une table (radio program), 143
Touré, Sékou, 172–73
tours, 23, 85, 91, 93–94
transatlantic exchange, 149
transistor radios, 144–45, 154, 170
translations, 64–65, 67, 118–19, 124, 140, 142, 155, 180, 201n12, 231n85. *See also* language
Treat It Gentle (Bechet), 91